Complete Home
Landscaping

Complete Home
Landscaping

Catriona Tudor Erler

CREATIVE HOMEOWNER®, Upper Saddle River, New Jersey

Editorial Director: Timothy O. Bakke
Art Director: W. David Houser
Production Manager: Ann Bernstein

Editor: Nancy T. Engel
Copyeditor: Anne Halpin
Consulting Horticultural Editor: Elizabeth P. Stell
Photo Researcher: Amla Sanghvi
Editorial Assistants: Dan Lane, Stanley Sudol
Editorial Intern: Sarah Sutcliffe
Technical Reviewers: Ken Badgley, Carole Ottessen,
    Mike Stoll, Brian Trimble
Design and Layout: David Geer, Heidi Garner
Front Cover Design: Heidi Garner
Front Cover Photography: Charles Mann
Back Cover Design: David Geer
Back Cover Photography: Catriona Tudor Erler,
    photo of author by James Walsh Erler

Manufactured in the United States of America

Current Printing (last digit)
10 9 8

Complete Home Landscaping
Library of Congress Catalog Card Number: 99-069397
ISBN: 1-58011-072-X

CREATIVE HOMEOWNER®
A Division of Federal Marketing Corp.
24 Park Way, Upper Saddle River, NJ 07458
www.creativehomeowner.com

Safety First

All projects and procedures in this book have been reviewed for safety; still it is not possible to overstate the importance of working carefully. What follows are reminders for plant care and project safety. Always use common sense.

- *Always* use caution, care, and good judgment when following the procedures in this book.
- *Always* determine locations of underground utility lines before you dig, and then avoid them by a safe distance. Buried lines may be for gas, electricity, communications, or water. Contact local utility companies who will help you map their lines.
- *Always* read and heed tool manufacturer instructions.
- *Always* ensure that the electrical setup is safe; be sure that no circuit is overloaded and that all power tools and electrical outlets are properly grounded and protected by a ground-fault circuit interrupter (GCFI). Do not use power tools in wet locations.
- *Always* wear eye protection when using chemicals, sawing wood, pruning trees and shrubs, using power tools, and striking metal onto metal or concrete.
- *Always* consider nontoxic and least toxic methods of addressing unwanted plants, plant pests, and plant diseases before resorting to toxic methods. Follow package application and safety instructions carefully.
- *Always* read labels on chemicals, solvents, and other products; provide ventilation; heed warnings.
- *Always* wear a hard hat when working in situations with potential for injury from falling tree limbs.
- *Always* wear appropriate gloves in situations in which your hands could be injured by rough surfaces, sharp edges, thorns, or poisonous plants.
- Always protect yourself against ticks, which can carry Lyme disease. Wear light-colored, long-sleeved shirts and pants. Inspect yourself for ticks after every session in the garden.
- *Always* wear a disposable face mask or a special filtering respirator when creating sawdust or working with toxic gardening substances.
- *Always* keep your hands and other body parts away from the business end of blades, cutters, and bits.
- *Always* obtain approval from local building officials before undertaking construction of permanent structures.
- *Never* employ herbicides, pesticides, or toxic chemicals unless you have determined with certainty that they were developed for the specific problem you hope to remedy.
- *Never* allow bystanders to approach work areas where they might by injured by workers or work site hazards.
- *Never* work with power tools when you are tired, or under the influence of alcohol or drugs.
- *Never* carry sharp or pointed tools, such as knives or saws, in your pocket.

Dedication

To my husband, Jim, and my sons Nicholas and Ashton.

Acknowledgments

Of the many people who helped this book see the light of day, I would like to give particular thanks to Neil Soderstrom, Anne Halpin, and Nancy Engel, who with their clear vision and sharp editing skills each contributed to make this book as fine as it could be.

Many people opened their homes and gardens to me, sharing their gardening experiences and stories, and allowing me to photograph their private domains. A special thank you to the following people for their generous, gracious hospitality: John and Laura Alioto, James and Becky Allen, Kerry Blockley, Pam Bruce, David and Marjorie Casey, Roger Cornell, Elsa Dekking, Becky Dembitsky, Claire Dwoskin, Lani Freymiller, Wallace Gusler, Susannah Haber, Michael and Caroline Hill, Penelope Hobhouse, the Leightons, Calder Loth, Betty Mackey, Marnie Mahoney, Linda Moule, Allen Mushinsky, John and Alma Paty, Ed and Regina Potter, Philip Power, Gail Raiman, Patricia Smith, F. Turner and Nancy Reuter, Glenn and Pam Rosenthal, Holly Shimizu, Marian Staver, Judith Terra, Frank Varcolik and Maribe Gardiner, Rosemary Verey, Margo Washburn, Pat Welsh, Penny West, Dorothy Williams, Joan Williams, Peter and Betty Williams, Michael and Audrey Wyatt, and Agatha Youngblood.

Thank you also to Jim Erler for being such a cooperative model in the how-to photo sequences, and Nicholas and Ashton Erler for helping in several photographs. I am also grateful to John Yockey and his team at Green Wave Landscaping, Inc. in Vienna, Virginia for their patience when I photographed them installing a stone path and dry stone wall; Chris Carr, owner of Stonecraft, for letting me take pictures of him laying a stone path; and to John Hansel of Dominion Masonry in Falls Church, Virginia for allowing me to photograph him laying a brick path and building a brick staircase.

CONTENTS

Introduction

Complete Home Landscaping is designed to take the mystery out of home landscaping. Whether starting from scratch for a brand new house or modifying an existing space, creating and planting a garden does not need to be a daunting task. With the help of this book, it can be a satisfying and fun creative project.

Here is a one-stop reference for conceiving your landscape plan, implementing it, and caring for your garden once it's designed and planted. You'll find valuable information on design principles, as well as ideas for creating your own personal landscape and how-to instructions for a wide range of landscape projects. The early chapters present the basics of planning and design; later in the book you'll find out how to create the finishing touches that make each landscape special and unique.

▲ **Roses, hollyhocks, delphinium, Euphorbia, and rose campion** *make a summer display rich with varied textures and shapes in this herbaceous border.*

A narrow stepping-stone path *winds through the garden bed and disappears from view, thus drawing the visitor forward to find out what's around the corner. The iron arch at the entrance to the path adds a pleasing vertical element to the design.*

Many garden installation projects, such as laying a stepping-stone path, are fairly easy once you know how to do them. Here you'll find clearly written and illustrated step-by-step instructions for tasks that are typically needed to implement a landscape design. Each sequence is rated as Easy, Moderate, or Challenging so you can make an educated decision about whether you feel up to tackling the job. With this book you have the potential to save hundreds of dollars on hired labor costs.

To make it easy to use, the book is divided into three parts: Preparing to Landscape, Setting the Stage, and Planting and Growing.

PART ONE: PREPARING TO LANDSCAPE

Part One explains how to envision your ideal landscape. At this stage of planning, anything is possible. This is the time to determine what kind of space you want to develop. Someone with a passion for plants may want lots of beds filled to overflowing with a wide variety of shrubs, perennials, annuals, and bulbs, while another family may want an easy-to-care for garden with a play area for the children. The garden may be

▼ **In this ornamental vegetable garden,** *designed by Rosemary Verey, golden leafed hosta, iris, allium, and roses live harmoniously with broccoli and peas. This design is proof positive that a vegetable plot does not have to be an eyesore.*

Practical and Affordable Landscaping Projects.
It's tempting to create a book filled with fabulous design ideas that require a huge amount of space and money to make them work. Here the temptation was resisted. Within these pages you'll find practical ideas that will work for a suburban or city landowner who wants to create an attractive landscape, but doesn't have an unlimited budget or untold hours to make it happen. The designs and ideas presented in this book are realistic to achieve.

needed as a retreat where you can relax, or a place for outdoor entertaining. Here you'll learn how to renovate an existing landscape or start from scratch, and how to minimize the liabilities and maximize the assets.

Make Your Dream Landscape a Reality. Look for tips to help you envision what your dream landscape would look like, and then information on how to make that dream a reality. Learn how to make a site analysis of your property, and then how to put your design down on paper. If you're having trouble coming up with a satisfactory plan, you may want to turn to a landscape designer or landscape architect for help. In Chapter 1 you'll read about the difference between the two and how to select the one that best meets your needs.

Gardeners with small properties will appreciate the section on designing for small spaces, which is full of visual tricks and information about design techniques that make a small space feel much bigger than it really is. The perfect plot of land is rare if not nonexistent. Find out how you can maximize your property's assets and minimize the faults—or even turn them into advantages.

▲ **Edible flowers and vegetables** combine to create a profusion of color. Plant layering, with low-growing specimen in the foreground, medium in the middle, and tall shrubs and vines in the back, gives this garden a rich look.

▲ **This short flight of natural stone steps** interplanted with ferns draws the eye upward and invites passage. The owner has created a moist, wild woodland environment in a home landscape.

▶ **Large chunks of Portland stone** support the slope and are a beautiful foil to the conifers and heather plants growing in this terraced rockery. In early March, crocus and daffodils flower, adding to the display.

▲ **Bougainvillea** *growing over the simple arch adds a pleasing vertical highlight to the garden. This plant is a vigorous and rampant growing vine once it is established; make sure any support for* Bougainvillea *is able to sustain its weight.*

▼ **Bright red roses** *scrambling over the white, dome-topped gazebo create a flowery bower for outdoor sitting. The brick path, laid in running bond, leads the eye to the gazebo, and contributes to the formal feel of the setting.*

PART TWO: SETTING THE STAGE

Before you begin planting a garden, you need to decide what structures and "hardscaping" elements such as paths, patios, walls, and pools you plan to have. You also want to complete projects such as soil amendment, drainage, installing an irrigation system, and possibly garden lights. Ideally these elements should be in place before you plant so roots and foliage aren't disturbed or damaged in the process of digging and construction.

Building a Strong Garden Foundation. Learn how to tackle the important, "invisible" tasks such as soil amendment, improving drainage, and putting in irrigation and lighting systems. Compared with building a patio, putting in a pond, or planting up a bed, there's not a lot to show for in the landscape once these more mundane jobs are complete, but like wiring and plumbing in a house, they make all the difference to the garden once they're done.

Find out how to incorporate paths and steps into your garden to enhance the overall design, and how to use ornaments and accents, such as bridges, arbors, and sculpture to give your garden a signature touch that reflects your unique personality.

▲ **Moisture-loving hostas,** *such as 'Sultana' planted in the foreground, are ideal to rim a garden pond, softening the edges for a natural look. In the water, iris and water lilies enhance the verdant picture.*

PART THREE: PLANTING AND GROWING

Healthy, thriving plants are essential for a successful garden. In this section you'll learn how to choose plants that are suitable for your particular garden, and how to keep them flourishing. The book is rich with plant lists. Every growing environment on the continent is represented, including warm and cold climates, drought areas, and coastal gardens.

Organic, Efficient Gardening Practices. You'll also find labor-saving techniques and tips on how to maintain healthy soil, minimize weeds, and reduce the need for watering. Find out about companion planting to create pretty combinations as well as to increase the vigor of the paired plants. The emphasis here is on practical organic care so you can keep your plants thriving with a minimum of poisons and synthetic materials. The organic philosophy pervades the entire book, but Chapter 14 in particular focuses on ways to control pests and diseases without resorting to damaging chemicals.

In this section you'll get ideas for making the most of a well-established, but overgrown garden. Instead of getting rid of mature trees, you can transplant them to more appropriate locations. You'll appreciate the easy-to-follow, step-by-step transplanting instructions. If a plant is too large to move, you can bring it back into scale with the rest of the garden with careful pruning, which is also clearly explained.

Lawns are a major feature of most gardens in North America. In Chapter 11, you'll find detailed instructions for planting, caring for, and renovating lawns, as well as

Clipped with architectural details, this boxwood hedge creates a garden room that is a formal centerpiece to a series of paths that converge from different parts of the garden. Notice the statue which draws the eye down the length of the garden.

suggestions for low-maintenance alternatives to turf. Look for the charts that help you determine the best type of grass for your garden, and to find out the best mowing height for your grass.

Flowers, herbs, ornamental grasses, and vegetables get full attention, with plenty of beautiful pictures to inspire you to create memorable garden scenes, as well as detailed information on planting and caring for them.

In his book, *A Love of Flowers*, H.E. Bates wrote, "A garden that is finished is dead. A garden should be in a constant state of fluid change, expansion, experiment, adventure; above all it should be an inquisitive, loving but self-critical journey on the part of its owner. It should in fact reflect its owner." Use this book to guide you on your adventure of making a personal landscape.

◄ *Yellow-flowering ice plant covers the ground while iris leaf spikes and bright red bee balm provide a pleasing contrast to the mounding plants in this drought-tolerant garden. Dense planting keeps weeds to a minimum.*

▶ *Edged with curly parsley, this narrow path gives access to the vegetable garden without taking away too much growing space. Generally vegetable beds should be designed so you can reach across the bed to tend the plants without stepping on the soil.*

Horticultural Nomenclature

Carolus Linnaeus, a Swedish botanist in the eighteenth century, was the first to classify plants using the two-name, or "binomial," system, which we still employ today. Linnaeus chose Latin as his language of preference because at that time most educated people could both speak and write Latin. In the right circles, it was a universal, international language; the Latin names of plants still provide the best way for two people to be sure they're talking about exactly the same plant.

The two scientific names identifying a plant are based on the genus and species. A genus is a group of plants marked by common characteristics. For example, plants from the yarrow genus are all named *Achillea* after the Greek hero Achilles who, according to legend, used yarrow to heal his soldiers' wounds during the Trojan war. All oaks are classified under *Quercus*, and maples as *Acer*, indicating their general commonalities.

The species is a subdivision of the genus, identified separately from the genus because of more specific qualities. If English were used for the world of animals, dog would be the genus and dalmation the species. *Achillea millefolium* is a species of yarrow with leaves divided into a thousand tiny parts. (*Mille* refers to thousands, and *folium* refers to leaves or foliage.) Another species, woolly yarrow, in Latin is *Achillea tomentosa; tomentosa* refers to its hairy leaves.

In a plant's scientific name, the word identifying the genus always comes first and is capitalized as a proper noun. The species name is a descriptive word used as an adjective to modify and further describe the noun; it is always lower case.

Occasionally there is a third Latin name denoting a variety or subdivision of a species that arises in nature spontaneously. For example, the beach or shore pine is *Pinus contorta*. The lodgepole pine, a variety of that species, is *Pinus contorta* var. *latifolia. Pinus* indicates both are from the pine family, *contorta* describes the twisted form in which the trees grow, and—in the case of the lodgepole pine—the variety name *latifolia* explains that the leaves (needles) are broader than those of beach pine.

If a plant is of garden origin, that is it doesn't exist in the wild, it will have an additional name listed after the Latin name in single quotes; this is the cultivar. The geranium cultivar 'Johnson's Blue' has become a staple in the perennials section of nurseries, as has the yarrow 'Moonshine'.

Although the scientific names may seem confusing, with too many syllables strung together, they are valuable. Common plant names are charming but can lead to confusion since they often vary from region to region and country to country. In addition, often several plants with very different characteristics share the same common name. The scientific name is precise and descriptive. With a little Latin under your belt, you can learn a lot about a plant just from its name. For example, *reptans* means creeping. You know a plant with *reptans* in its name will be low to the ground and spreading. If a plant has *officinalis* in its name, you can bet it was at one time used for medicinal purposes. A *sempervirens* will stay green throughout the year in most climates; *semperflorens* is ever-flowering.

What's in a Name?

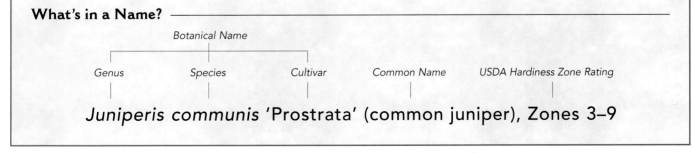

Botanical Name

Genus Species Cultivar Common Name USDA Hardiness Zone Rating

Juniperis communis 'Prostrata' (common juniper), Zones 3–9

Hardiness

Plants thrive in an environment that approximates their native habitat. For many years, plants have been labeled with their USDA (United States Department of Agriculture) hardiness zone rating, which indicates their tolerance to cold. All of the plants listed in this book are labeled with their USDA Hardiness Zone rating.

Although the USDA ratings are a good starting point, several factors can affect their accuracy. For example, city temperatures tend to be 5° to 10°F warmer than those of the surrounding countryside, raising the hardiness rating of a city garden by a full zone.

Every garden has microclimates that may be warmer or cooler or drier or more humid. The longer you garden in one location, the more familiar you will become with its microclimates. A hardiness rating of "Zones 4 or 5–7 or 8," suggests that the plant may survive the winter cold with protection in the warmer parts of Zone 4, but is safer in Zone 5. And, that same plant may need shade to protect it from the sun's heat in Zone 8, but is more likely to thrive in Zone 7. A plant that is surviving, but not thriving is under stress, and therefore more vulnerable to pests and diseases. Don't be dissuaded from growing a plant at the extremes of its stated cold tolerance. But be prepared to give that plant more attention.

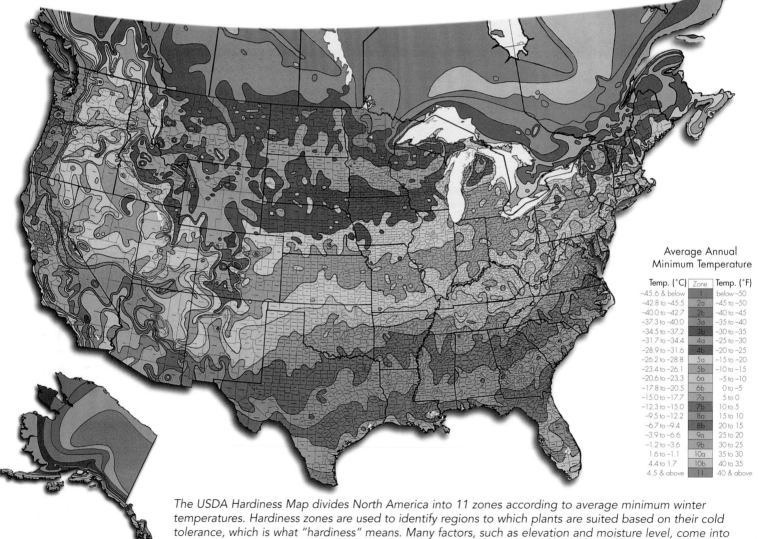

Average Annual Minimum Temperature

Temp. (°C)	Zone	Temp. (°F)
−45.6 & below	1	below −50
−42.8 to −45.5	2a	−45 to −50
−40.0 to −42.7	2b	−40 to −45
−37.3 to −40.0	3a	−35 to −40
−34.5 to −37.2	3b	−30 to −35
−31.7 to −34.4	4a	−25 to −30
−28.9 to −31.6	4b	−20 to −25
−26.2 to −28.8	5a	−15 to −20
−23.4 to −26.1	5b	−10 to −15
−20.6 to −23.3	6a	−5 to −10
−17.8 to −20.5	6b	0 to −5
−15.0 to −17.7	7a	5 to 0
−12.3 to −15.0	7b	10 to 5
−9.5 to −12.2	8a	15 to 10
−6.7 to −9.4	8b	20 to 15
−3.9 to −6.6	9a	25 to 20
−1.2 to −3.6	9b	30 to 25
1.6 to −1.1	10a	35 to 30
4.4 to 1.7	10b	40 to 35
4.5 & above	11	40 & above

The USDA Hardiness Map divides North America into 11 zones according to average minimum winter temperatures. Hardiness zones are used to identify regions to which plants are suited based on their cold tolerance, which is what "hardiness" means. Many factors, such as elevation and moisture level, come into play when determining whether a plant is suitable for your region. Local climates may vary from what is shown on this map. Contact your local Cooperative Extension Service for recommendations for your area.

Heat Tolerance

Researchers have recently discovered that plants begin to suffer cellular damage at temperatures over 86°F (30°C). The American Horticultural Society's Heat-Zone Map divides the country into 12 zones, based on the average number of days each year that a given region experiences "heat days," or temperatures over 86°F. The zones range from Zone 1 (no heat days) to Zone 12 (210 heat days).

In the near future, plants will be labeled with four numbers to indicate cold hardiness and heat tolerance. For example, a tulip may be 3–8, 8–1. If you live in USDA Zone 7 and AHS Zone 7, this label indicates that you can leave tulips outside in your garden all year.

It will take several years for most garden plants to be labeled reliably for heat tolerance. Unusual seasons with fewer or more hot days than normal will invariably affect results. The AHS Heat-Zone ratings assume that adequate water is supplied to the roots of the plant at all times. The accuracy of the coding can be substantially distorted by a lack of water, even for a brief period in the life of the plant.

Both the Cold-Hardiness Zone Map and the Heat-Zone Map are tools. After growing plants in one place for several years, gardeners will know what plants they can and cannot successfully grow.

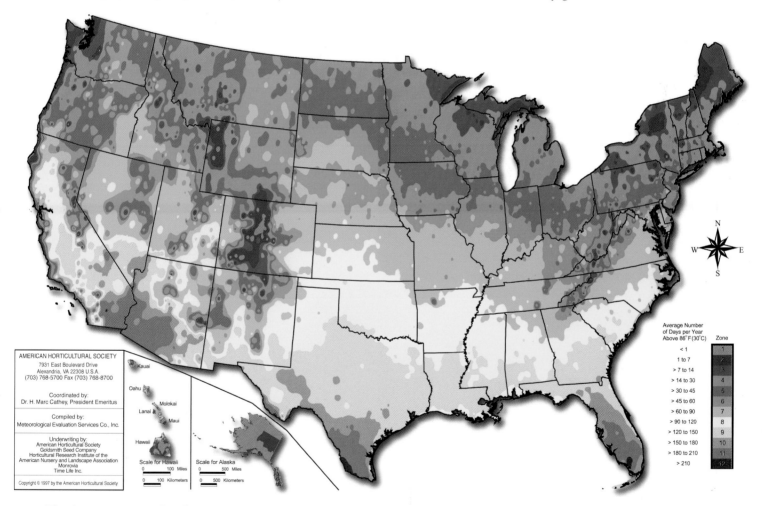

AMERICAN HORTICULTURAL SOCIETY
7931 East Boulevard Drive
Alexandria, VA 22308 U.S.A.
(703) 768-5700 Fax (703) 768-8700

Coordinated by:
Dr. H. Marc Cathey, President Emeritus

Compiled by:
Meteorological Evaluation Services Co., Inc.

Underwriting by:
American Horticultural Society
Goldsmith Seed Company
Horticultural Research Institute of the
American Nursery and Landscape Association
Monrovia
Time Life Inc.

Copyright © 1997 by the American Horticultural Society

Average Number of Days per Year Above 86°F(30°C)	Zone
< 1	1
1 to 7	2
> 7 to 14	3
> 14 to 30	4
> 30 to 45	5
> 45 to 60	6
> 60 to 90	7
> 90 to 120	8
> 120 to 150	9
> 150 to 180	10
> 180 to 210	11
> 210	12

The American Horticultural Society Heat-Zone Map divides the United States into 12 zones based on the average annual number of days a region's temperatures climb above 86°F (30°C), the temperature at which the cellular proteins of plants begin to experience injury. Introduced in 1998, the AHS Heat-Zone Map holds significance, especially for gardeners in southern and transitional zones. Nurseries, growers, and other plant sources will gradually begin listing both cold hardiness and heat tolerance zones for plants, including grass plants. Using the USDA Plant Hardiness map, which can help determine a plant's cold tolerance, and the AHS Heat-Zone Map, gardeners will be able to safely choose plants that tolerate their region's lowest and highest temperatures.

PART ONE

Preparing to Landscape

Before you plant a single tree or shrub, you must first envision your dream landscape. What kind of space do you want to develop? One where you can indulge your passion for plants, or somewhere you can relax? Do you need to incorporate a place for the children to play or where you can entertain outdoors? Have you always longed to bring the sound of water into your garden? Are you renovating an existing landscape or starting from scratch? What are the liabilities and assets of your property?

Chapter 1: Designing Your Landscape *will help you determine what features your dream landscape must contain, what you can live without, and how to make the best of your existing property. It will then explain how you can turn these ideas into a cohesive design.*

Chapter 2: Developing a Plan *will give you the tools you need to put that design down on paper. After you've read this chapter, you should be able to generate a master plan from which you or a professional landscape designer can work. A plan is essential whether you intend to finish your whole landscape all at once or work on it over many years—a section at a time.*

Sit back, and prepare to make your dream landscape a reality.

Designing Your Landscape

Your home landscape offers the opportunity to express yourself as though you were a landscape painter, by creating something beautiful from a "blank canvas." But instead of paint, your media will be plants, stone, and perhaps brick, sculpture, and garden furniture.

PERSONAL PARADISE

Today's homeowners have access to an amazing palette of plants, and new, improved hybrids are introduced yearly. The fun—and challenge—is working out a combination of plants that serves specific design functions, looks beautiful together, and grows well in your region. You can then combine the plants, often called *softscaping*, with *hardscaping* elements, such as stones, paths, patios, and walls, to create an environment that pleases you. In this process, you'll begin expressing your own vision of paradise—a place of bliss, felicity, and delight.

The landscaping of many suburban front gardens usually features a house with shrubs hugging the foundation, a walkway leading from the driveway to the front door, and a sapling that may one day become a tree. Sometimes, the front lawn also features an island bed with shrubs and ground covers. Typically, in the backyard, there's a patio or deck and a lawn surrounded with perimeter beds of shrubs, one or two perennials, and maybe some roses.

Rethinking the Front Yard. The style of landscaping that creates a yard has prevailed in North America for more than 100 years. However, it is not very interesting, and could do with some rethinking and updating. But it takes courage to try innovative designs in communities where all of the yards look alike.

Rosalind Creasy, a landscape designer and author, tells of the time she planned to replace the lawn and shrubs in front of her house with a vegetable garden. Most of her neighbors knew her skills as a designer and gardener and were excited about her plans. However, a man who'd recently moved in next door was skeptical, and he wasn't shy about

▲ **This unusual front landscape** features a lush collection of daisies, daylilies, and black-eyed Susans. The raised bed gives the planting more presence and hides the base of the lamp.

▶ **Breaking with tradition,** landscape designer Rosalind Creasy planted a vegetable and flower garden in her front yard instead of the more conventional lawn and foundation shrubs. One neighbor was initially skeptical about this entry garden, but he came around eventually.

expressing his concerns. However, the story has a happy ending. Creasy's vegetable garden is beautifully interplanted with flowers. It became a showpiece, and all of her neighbors were delighted.

LOOK WITH A FRESH EYE

Innovative garden design doesn't need to go as far as planting vegetables in the front yard. But it does require that you view your property with a fresh eye. For example, instead of leaving the front of the house exposed to the street with just a lawn as a buffer, consider creating a private garden room that serves as a foyer to your home. You can do this by planting shrubs around the edge of the front of your property instead of crushing them up against the house foundation. This border could be a hedge of one type of plant, such as yew, or a mixture of shrubs and small trees planted to create either an informal hedgerow or a tapestry-like hedge of different foliage colors and textures. Depending on your taste and the style of your garden, you can create a hedge in a straight line or place the shrubs off center from each other to make a soft, meandering line. If you fear that a shrub perimeter would appear antisocial, you can still achieve a sense of enclosure by planting perennial beds along the edges.

▼ **To create a private front garden,** plant a border of shrubs around the periphery of the property instead of tucked up against the house. Here, brilliantly flowering rhododendron define the borders.

A fresh approach to large swaths of front lawn is to use ornamental grasses and daylilies, as the design firm of Oehme, van Sweden did in this Arlington, Virginia, garden.

Playing Down the Lawn. The Washington, D.C., landscape design firm Oehme, van Sweden & Associates has garnered an international reputation by replacing public front lawns with more private spaces. In addition, they have incorporated plants such as Joe-Pye weed that designers formerly rejected as undesirable. Whatever plants the designers select are employed in innovative ways. Instead of using standard turf grass to create swaths of lawn, Wolfgang Oehme and Jim van Sweden often plant ornamental grasses in masses of flowing, wavelike drifts that mingle in abstract patterns with perennials such as rudbeckia and asters. Sensitive to the form and texture of each plant, Oehme and van Sweden achieve almost year-round interest. In these garden designs, floral color plays a part, but not necessarily the lead role.

Lawns play a minor role in their designs. Writing in their book *Bold Romantic Gardens*, the designers explain: "Pools and lawns, along with paved terraces, provide open spaces in contrast to layered volumes of plants. Lawn, however, is not a given in these gardens. Its long-term costs—labor, watering, and chemical treatment—are difficult to justify, so we require that any lawn address a specific purpose and scale it to suit that role. Some legitimate uses might include entertainment or children's play. We advise clients to think of the lawn as just one part of the overall garden and to retain only as much as needed."

The Oehme, van Sweden designs are not for every taste, but they suggest the many opportunities for creative design available to any homeowner wishing to break from the predominant suburban landscape style.

Before a landscape designer created a blueprint, this front garden was a bleak, bare space that made the house look uninviting and run-down. The redesigned entry is a welcoming place full of different plant textures, colors and forms. The owner, John Paty, cut costs by using fewer plants than were recommended on the plan and putting them in himself.

Planning on a Budget

Dream landscapes, even fairly simple ones, do not come cheap. Nevertheless, with careful planning and a willingness to do some of the work yourself, you can cut costs. Keep in mind that it is not necessary to implement a landscaping plan all at once. In fact, there are advantages to developing the landscape over time. As you live with your garden, you may decide there are modifications you want to make to the original plan. To spread out the costs, start with a master plan, and then complete it in stages. Start with the basic structure of the garden, putting in the hardscape. Follow immediately with slow-growing trees and hedges. Then add to the plan as you have the time and money. Keep in mind that heavy equipment can tear up plantings and compact the ground. Thus, it is wise to finish any major hardscaping project before the plants are in place.

INVESTING IN A MASTER PLAN

John Paty owns a rental property on Capitol Hill in Washington, D.C. He decided that an attractive landscape in front of the townhouse would attract good tenants, but he couldn't afford to spend much on the project. Realizing that a good master plan was basic to his success, he hired a top landscape design firm to create the design (shown below). They gave him a blueprint for the design, and a personalized booklet listing the recommended plants and explaining their care.

With blueprint in hand, Paty purchased the plants and put them in the ground himself. He also cut his costs by reducing

Before

After

the number of plants recommended on the blueprint in cases when he knew the plants would spread quickly to fill in the space. Savvy buyers are aware that even reputable landscape firms often recommend overplanting for instant gratification to the client and better profits.

Start Small. Another technique that saves money is to start with small plants. Instead of purchasing plants in 5- or 10-gallon containers, try to find them in the 1-gallon size or, in the case of herbaceous perennials, the 1-quart size. The smaller plants will cost considerably less because the nursery hasn't had to store and care for them while they were growing to the larger size. In many cases, small plants will adapt to being transplanted and start growing faster than their larger counterparts. As a rule, the larger the plant, the longer it will need to adjust to being moved.

Grow Your Own. Patient gardeners save money by propagating plants. If you are an experienced gardener, consider spending time rooting cuttings, dividing established clumps of plants, and growing plants from seed rather than buying new plants.

Many plants that propagate easily by division, such as daylilies and hostas, can be divided even when you first purchase them. When buying new plants, look for the ones with a lot of growing points that can be split into several new plants. Within a year the divisions will have grown into substantial plants. Ask friends if they are willing to divide an overgrown clump of plants and share the extras with you. If you offer to help do the job, they'll be especially open to sharing.

Free wood chips were a bonus for this homeowner's landscape budget. A local tree-trimming company was delighted to save the time and cost of a trip to the city dump, and the owner saved money.

Choose Paving Instead of Grass. Lawns are relatively inexpensive to plant, especially if you start one from seed rather than laying down sod. But in the long run, they are terribly expensive because of their maintenance costs. Even if you do all the labor of mowing, fertilizing, and aerating yourself, the annual cost of fertilizer and water adds up quickly. A paved or mulched surface might be less costly and more friendly to the environment over time.

Brick and stone are delightful paving materials for gardens because they too are of the earth and therefore blend in beautifully with their surroundings. But they are expensive. To save money, you may need to look at less costly alternatives. Flagstone is generally less pricey than brick, and local stone will always cost less than imported stone. In addition, local materials usually blend effortlessly with the landscape.

For paths, consider inexpensive material such as wood chips or shredded bark. These natural materials are especially attractive in an informal or woodland garden. Although bark and wood-chip paths need to be restored once a year because the wood breaks down, it's possible to get wood chips for free. Try calling town or county road departments or local tree-trimming companies. They may be willing to deliver a load to you for little or no charge. It saves them a trip to the dump.

Gravel is another less-expensive substitute for paving paths, and it makes a pleasing crunching sound when walked on. However, gravel can be a terrible nuisance if you allow it to drift into the surrounding garden. For a gravel path, always provide a containing edge, and avoid using gravel at the bottom of a slope. (See Chapter 4, pages 106–107 for directions on making a containing edging.) Otherwise, soil will wash down the slope and contaminate the gravel.

In dry regions, you can save money on your water bill by planting a garden of drought-tolerant plants. This type of landscape design is known as "xeriscaping." The increased demand for these low-water users has spurred nurseries and horticulturists to create hybrid plants that improve on existing drought-tolerant plants and to breed for that quality in new plants. Each year the selection of attractive plants for xeriscaping increases.

Don't Skimp on Soil. Soil improvements are one of the greatest up-front costs for developing a garden. However, this is one place where you shouldn't cut corners. You can save money by making your own compost and collecting fallen autumn leaves and by doing all the digging and rototilling yourself. Just make sure the soil is top quality before you begin to plant. Your landscape is an investment in time and money and in the overall appeal and value of your home. Good-quality soil will support and nourish your plants, the foundation of that investment.

Lower water costs by installing a drought-tolerant garden in places like San Diego, where 9 inches of rain a year is average. Here, the South African native plant Bulbine, which blooms throughout the winter in mild climates, adds fresh color to the xeriscape garden.

Hiring a Professional Versus Doing It Yourself

Some people have a natural design sense. But for those who need help, there are several professional options. For the initial design, you must choose between a landscape architect or a designer.

◖ *Landscape architects* are more expensive than designers because architects have more extensive formal training. To be certified, a landscape architect must have graduated from a course in landscape architecture that includes education in engineering, horticulture, and architectural design. Many states require that this course work be validated by passing the Landscape Architect Registration Examination (LARE), which tests the candidate's knowledge of grading and drainage, landscape construction, landscape design and history, and professional ethics.

◖ *Landscape designers* are knowledgeable about design principles and plant materials, especially those frequently used where they live and work. They are not required to have any formal training. These designers often are employed by large nurseries that provide free design services if you purchase the plants from them.

Loose gravel is an inexpensive paving material. Here, it is contained from drifting into the beds by a dense planting of ferns on one side and a tight edging of Mondo grass and low-growing azaleas on the other.

🔥 *Landscape contractors*, a third professional category, are individuals trained to lay patios and paths, build decks and structures, install irrigation systems, and install plants. Landscape contractors also carry out the construction plans of landscape architects.

CHOOSE THE RIGHT PERSON

If you have a complicated project that includes grading for terraces, sophisticated drainage, hardscaping, or ponds and swimming pools, you would be wise to hire a landscape architect—who has the engineering and design training necessary—along with a contractor. On the other hand, for much less money, a creative landscape designer can usually provide a satisfactory plan for beds and borders with a pleasing assortment of plants.

Be Selective about Services. If you decide to use both a landscape architect and a contractor, remember that you don't need to use all of their services. Most landscape architects are willing to draw up your plans and then allow you to implement them at your leisure. You may need to call in a professional to build the pond, but you may want to lay the paths and install the plants yourself. You are in charge, and you can negotiate whatever arrangement best suits your needs and budget.

Once you've decided whether you need a landscape architect, designer, or contractor, it's important to find the right person for the task. Start with a garden that you especially like. Most people will be flattered if you contact them to inquire who did their work. Also ask for referrals from friends. Once you've found one or two possibilities, meet with them, look at their portfolios, and discuss how they work with their clients.

You'll know after meeting with a couple of designers whether they will work with you as a partner or impose their own vision on your property, giving you little say. You are embarking on a team effort, with lots of creative decisions to make, and you want it to be a happy experience.

When starting from scratch, *put the hardscape (paths and stairs) in first. Keep equipment and vehicles off the beds so the soil doesn't get compacted. Amend the soil next. Finish off with the plants.*

Check References. Ask for a few references, and call them all. Find out whether the projects came in on budget and the agreed schedules were maintained. And don't be shy about requesting to see the properties. Although photo portfolios are helpful, they often distort the scale of the landscapes. Also, it's easy to frame a photo so that an eyesore is left out. Nothing can replace visiting the site to see a landscape design and understand how all the components blend and interact.

Another option: Consider enrolling in a landscape design course or at least attending local lectures. Once you're in the network, you'll hear about outstanding designers in your area. In addition, with a little training you'll be a more informed customer, and your increased knowledge will heighten your pleasure in the process.

Starting from Scratch

Although making a garden from a patch of bare, bulldozed ground may seem daunting, it is really a grand opportunity. With time, creativity, and money, that barren ground can be transformed into anything you like. A property with no landscaping has advantages over a home landscaped by previous owners because you're not faced with correcting other people's mistakes. You don't need to deal with trees and shrubs that have outgrown their situation and maybe shouldn't have been planted there in the first place. Nor do you need to change the course of a path that makes no sense from a practical or aesthetic standpoint.

Marry House to Landscape. A landscape architect's dream project is one for which the planned house is still in the blueprint stage. That gives the landscape architect the opportunity to take part in early decisions, such as where the house will be situated on the lot, and whether to save existing trees or shrubs. These choices and many others have a major impact on how successfully the house can be married to the property, and how well the entire property fits with its surroundings.

A well-paired house and landscape occupy this small lot. A swimming pool and space to entertain outdoors were obviously important to these homeowners. Thus, in this well-designed property, there is easy access to the outdoors from the house. The shape of the house and the terraced patio take full advantage of the slope.

Remember the Basics. Whether you choose to work with a landscape architect or not, there are basic tasks, such as amending the soil and solving drainage problems, to be tackled before plants go into the ground. To most homeowners, these efforts don't seem as interesting or rewarding as seeing plants transform bare ground, but they are as essential as wiring and plumbing in a house. Chapter 3 (page 66) provides details on installing your landscape's infrastructure. Remember, the advantage when you start from scratch is that you can ensure that each project contributes to your ultimate design.

Do have a master plan to give you a frame of reference and to help you avoid heading off on tangents. Many a garden is full of plants purchased spontaneously at a nursery or garden center that were appealing at the time but do nothing to advance the overall landscaping goals. As Hugh Johnson warns in his book *The Principles of Gardening,* such a "garden eventually becomes a magpie's nest of ill-assorted plants bought on impulse, with neither unity nor harmony, plan nor purpose."

Assessing Your Needs and Desires

Before you put pen to paper to map out a garden design, your first task should be to determine the features you need and want. The odds are that you'll need to make compromises on your ultimate desires because of space or budget constraints. But at this stage, try to list every feature you would like under ideal circumstances. It's wise to make this a family brainstorming session with assurance to all that no idea will be considered too silly or far-fetched. Later you can sift through all ideas to determine which are most important to you and most feasible. Study books and magazines that are rich with photos of garden ideas. Use them for inspiration in the same way you might use home magazines to gather ideas for interior decorating. Mark or save the pages with gardens you like; then consider what qualities in those gardens appeal to you.

Don't be afraid to consider designs on much bigger properties than yours, as well as designs in different regions. With creativity, you or a professional designer can adapt and scale designs you like to fit your property, substituting plants suitable for your locale.

Successful Landscape Design

Each of the following steps plays an equally important role in successfully designing your landscape:

1. **Identify Your Dream Landscape**
   List every feature you want, no matter how frivolous it seems.

2. **Establish a Budget**
   This will determine whether you need to scale back and plan to do some work yourself.

3. **Determine Your Style**
   What are your tastes? What makes sense for your property?

4. **Understand the Elements of Design**
   Proportion, light, color, mass, and texture are the key concepts of landscape design.

5. **Develop a Concept**
   Now that you know what you want, you can start to make it a reality.

6. **Start Planning**
   Take photographs, make notes, and draw sketches to commit your ideas to paper.

The Jackson family in California used this brainstorming process to develop a landscape plan that met the needs of the parents and their two children. They worked with landscape architect Ned Bosworth, who listened to each family member's vision for an ideal landscape. "I created what I call a fantasy space for each member of the family," said Bosworth. "Everyone got what they wanted."

The Jacksons invested a lot of money in their landscape, but no more than they might have spent on a major house addition. In fact, the family got far more living space with the garden addition than they could have gained by enlarging the house.

MAKE A WISH LIST

When you sit down to make your garden wish list, keep in mind the following considerations:

❧ *Amount of time you want to spend working in the garden.* If work and family demands make it difficult to spend more than a few weekends a year keeping the garden tidy, then you'd be smart to consider a design that minimizes labor. Hardscaping is more expensive up front, but requires much less time and lower upkeep expenses over the long run than lawns and beds. For softscaping, choose shrubs that need minimal pruning. (See the box on page 26.) Mulch your plants or plant your beds densely so weeds can't intrude.

❧ *Places to entertain.* If you enjoy hosting parties and you want guests to be able to walk outdoors, plan to create patios and decks with seating space.

❧ *Play areas for children.* A place for children to play may take the form of a grassy area for them to romp on or an area for a sandbox, swing set, and playhouse. Small children with tricycles and other wheeled vehicles appreciate a paved or hard surface. You may want to plan a large patio with paths looping through the garden and back to the house. Such a path provides a great freeway for the children, as well as a pleasing route for a garden stroll.

❧ *Private places to retreat.* For most people, secret gardens have enormous appeal because they provide a place to withdraw and restore their mental peace. Even on a small lot you can screen off an area with a trellis or hedge, provide a comfortable place to sit, and add plants (and perhaps a statue or birdbath) so that the space is a special, restful place.

▲ **This alfresco dining area** is conveniently located near the house. The low plants bring the garden to those seated without hemming in the patio, while the tall trees in the background shelter the space.

◀ **A private retreat spot** is essential in every garden. What could be more inviting than strolling barefoot over this no-maintenance path to the shaded hammock without worrying about mowing the lawn?

Shrubs That Need Minimal Pruning

While the following shrubs can get by with no pruning, they'll look better if you give them just a few minutes of care each year. Remove any dead, broken, or diseased twigs and branches. Then cut back any branches that stick out so far that they look odd.

Aronia arbutifolia (red chokeberry), Zones 4–9

Aronia melanocarpa (black chokeberry), Zones 3–9

Aucuba japonica (spotted laurel), Zones 7–10

Berberis (barberry), zones vary with species
and variety

Camellia species, zones vary with variety

Carissa macrocarpa (natal plum), Zones 9–10

Ceanothus species (California lilac), zones
vary with variety

Choisya ternata (Mexican orange), Zones 8–10

Cistus species (rock rose), Zones 7–9

Deutzia scabra (fuzzy deutzia), Zones 5–9

Enkianthus perulatus (white enkianthus),
Zones 6–9

Euonymus alatus (winged spindle tree), Zones 4–9

Fothergilla major, Zones 5–9

Hebe species, zones vary with variety

Hibiscus syriacus (rose-of-Sharon), Zones 5–9

Hydrangea species, zones vary with species

Lavatera olbia (tree mallow), Zones 8–10

Magnolia stellata (star magnolia), Zones 4–9

Mahonia japonica (Oregon grape), Zones 6–8

Myrtus communis (myrtle), Zones 9–10

Pieris floribunda (andromeda), Zones 5–8

Pieris japonica (Lily-of-the-Valley bush), Zones 6–8

Pontentilla fruticosa (shrubby cinquefoil), Zones 2–7

Prunus mume (Japanese flowering apricot),
Zones 6–9

Rhododendron species and cultivars (azalea
and rhododendron), zones vary with species
and variety

Viburnum plicatum f. tomentosum (double file
viburnum), Zones 5–8

Fothergilla major

Magnolia stellata

Rhododendron

This water feature, *a swimming pool, looks like a natural pond in a woodland clearing. With the bottom painted black and planting beds tucked into the curves, the pool is an integral and attractive part of the overall landscape design.*

❧ *A water feature.* Water can be a magical garden element. You may want a splashing fountain as a musical backdrop or simply as a means of masking the sound of street traffic. A large reflecting pool provides an ever-changing echo of the real world. Also consider a fish pond, which has a life and movement of its own. Or for recreation, a swimming pool and spa can be a delight. Remember, a swimming pool need not be a jarring element in the landscape. When skillfully designed, the swimming pool can be an integral and attractive part of the overall design. (See the photo above.)

❧ *Theme gardens or plant collections.* You may want to plant a vegetable garden, rose garden, or herb garden. Perhaps you're fascinated with the hundreds of hybrid daylilies, irises, hostas, or fuchsias, or the amazing diversity of ferns. These collections can be integrated into the garden and mixed with other plants. Or you may want to set aside a space just for plants that interest you most.

❧ *Views from the house.* If your house has large windows, capitalize on that feature by creating a pretty garden you can enjoy from inside. Use the window to frame the scene; design the visible space as a picture contained within that frame. You may want to create an intimate, contained garden room visible only from the window, or use the view to lead the eye down a central axis to a vista or focal point in the distance.

A collection of lilies and roses *makes a vibrant summer display. The foliage of the daylilies effectively hides the bare stems of the roses and the Oriental lilies.*

Looking from the inside out. *When designing, think of how the landscape will look from inside the house. Here, the bright red barberry (Berberis Thunbergii 'Atropurpurea') beckons those inside to come out for a closer look.*

Work space and unsightly views. Let's face it: You need somewhere to store your tools. Although an air-conditioning unit is an eyesore, it is necessary in hot climates. Then too, unconcealed garbage cans can be unsightly. Plan for utility areas by screening them off from the ornamental parts of your garden. If you enjoy growing plants from seed and rooting cuttings, you may want to create a garden workstation with a table and storage space for all the equipment.

▲ **Imagine the unsightly view** of this building, without screening, looming over the tiny courtyard garden. The hulking presence of the building served as a constant reminder of the urban setting and lack of privacy.

▼ **Diffuse ugly spots** or work areas with a simple bamboo screen. This screen is just high enough to hide the large brick building visible in the picture above. The light color and texture of the screen save it from becoming overpowering.

Determining Your Own Style

The overall style of your landscape should be determined by two factors: your own taste and what makes sense within the context of your property. Although your garden should be a unique expression of you, it should also be in harmony with its surroundings. For example, a picket fence with old-fashioned flowers spilling out between the slats may be the perfect adornment for a traditional or country-style home with a symmetrical facade. But that homey style would look out of place in front of a modern home or a mansion.

The scope for different style possibilities is vast, and you can always modify an existing style to better represent your needs and situation. For example, you can soften the clean, straight lines of a formal garden by allowing plants to intertwine and spill onto pathways. If you like Japanese gardens but don't want the precision design typical of that style, you can introduce elements from traditional Japanese gardens without being a slave to the style. Plants such as the red laceleaf Japanese maple (*Acer palmatum* 'Dissectum Atropurpureum'), with its wonderful twisted branches, and stone lanterns or basins, instantly evoke the Japanese motif.

▲ **The Japanese style of landscaping** can be evoked with a single plant, such as this red laceleaf Japanese maple (Acer palmatum 'Dissectum Atropurpureum'). The twisted trunk is sculptural and very decorative.

FORMAL STYLE

Characteristic elements of formal design include straight lines, geometric forms, symmetry, and a central axis, usually leading to the house. In a large garden, there may be several axes that link the different areas.

Because formal gardens have a strong sense of structure delineated with hedges, walls, and paths, they are usually interesting and attractive throughout the year. This type of garden is much less dependent on seasonal blooms for its beauty than other garden styles.

INFORMAL STYLE

Informal gardens are designed with curving, instead of straight, lines. The idea is to mimic nature rather than force it into unnatural forms and shapes. Curiously, it can be much more difficult to create a well-designed informal garden than a formal one, perhaps because informality is a newer design form and the concepts are more abstract and challenging. What looks right and pleasing to the eye is less obvious in an informal garden.

This formal garden, composed of symmetrical plantings, pleasing proportions, and elegant lines, is a comfortable, restful place. The focal point visible through the arch in the distance draws the eye and keeps the design from being too static.

Most of the same principles that govern formal designs apply to informal gardens, with the exception of balance and geometry. Instead of working with straight lines, you are designing with curves. These curves should serve to soothe the eye with loose, flowing forms rather than tight, sharp zigzags. But if you put too many curves into the garden, the design may become busy. Also avoid the temptation to introduce too many different plants into an informal design. Especially avoid dotting plants about randomly. Otherwise, instead of having a natural look, the garden will look sparsely planted. Work to create a rhythm and flow in your design by repeating plants and shapes, placing them in purposeful relationships. A rule of thumb is to group plants in clumps of three or more. A single plant massed in drifts is particularly effective.

◀ *Informal landscapes* have an organic rhythm and flow. This landscape is unified by the deep purple and red flowers and the round shapes of the plants. The patches of monochromatic yellow also tie the garden together.

▶ *The best informal designs* mimic nature while maintaining a sense of order. Groups of plants in twos or threes work better than single plants randomly arranged, which too often look chaotic.

COTTAGE STYLE

Typically a cottage garden belongs with a cottage-style house. Its hallmark is a profusion of plants: flowers and herbs, fruits and vegetables, and close-growing shrubs. Vigorous vines such as climbing roses, honeysuckle, and clematis may scramble around the front door, be trained as eyebrows over windows, or soften broad expanses of walls—conveying a sense of coziness and abundance. The controlling element to all this unbridled profusion is the structure of the garden. Traditionally, a cottage garden is enclosed by a hedge, wall, or fence, with a gate giving access to the property and a straight path leading to the front door. While the beds flanking the path need not be mirror images, there should be repeating patterns of plants and colors on each side.

Petite Flowers. Old-fashioned plants are ideal in cottage gardens. The old varieties tend to have small, delicate blossoms that mix happily with other flowers and plants, none competing for center stage. A cottage garden planted with too many large, brightly colored modern hybrids risks becoming an overwhelming cacophony of color and form. Among the old-fashioned flowers, consider using clove-scented pinks, honeysuckle, mignonette, primroses, lavender, hollyhocks, roses, foxglove, columbine, daffodils, and lilies. Because plants are spaced closely in a cottage garden, weeds tend to be shaded out, which is a great boon. Nevertheless, the garden still requires care. Although Marjorie Fish, one of the most famous cottage gardeners of the twentieth century, claimed that the plants she used were "good tempered" and not particular about soil, a cottage garden is an intensive growing situation. For best success, start with high-quality soil, rich in humus, and top-dress it each spring with well-rotted manure or other organic amendments.

Traditional cottage gardens typically contain flowering plants that cover the ground and grow up and over structures. Here the climbing rose 'Albertine' reaches across the top of the window to form a decorative "eyebrow."

▲ *The plants are closely spaced* in Rosalind Creasy's cottage garden. This classic garden is brimming with flowers, herbs, and vegetables that mix well together. The ivy-covered walls and the arbor contain the garden.

◄ *This low, old-fashioned house* is the perfect setting for a cottage garden. A profusion of delicately colored plants is growing with abandon while the hot-pink plants add a modern punch. The climbing vines complete the abundant look.

Japanese Style

The distinctive look of Japanese gardens is easy to recognize but difficult to achieve. It appeals to many American gardeners, perhaps because these gardens provide an oasis of serenity in an otherwise chaotic world. Full of symbols that convey the philosophy of Zen Buddhism, Japanese gardens are meant to be both a visual and a spiritual experience.

The three main elements of Japanese gardens are trees and shrubs, water, and stones. With the exception of a few deciduous trees for spring flowers and autumn foliage, most trees and shrubs in Japanese gardens are evergreen. Typical trees and shrubs include Japanese maples, pines, evergreen azaleas, and camellias. Bamboo also is favored, along with certain ornamental grasses such as Japanese blood grass (*Imperata cylindrica* 'Red Baron'), and grasslike plants such as *Liriope*. Flowers play a minimal role, with interest and variety created by shaping the plants and combining interesting leaf color and texture. When flowers are used, they are generally grown in swaths, such as a mass planting of Japanese irises.

The second element in Japanese gardens is water, which symbolizes the source of life. If actual water isn't feasible, then water is suggested with "rivers" of stone, or gravel raked in patterns to represent river currents. The steeply arching bridges, so evocative of Japan, span ponds or dry river beds and symbolize a rainbow. When running water is possible, sophisticated Japanese gardeners make a high art of regulating the flow to shape the sound, thus creating musical effects.

Stones are the third key element in Japanese gardens. Decorative stones are placed carefully for aesthetic as well as symbolic reasons. Each stone is assigned a name and meaning, such as Moon Stone, which represents solitude. Each stone's placement, in relationship to the others, also communicates its meaning.

Westerners perhaps best appreciate the Japanese stroll garden with paths that meander, opening new vistas or revealing another intimate moment of wonder with each twist and turn. This type of garden is a pleasing, unfolding experience as new sights greet the stroller around each bend and curve in the path. Another type of Japanese garden is the austere meditation garden, consisting of perhaps one stone or ornament, one or two plants, and gravel meticulously raked into flowing patterns.

The atmosphere of the Far East is evoked with the Japanese flag iris and the arched bridge.

Heavily pruned evergreens on an island of rock are very symbolic.

The sand garden conjures up images of currents in the sea moving around stone islands.

WILD AND WOODLAND STYLE

The father of wild or woodland gardens is the English garden writer William Robinson (1838–1935). While he believed that gardens close to the house should be designed with traditional formality, in his landmark book *The Wild Garden* (originally published in 1870 and still in print), he advocated allowing the garden to become more rustic and informal as it moved away from the house until it blended seamlessly with the surrounding countryside. He encouraged the use of hardy native plants and wrote eloquently about the merits of wild and roadside plants, such as foxgloves, daisies, and columbine, that were spurned in formal Victorian borders. Because these plants are hardy and well-suited to the English climate, he explained, they can be left to naturalize in wild gardens. "The whole success of wild gardening," he wrote, "depends on arranging bold, natural groups with a free hand."

In North America, we have adapted this concept to woodland, meadow, and prairie gardens.

Woodland gardens are the perfect choice for tree-filled properties such as the one above. Here creeping phlox, fringed bleeding heart, and Celandine poppy thrive in the shade.

◄ *A meadow* can be made in an enclosed space. In this bed, the red, purple, pink, and white flowers crowd against the stone edging in wild abandon.

Combine landscape styles by using informal plants in a woodland-style border. Shown here, peonies shelter shade-loving columbine, wild sweet William, primroses, and coral bells. The result is a relaxed version of a formal border.

COMBINING STYLES

On large and even moderate-size properties, you can indulge in two or more different garden styles if you divide up the space into distinct garden "rooms." Pat Welsh, author of *All My Edens,* has created several different gardens on her small lot. Next to the house is a lath-covered patio, which she enlivens during the summer months with pots and hanging baskets spilling over with colorful annuals and fuchsias.

To one side of the patio, under her bedroom window, she has created a Japanese garden vignette. The bed is planted with a large-scale bonsai cedar, dwarf heavenly bamboo, dwarf Mondo grass, bamboo, and ferns. Japanese accents include a dry "pond" made from blue beach rocks, three bronze Japanese cranes, decorative moss-covered rocks, and a stone lotus-shaped water basin, with a hollow bamboo "deer scare" slowly dripping water into the basin.

A steep slope separates the level patio area near the house from a lower garden that contains drought-tolerant plants growing in delightful profusion. In keeping with the informal nature of the design, the paths in the lower garden are covered in shredded bark. Off to one side, Welsh built an oval, raised bed, which she plants as a meadow. The floral display begins in mid-December in the mild southern California climate, and continues through the summer as the early spring flowers give way to the summer bloomers.

A pergola draped in Chinese wisteria (*Wisteria sinensis*) blooms prolifically each spring with long panicles of purple flowers; it covers the path between the driveway and the front door, connecting as well as partitioning the different parts of the garden.

Regional Style

Each part of North America has a distinct climate, topography, and cultural history that influences its landscape styles. For example, gardens in southern California and the Southwest often reflect the Spanish influence of the early missionaries.

The Pilgrims in New England brought plants with them from Great Britain to remind them of home. Nevertheless, they were coping with a much harsher climate and with a different topography. The indigenous forests were thick, and when the settlers felled the trees to create fields for farming, they discovered their land was rich in stones. Every spring the plow unearthed a new crop. These nuisance stones were put to good use: They are the material of the stone walls and rock gardens that are associated with New England gardens.

Whatever style you choose for your property, be sensitive to the region in which you live. If your landscape is in harmony with the constraints and assets of your particular climate and topography, it will be a more beautiful place. While you need not use only native plants, at least try to select plants that are well adapted to your region, rather than struggling to make a plant survive in a climate foreign to its nature.

Indigenous stones add interest to this garden stream. The banks are planted with native wetland plants.

Southwestern landscapes often contain a Spanish influence. A hedge of Yeddo hawthorne encloses the space.

This regional-style landscape features an irregular local-stone path lined with plants that fit the scale and style of the house.

The old farmer's wall in this New England garden makes good use of the abundant native stones.

Elements of Design

Harmony and unity; proportion and scale; light and shade; mass and space; and texture, pattern, and color are all aspects of a successful landscape design. The truly great gardens use these factors in evoking delightful tensions between restfulness and stimulation. They are harmonious without being repetitive and boring. A well-designed garden is balanced and unified, and at the same time surprising.

HARMONY AND UNITY

In any truly successful design, the plants, hardscape, and ornaments combine to create a cohesive whole in harmony with itself and its surroundings. There are many ways to achieve a sense of harmony and unity in a landscape. Once this sense is achieved, it looks simple and obvious, as if the garden could never have been any other way. But attaining that goal takes great skill and planning:

Grow healthy plants. A garden with plants that are struggling to survive, languishing in a less-than-ideal growing environment, is an uncomfortable place, one lacking in harmony. Before you buy plants, research their cultural requirements. If the conditions where you intend to set a plant aren't ideal, substitute another plant.

Group plants that have similar needs. For example, there is nothing more jarring than to see primroses, which enjoy moisture, growing with plants with gray foliage, such as lamb's ears, that prefer dry conditions.

Keep in mind the native habitat of a plant. Most people appreciate that a Bengal tiger would survive no better on Antarctic ice than a penguin would in a tropical jungle. We should have the same appreciation for the environmental needs of plants. For example, hostas are adaptable. They adjust to wet or dry conditions, as well as semi-shade and even quite dark situations. Still, they usually look more attractive when grown with ferns, astilbe, and other woodland denizens than in a flower bed with sun-loving roses and lilies. Another inharmonious combination would be California poppies, which are native to the dry hillsides of California, and rhododendrons, which are woodland shrubs. While you might succeed in growing those combinations, the final result would appear inharmonious.

Plant Shape. How we shape a plant also affects the garden's sense of unity and harmony. In a formal garden, hollies, yews, and boxwoods generally are sheared into clean, geometric forms, in keeping with the ordered, symmetrical nature of the formal design. Yet in a woodland garden, those same plants, which adapt to both sun and shade, will fit their setting better if allowed to grow in a looser form. The shrubs still may require pruning, but the goal in this situation is to shape the plants in harmony with the open, spreading canopy of taller trees.

Many shrubs used as hedges lend themselves to severe pruning. Others such as forsythia, spirea, and mock orange—whose natural growth pattern is a graceful, spreading form like a fountain—look silly when pruned into tight balls or boxes. Sadly, unknowing gardeners often shear plants such as forsythia, destroying their relaxed natural form, and with it one aspect of the garden's sense of harmony.

▶ **Shaping forsythia** in balls is discordant and looks wrong. The highly pruned shrubs require heavy maintenance and do nothing for the front garden.

▶ **Perfect harmony** results when forsythia is allowed to grow in its natural form. The dramatic, fountain-like spray of sunny yellow flowers is stunning in the spring against the dark evergreens.

*A **satisfying rhythm** and pattern of repeating forms is created by this avenue of cedar trees. Throughout the day, the trees' moving shadows add another pattern to the design.*

Landscape Views. Just as plants should be in harmony among themselves, the overall garden should be in harmony with its site. A walled garden can be its own unique environment, set apart from the rest of the world, and as such, can be a place of fantasy and mystery. However, when a garden has views beyond its boundaries, what you plant should have some relation to the local terrain. For example, a garden in the Southwest with panoramic views of rugged mountains and scrubland will feel more harmonious when it is united with the scene beyond. Techniques that achieve unity include growing native plants; using indigenous rock in your design; and echoing a dominate shape, color, or form from the scene outside the garden.

Repetition and Rhythm. Repeating a color or planting theme in different parts of the garden also helps create unity. Joseph Haber planted a row of pink wax begonias along his outdoor spa in his large garden in Del Mar, California. He repeated the planting around the corner in a border that ran the length of the lawn. Although the two begonia displays could not be seen at the same time, they remain in memory, unifying the garden. Other

*This **landscape harmonizes well** with the borrowed view of the fields and meadow. The wild phlox, columbine, and ferns blend beautifully with the field beyond the fence.*

planting themes that unify include the repeated use of plants with gray foliage or multiple uses of boxwood.

Patterns and shapes repeated throughout a garden can also provide a pleasing rhythm that unifies. A straight line of trees, with tall trunks, makes a vertical pattern that casts interesting shadows. If your walkway curves, try to repeat that line in the shapes of the beds and even in the mounding shape of some plants.

Another landscape architect, Gary Stone, also repeated an architectural detail from the house when he designed John and Laura Alioto's garden. In this case, Stone chose to echo the cutout squares that decorated the Alioto's post-modern house by saw-cutting a large square grid in the drive and walkway. He repeated the grid pattern in a low stucco wall that zigzags from the entryway to the street and defines the front walk space. "I wanted to bring the stucco from the house to the street," said Stone. "It is a marriage of the inside and the outside. I've included a narrow planting of Mondo grass along the wall to float the wall, rather than bringing the concrete right up to the edge."

*A **landscape in synch with its site:** The cutout squares in the Alioto house are echoed in the square blocks in the driveway and in the square planters.*

In addition to echoing architectural features from the house, plan to use materials in the landscape that are consistent with the house. If your house is brick, then brick pathways can enhance unity in the same way a picket fence complements an old-fashioned clapboard house. Both your house and garden will be more unified if you choose local, natural building materials rather than imported ones.

Develop a Concept. A clear sense of purpose and intent has a strong unifying effect. As Sylvia Crowe says in her book *Garden Design,* "… all the great gardens of the world have a unity both of execution and conception which shows that they were created in singleness of thought. Their makers knew what they wanted and were able to express it as a complete whole."

What you need or want in a garden will be unique to you and your personal goals. For example, in seventeenth-century French gardens, the grand allées, elaborate parterres, and flower gardens with beds and paths arranged in patterns reflected the owners' desire to project an image of wealth and power. Their control extended to manipulating growing things and creating exacting, punctilious order in their gardens. The sophisticated geometric designs also grew out of the period's fascination with René Descartes's invention of analytic geometry. This was the Age of Reason, where logical, rational thinking was considered the sole test of truth.

Keep it Individual. Your landscape should be a reflection of you and who you are. Determine what you want your garden to be, and then work toward that goal undistracted by other attractive, but perhaps contradicting, possibilities. Crowe states, "… if gardens are to fill their historic role of compensating the individual for the incompatibilities of the outside world, the private garden must be more individual than it has ever been before."

The proportion of the gardens was off when the boxwood parterres at Oatlands Plantation in Leesburg, Virginia were allowed to grow too large. Once the boxwood was trimmed down to the proper height of 12 inches, the garden felt "right."

PROPORTION AND SCALE

A large piece of furniture, such as a couch, can look enormous in a small room. Yet the same couch in a large room may look quite small. The phenomenon at work here is scale. The same object will look larger or smaller depending on the relative size of its surroundings.

In a sense, a garden is a decorated outdoor space where the same principles of scale and proportion apply. A large garden needs a sense of boundary to set the space apart from the expanse of sky and horizon and define it as a special, protected place. In addition, large trees and shrubs serve as transitions between the garden and the vast scale of the world outside. On the other hand, a garden in the city, with tall buildings looming over the property, usually needs shrubs and smaller trees that establish an intimate scale and separate the garden from its surroundings.

A common mistake, especially in small gardens, is to have too many diminutive features. Instead of making the garden feel bigger and in proportion with its space, small features make it feel busy and lacking in focus. Even in a pint-sized space, try to provide some sense of bulk and stature. For example, plant one tree or massive shrub as an important statement, and then use that plant as a reference, relating the scale and proportion of the rest of the plantings and ornaments to it. Also try to include a vertical element such as a tree, trellis, or arbor to draw the eye from the close boundaries of the property.

ESTABLISHING PLEASING PROPORTIONS

Alfredo Siani, who restored the historic gardens of Oatlands Plantation in Leesburg, Virginia, remembers the overgrown plants when he first arrived. Boxwood parterres had grown 7 feet tall. It took years of annual pruning to reduce the plants to their proper height of 12 to 18 inches, but once the job was complete, the difference astounded people. "One of the most difficult things in a garden," said Siani, "is achieving a sense of proportion and structure. When I finally got the box to the height I wanted, people responded that the garden was now 'right.' What had happened was the garden's structure was finally in proper proportion."

Follow Nature's Guidelines. Any garden, whether formal or informal, will be most successful when the elements are combined in pleasing proportions with objects properly related to one another by size. As early as the thirteenth century, mathematicians worked to codify rules and ratios for pleasing proportions. One of the most respected formulas was developed by Leonardo Fibonacci, also known as Leonardo of Pisa. In 1202 he discovered a series of numbers now known as the Fibonacci sequence. The sequence is created by adding together the two numbers that precede the next. For example, the first two numbers, 1 and 2, added equal 3. Two plus 3 equals 5, the next number in the series, and so on (1, 2, 3, 5, 8, 13, 21, 34, ad infinitum).

According to Fibonacci's formula, pleasing dimensions for a space are determined by adjacent numbers in the series. Thus a well-proportioned room, either in a house or garden, would be 8 feet by 13 feet, 13 feet by 21 feet, or any other size combination that fits the formula. Interestingly, this mathematical series closely matches the natural growth patterns of many plants, including the distribution of branches, leaves, and seeds. The mathematical sequence can be seen in the intersecting curves appearing in the seed arrangement of a ripe sunflower and in the seed cones of fir trees.

Keep Height and Width in Balance. Although few people today know of Fibonacci's work, it lives on in guidelines for proportions recommended by modern garden designers. For example, designers recommend that the depth of a border should be at least two-thirds the height of the structure behind it. According to that

Nature displays perfect proportions. *As can be seen in this photograph of a single pachysandra plant, each leaf is positioned to receive maximum sunlight without being in the shadow of other leaves. If this pattern was translated into numbers, it would nearly match Fibonacci's formula for pleasing proportions.*

rule of thumb, a border planted in front of a 6-foot tall fence or hedge should be at least 4 feet deep, measurements very close to the proportions in Fibonacci's number series (4:6 = 2:3).

Scale Foundation Plants Properly. An exception to the height-width rule is foundation plantings around a house, which should be low enough to leave windows unobstructed. It would be impractical—and out of proportion to the property—for the bed to be two-thirds the height of the house. Instead, the foundation planting should be about as wide as the height of the tallest shrub in the bed. Taller foundation plants should be sited against blank walls or between windows.

Similarly, in a small garden the enclosing fence should be no taller that half the width of the garden itself. Any taller, and the fence will feel oppressive. If you have a tiny space and want a high enclosure for privacy, consider putting an open trellis on top of the solid partition.

Another widely accepted guideline is that the tallest plants should be no taller than twice the depth of the border. For example, a 3-foot-wide border would accommodate plants whose mature height is about 6 feet, such as Joe-Pye weed, mixed with plants of shorter stature.

When planning your landscape, consider whether the plants you assembled on paper are in pleasing scale to themselves and to the rest of the garden. Also consider whether the different elements in the garden are attractively proportioned.

LIGHT AND SHADE

Lack of variety, or too much of a good thing, diminishes the pleasure of a garden. A garden that is totally exposed to the sun, with no shady retreat for contrast and relief, is exhausting. Similarly, a garden that has nothing but deep shade becomes oppressive. Try to use light and shade in your garden to provide pleasing contrast and show off the different effects of light on floral color.

Because the sun tends to fade flower colors, many flowers will appear to be brighter in a slightly shaded spot than in full sun. In addition, the quality of light varies in different parts of the country, affecting how colors look. One of the reasons vividly colored tropical flowers are perfect in their native habitat, but can look garish in other places, is that the bright sunlight typical of the tropics fades bright colors. In the softer, more diffused light typical of northern localities, where the sun's rays are less direct than those near the equator, those same tropical flowers scream with color. In regions with less intense light, the soft pastels come into their own, enlivening the garden with their glow. There, pale colors appear more brilliant in contrast to the duller light.

You can use shade as a cool retreat in your garden, as an escape from the hot sun. In a small space,

when the farthest corner is a shady bower, the dark in the distance will make the corner recede visually, so the garden appears larger. You can use the patterns created by shade to add movement. If you plant an evenly spaced row of straight-trunked trees, you can enjoy the stripes of shade that move across the ground as the sun arcs through the sky. And trees with high, light canopies can cast a delightful, dappled pattern that migrates as the day progresses.

Seek Inspiration in Impressionist Paintings. One way to get inspiration for your garden is to go to art museums and study the works of landscape painters. The French Impressionists explored nature in terms of color and light. Monet painted his gardens at Giverny over and over at different times of the day and in different weather conditions. Looking at paintings of gardens can give you a new understanding of color, light, and shadow.

Color and light were explored over and over again by the Impressionist artists. Claude Monet's painting, "The Garden, Giverny," shows how the interplay of color, light, and shadow affects the overall mood of the landscape. A good way to get inspiration for your own landscape design is to study Impressionist paintings.

MASS AND SPACE

An ideal design should contain a pleasing mix of mass and space. If there is too much mass, the garden will appear heavy and dark. If there is too much horizontal space, the garden will feel empty.

Large, solid plants have mass, especially if their color is dark. They take up more space in the garden—both physically and visually—and so help define and fill space. They also provide resting places for the eye when a landscape is busy with bright floral and other ornamental interest. These large plants also give form to the design.

Winter is the best time to judge whether your landscape has adequate mass. Then all the frills and distractions of summer's bounty are gone. Evergreens, hedges, and the exposed form of monumental deciduous trees stand out. If your design is well done with enough mass, the garden will be interesting even in this bare state.

Besides mass, you also need horizontal breaks or space. An expanse of patio, a change in level, a swath of lawn, or a reflecting pool all provide such breaks. These open areas are visually and physically inviting. They allow the viewer's eye to rest and encourage visitors to explore these areas and even to linger on a well-placed bench or chair.

Judge the mass of your garden in the winter. If the mass and space are balanced, your landscape will remain attractive during this bare time of the year. The bench provides a focal point.

PATTERN, TEXTURE, AND COLOR

Garden patterns are provided primarily by the physical layout. Whatever the pattern, whether symmetrical and ordered for a formal garden, or flowing and abstract for an informal design, it will establish the essential character of the garden.

To consider pattern in your garden, take graph paper and mark off the shapes of paths and beds. A static design, perfect for a small, enclosed garden that has no view to the outside to draw the eye, is one in which your eye focuses on the pattern itself rather than being lured to move through the space. Such a design can be formal or informal, abstract or geometric, but it should capture

The light-colored steps soften the mass of the dark trees and shrubs. The stone lantern and bench punctuate the mass of the steps and encourage strollers to take a closer look.

The pattern of the crazy-quilt paving enlivens the almost straight stone path and serves as a dramatic backdrop for the boldly colored border of Alstroemeria and daylilies.

attention because of the interest in the pattern. On a smaller scale, you can create additional patterns in your garden with bricks or stones laid out in designs.

By contrast, a pattern with movement, such as a diagonal that stretches in either straight or zigzagging lines across the property, will urge the eye to follow the flow. Part of the excitement of that pattern will depend on what your eye sees. If, after following a dynamic line to it's logical end, your eye finds nothing interesting to see, the result tends to be disappointing.

Leaves and Flowers Provide Texture. Leaf and flower forms and surfaces are the primary sources of texture. You can create different effects by experimentally combining contrasting textures. For example, combine a plant with spiny leaves, such as a dwarf pine tree, with the softer-looking, feathery foliage of the golden-hued *Cedrus deodara* 'Aurea'. Or try the straplike foliage of plants such as daylilies with broad-leaved plants such as large hostas, *Gunnera*, and *Rodgersia*.

Contrasting textures *are the dominant theme in this bed of lacy ferns, spiky iris, and flowing ornamental grass. The yellow iris flowers, gold grass, and yellow flowers on the shrub in the background unite the disparate elements.*

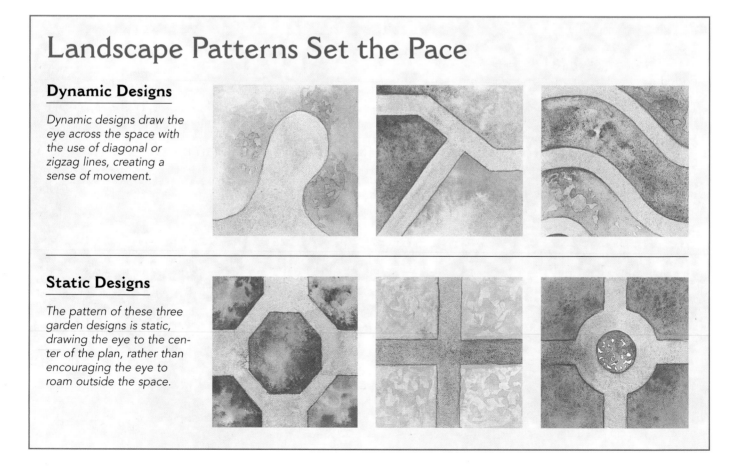

Landscape Patterns Set the Pace

Dynamic Designs

Dynamic designs draw the eye across the space with the use of diagonal or zigzag lines, creating a sense of movement.

Static Designs

The pattern of these three garden designs is static, drawing the eye to the center of the plan, rather than encouraging the eye to roam outside the space.

Brightly colored, variegated hosta leaves create a bold display. The solid green yew in the background tempers the scene. The tiny yew leaves are a pleasing textural contrast to the large hosta leaves.

Large-leaved plants are bold in texture, creating a strong, assertive look. Small-leafed plants tend to have a more delicate look. Too much of either will probably make a less successful design than a balanced blend of textures.

Flower form also contributes texture. Again, the most interesting designs will combine different shapes and textures. For example, the famous English herbaceous and perennial borders show a pleasing mixture of flowers with round heads; tall, pointed spires; airy sprays of small blossoms; umbrella-shaped blooms; and tiny-petaled flowers. The variety of textures, blended into an attractive whole, contributes greatly to the appeal of these borders.

Contrasting shapes, textures, and colors combine in this visually pleasing border. Here, the gray, fuzzy foliage of lamb's ears, the spurred columbine flowers, bell-shaped campanulas, and upright lupines work beautifully together.

Add interesting texture to the landscape by combining flowers of different shapes. The tall, white spires of the lupines provide a pleasing counterpoint to the rounded, full peony blossoms.

Color lights up the landscape. The yellow garden room at Ladew Topiary Gardens in Maryland glows on the dullest day. Plants include golden arborvitae, golden privet, goldtip yews, hostas, golden juniper, golden dogwood, and Japanese maples.

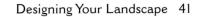

This color scheme is restful and easy on the eyes. Muted flowers in blues and soft yellows combine harmoniously with the blue foliage of the fescue grass and the gray and beige pebbles in this drought-tolerant garden.

there are many shades of pink, red, and purple. For spice, variegated leaves are striped, streaked, dotted, splashed, or mottled with two or more colors.

Of course, flowers are available in almost any conceivable color and combination. Be careful when buying from flower catalogs or nurseries not to be lured too far afield by outrageously colored flowers. Whether you choose a bold palette of reds and yellows, a striking composition of complementary colors such as blue and orange, or opt for softer pastel tones, you won't want the final combination to clash.

That said, be willing to experiment. Planning plant combinations, especially for beginning gardeners, is partly a process of trial and error. There is no harm in changing your mind and moving plants around; most will survive the move. If you persevere, you can create a garden that combines pattern, texture, and color in a way that pleases your eye and satisfies your soul.

Color Sources. Color is available to the gardener both in foliage and flower. In the plant kingdom the range in leaf color is remarkable. Some leaves are yellow—from bright gold to softly glowing yellow-green. There is every imaginable shade of green from pale, almost translucent spring greens to deep forest greens. There are blues from deep and dusky to gray. And

Combine colors boldly. The deep violet blossoms of the cranesbill (Geranium 'Johnson's Blue,') are striking growing next to the hot pink Dianthus chinensis x barbatus 'Princess Crimson Eye'. Although this is an unusual combination, the result is quite pretty.

Teaming with Neighbors

In neighborhoods where homes are close together, what happens on the next-door property, especially close to your property line, can have a huge effect on the beauty of your own landscape. For instance, large, overgrown, unpruned trees along a boundary may create too much shade and messiness from falling leaves. One woman solved that problem by offering to pay to have her neighbor's trees thinned. The neighbors were delighted with her proposal, which benefited both the neighbors as well as the neglected trees.

Fence Design Brings Continuity. Holly Shimizu wrote in *Horticulture* magazine how she and her husband, Osamu, gained much-needed privacy for their small garden in Maryland. "We replaced the chain-link fence with a lattice-topped, 6-foot-tall board fence that suited the character of Glen Echo, but first we talked to our three adjoining neighbors to see if they would like to purchase the same fence for their gardens. We offered to deliver the fence ourselves and help them with the installation. They agreed, and the result is a wonderful sense of continuity between our adjoining yards. Still, being in need of some additional height to screen our rear deck, we asked whether we might plant some evergreens next door. To our delight, the neighbors were thrilled by our proposal to plant incense cedar, Leyland cypress, and American hollies. They had been wanting privacy as much as we had. Their generosity allowed us to keep the much-needed space where we intended to build our waterfall, and it took only two years for both families to enjoy a welcome sense of privacy."

Shared Garden. In another case, a 12-foot strip of land divided the two driveways of neighboring properties. One of the families wanted to develop their half into a rose garden, but they were concerned that the weedy patch on the neighbor's side would spoil the effect. When they installed a sprinkler system through-

The unclipped shrubs near the house separate two properties, one of which is Monet's garden (background). The foreground once belonged to American impressionist artist Lilla Cabot Perry.

out their property, they offered to share the water delivered to that section of the garden if the neighbors would plant the space as well. The neighbors were pleased to have an opportunity to improve the strip of land and agreed to plant roses in their half of the strip.

Cooperative Pest Control. In another neighborhood effort, one member of the community negotiated a wholesale price for a large order of milky spore disease to control Japanese beetle grubs, and then sent a letter to everyone concerned explaining the importance of treating the entire neighborhood and offering the product at the reduced price. Since the beetles are flying insects and can lay eggs over a large area, a space with a radius of 300 feet needed to be treated to be effective. Seeing a solution to the frustrating damage caused by the beetles, everyone was delighted to participate.

Seeking privacy, yet continuity, Holly Shimizu and her husband replaced a chain-link fence with the board fence shown here. They asked their adjoining neighbors if they would like the same fence along their property line. The neighbors agreed; the result is a strong sense of continuity between the yards.

CHAPTER 2

Developing a Plan

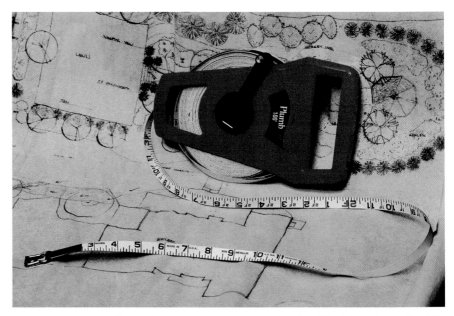

Whether you wish to landscape your property all at once or plant one section at a time as budget and schedule allow, it is a good idea to create a master plan. This plan is basically an overhead map of your property that shows its features, including your intended plantings. Over time, you may amend this master plan, but it will continue to serve as your basic road map and keep you on course.

Measuring your property can be simplified by using a flexible steel or fiberglass hand-winding tape measure that is long enough to stretch the full length of your garden. Retractable measuring tapes are typically not long enough for landscape dimensions, and they are likely to be ruined if you get dirt in the winding mechanism.

Conducting a Site Analysis

The first step, before drawing the plan, is to make a site analysis of your property. This is simply an inventory of all features that relate to the present landscape. Record this information on a base map, drawn to scale. The map should show your property boundaries as well as your house and any other structures. Even if you opt to employ a professional designer for the landscape plan, you'd be wise to record information yourself on the site analysis. The process will help you gain a deeper understanding of the features of your property. Armed with that knowledge, you'll be better equipped to care for your property over the years and to select plants and design elements.

A site analysis is a thorough inventory of the features on a property, including any structures, major trees and specimen plants, utility easements, equipment such as

air-conditioner units, and the topography of the lot—significant slopes, dips, and hills. A really thorough analysis will also record any aesthetic factors, including attractive or unsightly views, and information on conditions that affect plant growth, such as wind patterns, warm microclimates, and low spots where cold air settles.

Most homeowners can record the necessary information in a couple of hours. However, if you are new to the property and it is already planted, you may want to record changes throughout a whole year. Do a site analysis in the spring and in the winter to capture the important aspects of your landscape.

BEGIN WITH A BASE MAP

You can create a base map from a copy of your plat (or property survey) prepared by surveyors, which most homeowners receive when they purchase their house. A plat typically shows several individual properties and may or may not show structures, including houses. If you don't have a plat, request one from your tax assessor's office; copies are usually available at no cost or for a nominal fee.

In addition to showing locations of property lines, a footprint of the house, and any other significant structures, the plat should show easements and the location of overhead and underground utility lines owned by the county or city. It should also have a legend indicating its drawing scale, which is typically 1:20, meaning that every inch on the paper is equivalent to 20 feet on your property. If the scale isn't shown, you can calculate it by measuring a distance on the plat in inches, and then correlating that with the same actual distance on your property.

Make Several Enlarged Copies.

Property surveys and plats are usually a standard size, which is tiny considering all the information you want to record. Take your plat or property survey to a copy shop or blueprint company to get an enlargement. While you're there, you might as well have them make four or five copies, one for your site analysis, one for drawing your design, and extras for updates and changes over the years. If you can, have the blueprint company enlarge the original scale to at least 1:12. This will give you more room to draw garden features.

Even if your map shows the primary dimensions of your property, you'll need to take other measurements. This task will be easier if you use a fiberglass, nylon-clad steel, or chrome-steel measuring tape on a reel. These tapes, noted here in order from least to most expensive, come in longer lengths than the retractable type and are more suited to measuring larger spaces.

Typical Plat Map

A plat map shows the precise boundaries, the measurements of the lot, and the position of the house, garage, and existing easements. Plat maps are available free or for a nominal charge from the tax assessor's office. Make sure you understand where the property lines are and whether any easements exist before you start landscaping.

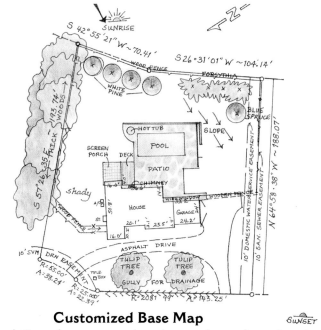

Customized Base Map

Completing a base map, such as the one shown above, is an important first step in landscaping. Here the owner has indicated where the sun rises and sets; the shady spots; how the footprint of the house has been expanded to include a patio, pool, and screen porch; where the property slopes; some major plantings; and a fence.

Kinds of Information to Gather. The following pages outline the kinds of information you should gather. Although the list is long and comprehensive, don't feel overwhelmed. A site analysis will greatly help you in making informed design decisions. Simply use the text as a guide, and disregard items that do not apply. However, bear in mind that an accurate site analysis can prevent expensive design errors. The last thing you want is to damage a utility line while digging. Remember, by law you must call your utility company before you dig. Another expensive mistake would be to build a garden pond for water lilies where there's not enough sun for them to flower.

Lot Boundaries and Shape

If you're starting with an official drawing of your lot, it will show property boundaries accurately. You can next measure other useful distances that aren't recorded on the plat, and write them down. For example, you will want to know the length of the front walk, the size of an existing patio, the distance from the patio to the back of the lot, and so on. If the surveyors' pipes or markers are no longer in place, be sure you find and indicate the exact locations of property corners and edges. (You may need the help of a surveyor.) An error of even a few inches beyond your property line can lead to a dispute with the affected neighbor, especially if you build a fence or plant a hedge. If you don't have an existing plat to work from, measure the property carefully, and draw the boundaries to scale on graph paper. With your boundaries correctly drawn, you'll have a bird's-eye view of your property.

The House

On the plat, draw the perimeter, or *footprint*, of the ground floor of your house. Note doors leading outside, windows, chimneys, stoops, overhangs, eaves, the garage, and other outbuildings. Indicate dimensions of each feature as close to scale as possible. Also record the height from the ground to the first-floor windowsills. A common mistake is to put plants that will grow too big under windows. Although they may be small and cute at the beginning, in a few years those plants will grow and begin blocking the light and the view. If you know the projected mature height of the plants you choose and have noted window heights and dimensions, you can avoid that mistake.

Turn a utilitarian side entrance into a pleasant landscape feature, as the homeowners did with this pretty dooryard garden. Petunias, lobelia, nasturtium, and snapdragons soften the pavement and steps, and make the entrance inviting.

While recording this information, think about the natural traffic flow from your house to your garden areas and about views from windows that you might want to improve or emphasize. A typical drawback of older houses is that they often have a side door rather than a back door, and this side door often opens onto the least attractive portion of the property. Instead of remodeling the house to install a back door, you can convert the side-door problem to an asset by creating a small garden next to the side door, with a path that leads to the front and back garden areas.

Structures and Pavings

With your house and its first-floor features drawn on your base map, begin drawing other existing structures such as gazebos, fences, walls, and hedges. Also include play structures such as swing sets, basketball hoops, and sandboxes, as well as patios, terraces, decks, ponds, and pools. Lastly, draw in the driveway, walkways, and garden paths, noting the types of paving material.

The most direct route from the driveway to the front door is across the lawn. Here the homeowner laid a stepping-stone path across the route, which saves the grass from wear and tear and keeps shoes dry.

Combine Convenience and Aesthetics. Although you want your property to be aesthetically pleasing, it should also be convenient to use. Try to keep human needs in mind. For example, while you're noting the paths and walkways, think about how convenient they are to use. Does the path follow a route that family members actually walk, or do they tend to cut corners and step through planting beds? Is the driveway wide enough, or do vehicles often drive off the edge, damaging adjacent lawn and plantings?

SUN AND SHADE PATTERNS

Knowing the light intensity at different locations on your property is extremely important when choosing plants. While a wide variety of plants thrive in dappled sunlight or in shade where the light is fairly bright, your choice of plants is more limited for deeply shaded areas.

Patterns of sun and shade will change throughout each day and over the course of the year. Because the pattern of shadows is constantly shifting, it is important to record where the shady spots are at different times of the day and year. In the early morning and late afternoon, the sun will be low in the sky, casting long shadows. At noon, shadows will be short. During winter months, the sun remains low in the sky throughout the day, although a property with deciduous trees may receive more sunlight in winter, when the leaves have fallen, than in summer. The sun is high in the sky in summer, when its warmth and light intensity are increased.

It's not necessary to record the shadow cast by every structure on your property every minute of the day. But do make note of spots such as the north side of the house that are in deep shade for most of the day as well as other areas that may get only three or four hours of sunlight per day.

Although shade is an important consideration, so too is sun. You may want to reserve the sunniest spots for a swimming pool or a vegetable garden. Also consider the

The sun and shade patterns change over the course of the year. In the winter, when the sun is low in the sky, the shadows cast by the deciduous tree and shrubs are longer than those cast in the summer sun.

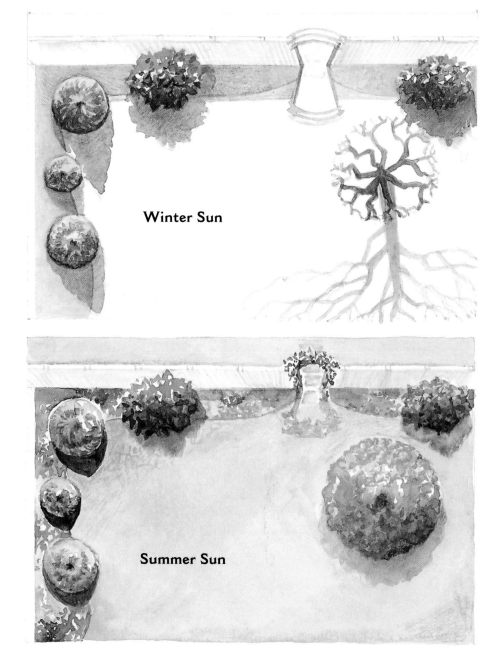

Winter Sun

Summer Sun

Notice how the sun patterns *change through the day. In the scene above, the large tree casts a shadow across the lawn in the afternoon. However, earlier in the day the space receives more light and smaller shadows.*

time of day you are most likely to use such spaces. If you plan to sit outdoors in the sun after work, you won't want the patio on the east side of the house, which gets only morning sun. On the other hand, an eastern exposure is ideal for *al fresco* breakfasts.

UTILITIES AND EASEMENTS

Again, you need to know the location of underground utilities such as electric cables, water pipes, and sewer pipes or a septic system in case you plan to dig anywhere near them. In addition, you need to know about any easements on your land that are subject to public use. If this information isn't provided on your plat, call your utility company and municipal jurisdiction to determine exact locations and depths. Buried cables and pipes generally aren't an issue if you're putting in shallow-rooted plants, but utilities could pose hazards if you dig deep holes for trees, pools, and ponds, or if you excavate for foundations or terracing. Also record any overhead wires and their approximate height so you can choose trees that will comfortably fit. Too many lovely trees eventually need to be heavily pruned to keep their branches away from overhead power lines.

In addition to belowground utilities, remember to indicate locations of utility meters and air-conditioning units. Consider planting shrubs or building a trellis to screen these unsightly necessities from view. Also, try to avoid placing a patio too close to a noisy air conditioner.

IS THE LIGHT RIGHT?

When you plan your landscape, consider the availability and intensity of light throughout the year. Most plants tolerate a range of light but have specific conditions in which they perform at their best. To determine optimal light conditions for particular trees, shrubs, and plants, look up the plants or ask your supplier. The following definitions will help you determine which conditions you have on your property.

- **Full Sun**—a daily minimum of six hours of direct unobstructed sun.

- **Semisunny or partial shade**—a daily minimum of four to six hours of direct sun.

- **Light shade or dappled shade**—sunlight under tall trees and under trees with sparse foilage.

- **Shade or full shade**—no direct sun; this occurs on the north side of structures and under dense leaf canopies.

- **Dense shade**—shade so deep that no shadows are cast; this occurs between tall buildings and in woods with a dense canopy.

Sun/Shade Log	Date _____		
Property Section _____			
Hour	**Full Sun**	**Partial Sun**	**Full Shade**
6:00 AM			
8:00 AM			
10:00 AM			
12:00 NOON			
2:00 PM			
4:00 PM			
6:00 PM			
8:00 PM			

To create a sun/shade log for various parts of your property, make photocopies of this chart. Then, monthly during the growing season, check off the hours of full sun.

TOPOGRAPHY AND DRAINAGE

Use angled arrows to indicate slopes and any other changes in elevation. On a lot with abrupt changes in elevation, you'll need to decide whether to work around the natural topography or do major grading or terracing.

Study your land during and after heavy rains to understand how runoff flows. Look to low-lying spots where water accumulates, and note how long they remain wet. Prolonged wetness may indicate poor grading or clay soil that doesn't allow water to be absorbed readily. If your property doesn't handle water well, you may need to install drainage trenches. Also note runoff routes and evidence of erosion. If runoff hasn't already been channeled away from your house by foundation perimeter drains, you may need to build a berm (mounded earth) or find another way to redirect the flow.

Draw in the locations of house and outbuilding downspouts on your site map, and show any buried pipes that lead the water away. After heavy rains, check to ensure the drains are open and functioning properly.

◀ **Drainage problems** can be solved creatively, as was done here with a dry stone riverbed. The excess water flows harmlessly toward an underground drain. The "riverbed" is planted with Miscanthus sinensis.

Indicate slopes on a site plan with angled arrows. The slope in the front garden shown above presents an attractive view to the neighborhood. It is planted with clumps of drought-tolerant, blooming perennials and small shrubs.

MICROCLIMATES AND PREVAILING WINDS

Most properties have pockets where temperatures and growing conditions vary from the prevailing climate. For example, a south-facing wall will catch the sun and radiate heat and light, warming that section of the garden early in the spring and helping maintain the warmth late into autumn. Also, cold air collects in low-lying areas, potentially injuring sensitive plants. And windchill can lower temperatures significantly in exposed areas of the garden. Try to keep all of these factors in mind as you map your site, develop your landscape plan, and choose plants.

If your property is windy, you may want to install windbreaks. These can consist of trees or shrubs, open board or latticework fencing or walls, or a glass wall that preserves your view. If you garden in coastal conditions, be mindful that the salt content of sea winds can damage some plants. In that case, be sure to choose plants that will tolerate the salty air. Local nurseries can usually provide advice. In general, plants with silver, gray, or fuzzy leaves do well near the shore.

Cold air tends to settle into low-lying pockets, creating a frigid microclimate. Notice air patterns in your garden, and mark spots on your site plan that are noticeably hotter or colder than the norm.

Rather than cut down *this grand old tree, the owners incorporated it into their deck. The tree creates a fun conversation starter and provides welcome shade on hot summer days.*

EXISTING PLANTINGS

Be alert to the potential for conserving existing plants in your new design. Record the locations of trees, shrubs, and planting beds on your base map. Draw the shapes of beds to scale, and indicate what is growing in them. Represent trees and shrubs with circles scaled to approximate circumferences. If you know tree and shrub names, label them. In addition, note the general health of these plants.

Because deciduous trees lose their leaves in winter, they can be a boon for temperature control. If they are planted near the house, they provide much-wanted shade in the summer and allow the sun to warm the house in winter. On the other hand, too many trees can turn a house into a dark cave. Consider whether your house needs any shade trees to provide protection from the hot summer sun. Also consider whether trees which now provide shade need to be thinned or removed. See Chapter 9, pages 196-197 for specific information on thinning trees.

If you have a spectacular tree, you will probably want to keep it and plan your landscape around it. However, you may have valuable shrubs planted where you don't want them. Right plants in the wrong places can potentially save you a lot of money. When handled properly, most shrubs and small trees can be successfully transplanted. On the other hand, you may not need to move them, as a little pruning can transform many overgrown plants and give them a new look and a new life. (See Chapter 9, pages 198-199, "Transplanting Large Shrubs and Trees.")

VIEWS, NOISE, AND ODORS

Indicate any attractive views that you would like to emphasize, as well as unsightly scenes that you would like to hide or disguise. A good view doesn't need to be a vast panorama of mountain ridges or ocean. It might be as simple as a tall, beautiful tree on your neighbor's property, or a tiny slice of a view of the surrounding countryside. Mark trees or shrubs that need to be removed to open up scenic vistas. For ideas on how to be creative with good views and bad ones, see "Maximizing Assets and Minimizing Faults" on page 53.

Our world is full of ambient noise. Some of it, such as bird song, is pleasant to the ear, but there are other sounds we would rather not hear. Make a note of the source of unpleasant noise, such as traffic sounds. You might be able to reduce the noise with a dense planting of shrubbery, or with a fence or wall. Another possibility is to mask the unpleasant noise with a splashing fountain. A third technique is to practice avoidance—keep outdoor seating areas away from noisy air conditioners, for instance.

Also, when you locate your patio, keep potential odors in mind. You could do a marvelous job of screening your trash bin from view, only to have your nose be reminded of its proximity on hot summer days.

LIGHTS AND SPRINKLERS

If your property has outdoor lighting, mark the locations of the fixtures, and if possible, indicate where the wiring is buried. Also draw in weatherproofed outdoor outlets.

Mark existing light fixtures *on your site plan, including, if possible, where the power lines run. Low-voltage lights can be easily moved around, but 120-volt systems are more permanent.*

If you wish to install outdoor lighting, now is the time to plan for it. Especially if you opt for a traditional 120-volt system, which requires digging trenches to bury wires that are encased in waterproof conduits. You won't want to do such disruptive digging after you've planted. As an alternative, you might consider low-voltage lighting, because its wires do not need to be buried. For more on lighting, see Chapter 3, pages 89–92.

Draw in the locations of sprinkler heads on your base map, along with their water lines and spigots. Make plans for any underground watering system in the early stages of your design. For an easier option, consider drip irrigation systems, which deliver water directly to the root system at a slow rate. Drip systems soak in deeply without watering the leaf surfaces. Drip-irrigation lines can be moved as your needs evolve. For more on drip irrigation systems, see Chapter 3, pages 80–83.

Planning Your Landscape Design

An ancient Roman maxim states, "It is a bad plan that admits of no modifications," and a plan for a landscape design illustrates this point perfectly. A good landscape design is the foundation upon which you will build for years to come. You'll likely make adjustments—moving the pink rose bush closer to the wine-colored Japanese maple or adding royal purple crocus to the bed of golden daffodils—but the basic structure of a well-designed landscape will help guide you. Begin by considering the permanent elements of the physical landscape, such as large trees, neighboring structures, and microclimates, as well as certain regulations imposed by your local authorities. Then start planning.

LOCAL CODES AND REGULATIONS

Rules and regulations on issues such as fence height, pools, spotlights, decks and other construction projects vary from community to community. Before you embark on any hardscape project, check with your local building authorities to learn whether permits are required and whether any restrictions will apply.

If your property has any public rights-of-way or set-backs (areas along property boundaries where construction is prohibited), be sure you know their exact locations. Be aware that your property may not extend

Enlarge a photograph *of your property that gives good perspective to help you visualize a landscape design. Cover the enlargement with a clear sheet of plastic, and use water-based markers to draw proposed garden features.*

all the way to the public road. In many communities, the town or county may own as much as 20 feet of what may look like your property. If you plant a hedge along the road on municipal property, you might be required to remove it.

USING PHOTOGRAPHS TO VISUALIZE PLANS

While a landscape map can give a good two-dimensional, top view of your property design, it doesn't give you the perspective that you have on foot. For this, you need what architects call a *frontal elevation*. It's a simple matter to create this view using a photograph.

Find a vantage point that gives you a good overview of your property. If your property is too wide to fit into one frame, shoot several photo prints and tape them together, or borrow a camera with a wide-angle lens. Request 4×6-inch prints or larger; then have a copy center make enlarged copies up to 11×17 inches.

A black-and-white photo or photocopy is an excellent means of assessing the strengths and weaknesses of an existing design. Without the distraction of color, you can better analyze the design in terms of form and texture. Plus, oversize photocopies are less expensive in black and white (for the clearest black-and-white photocopies, start with black-and-white prints).

For evaluating color schemes or coordinating with house colors, you'll need color prints. A photograph, whether in black and white or color, is uncompromising in capturing a landscape as it really is, whereas your eye tends to overlook design flaws in the same way that your ears screen out unwanted background noise.

Add New Features. Place a clear sheet of plastic over the photograph and draw on it with water-based markers. Plastic makes the use of different colored pens easier, giving a sense of form in your design as well as its colors. And it lets you easily erase.

As an alternative to plastic, tape a piece of tracing paper over the enlarged photocopy, and draw in the existing plantings and features you plan to keep. Then draw in the new landscape elements you have in mind. It's not necessary to give an artistically accurate rendering of the plants. Simply capture the basic shapes, and draw them as close to scale as possible. Be sure to draw the plants at their mature size so that you can see how the design will look when it has grown, and can gauge how many plants you'll need. If you don't like the design, no problem: just try again with a new piece of tracing paper.

Another photo option is to shoot a slide of your garden and project it onto a wall where you've taped a large piece of paper. Simply trace the outline of the house, including the windows, doors, and roof line, as well as existing plants. Then add the new elements.

To give you a better sense of scale, it may help to position reference markers before you take the photograph. Place several 6-foot vertical stakes at different points on your property to serve as guides to height. When you draw in your plants, 3-foot plants will be half the height of the pole. This technique is especially useful if you are designing a bed or border.

OTHER PLANNING TOOLS

Today there's a wide selection of computer programs that allow you to experiment with plant combinations and move plants around easily without the effort of drawing and redrawing on paper. Some of the programs include information on each plant's growing requirements. In others, you can input plants when they are young and small and then push a button to see how much they will grow in five years. The programs include predrawn mapping symbols for trees, shrubs, annuals,

Computer-generated *landscape design programs allow you to move plants around and try different designs almost effortlessly. The programs help you to visualize how a proposed design will actually look.*

and perennials. There are even shapes and symbols that represent hardscape elements such as decks, stone walls, fences, and pools, and different textures to represent paving materials such as gravel, mulch, and brick.

If you'd prefer to arrange landscaping symbols with your hands rather than draw them or manipulate them on a computer, consider the various garden design books and kits that include grid paper and reusable, movable flower and plant images. The better products include plant lists with cultivation information, as well as valuable comments on regional differences. They also indicate how the plants will relate to one another by color, height, and bloom time, as well as by shape and texture of flower and leaf.

For a more hands-on approach, *you can position stick-on trees, shrubs, and flowers with kits such as the one shown above. The "plants" come in different sizes and are scaled to fit the grids to which they adhere.*

Maximizing Assets and Minimizing Faults

"Accentuate the positive, eliminate the negative." So goes an old song by Johnny Mercer and Harold Arlen. The same philosophy applies to landscaping. Try to showcase the positive features of your property, such as a beautiful view, established trees and shrubs, large windows in your home that look onto the garden, or cooling summer breezes. Work to create designs that emphasize and enhance these good features.

If your land is evenly rectangular, you may want to make it appear more interesting by breaking up the space so that the entire back or front garden can't be seen at once. A screen of plants, a trellis, or a wall can divide a property, creating separate *garden rooms.* An unevenly dimensioned lot offers both a challenge and an opportunity. For example, on a triangular lot, you can partition the narrow end from the rest of the lot by means of a hedge or fence. Include a narrow gate or doorway to give access to a secret retreat.

You can draw attention to a pretty view by framing it with a pair of trees, an arbor, or a pair of statues. Preserve panoramic views by keeping the plantings low so that the vista isn't obscured. If a distant view is just visible through a gap in the trees or between two buildings, use paths or other landscape elements to draw attention to the distant scene. Above all, if you have a good view, create a comfortable place where you can sit and enjoy it. This viewing place can be a patio or deck or simply a couple of chairs placed where the outlook is best.

Large windows give you a wonderful opportunity to enjoy your garden from indoors as well as outside. To improve this view, you can design a vignette (a small, room-like garden) centered on the window, or design plantings around an axis from the window into the garden that invites viewers to look outside. It's often best to conclude the scene with a pleasing focal point at the end of the axis. For evening viewing, you can install

An awkward triangle-shape lot is divided into two garden rooms, transforming a challenging space into an asset. The front garden has a more usefully proportioned shape, and the hidden, pointed garden beyond is a gem.

garden lights. Place plants with sweet-smelling foliage or flowers near the windows so you can enjoy their fragrance when the windows are open. Good choices for fragrance include gardenia, apothecary rose, Oriental lilies, flowering tobacco, daphne, honeysuckle, star magnolia, and many others.

TAKING ADVANTAGE OF BREEZES

Because a cooling summer breeze is a major asset in hot climates, try to locate seating areas in the path of cool moving air. Where summers are cool, look instead for a sheltered, sunny spot, and furnish it with comfortable chairs. Also consider planting fragrant shrubs and herbs in the path of the breeze.

Maintain Established Trees. Beautiful, established trees and shrubs are a landscape treasure, giving a sense of permanence and history. Their value will be increased if you take care of them. Keep them pruned so that they stay in good health and maintain an attractive form and scale. You may want to feature a rare or special specimen plant as the central focal point of a garden.

Wyatt and Dorothy Williams were dismayed when water from a newly built pond seeped underneath the pond and collected at the far end, drowning the oldest and largest tree on their property in Virginia. The Williamses turned that tragedy into a triumph when they built a gazebo where the tree had been. The gazebo adds architectural interest to the garden and provides a pleasant place from which to view the pond.

SCREENING BAD VIEWS

A property's negative features are generally more challenging than its assets, but with skill and creativity you can turn a problem into an advantage. Unsightly views and lack of privacy are common problems facing homeowners today. While the neighbor's house may be attractive, most people nonetheless want their garden to be a private retreat, out of sight of the neighbors' houses and yards. Although many communities have restrictions on the height of fences and walls, you can create wonderful screens using trees, shrubs, hedges, and tall ornamental grasses.

If you already have a chain-link fence, you can mask it with a dense-growing evergreen vine, such as ivy. In just a few years, unattractive fencing will all but disappear under the thick vine. In restricted spaces where a

Change a garden problem into an attractive solution. *The Williams family built a gazebo on the spot where a large and ancient tree died due to water seeping from a new pond.*

Screen unsightly areas *with trellises or lattice panels. Lattice is a particularly effective way to hide an unwanted view, provide privacy and shade, and add height.*

tall wall or fence would take up too much room or would be too imposing, consider building a trellis. It can become an effective screen without being visually heavy. Turn the trellis into a stunning vertical element by covering it with flowering vines. You can add to your privacy by topping existing fences or walls with an extra few feet of lattice or vine-covered trellis.

MANAGING SLOPES

Many people address the mowing problem and reduce erosion on steep slopes by planting masses of low-maintenance shrubs or ground covers. While that solution is functional, it sometimes misses an opportunity to create a really special place.

Terraces for a Hillside. Consider terracing a slope or turning it into a stroll garden with stepping-stone paths that zigzag across the face. A hillside is an excellent place for a rock garden because the slope presents the garden, making small plants readily visible. Consider building a retaining wall at the bottom of the slope, filling the space behind the wall with soil to create a planter, and incorporating cascading plants. (See Chapter 6, page 137 for "How to Build a Dry-Laid Stone Retaining Wall.") For a more ambitious design, create a series of waterfalls that run down the slope into a pond at the bottom. (See Chapter 7, page 162 for information on waterfalls.)

▲ **One way to manage a slope** is to create a stroll garden. Here, shallow steps allow visitors to climb the hill safely, while encouraging them to pause to examine the garden nestled against the edge of the stairs.

▶ **A shady retreat** from the bright Southern California sun was created by building this pergola. It is covered in vining Stephanotis, which produces sweet-smelling flowers often used in bridal bouquets.

DEALING WITH TOO MUCH SUN

In hot climates, a shady retreat is especially welcome. But shade trees take many years to grow. Nevertheless, they are an investment worth making. In our society, statistics show that people, on average, live in one house for only five years. With prospects of a possible move, you might find it tempting to go for instant results rather than long-term benefits. Instant gratification makes sense to a point, but it is often carried too far. Gardens throughout North America are being planted with fast-growing trees and shrubs that may be past their prime and dying in just 15 to 20 years. Even if you don't plan to be around to see a slow-growing sapling mature to a tree, prospective buyers of your home will appreciate your foresight, perhaps by being willing to pay a better price. So when you are designing a landscape, it's best to plan for the future. Who knows, you might decide to stay for decades yourself.

Instant Shade. While waiting for the trees to grow, you can achieve instant shade and add an attractive architectural feature at the same time. Consider a lath-covered structure, such as a pergola or arbor, over a patio or deck. You can grow flowering vines up the support posts and hang flower-filled baskets from overhead beams. Plant the baskets with colorful shade-lovers such as wax begonias and cascading fuchsias. If possible, position the lath strips to run north and south so that the shade will shift as the sun moves during the day from east to west. If the lath shelter connects with your house, construct panels in the section nearest the house so that you can remove them in winter, allowing more light to enter the house.

Portable shade is delivered by a large, market-style garden umbrella set into a heavily weighted stand. The umbrella can be moved to follow the sun, and it is an attractive landscape feature.

A garden umbrella is an even easier source of shade. You can buy umbrellas that fit into the center of a garden table or into a weighted stand, which allows you to move the umbrella wherever it's needed.

COPING WITH DEEP SHADE

While wooded property can be lovely, too many trees create dense shade and block light to the house. Many people are loath to cut down trees. Yet when you thin a woodland, the remaining trees will show to better advantage. In addition, they will be healthier and will develop more-beautiful forms because they will not be competing as much for light, space, water, and nutrients.

Pruning Lower Branches. You'll gain a surprising amount of light in your garden if you prune off lower branches of surrounding trees. On very tall trees, you can trim as high as 30 or 40 feet, creating an open, airy understory that is protected by the high foliage canopy. This shady but bright environment is ideal for a wide range of plants that prefer shade or partial shade.

Over time, even trees known for their loose, open canopies will become overgrown. Trim them to remove excess branches and twigs. In addition to allowing more light into the garden, a properly pruned tree will have a more attractive form. (See Chapter 9, pages 184-189 for information on pruning trees.)

It is possible to have a shady area of your garden that is quite bright because of reflected light. Such a location will support a wider variety of plants than a spot that gets an hour or two of direct sun but is very dark for the rest of the day. You can create reflected light and brighten dark spots in the garden, in addition to visually cheering up the space, using white or light-colored walls and paving. Researchers have found that even a small percentage increase in light will improve a plant's growth and flowering. Light-reflecting walls and pavings can make a huge difference.

A variety of plants will grow in dappled or partial shade, but the choice is limited when the shade is dense. Ivy is one stalwart that will grow in almost any situation, including deep shade. It also can withstand the dry conditions created by a heavy tree canopy and dense root systems.

Pruning lower branches, or "limbing trees up," as high as 30 or 40 feet, is a creative way to add enough light to grow a healthy lawn and a wide assortment of plants. The dappled light under these stately tulip trees is perfect for shade-tolerant plants such as azaleas and even for sun-loving iris.

DESIGNING FOR SMALL SPACES

As the population grows and land becomes ever more valuable, building lots tend to become smaller and smaller. As a result, many people are faced with creating a garden in a pocket-sized space. Fortunately, small gardens can be gems, and there are all sorts of tricks to make a tiny plot look much bigger than it really is.

Optical illusions, the basis of magicians' tricks, can work wonders in your landscape as well. With a little trickery, you can fool your eye into believing that the tiniest of gardens is spacious or at least less cramped. The tools are the same as those used by painters and interior decorators to create a sense of space: the use of scale, perspective, color, light, and shadow. If you are fortunate enough to have a large property, you may want to consider subdividing an open expanse of space into more intimate garden rooms.

Scale. For a small space, use dwarf varieties of your favorite plants. In most cases, these diminutive versions of their full-size counterparts have all the beautiful qualities of form and texture but not the large size.

Also look to trees and shrubs that are naturally small and compact in growth. Instead of a tree that can grow to 60 feet tall at maturity, choose one that grows to only 20 or 30 feet. Excellent trees that are suitable for small gardens include dogwoods, some varieties of magnolia, crape myrtle, and some varieties of birch.

Keep plants in scale with their surroundings. The dwarf conifers shown here are in pleasing proportion with the raised bed and the landscape. They will stay small without pruning, making them a great addition to a low-maintenance design.

Choose naturally small trees, such as crape myrtle, shown above, for small gardens. Some hybrids will grow only 8 feet tall, while others will mature at 25 feet. In late summer they glow with brightly colored flowers.

Many large trees can be pruned to the right scale for the garden and maintained there with frequent pruning. In fact, an evergreen that normally would grow to 50 feet can be kept as low as 3 feet high if you shear it on a regular basis.

This *prune-to-size* method is a good choice if you like the tailored look of well-pruned plants. In a small garden, pruned plants add sculptural interest, but you'll need to keep cutting them back that so they stay in proper scale. But remember, if you choose an evergreen that is naturally short, you'll save yourself a lot of effort.

Perspective. The discovery of perspective revolutionized the art of painting during the Renaissance. Perspective is one of the most useful illusory tricks up the magician's sleeve. With perspective you can make close-up objects seem farther away and objects in the distance look closer. In much the same way, you can transform your garden by using perspective to alter the way you perceive it.

A project by Daniel Stewart, a landscape architect based in San Clemente, California, demonstrates a masterful use of perspective. His goal was to visually enlarge a long, narrow brick patio only 12 feet deep and 30 to 35 feet wide that is surrounded by walls. Stewart cut the bricks farthest away from the house to one-third their normal length, gradually increasing their length as they neared the house until they were back to the original length where the patio met the home's exterior wall. This trick makes the patio look much deeper than it really is.

Statues and Perspective. You can apply the perspective principle to statuary as well. Place a small statue at the end of a small garden. Its small size will trick your eye into seeing it larger and farther away than it really is.

British garden writer Roy Strong tells about a 6-foot-high obelisk he placed at the end of a narrow walk on a slight rise in his own garden. "It looks twice the height (that it really is) … as long as no one stands next to it."

Other Perspective Tricks. Just as the lines of a road in a painting slowly converge to a single point to create a sense of distance, so too can your garden path. If your path is straight, narrow it slightly as it moves away from you. To add to the effect, prune the shrubs at the far end of the path so that they appear smaller than those that are up close. If you do this skillfully, the perceived distance may appear to double.

Vary Plant Heights and Texture. Staggering plant heights also gives a greater sense of depth. This is a good option for people who have small gardens but want lots of plants. Start by planting a vine, tall shrub, or small tree at the back of the bed. If you use a shrub, choose one that won't spread so much that it will intrude on the rest of the space. In front of it, plant something shorter; continue layering in this manner, finishing off with low-growing shrubs or edging plants.

Use leaf texture as another perspective tool. Shrubs with small, fine leaves will appear farther away than those with large or coarse leaves. Be bold. Plant a large-leaved shrub near the front of a small garden with a finely textured shrub as a counterpoint in the background, and watch the perceived size of your garden grow.

A small statue enlarges a landscape *by fooling your eye into seeing the statue as being larger and farther away than it is in reality. The twin rows of trees converge on the statue, adding length. These perspective tools, although often employed on large properties, have equal value on small landscapes.*

Stagger plant heights *to give a greater sense of depth. This design option works well for people who don't have a lot of space but want a lot of plants. Put tall plants at the back of the bed, with something shorter in the middle, and low plants in the very front.*

Small spaces can be made to appear larger than they are in reality. This front walk gives the impression of greater depth because it narrows as it moves away from the viewing point.

Pale, pastel colors recede and lend a sense of depth when placed at the end of a landscape view. The pink dogwood blossoms add a splash of color between the dark green yews.

Color. Generally, warm colors such as yellow and red appear to advance toward you, while pastels and cool colors such as blue and green appear to recede. By putting this color principle to work in your landscape, you can visually enlarge it by placing cool colors in the back, making the rear boundary seem farther away.

If you are lining a path with flowers or creating parallel rows of perennial borders, place the warm-colored plants closest to the house and those with cool colors farther away. By the same token, plants with red or yellow foliage should be up close, and shrubs and trees with blue foliage should be in the distance to create a feeling of depth.

Light and Shadow. Enlarge your garden with a dark, shady corner at the far end. Forms become indistinct in a dim spot, leaving it unclear where the boundaries are. Your eye will be tricked into seeing that the end of your garden is somewhere deep in the shadows. In addition, this shady nook can be a pleasant retreat from the sun as well as a private getaway. Furnish it with a comfortable bench.

Creating Grand Illusions

"Illusion is everything in a garden," says San Diego landscape designer W. F. Sinjen, who transformed his own 40×100-foot lot into a tropical forest of winding paths that loop back on themselves to increase the sense of space. The plantings are tall and dense enough to screen the view to an adjoining path that is actually just a few feet away, and they give an enormous sense of space and privacy. You can take quite a long walk in his modest-size garden. The stroll is enchanting because around each corner is a special plant or ornament to delight the eye and stimulate interest.

Sinjen's garden is evidence of a paradoxical truth: a small space will appear larger if it is divided into two smaller spaces. Because you never see the entire space at once, it gives the sense that there is something more beyond. For example, a townhouse garden may feel larger if the space is partitioned by a hedge or screen that blocks the view to the area where the garden ends.

"Many people respond [to a small garden] by following meticulously the lines of the site boundaries with narrow borders combined with the largest possible area of lawn … this design fully reveals the shape and extent of the site," write Andrew Wilson and Peter Thurman in *The Garden*. The authors go on to say that it's better to draw attention away from the site boundaries by "allowing blocks of shrub planting or perforated screens like trellis to penetrate the main garden space, breaking away from the boundaries."

By doing this, the opposite effect is achieved, say the authors. "The full extent of the site is concealed rather than revealed, an air of secrecy is created, and the whole garden layout remains a mystery."

Visual Tricks. There are many other ways of enhancing the illusion of space in a small lot. Consider installing a gate or doorway in the fence or wall, even if it leads nowhere. People will assume there is another part of the garden, and the actual space will therefore feel larger. Another idea is to put an arbor along the property boundary so that it appears to be a passageway into another part of the garden. To give the arbor a purpose, put a bench inside so that you have a cozy place to sit.

Trelliswork, or *treillage,* built so that the slats create a false perspective, is another means of dressing up a fence or wall and creating a sense of distance. In this case, you want to suggest a retreating tunnel. Plant a pair of trees on either side of the trellis to anchor the design, or train a hedge or vine alongside and across the top of the trellis. *Pyracantha* is a great choice for this. It features clusters of creamy white flowers in spring and bright red or orange berries in winter. With a trellis built to resemble a receding tunnel, you can create a greater sense of depth and space in your landscape while adding interest to an uninteresting wall or fence.

Visually enlarge small spaces by adding a fence or gate. The arch set in this fence makes the property appear bigger because it suggests a passageway into another garden room. This arch breaks the monotony of the long run of fence and adds pleasing height.

Draw attention away from the boundaries by extending the beds toward the center of the property, rather than following the perimeter. Here, the shrubs add interest and obscure the view of the property's edges.

Small gardens magically grow if they are divided into rooms with different functions. The flowering plants and shrubs create one room around the lush lawn, the hedges around the patio create a second, while the fence contains a third room.

Creating a Vista. A *vista* (an avenue or line of sight that allows a distant view) can enlarge a small space by drawing the eye to the distance. While we associate vistas with large estate gardens, in fact you can create a vista in quite a small space.

A straight path or an expanse of lawn running down the center of a garden, even if it's only 15 to 20 feet long, can create a vista. Put a bench, a gate (even if it leads nowhere), a three-sided gazebo, an arbor, a specimen plant, or an ornament at the end to draw the eye and provide a satisfying finish to the scene.

If an uninterrupted straight path is too linear for your taste, you could create a short path that leads to a rectangle of lawn, and then continue it on the opposite side. Surround the little rectangle of lawn and paths with plants, and install a specimen plant or garden ornament at the far end to create a focal point. You might also consider placing a statue, sundial, birdbath, or gazing globe in the center of the lawn to break the horizontal monotony of the design.

Base Your Designs on the Diagonal.

Another option is to base your design on the diagonal. "The diagonal provides the longest dimension in square or rectangular gardens," note Wilson and Thurman. "Designs based on this angle benefit from the extra

Create a vista in a small garden with a straight path leading to a focal point at the far end. Orange and yellow deciduous azaleas add drama to this garden path. In summer, the roses on the right will provide the color.

length, and the resulting deep areas of planting disguise the boundaries—an effective technique in small gardens." Whether the vista created by a diagonal design is full length or shortened by screening plants, the diagonal itself gives a sense of urgency and excitement to the design, drawing the eye with its power.

Vistas draw the eye to the distance and enlarge the landscape. Something as simple as a small, well-tended lawn, even if it is not long, can create a vista as shown in the plan view (below left) by ending with a garden accent that serves as the distant focal point. In the perspective view (below), the plants are shown in more detail. The homeowner has chosen low-growing plants that frame the ornament without obscuring it.

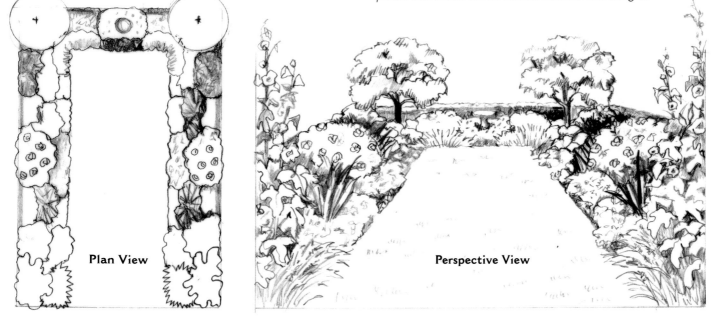

Plan View

Perspective View

Plan View

A meandering "stream" is effectively simulated by this gently curving path. In the plan view (above), it's clear to see the path as a stream. In the perspective view (right), the large groupings of plants, low ground covers hugging the banks, and water plants such as iris and ornamental grass complete the streambed effect.

Perspective View

A Vista of Flowers. You also can form a vista with a mass planting of flowers that runs like a river from one part of the garden to another. Again, the strong lines draw the eye and the vista gives a sense of space and distance. In addition, it encourages the viewer to move through the garden.

Vistas do not need to be straight lines. A meandering path in an informal garden can draw the eye just as effectively as a straight one. The sense of mystery and of being beckoned is heightened when the path curves out of sight, obscuring the view into other parts of the landscape, whether or not there is more to be seen.

This path borders a swath of flowers, which flows like a river from one part of the garden to the next. Stepping-stones accentuate the feel of crossing a river, hopping from stone to stone to keep your feet dry.

If possible, create a vista that you can see from a window or doorway in your home. In addition to making the garden feel bigger, a garden vista will make the house feel more spacious. The view will be a constant lure into the garden.

FRAMING THE VIEW

Just as a picture frame can lend importance to a painting or photograph and give it an appropriate setting, so can a framed view in a garden lend importance and enhance perspective. If an arch doesn't suit the style of your garden or your budget, consider framing a vista with a pair of trees or shrubs. The support posts of a patio cover can form an attractive frame if the vista is centered between the two posts. Here you can grow vines up the posts and allow them to crawl across the top of the cover and droop over the edge. The view will then be framed by a semitransparent curtain of foliage and flowers creating a magical spot.

Also consider a *borrowed landscape*. Even though your garden may be spacious, there's no law against borrowing the view of a spectacular tree growing outside your property and making it look as if it's growing inside by planting complementary trees and shrubs that disguise the property line or even screen out a neighbor's wall or fence.

If you are lucky enough to have an attractive view beyond your property, be sure to make it part of your landscape vista. In Sinjen's small garden, for example, you get a glimpse of San Diego's Mission Bay through the trees. To capitalize on this view, Sinjen built a fish pond that appeared to join with the bay. "It looked like the bay came right up into the garden," he said. "I would tell people it was my personal fjord. Illusion is everything—the illusion of space and grandeur."

Frame a view of the landscape by planting vines on a patio cover. The vines shown here, growing up and over a patio, dress up the cover, much like curtains on a picture window.

This lovely seaside view is framed by the simple fence and two sides of hedges; the straight expanse of lawn leads your eye to the view. This homeowner has wisely chosen subdued plantings that accentuate the view while not overpowering it.

PART TWO

Setting the Stage

Now that you have a plan, it's time to get down to work. Think of plants as temperamental stars who won't deliver their full potential unless the stage is set just right. However, if you take the time now to create the optimal conditions, your plants will perform at their peak for years into the future.

Chapter 3: Laying the Groundwork *explains how to give your new landscape a strong foundation. You will learn how to create fertile soil, improve the drainage, install irrigation systems, and even add lighting.*

Chapter 4: Paths, Edgings, and Steps *gives you access to all of the parts of your landscape, from the driveway to the front door, up steep hills, or across boggy fields.*

Chapter 5: Patios, Decks, and Swimming Pools *increase the value of your landscape by giving you outdoor living space and providing a good platform from which to display and appreciate your plants.*

Chapter 6: Walls, Fences, and Other Structures *contain your landscape, providing privacy and boundaries.*

Chapter 7: Water Gardens *transform any landscape into a serene oasis. In this chapter, you will learn how to build a pond, bring in fish, and grow water plants.*

CHAPTER 3

Laying the Groundwork

Once you've put your landscape design on paper, the next step is to lay the groundwork. This includes the soil and drainage; it may also include irrigation and lighting systems. Garden lighting and irrigation systems can be optional niceties, but good-quality soil and proper drainage are essential to success. While few people find preparation of the infrastructure as visually and emotionally satisfying as planting, these tasks are as important to a landscape as utilities are to a house.

Soil and Drainage. Good soil is essential for your plants to grow properly. For a garden to flourish with healthy plants that are strong enough to resist pests and diseases, you must first invest in improving the soil. Unless your property drains sufficiently so that rain water doesn't cause flooding or erosion, you may need to improve the drainage.

Irrigation. An irrigation system may be a seldom-needed convenience in regions that only occasionally experience extended dry periods. However, as droughts become more widespread, an irrigation system is almost essential unless you have lots of time to move the garden hose about. Often when a garden is hand-watered, some areas get more than enough water while other parts are slighted.

Lighting. Landscape lighting may seem like a luxury, but it can improve the security of your property, as well as making paths safer after dark. On warm evenings, it also extends the number of hours when you can enjoy your landscape. Throughout the year, a well-lit garden makes a dramatic backdrop to uncurtained windows after dark.

From properly prepared soil, healthy seedlings emerge and grow strong (top). Neatly divided raised beds provide a well-drained planting space, while the geometric pattern creates an ornamental display for vegetables and herbs.

Soil

Unless you purchase a home where the previous owners were avid gardeners and worked the soil for some time, the odds are high that the quality of soil on your property is poor. Once you commit to improving the soil, have it analyzed to find out its pH level and nutrient content.

Soil is a living organism, constantly changing. To keep abreast of any changes in pH and nutrient balance, you should test your soil every three to four years. The trouble and expense are small costs for the advantage of knowing exactly what nutrients or soil amendments your plants need to perform at their best.

SOIL ANALYSIS

Cooperative Extension agents get many calls from people whose plants are ailing. Agent Patricia McAleer in Fairfax County, Virginia, says, "The first question they ask me is what spray should they use. Instead they should be asking if there is something wrong with the soil."

The basis of a healthy garden is its soil. Pests may annoy and diseases may intrude, but in most cases if the plants are growing in good soil, they will be resilient enough to overcome these travails. On the other hand, if the soil is missing a key nutrient or if the pH is off for a particular plant, the plant will begin to fail and will then be vulnerable to a host of pests and diseases.

pH Levels. The pH level is a measure of how much hydrogen is in the soil, which in turn affects how available nutrients are to your plants. Most ornamental plants, vegetables, and herbs do best in soil with a pH between 5 and 7. Woodland plants, including rhododendrons, azaleas, ferns, and astilbes do best in slightly acidic, or "sour," soil (below 5), while plants such as clematis prefer alkaline, or "sweet," soil with a pH of 8 or higher. Turf grass does best with a pH of 5.8 to 6.6. Soil pH figures are always given in a range. But, be aware that

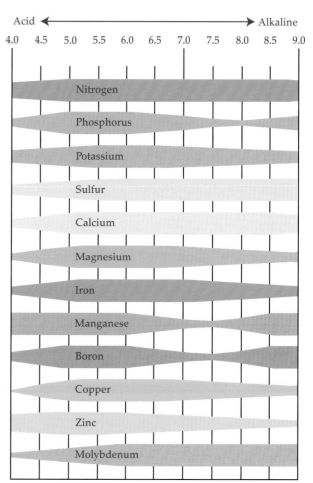

How pH Affects Plants

Acid ⟵——————————⟶ Alkaline

4.0 4.5 5.0 5.5 6.0 6.5 7.0 7.5 8.0 8.5 9.0

Nitrogen
Phosphorus
Potassium
Sulfur
Calcium
Magnesium
Iron
Manganese
Boron
Copper
Zinc
Molybdenum

This chart suggests the importance of conducting a soil test before planting new trees or shrubs or attempting to chemically amend existing problems. For most plants, the ideal soil pH ranges from moderately acidic (5.5) to neutral (7.0). A low pH number (4.5 or lower) indicates high soil acidity; a high pH number (10.0 or higher) indicates high soil alkalinity. Relative acidity greatly affects the availability of nutrients to the plants.

The bar widths in this chart approximate the availability of essential nutrients at various pH levels; the narrower the bar width, the less available the nutrients. The first six elements are needed in larger amounts. Based on USDA charts showing the availability of nutrients in various kinds of soil, the chart represents only an approximation of nutrient availability in hypothetical "general" garden soil.

pH figures change exponentially. If your soil is at the extreme ends of the range or outside the suggested figure, you will most likely need to add amendments.

Most garden centers sell pH test kits with which you can test your own soil. However, for a nominal fee, the Cooperative Extension will measure the pH, and more importantly, give you a report indicating what, if anything, should be added to the soil and in what amounts. The Extension agent will determine whether the soil is sandy, clay, loam or some combination of the three. This is important information because it affects the amounts of amendments needed.

Acidic and Alkaline Soil. Typically parts of the country which receive plenty of rain, such as the eastern third of the United States and Canada, tend to have acidic soil. Dry regions, such as the southwestern United States, usually have alkaline soil. However, don't assume that the soil on your property matches what is typical for the region. Parts of your property could have significantly different pH levels if the soil was heavily fertilized, if it's located at the end of a flood runoff, or if mineral substances ever leached into the soil. If you are new to the property, it's a good idea to bring in several samples for analysis.

How to Take a Soil Sample

Difficulty Level: Easy

The directions are the same whether you are measuring the pH or nutrient content. Indicate what you plan to grow because lawns, vegetables, and perennials have different pH requirements. Collect samples from several spots for an average reading. Mix the samples in a jar or plastic bag; allow the soil to thoroughly air-dry before testing it.

Tools and Materials: Trowel, plastic bag, soil-testing kit.

Step 1: Dig Down 8 Inches. *Bag the soil. Remove soil from several spots in one bed and mix them together.*

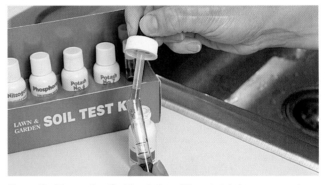

Step 2: Test the Soil with a Kit. *Add the appropriate solution to a measured amount of the soil sample.*

Step 3: Shake the Solution. *Cap the tube and shake it until the soil and solution are thoroughly blended.*

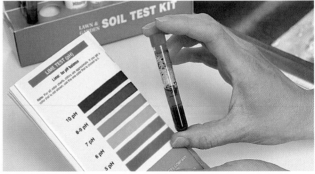

Step 4: Read the Results. *Match the color of the resulting solution with the chart to determine the pH.*

Nutrient Analysis. A nutrient analysis requires serious chemistry. It's usually best to pay the fee for a soil analysis from your Cooperative Extension Service or from a commercial laboratory that includes information on soil pH as well as a breakdown of the soil's nutrients. The report will include recommendations on the amounts and types of amendments and fertilizers needed. Nitrogen is the one basic nutrient that usually isn't included because nitrogen levels in soil fluctuate daily, making that measurement meaningless.

Testing and Treating Lawns. Because lawns cover a large proportion of most properties, they are particularly important areas for soil testing. Although many people regularly lime their lawns, frequent applications of lime-stone may be unnecessary or even harmful to your grass. Save money by applying lime only when a soil test shows your lawn needs it. Grass needs a different balance of primary nutrients (nitrogen, phosphate, and potassium) than ornamental plants, so be sure to specify that the tested soil will be used for a lawn. Excessive use of fertilizer is not only a waste of money, it disturbs the natural balance of microorganisms and makes lawns more prone to disease and thatch build-up. Plus the excess fertilizer may wash into water sources and pollute them. If you have a complete soil analysis done on your lawn every few years, you will know how much fertilizer to buy and whether the soil needs any additional lime. As a result, you will be able to make informed and environmentally responsible decisions on the best balance of nutrients to apply.

UNDERSTANDING SOIL TEXTURE

In addition to having an appropriate pH and blend of nutrients, your soil should have a good structure, with spaces for air and water. Structure can be improved, although the texture—clay, sand, or loam—will not change.

Clay Soil. To determine the soil texture squeeze a handful in your palm. Heavy clay soil will form a tight ball. Clay is composed of extremely fine particles that pack together closely, so water drains slowly. Clay soil contains very little oxygen. Because it is dense, roots have a hard time pushing through.

Sandy Soil. Sandy soil, by contrast, will not hold together at all. Its loose, coarse particles allow space for lots of oxygen and easy root growth. Water can drain easily, but it can also leach out essential nutrients. Another disadvantage of sandy soil is that it dries out quickly; water drains so easily that it disappears before plants can use it.

Silty Soil. Silty soil feels silky or even soapy. Silt is sedimentary material that is coarser than clay but still comprised of fine particles. It compacts easily.

Soil Texture

Loamy Sand

Sandy Loam

Loam

Silt Loam

Humus

Clay Loam

Soil texture is determined by the percentage of sand, silt, and clay. Sand particles can be as large as $\frac{1}{2}$ inch, while clay particles are as tiny as $\frac{1}{12,500}$ inch. However, most soil is a mixture of particle sizes and is described by the dominant material, as shown here. Loam is ideal garden soil with a combination of sand, silt, and clay.

Healthy soil is alive with beneficial organisms. In addition to worms, which till the soil as well as add nutrients in the form of their castings, loam is rich in microscopic life which performs a wealth of valuable functions for plants, including making nitrogen available and feeding on plant pathogens.

Loam. The ideal soil is a rich loam balanced in its composition of clay, silt, and sand particles, and containing plenty of organic material such as humus or manure. When you squeeze loam in your hand, it will form a shape, but then crumble easily. Loam retains enough water for plant roots, but it still drains freely and is well aerated.

You can't change the texture of your soil, but by improving soil structure you can make any soil behave more like ideal loam. The easiest way to improve the structure of any soil is to add organic matter.

Organic matter lightens up heavy clay soil, improving drainage by creating more spaces for air and water. It also improves the structure of sandy soil by acting as a sponge to help hold water and nutrients so they aren't so easily washed away.

Amending any soil with organic materials brings its structure as close as possible to the ideal for growing plants, and at the same time enriches it with microorganisms that increase the soil's (and therefore your plants') health.

Improving the Soil

SOIL AMENDMENTS

"Put a five-dollar plant into a ten-dollar hole" is common advice. If you've invested money in a plant, you'd better invest even more in creating an environment where it can grow and be healthy.

Soil scientists have identified about 4,000 species of beneficial microorganisms. These unseen creatures perform a host of valuable functions. Some convert nitrogen from the air into water-soluble compounds, making the nutrient available to plants. Others promote the decay process which transforms garden waste into nutrient-rich humus. There are microbes that feed on harmful plant pathogens and others that interact with plant roots to help them absorb mineral nutrients. Another group works to bind together the mineral particles in soil with the organic additions. Soil without these beneficial microorganisms is literally dead.

Once you've committed to amending the soil in at least a small area, the next step is to check the moisture content. Slightly moist soil is easiest to dig. If a handful feels moist and crumbles easily, you're ready to go. If soil feels dry, water the ground thoroughly and wait a couple of days. If the handful feels wet or leaves mud on your hands, wait a few days and retest. Soil structure can be severely damaged if you try to work wet soil.

Organic Soil Amendments

Amendment	Significant Source of Organic Matter	Provides Nutrients/Minerals
Alfalfa Meal	Yes	Trace Minerals
Crab Meal		Nitrogen
Greensand		Potash, 32 Trace Minerals
Kelp Meal		Potash, Trace Minerals
Peat Moss	Yes	
Rock Phosphate		Phosphate, Calcium, Silicas, 11 Trace Minerals
Sul-Po-Mag		Potash, Magnesium
Manure	Yes	Many Nutrients
Worm Castings	Yes	11 Trace Minerals

COMPOST: THE BEST SOIL AMENDMENT.

Compost is the result of a marvelous alchemy that transforms garden and kitchen waste into garden gold. When piled together for a period of time, everyday garden ingredients, including fallen leaves, garden trimmings, weeds, grass clippings, and kitchen scraps decompose into a crumbly black, organic material rich in earthworms and healthy soil bacteria.

This free garden resource, often referred to as "black gold," is ideal for amending soil, topdressing lawns and beds instead of using chemical fertilizers, mulching beds, improving the texture and moisture-retentive properties of soil, and even using straight as a planting medium.

Use Compost to Improve Soil Texture.

Compost loosens clay soil, improving its structure and tilth (workability) so that the soil is easy to cultivate and holds moisture well. In sandy soil, compost acts like a sponge to hold nutrients and water. In any soil, compost supplies nutrients and beneficial microorganisms. Compost also brings the pH closer to neutral. Don't worry about overdosing the soil with organic amendments. You never can have too much.

Compost happens naturally. Walk through an old-growth forest and notice the spongy, rich soil under the trees, which is the result of centuries of decomposing leaves breaking down into humus. However, you can speed up the natural process. To work most efficiently, the microorganisms that cause composting need a balanced diet of carbon and nitrogen as well as air and moisture.

Composting is easy. Anyone can create their own black gold regardless of the size of their garden. No fancy equipment or special expertise is needed. At the end of the season, you'll reap the rewards of finished compost, knowing that you made it all by yourself.

CONTAINERS FOR COMPOSTING

There are more than 100 composting bins currently on the market, as well as a lot of do-it-yourself designs such as suggestions for creating compartments with stacked cinder blocks or wire cages supported with stakes. While an especially designed bin may be useful, it is not essential. Don't let the lack of a container keep you from composting. Many gardeners successfully make wheelbarrow-loads of compost simply by piling all the material directly on the ground.

Compost breaks down fastest if you layer the "brown" and "green" material. The other ingredients for successful compost are air and water. Here the wire cage allows for ample air. Water your compost heap during periods of drought.

Create disposable compost bins with bales of straw. The straw will decompose along with the other garden waste, eventually contributing to the compost supply. These bins are based on a design by organic gardening specialist Elliot Coleman.

One pound of worms will turn a pound of kitchen waste into compost every day under average conditions. An outdoor wormery should be in a sheltered spot where temperatures do not fluctuate greatly. Worms thrive in temperatures ranging from 60° to 70°F.

Recipes for Compost

The ideal compost heap should be 3 feet wide x 3 feet deep x 3 feet tall. It quickly will shrink by as much as 50 percent. That's a good sign that the material is breaking down. Another way of checking if everything is working is to reach inside. It should feel warm.

A compost pile should be contained so it attains a minimum height of three feet. A simple three-sided wire mesh fence on posts, or a specially created wire bin works fine. If you are starting your first compost pile, dig a shallow hole and build on top of that. This will help introduce earthworms to your pile and bring in the microorganisms. If you are using a pre-made container with a closed bottom, put a shovel-full of dirt into the bottom.

Alternate 4- to 6-inch thick layers of brown material (dry leaves, straw, and wood shavings) that are high in carbon and green matter such as grass clippings, manure, and kitchen scraps (except meat and dairy products), and garden scraps which are high in nitrogen. Sprinkle a little water and garden soil between each layer to help things along. Or apply a compost inoculant to boost the microbial activity of the heap.

About once a week, turn the pile with a pitchfork. Turning adds oxygen which stokes the stove and helps the compost to cook faster. Keep the pile watered. The compost is properly moist when it feels like a wrung-out sponge, neither soggy nor bone dry. Using this technique, it takes about six weeks to produce finished compost.

The microorganisms working busily in your compost need about three times as much carbon as nitrogen. Heavy doses of carbon also speed up the process. But, most home gardeners usually end up with all nitrogen-rich material in the spring and summer, and only carbon (dried leaves) in the fall. An easy solution is to stockpile leaves collected in the fall and add them a layer at a time.

You'll never have enough compost. The more you make, the more uses you will find for compost.

Compost Ingredients

Browns (carbon)

Need 2–3 times as much Browns as Greens (nitrogen)

- Dry leaves
- Brown plant wastes
- Shredded newspapers, cardboard
- Wood chips, sawdust
- Corn stalks
- Used potting soil

Greens (nitrogen)

- Manure
- Grass clippings
- Garden waste
- Kitchen waste
- Kelp meal
- Blood meal
- Alfalfa
- Human hair

How Compost Happens

Combine Organic Matter. *An apple core, banana peel, lemon rind, egg shell, and garden clippings are the raw materials.*

Decomposition Has Begun. *The ingredients have started to turn crumbly and brown, but are still recognizable.*

Finished Compost or Humus. *The humus has a rich, earthy smell. This "black gold" is found at the bottom of the pile.*

OTHER SOIL AMENDMENTS

Rotted Manure. Rotted manure from cows, chickens, horses, or rabbits is another excellent soil amendment, especially for sandy and heavy clay soils. Rotted manure provides key nutrients as well as organic matter. Make sure the manure is properly rotted (six to 10 weeks) to prevent the risk of burning plants. You also can buy composted and bagged manure. Spread at least 1 to 2 inches over the ground.

Leaves. Leaves are an inexpensive soil amendment. In autumn, pile leaves on the plot you plan to amend and leave them to rot during the winter. If the leaves are large, such as those of oaks or maples, shred them before spreading them on the garden, or use a lawn mower. In communities that collect fallen leaves, you usually can arrange for a truckload delivery of leaves for free or for a nominal charge. Come spring, you should either dig or till the rotted leaves into the soil.

Commercial/Organic Amendments. There are many organic soil amendments on the market. Depending on where you live, you can find products such as kelp meal, alfalfa meal, crab meal, or rotted manure bagged and ready to use without the bother of making your own.

WORKING IN AMENDMENTS

The size of your plot will influence whether you rototill or dig in amendments. If you are working a large area, a gas-powered tiller is a great labor saver, although even the large machines cannot penetrate the soil as deeply as you can if you dig by hand. To get the best results with a tiller, use a rear-tined machine with blades that can penetrate up to 10 inches.

Single and Double Digging. There are essentially two options for systematic hand digging soil: single digging, which turns the soil to a depth of 8 to 12 inches, and double digging, which loosens the soil to twice that depth. (See the illustration below.) If you have heavy clay soil, level soil that doesn't drain well, or a garden that has never before been cultivated, double digging is worth the time and effort.

The next step is to check the moisture content; slightly moist soil is the easiest to dig. If a handful feels moist and crumbles easily, you're ready to dig. If the soil feels dry, water the ground thoroughly and wait a few days. If the handful feels wet or leaves mud on your hands, wait a few days and recheck. Avoid working soil when it is too wet. Soil structure can be severely damaged if you try to work wet soil.

Single and Double Digging

Double digging is a process used to aerate a bed to double the depth of a shovel or spading fork—approximately 20 inches. To single dig a bed, follow the directions below, but do not use the spading fork to loosen the ground at the bottom of the trench.

Step 1: Dig Out the First Trench. *Divide the bed into sections, and dig out a 12-inch layer of earth from the first trench, setting aside the removed soil for the final section.*

Step 2: Add Soil Amendments. *Spread amendments into the bottom of the trench. Use a spading fork to loosen the soil on the bottom of the trench another 10 inches. (Single diggers can skip the spading fork step and proceed to Step 3.)*

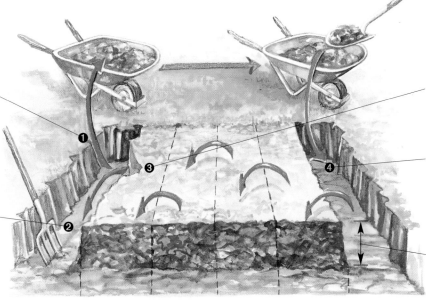

Approx. 8"–12"

Step 3: Dig Out the Second Trench to 12 Inches. *Move the soil dug from the second trench into the first trench. Repeat Step 2 in the second trench.*

Step 4: Continue to Dig Trenches. *Add the soil dug from the last trench into the adjacent newly dug trench.*

Trees and Shrubs for Poor Soil

Intense soil amendment is particularly important if you are planting perennials, annuals, or vegetables. If you are planting trees and shrubs, which have root systems that will delve far deeper than you can amend, your best bet is to choose plants that are adapted to the native soil. Below are lists of trees and shrubs that are proven performers in specific soils.

CLAY SOIL

Trees

Alnus glutinosa (common alder), Zones 4–7
Cedrus libani ssp. atlantica (Atlas cedar), Zones 7–9
Cryptomeria japonica (Japanese cedar), Zones 6–9
Fraxinus species (ash), zones vary with species
Juglans nigra (eastern black walnut), Zones 5–9
Lagerstroemia indica (crape myrtle), Zones 7–10
Metasequoia glyptostroboides (dawn redwood), Zones 5–10
Oxydendrum arboreum (sourwood), Zones 5–9
Populus species (poplar), zones vary with species
Quercus palustris (pin oak), Zones 5–8
Quercus robur (English oak), Zones 5–8
Salix x sepulcralis var. chrysocoma (golden weeping willow), Zones 4–9
Salix matsudana 'Tortuosa' (contorted willow), Zones 5–8
Salix purpurea (purple osier), Zones 4–9
Sambucus racemosa (red-berried elder), Zones 4–7
Taxodium distichum (bald cypress), Zones 5–10

Shrubs

Aronia arbutifolia (red chokeberry), Zones 4–8
Calycanthus floridus (Carolina allspice), Zones 5–9
Cornus alba 'Sibirica' (red-barked dogwood), Zones 2–8
Cotoneaster species, Zones 5–9
Kalmia latifolia (mountain laurel), Zones 5–9
Ledum groenlandicum (Labrador tea), Zones 2–6
Magnolia virginiana (sweet bay), Zones 6–9
Photinia serratifolia (Chinese photinia), Zones 7–9
Pyracantha species (firethorn), Zones 6–10
Viburnum lentago (sheepberry), Zones 3–8
Viburnum opulus (European cranberry), Zones 4–8

SANDY SOIL

Trees

Abies grandis (grand fir), Zones 7–9
Acacia dealbata (silver wattle), Zones 9–10
Acer negundo (box elder), Zones 3–9
Betula pendula 'Dalecarlica' (cutleaf European birch), Zones 3–8
Castanea sativa (Spanish chestnut), Zones 5–8
Celtis australis (European hackberry), Zones 6–9
Cupressus leylandii (Leyland cypress), Zones 6–9
Eucalyptus ficifolia (red-flowering gum), Zones 9–10
Gleditsia triacanthos (honey locust), Zones 5–9
Phoenix canariensis (Canary Island date palm), Zones 9–10
Pinus pinaster (cluster pine), Zones 7–9
Pinus radiata (Monterey pine), Zones 7–9
Pseudotsuga menziesii ssp. glauca (Rocky Mountain Douglas fir), Zones 5–7
Quercus ilex (holly oak), Zones 7–9
Schinus molle (California pepper tree), Zones 9–10

Shrubs

Acanthus spinosus (spiny bear's breech), Zones 5–9
Calluna vulgaris (Scotch heather), Zones 5–7
Cercis siliquastrum (Judas tree), Zones 8–9
Cistus species (rock rose), Zones 7–10
Cytisus scoparius (Scotch broom), Zones 6–9
Genista tinctoria (dyer's greenweed) Zones 2–8
Juniperus species (juniper), zones vary with species
Rosa pimpinellifolia (Scotch rose), Zones 4–9
Spartium junceum (Spanish broom), Zones 7–10
Yucca gloriosa (Spanish dagger), Zones 7–10

Grading

The reasons for grading range from aesthetic to utilitarian. You can add visual interest to your garden by varying the contours and levels, or make a dangerously steep slope easy to navigate by altering the grade. Always contact your local building department before embarking on any landscape construction project. And leave larger earth-moving jobs to a professional, such as a landscape architect or civil engineer. It's too easy to create flooded basements, or an accidental pond in a neighbor's yard.

Writing in her book *Rosemary Verey's Making of a Garden*, garden designer Rosemary Verey says, "If a client's garden is naturally flat, I wonder where and how a change of level can be created." She loves formal sunken gardens because they let you stand at the top and enjoy the pattern of the beds. If that is not practical, she recommends a raised bed, "to enable you to see the plants from a different viewpoint. Its retaining wall can be comfortable to sit on and gives the opportunity to use plants which love to cascade down."

A gentle slope is an opportunity to "present" plants; the slope raises successive plants slightly so they can be viewed from a perspective not possible on flat soil. A slope is also an ideal situation for a rock garden where small plants that would get lost in a larger envi-

This Japanese-style graded landscape divides a hill into two slopes. A simple wooden bridge spans the slopes and leads to a stepping-stone path which follows the contours of the sloping ground.

ronment can be showcased by tucking them next to attractive rocks.

Grading is often required for paved paths and patios. If your proposed patio site is near your house and is relatively flat, it's easy to create a level surface with a slight slope or grade that drains away from the house foundation. A slope of ¼ in. per foot is usually adequate. If the patio won't be near a structure, create a single central high point to avoid puddles. See Chapter 4, pages 100–05 for instructions on laying paths and Chapter 5, page 120 for instructions on building a patio.

GRADING A SLOPE

Before it was graded, the large hill dotted with randomly-placed trees was not a landscape asset. And the sloping lawn was a nuisance to mow. A small bulldozer was sufficient to move the earth about to create two terraces connected by a steep slope as well as to move the large trees to more logical places in the garden. The short, steep hill that remains after grading is ideal for a rockery, using the slope to show off small but fascinating plants.

Drainage

Soil should be contoured to direct water away from the house foundation into storm drains. When builders construct a new house, they usually design for water runoff with downspouts, swales, and drainage ditches. However, you may need to add to the existing drainage plan to cope with the freak storms that drop enormous amounts of water in minutes, creating rivers down slopes.

There are many kinds of drainage options, ranging from simple measures to elaborate underground systems that might include gravel-filled trenches or drain tiles. Because underground systems are so labor intensive, it's wise to search for the simplest solution.

If you plan major digging, you may need a permit from local building officials. Even if no permit is required, make certain you know the locations of underground lines for telephone, water, electricity, and so on. When digging trenches by hand, use a straight-edged spade, rather than a rounded shovel, so the walls of the trenches remain square. Also slope your trenches gently down hill at a rate of at least 1 inch per 8 feet. Several drainage options are described below.

BERMS

A berm is a mound of earth that allows you to direct water away from the house or from an area that's vulnerable to erosion. In addition to directing water, a berm can serve as a lovely raised planter. Berms are also useful for creating privacy, for noise control, and to deflect winds.

Determine the approximate amount of soil you will need for the berm, based on its length, width, and average height. Soil is sold by the cubic yard, which is 3 feet × 3 feet × 3 feet. Order soil by the truckload. Be sure to specify that you want landscape-quality topsoil. When the dirt arrives, check it before they dump it. Topsoil should be dark, loose and crumbly, not full of rocks or sticks. To avoid tire damage from the delivery truck, you may need to dump the load some distance from the berm site and haul the soil in a wheelbarrow. Grade the sides of the berm to a gentle slope. Then plant ground covers, shrubs, or perennials so the roots will hold the new soil in place.

A stone "river bed" is an attractive landscape feature, and is particularly useful to protect a slope from erosion when rain runoff is heavy. It is essentially an earthen ditch lined with stones.

Without the berm *running parallel to the hillside, water runoff down the slope would settle at the house foundation where it can create problems. The berm keeps the water away from the house, channeling it toward the street.*

SWALES AND DRAINAGE DITCHES

A swale is simply a dip or depression. A drainage ditch can route water from the swale away from your house. In some neighborhoods, the drainage ditch running along the front of the property is cement. Within residential properties, earthen ditches are often planted with grass or a ground cover to prevent erosion. If you already have such a ditch, you could transform it into an attractive "dry riverbed" by lining it with stones and edging it with plants that enjoy moist soil such as Louisiana iris, forget-me-not, or meadow rue.

A dry well is useful if you do not have storm drains to collect excess water. Direct drainpipes so they empty into a gravel-filled hole 2 to 4 feet in diameter and 3 feet deep. From there the water can disperse gradually through the surrounding soil. Cover a dry well with a concrete slab or other paving material, or lay sod on top as shown here.

*Install a **catch basin*** at a low point in the garden where water settles. The collected water will flow through the pipe at the bottom of the basin. The pipe should empty into a storm drain or area where the water can disperse without causing any damage.

CATCH BASINS

Standing water and soggy soil in low spots often can be handled by catch basins. Purchase a ready-made catch basin and install it underground at the lowest point where the water gathers. From the catch basin, dig a trench for a drain pipe that will funnel water away to a storm drain or area where it can flow away properly. Catch basins typically have a grate at soil level and a holding reservoir where water can collect before draining away through the pipe. Inside the basin is a sediment trap that catches any leaves or debris. Remember to clean out the trap periodically so debris doesn't accumulate and block the drain pipe.

DRY WELLS

If you don't have a storm drain or other convenient place to dispose of excess water, build a dry well at the lowest part of the area to be drained and run all the drain lines to it. A dry well holds excess water until the surrounding soil can absorb it. The size of the dry well will depend on the local rainfall. Dry wells 2 to 4 feet in diameter and 3 feet deep are generally adequate in parts of the country with moderate rainfall, where it does not usually flood. Dig the hole, run the drain pipes into the hole, and fill the hole with gravel or rocks. Cover the hole with a concrete slab or other paving material, sod, or topsoil.

FLEXIBLE DRAINPIPES

Use flexible drainpipes to move runoff water away from structures and to channel it to areas where it can percolate into the earth or drain away. Dig a trench wide enough to accommodate the flexible pipe and about 1 foot deep. Be sure to make the trench slope (at least 1 inch for every 8 feet) so the water will run down hill away from its source. Lay the pipe in the trench, connecting it to downspouts with specially designed sleeves.

If you are using perforated pipe, line the bottom of the trench with 2 inches of gravel and lay the pipe on top with the holes facing down so they don't get clogged with dirt and debris. Fill in the trench with soil and cover with sod or backfill with gravel. Be sure to keep the exit end of the pipe open and clear so that water can escape freely, either into a swale or soak away into the surrounding soil. If you plant around the exit to disguise it, avoid blocking the water flow.

Terracing

Terracing a steep hillside is a time-honored way to transform unused land into broad level "steps" for garden beds or paved areas. If you want several terraces to traverse a slope, connect them with steps made of stone, pavers, or wood, depending on which material would look best in your overall design.

Some communities have regulations against homeowners building retaining walls more than 4 feet high. If your embankment requires a taller wall, either build a series of terraces with shorter retaining walls, or hire a professional engineer to design your wall and a contractor to build it. Many communities require permits for walls 3 feet or taller, so be sure to check with your local building inspector before you begin.

Even well-packed soil is not completely stable on a slope. If you need to do extensive grading to create your terraces, contact a soil engineer or landscape architect to ensure that the final terracing will be structurally sound. If you plan to attack the project without professional help, begin at the bottom, just below the slope. Build a retaining wall on ground that is already level. Use the soil from the low end of the slope near the wall to backfill the gap between the wall and the slope until you have created a level terrace. Continue until you have created the number of terraces you want. It is essential to provide drainage for a retaining wall so water doesn't build up behind it. Either build weep holes in the wall, or run perforated drain pipe behind the wall before you backfill with soil.

Materials for retaining walls include wood, stone, precast blocks, and concrete. Choose a building material that is suitable for the site, and that creates the overall effect you want. Details for constructing wooden retaining walls are given below. (See Chapter 6, pages 134–37 for information about brick and stone retaining walls.)

Wooden Retaining Walls

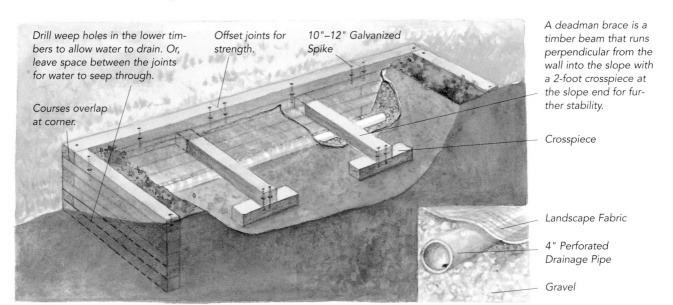

Drill weep holes in the lower timbers to allow water to drain. Or, leave space between the joints for water to seep through.

Courses overlap at corner.

Offset joints for strength.

10"–12" Galvanized Spike

A deadman brace is a timber beam that runs perpendicular from the wall into the slope with a 2-foot crosspiece at the slope end for further stability.

Crosspiece

Landscape Fabric

4" Perforated Drainage Pipe

Gravel

Wooden retaining walls are generally the easiest and least expensive way to tame a slope; they usually look less formal than terraces walled with stone or brick. Wood tends to survive longer in drier climates than wet ones and on well-drained slopes. On a large slope, where the wall must support tons of earth, you must use heavy lumber such as landscape timbers. To delay rotting, choose either pressure-treated lumber or wood that is resistant to decay such as redwood, cedar, or cypress. If you want to avoid digging deep holes for support posts, you can use deadman braces to give structural strength to a timber retaining wall. Deadmen should be installed along your wall in the second or third course from the bottom and in the second course from the top.

TERRACING A HILLSIDE

Difficulty Level: *Moderate*

These terraces were built so a vineyard and orchard could be planted on the sloping land. A home gardener built them in the spring when the ground was soft and the winter rains were finished. The northern California coastal soil was naturally porous with a gravel base; thus there were no drainage problems. The gardener does not recommend building such a terrace in clay soil without a retaining wall.

Tools and Materials: Gas-powered rototiller, shovel, wildflower seeds.

Step 1: Choose the Location. *Before the hillside was terraced, it was quite steep. But this area received the optimal sunlight for a vineyard and an orchard and had great potential. Some old hardwood trees block the wind.*

Step 2: Build the Terraces. *Using a gas-powered tiller and a shovel, the homeowner built the terraces. It required many passes with the tiller, which cut just 8 inches at a time. Each terrace was 4 feet, half filled and half cut.*

Step 3: Seed the Terraces. *Fast-germinating wild-flower seeds were well-established plants when the winter rains began. Vegetables also held the soil until the vines and trees were established.*

Step 4: Plant the Saplings. *Fruit trees were planted, and the homeowner hung wire between poles to support the grape vines. The wildflowers covered the terraces, and some reseeded themselves the following year.*

Irrigation Systems

Although hand watering can be a relaxing, therapeutic occupation, it is time consuming. Except for plants growing in containers, it's almost impossible to give plants the thorough soaking they need with just a watering can. Portable sprinklers do a better job and take less hands-on time, but they require that you remember to move them at regular intervals.

To save hours of hand watering and dragging hoses, consider installing systems that drip water directly into the soil, or sprinkle water through the air. If you include automatic timers with your system, you can ensure that your plants consistently receive the amount of water they need.

Installing your own irrigation system is a great do-it-yourself project, challenging enough to give a sense of accomplishment when the job is done but not so complicated that it takes a professional to do it right. In addition, the savings are significant. You can save 50 percent or more from the cost of a professional installation, and the time you spend on the project is minimal compared to the time you'd otherwise spend watering by hand over the years.

*A **drip irrigation system** is ideal for vegetable beds because the layout can be revised and amended as needed with each new crop. Set out the lines when the plants are young, and in a few weeks they will be completely hidden by the growing produce.*

DRIP IRRIGATION SYSTEMS

Drip irrigation is more versatile and flexible than sprinklers for most situations, other than lawns and ground covers. Drip irrigation delivers water at a slow rate directly to root systems. The long, slow delivery ensures that plants are deeply watered, even in clay soil where water absorption is slow.

With drip irrigation, there is no waste due to runoff and evaporation, and the deep watering encourages plants to grow deeper roots, making them more drought-tolerant. Because drip irrigation doesn't wet the foliage, plants are less likely to suffer from diseases resulting from damp foliage (which encourages some fungi), or from pathogens carried from upper leaves to lower ones in descending water droplets. Drip irrigation also reduces the need for pesticides, since damp leaves harbor some pests. Since the water is applied exactly where it is needed through custom-made emitters (holes) located only where water is needed, weed plants have a harder time getting their share. In addition, drip lines do not need to be buried. Thus you can move the lines around easily and adapt your system to any changes you make in your garden design. It is easy to add new lines, remove old ones, or plug the holes for old feeder lines that are no longer required.

Planning Drip Systems. Starting with a base map of your property that shows the location of buildings, walkways, patios, water sources, and a layout of your garden beds and plants, divide your garden into zones based on the types of plants and their watering needs. For example, plants growing in shade would be one zone, trees and shrubs in another, the vegetable garden a third zone, and containers and hanging baskets in yet another zone. Annuals, which require frequent shallow watering, should be in a different zone from trees and shrubs which require infrequent but deep watering. Ideally each zone should have a separate drip watering circuit that is connected to its own valve.

The kind of soil you have will be a factor in determining the rate of flow you want from each emitter (water delivery device), and how many emitters you will need. Because heavy clay soil absorbs water slowly, you will want long, slow water delivery and therefore fewer emitters. Because sandy soil soaks up water quickly, allowing water to drain straight down rather than spreading, you'll need more emitters spaced closely.

Plan your drip irrigation system by dividing your plants into groups or zones based on their water requirements. Here large trees that require deep, infrequent watering are on one line, the vegetable garden is a zone of its own, the flower beds are grouped together, and the containers have a separate system with drip lines running to each pot. Such a map is also useful for underground sprinklers with which you can water all of these plants plus lawns, but not containers. Also separate out plants growing in full sun, which will dry out faster than plants growing in shady areas.

DRIP WATERING ZONES

—— Trees & Shrubs

—— Vegetable Gardens

—— Container Plants

—— Flower Beds & Ground Covers

Materials. Supplies you will need for drip systems include ½-inch polyethylene hose (sufficient length to complete your design), hose fittings, an anti-siphon control valve for each watering zone, a pressure regulator, a filter to keep pipe debris from clogging the emitters, Y-filters to enable you to fertilize as you water, end caps, transfer barbs for extending lateral lines, polyethylene microtubing (the spaghetti-like lines that take the water from the main hose to the plants), and emitters.

Although not essential, an automatic timer is a real asset. Drip systems run for hours at a time, making it easy to forget that the water is running. With a timer, you don't have to remember to shut off the water. In the case of a large fruit or ornamental tree with a canopy spread of 15 feet in diameter, you should plan for six emitters. Smaller trees and shrubs require one emitter for every 2½ feet of canopy diameter.

Make a shopping list of all the supplies you will need to complete the system. Use the parts lists available from the manufacturers as a guide.

Watering Chart

Type of Plant	Water Needed Gallons/Week	Watering Frequency per Week		
		Moderate	Hot	Cool
Vines & Shrubs (2–3')	7	2	3	1–2
Trees & Shrubs (3–6')	10–15	2	3	1–2
Trees & Shrubs (6–10')	30–40	2	3	1–2
Trees & Shrubs (10–20')	100–140	2	3	1–2
Mature Trees (Over 20')	160–240	2	3	1–2
Flowers, Plants, Vegetables	3	2	3	1–2
Potted Plants	¾	2	3	1–2
Rows of Flowers or Vegetables	6	2	3	1–2

INSTALLING DRIP IRRIGATION

***Difficulty Level:** Moderate*

Drip systems are fun to design and easy to install. You don't need wrenches, saws, or glue, and if you make a mistake, it is simple and inexpensive to remedy. Drip lines can be installed aboveground or belowground, and the design can be expanded or relocated as your needs evolve.

Companies that manufacture drip irrigation supplies provide free brochures that give detailed instructions for designing and installing the systems. You can purchase kits with complete instructions for specific applications such as containers, vegetable gardens, and general landscape areas. Following is a brief summary of the usual steps.

Tools and Materials: Hosing, T-connectors, filter, timer, crimping rings, measuring tape, utility knife or garden shears, punch (available from manufacturers of drip systems).

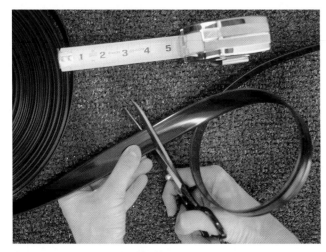

Step 1: Measure the Tubing. *Lay out the line, measure carefully and cut it to the proper length. This system is designed to water containers. The tubing becomes round when it is filled with water.*

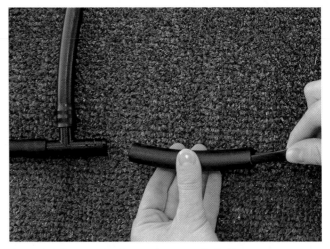

Step 2: Connect the Tubing at T-Joints. *These joints connect several lines to a single water source. Punch holes where you want the emitters. These holes can be plugged and new ones punched as the garden changes.*

Step 3: Attach a Filter to the Water Source. *Filters vary in size from very fine mesh to trap tiny particles to larger mesh openings. The sediment content of your water supply will dictate the type of filtering system necessary.*

Step 4: Set a Timer. *The easiest way to run a drip irrigation system is to put everything on an automatic timer, which will turn the water on and off at custom intervals. The duration of each watering can also be programmed.*

Installing Drip Systems. You can either bury the lines—being careful to keep the ends of the microtubing aboveground, cover them with mulch, or leave them above the ground. In annual and vegetable beds, the growing plants will soon hide most, if not all, of the aboveground tubing.

Maintenance. Sediment present in your tap water will accumulate in the irrigation lines and clog them. Every four to six months flush out the lines by opening the end caps and allowing water to run freely through the system for a few minutes. Also flush out the lines if they haven't been used for several months.

Filters should be checked monthly. Wash them under running water, checking for tears or other damage; replace any that are damaged. Y-filters need less regular maintenance. They handle up to 720 gallons per hour (gph) through a screen.

Every few months check the emitters to make sure they are working properly. Also check an emitter if you notice that a nearby plant is wilting, or an unusual wetting pattern. Clean any emitters that have become clogged, and replace damaged ones.

If a line is damaged, repair it with a slip-on coupling. In areas with winter freezes, drain the lines and shut off the system before the first major frost. You also should protect the control head from freezing. The best way to do this is to install the control head with a union on either side of it. When the weather turns cold, just unbolt the control head and store it indoors until spring.

This group of valves, called a manifold, shows a 3-circuit system. Anti-siphon valves (which are available with built-in backflow prevention) are always installed above ground. In-line valves (which require separate backflow prevention) are installed below ground, usually in protective boxes. PVC pipe is shown in this illustration. In areas where freezing occurs, poly pipe may be used instead of PVC downstream of valves. Check local codes for pipe recommendations and before installing backflow protection devices.

UNDERGROUND SPRINKLER SYSTEMS

These irrigation systems involve buried pipes with sprinkler heads placed at regular intervals. Sprinklers spray water over the plants, wetting them the same way that rain does, at a rate as high as 9 gallons per minute. Sprinkler systems tend to work better for lawns and ground covers than for garden beds.

Planning Your Underground Sprinkler System.

Excellent brochures by the major sprinkler companies give detailed step-by-step instructions for designing and installing their own sprinkler systems. In addition, some of the larger companies will create a custom design for your property free of charge. Call their hotlines if you need help or have questions.

Use a copy of the landscape base map you created earlier to work out and draw your sprinkler system's design. If you haven't yet created a base map of your property, as explained in the previous chapter, draw your property to scale on a piece of graph paper. (See Chapter 2, page 45 for how to make a base map.) Then indicate the location of your water meter and the location and length of the service line to your house. If your water supply comes from a well, rather than from the city water supply, show where the well and pump are located.

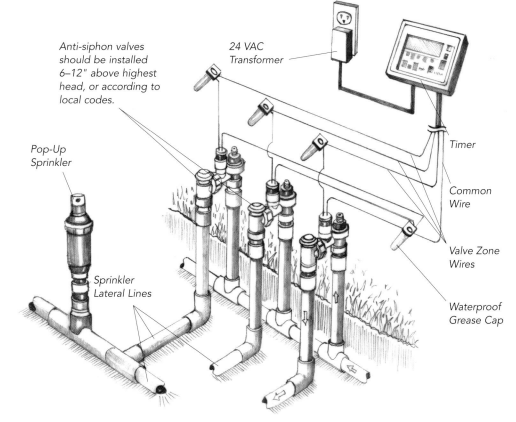

Anti-siphon valves should be installed 6–12" above highest head, or according to local codes.

24 VAC Transformer

Pop-Up Sprinkler

Timer

Common Wire

Valve Zone Wires

Waterproof Grease Cap

Sprinkler Lateral Lines

Divide Sprinklers into Circuits. You will not have enough water pressure to water the entire garden at once. Instead you need to divide the sprinklers into separate groups called circuits. Each circuit will be an independent sprinkler line. Group the sprinklers into sections or circuits, being careful not to mix areas with different watering requirements on the same circuit (keep lawns separate from flower beds). In general, plants with different water requirements will have different types of sprinkler heads (rotating, spray, bubbler), so you can usually organize circuits by the type of sprinkler head. The number of heads you can have in any section will depend on the gallons per minute your water system produces. Sprinkler manufacturers provide excellent guidelines to calculate the gpm. Once you've grouped your sprinklers into different circuits for valve control,

draw the piping system on your map, connecting each sprinkler group to a separate control valve.

Sprinkler Heads for Different Jobs. Sprinkler heads come in varied designs, each meant for a different job. Among the many options are bubblers for watering individual plants, such as roses; pop-up heads designed to spray in a full circle, half circle, quarter circle, or square; and shrubbery spray sprinklers, which are mounted on a riser pipe high enough to spray over shrubs. Each product brochure lists all available sprinkler heads and describes the purpose of each. For full coverage, you need to space sprinkler heads so their spray slightly overlaps. Sketch the position of the sprinkler heads on your site map, using arced lines (circles or portions of circles) to indicate the spray pattern.

Sprinkler Heads

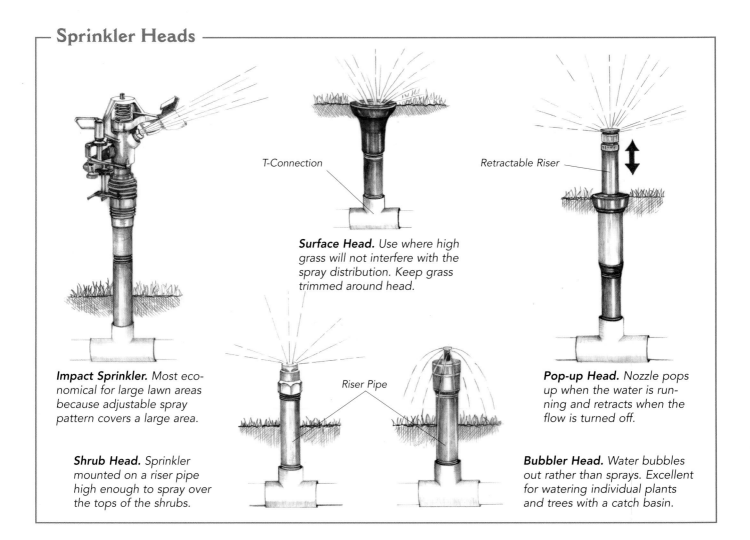

T-Connection

Surface Head. *Use where high grass will not interfere with the spray distribution. Keep grass trimmed around head.*

Retractable Riser

Impact Sprinkler. *Most economical for large lawn areas because adjustable spray pattern covers a large area.*

Riser Pipe

Shrub Head. *Sprinkler mounted on a riser pipe high enough to spray over the tops of the shrubs.*

Pop-up Head. *Nozzle pops up when the water is running and retracts when the flow is turned off.*

Bubbler Head. *Water bubbles out rather than sprays. Excellent for watering individual plants and trees with a catch basin.*

Materials. Once you've drawn a satisfactory plan, create a shopping list of all the materials you'll need. Also ask local building authorities whether you'll need a permit and if so, what codes apply. Some communities require a backflow preventor to stop water in the irrigation pipes from flowing back into the household drinking water.

Consider any accessories you may want. For example, it is very helpful to have a timer that turns the various sprinkler lines on and off automatically according to a preprogrammed schedule. With timers the garden continues to be watered even when you're away on a trip. Another possible accessory is a rain meter which measures the rainfall and turns off the watering system after a predetermined amount of rain. Rain meters are particularly useful for sprinkler sys-

tems. Still, another useful device is a soil moisture sensor, which activates the sprinkler system when the soil becomes too dry.

Be aware that sprinkler pipe is made from several materials. Two commonly available types are PVC (short for polyvinyl chloride) and "poly," (short for polyethylene). PVC is semi-rigid, and poly is flexible. Poly pipe is easier to install because you can bend it around corners, saving time on joints. However, PVC is generally preferred because it is less expensive than poly and holds up better under high water pressure. PVC pipe is stamped with a pressure rating on the side of the pipe. Use PVC rated with a lower pressure rating for regular sprinkler lines. Always use PVC schedule-40 rated pipe to connect the pipe between the service line and the control valves because of surge pressure.

PVC & POLY PIPE CONNECTIONS

*Difficulty Level: **Easy***

Poly pipes are quicker to install than PVC pipes because they bend around corners. Never use poly pipe to connect between the service line and the control valves where the surge pressure can be high. PVC pipe is less expensive than poly, and although you'll need to cut and join pipes more often, connecting pipes is easy.

Tools and Materials: PVC or poly pipe, elbows, clamp, screwdriver, PVC cement, rag.

Poly Pipe

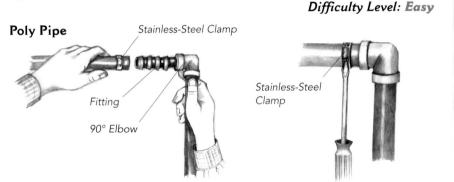

Step 1. *Slip a stainless-steel clamp over the cut pipe and then insert the fitting into the pipe.*

Step 2. *Position the clamp over the inserted fitting ridges and tighten with a screw driver.*

PVC Pipe

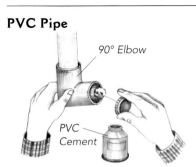

Step 1. *Clean off any burrs from the cut pipe, and then brush the cement evenly on the outside end of the pipe and inside the fitting.*

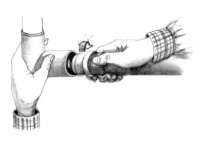

Step 2. *Quickly slide pipe into the fitting as far as it will go, twist to ensure a complete seal, and then hold for 10 to 15 seconds while the cement sets.*

Step 3. *Use a rag or paper towel to wipe any excess cement off the outside of the pipe.*

INSTALLING A SPRINKLER SYSTEM

As you plan how to tap into your service line, it is also important to determine your water meter size, the diameter of your water service line, and the water pressure. This information is important because it tells you how many sprinkler heads you can attach to one watering line and the rate in gallons per minute (gpm) of water delivery. The sprinkler manufacturer will specify a minimum rate of water flow for its system to work. If your water pressure is low, you will need more pipelines (known as circuits), with fewer sprinkler heads on each. The more sprinkler heads you have, the more water pressure you need to supply enough water fast enough to feed them.

Tools and Materials: measuring tape, screwdriver, hacksaw, shovel, pipe wrench, Teflon tape, PVC cement (also known as solvent), and PVC primer. Optional: a gasoline-powered trench digger will save hours of hand digging.

Step 1: Map the System. *On the base map, mark the water source and the circuits you will be watering. Dig the trenches 8 inches deep (or below the frost line in cold regions). Line the trench with sand or gravel.*

Step 2: Apply PVC Cement. *Measure and cut the pipe. Connect the risers. Brush PVC cement around the end of the pipe and inside the fitting. Quickly connect the two pieces.*

Step 3: Attach the Sprinkler Head to Riser. *After you've determined the type of head needed, attach it to the appropriate riser. For complete coverage, you will need to space the heads so their spray overlaps.*

Step 4: Test the Riser Height. *Shrub heads should be mounted high enough to spray over the tops of shrubs; surface heads should be at ground level, where they won't be damaged by the lawn mower.*

Difficulty Level: Challenging

In regions where pipes freeze in cold winters, you'll need a shutoff valve and drain to empty the system before the first freeze. This drain must be installed horizontally at the lowest point in each circuit line, and every pipe must run slightly downhill to it so that all the water will drain out. In cold regions, you will also have to dig the trenches below the frost line. The depth of the frost line varies; check with local authorities for specifics. As an added precaution, you can opt for an automatic drain valve that opens automatically to drain the pipes every time the water is turned off. With this device there is never any water standing in the pipes at any time. If you are concerned that your system isn't draining all of the water out of the pipes, there are garden maintenance companies that will come in autumn and blow out the lines with compressed air.

Step 5: Connect Water Shutoff Valve and Drain. *Every line must have its own shut-off. Locate the drain at the lowest point in each circuit line. Drain the system before the first frost.*

Step 6: Install the Anti-siphon Valve. *Close to the main water supply, attach the anti-siphon valve which prevents water from flowing backward out of the irrigation system into the main water supply.*

Step 7: Flush the Sprinkler Valves. *Wait four hours to ensure that the cement is fully dry. Then run the water to clear any debris in the pipes. Check for leaks and go back and re-cement any leaky joints*

Step 8: Program the Controller. *The controller (or timer) is the brains of the sprinkler system. It will turn the water on and off at intervals you determine, and will control how long each circuit stays on.*

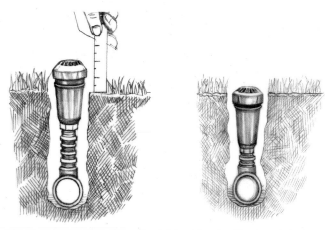

Check the Height of the Sprinkler Heads. *The head shown on the left is too high; the one on the right is flush with ground level and is correct. Measure and mark the pipe. Cut the riser if necessary and cement the pipe.*

Test the System. Once you have connected all the lines, wait four hours to ensure that all the joints have set completely. Then run the water to flush out the pipes and remove any dirt that may have collected while you were working. At the same time, check for leaks. If you find a leak, apply more cement to the joint. If that doesn't solve the problem, you need to cut out the leaky joint and connect new pipe. Also measure to see how far the risers are above the ground. For lawns, you want the sprinkler heads flush with the ground. Trim any risers that are too tall, then attach the sprinkler heads. Finally, bury the lines, using the soil you removed from the trenches. Be careful not to bury the sprinkler heads. If you saved your sod, replace it. Otherwise, you'll need to reseed.

Water will spray with more force from sprinkler heads closest to the water supply. To get a relatively even flow from all the heads on each line, adjust the main circuit valve so that the flow is greatest from the heads nearest the water source. Then put on your bathing suit, and beginning nearest the water supply, adjust each head (there's a screw you turn) while the water is running until each sprays about the same amount.

Irrigation Map. Keep the final map of your sprinkler design, showing the location of all pipes. You'll be grateful for the information if you need to dig for other projects or to make repairs in your system. You can bequeath the map to the next owner of your house. The map will remain a valuable piece of information.

OTHER SYSTEMS

Additional options for irrigation include soaker hoses and mist irrigation. Soaker hoses are porous hoses that weep water at a slow rate. They are the easiest form of irrigation to use. Laid on top of the soil, they are excellent for watering a row of flowers or vegetables that are planted close together. Soaker hoses can be installed in shrub borders and perennial beds for an entire season, hidden from sight under a layer of mulch. Use quick-release attachments to connect them to the ordinary garden hose that delivers water from the spigot.

In mist irrigation systems, the water is delivered as a fine mist through specially designed heads. If you have a greenhouse, you should also investigate mist irrigation systems.

Watering Tips

❧ Water early in the morning so wet leaves can dry off before the sun becomes too strong. The second-best time is early evening. Less water is lost to evaporation at these times, so more will reach plants.

❧ Avoid watering in the heat of the day, especially in bright sunlight, because water droplets on the leaves act like magnifying glasses in the sun, causing leaf burn.

❧ Avoid getting water on the leaves, especially after dark, because wet leaves are prone to fungal diseases.

❧ Allow the water to run slowly so it penetrates deeply. Plants will be much healthier and more drought-tolerant if you water thoroughly and less often than if you lightly splash them frequently.

❧ Avoid using sprinklers when it's windy. The wind will blow the water droplets away from where they're meant to fall, and the wind increases water loss through evaporation.

❧ Water newly planted trees and shrubs and young seedlings, frequently until their root systems develop.

❧ Mulch plants to reduce evaporation and minimize the amount of watering you need to do.

Landscape Lighting

Everchanging light transforms a garden's appearance throughout the day. A garden can look etched in sharp clarity in the bright sun of high noon. Bathed in the long, golden glow of the waning evening sun, the same garden can take on a rosy gilt. In early morning, when the sun shines through a mist, there's an ethereal, silvery quality to a garden's appearance. Come dusk, an unlit garden recedes and then disappears as twilight fades to night.

Outdoor lighting can transform night into an enchanting time, highlighting parts of the garden in new ways. Garden lights also prolong the time you can be outdoors, especially in the transition seasons of spring and autumn when the days are shorter but the temperature is still warm enough to be outdoors. Dining outdoors in the summer and lingering at the table late into the evening are added pleasures when your surroundings are bathed in soft light, perhaps occasionally punctuated by a dramatically uplit plant.

In addition to the aesthetic benefits, outdoor lighting can make your property safer both for walking and as a deterrent to burglars. To do its job, however, safety lighting must be installed properly. For example, a spotlight focused on the bottom of a set of steps or at a sharp change in a path may increase the hazard for a person moving from intense light into total darkness. A more general floodlighting is safer. Better yet, and more attractive, is a series of tier lights along a path or stairway, focusing light downward in even pools.

Well-placed lights *along this waterside garden path encourage an evening stroll, and add a sense of enchantment to the lovely scene.*

Burglars and prowlers tend to avoid well-lit properties, but all-night lighting wastes electricity. Rather than leaving lights on all night, you can install floodlight fixtures with sensors that respond to movement by switching the lights on for a preset number of minutes. One disadvantage of motion lights is that they also switch on when neighborhood pets pass through or, when breezes move tree branches or other plants that are growing within range of the motion detectors.

Installing a 120-volt garden lighting system is an expensive and labor-intensive job that requires buried waterproof pipes. As with other electrical projects, strict safety codes must be followed. Installation of a 120-volt system is usually best left to professional electricians.

Fortunately, there is an inexpensive alternative to 120-volt systems, called low-voltage outdoor lighting. Low-voltage systems use only 12 volts of electricity instead of 120. A typical six-light set uses less electricity than a 60-watt bulb, costing pennies per evening to operate. Best of all, most of the low-voltage systems are reasonably inexpensive and easy to install.

Landscape lighting *transforms a garden after dark from a black hole to a magical place where fascinating shapes and silhouettes are highlighted.*

INSTALLING LOW-VOLTAGE LIGHTS

Difficulty Level: Easy

The only hard part of installing low-voltage lights is deciding where you want the lights to be and which of the many effects you want to create. There are kits available designed for specific purposes. Check them out to help you make your decisions. For the sake of economy and tidiness, try to minimize the amount of wire you need. Once you're ready to connect the wires, the job literally takes minutes.

Lay out the wire in a direct route, which avoids crossing the wire back over itself or making tight, twisty turns, following the manufacturer's instructions. Be careful not to exceed the prescribed number of lights for each circuit. Plug the transformer box into a properly installed outdoor outlet. If you don't have an outdoor outlet, have one installed by a professional electrician following local codes.

Tools and Materials: lights, fixtures, wires, transformer box, measuring tape to mark the spacing between lights, wire cutters (with a stripper), pliers, screwdriver to assemble the light fixtures and connect wires.

Step 1: Connect the Wire Cable to the Transformer Box. *Wrap the wire around the terminal screws. For proper connection, make sure the wire insulation is clear of the pressure plates. Tighten the screws firmly, and plug the box into a grounded outlet.*

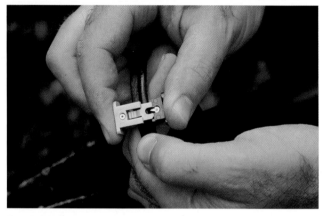

Step 2: Connect the Lamps to the Low-Voltage Cable. *Pinch the fast-lock connector, which is attached to the cable that runs from the light, onto the main line. You can undo the connection and move it at any time. The hole is tiny and the voltage is low, so there is no hazard.*

Step 3: Hide the Wires. *Pre-installed wires run through the light fixture and are connected to the main line. You can bury the cable lines underground. But if you think you may be moving the system, the lines are perfectly safe left aboveground.*

Step 4: Position the Lamp. *Anchor the lamp in place by pressing the lamp stake into the ground. In climates where heavy winter freezes cause heaving, dig a hole 8 inches deep and 6 inches wide for the lamp stake, and backfill the hole with gravel.*

DECORATING WITH LIGHTS

The two basic types of lighting are spotlighting and floodlighting. A spotlight is focused so the light beam strikes a defined area, creating a distinct line between the lit and unlit areas. A floodlight is more diffuse; it covers a wide general area with a gradual decline from well-lit to dark. In either case, the light can be intense or subdued, although in low-voltage systems the floodlighting is less bright than with 120-volt systems. Halogen bulbs produce the brightest light for low-voltage fixtures.

By positioning and combining spotlights and floodlights, you can create a wide variety of decorative lighting effects. It's often a good idea to experiment with portable lights to work out the effects you want, and then study a product list to determine which fixtures will produce those effects. The wiring for lights installed in trees can be vulnerable to falling branches, so secure the wire to the trunk of the tree to prevent problems. If you are using 120-volt lighting, run the wire up the tree trunk in a conduit that meets local building codes and is firmly attached to the tree.

Part of the art of designing is creating contrast. To be artistically effective, light should be complemented by shadow. Of course, you could floodlight your entire property so everything is as clearly seen as in the daylight; but your night garden will be more special, more mysterious, if you contrast lit areas with darker places. Change also adds interest to designs. With a low-voltage system, you can easily move lights around throughout the year. Highlight the blooming azaleas in spring, and then move the lights to showcase a summer display elsewhere.

Avoid going overboard with colored lenses or bulbs. Yellow colored lights can be useful near a patio or outdoor sitting area because they attract fewer flying insects. In general, however, you'll be more pleased with white lights, which enhance the natural colors of the plants and other features in your garden.

▶ *This decorative fixture illuminates a section of path at the edge of a bed. The verdigris copper has an organic look that blends with the landscape.*

◀ *This low-profile flare light accents a special plant. Several can be used to light a path, and to lead the way to a special destination. (Courtesy of Malibu Lights)*

▶ *This low-profile edge light emphasizes the texture of the pavers, while lighting the path. This light would cast interesting shadows. (Courtesy of Malibu Lights)*

◀ *This rectangular flood light illuminates a large area, but is less decorative. Try this light on main walkways, where optimal light is needed for safety and security. (Courtesy of Malibu Lights)*

◀ *The low-profile well light highlights the evergreen shrub, while casting a soft light on the river stones. The hood can be turned 360° to change the focus of the light. (Courtesy of Malibu Lights)*

LIGHTING EFFECTS

Uplighting. Fix a spotlight or well light at ground level and focus it upward at the feature you want to illuminate. Well lights are designed to be buried; they employ a shade or sleeve in the housing that conceals the light source. Well lights create highlights and shadows on the underside of leaves and branches.

Silhouetting. Conceal a strong light behind an object, such as a plant with a striking form and clean outline, to make it stand out in silhouette.

Downlighting. Illuminate objects or areas from above by mounting floodlights in trees or high on walls. You can also downlight paths or patches of ground with tier lights that reflect light downward.

Moonlighting. This variation on downlighting creates a moonlit effect by means of floodlights high in trees. The light filters down through the branches and leaves, casting complex shadows on the ground.

Moon Gardens

For centuries man has been fascinated by the idea of white gardens designed to be enjoyed during the day, as well as at night. Even a small bed, carefully planted with white or pale yellow varieties of annuals and perennials, can add aesthetic interest to your garden. Today, when people work long hours, a white garden designed to be seen by moonlight or artificial light is a simple luxury.

Plant a moon garden near your patio so you can enjoy the white blossoms shimmering in the moonlight when you dine outdoors. For another dimension of pleasure, choose fragrant flowers such as angels'-trumpets (*Brugmansia*), night jessamine (*Cestrum nocturnum*), gardenia, *Hosta plantaginea*, jasmine, sweet peas, honeysuckle, fragrant roses, and sweet-scented varieties of phlox. Or, cover an arbor with a white-blooming vine (preferably one with fragrant flowers), surround it with a few white-blooming flowers, then sit in its shelter on hot summer nights.

Add Night-Blooming Flowers. Many flowers, such as night jessamine and angels'-trumpets, release their scent at night to attract night-flying pollinators. Other flowers, such as moonflowers, four-o'clocks, *Datura inoxia*, and some water lilies open in late afternoon, saving their floral splendor for the evening hours.

For added interest in your white garden, consider including plants with grey foliage. Lamb's ears (*Stachys byzantina*) is a charming, low-growing choice that makes an attractive border for flowers. (Its soft, white woolly leaves make its common name most apt.) Dusty Miller, *Artemisia stellerana*, has a toothed, woolly white foliage that can add interesting texture to the garden.

Variegated Foliage Enhances the Effect. Foliage with splashes or ribbons of white variegation are another excellent addition to a moon garden. In the dogwood family consider *Cornus alba* 'Elegantissima' (variegated red-stemmed dog-

wood), *C. alternifolia* 'Argentea' (Pagoda dogwood), and *C. controversa* 'Variegata' (giant dogwood). Many of the hostas, including *H. albomarginata*, *H. Fortunei* 'Marginata-alba', and *H.* 'Francee', have different patterns of white in their leaves.

Moon gardens are special. As Barbara Damrosch wrote in her book, Theme Gardens, "A garden planted with only white flowers is by day a pleasing and unusual picture. By night it is an enchantment."

Variegated foliage and white flowers *light up this moon garden. Plants shown include:* Alchemilla vulgaris, Phlox divaricata, *and* Anemone sylvestris.

An all-white border *weaves a magic spell on summer evenings. The plants casting the spell include:* iris, Lupinus, hosta, *and* Orach.

CHAPTER 4

Paths, Edgings, and Steps

Garden Paths

"Paths are more or less essential … [to a garden], a pathless garden being not only a contradiction in terms but highly inconvenient, as anybody will agree who has ever had to hop across a cabbage patch in order to inspect a pedigree lobelia." So wrote Heath Robinson and K. R. G. Browne in their irreverent book, *How to Make Your Garden Grow*, published in 1938.

As Robinson and Browne suggest, paths and steps perform a practical as well as an emotional and aesthetic function in landscapes. Ostensibly paths are designed to lead comfortably from point A to point B, keeping the feet clean and dry. However, walking in a garden is a type of journey with different experiences available along the way. The sort of path you create will help determine the nature of that journey. You can use paths to choreograph the way visitors move through your landscape.

▲ **A woodland path** invites exploration and gives visitors a clear destination. The shredded bark is in harmony with the trees surrounding the path, while the loose—but manicured—stone edging indicates that these woods are tamed.

A mortared brick path brings structure to this landscape. The gentle curves disappearing into the distance lend a sense of spaciousness and mystery to the garden, while the wisteria pergola frames the view.

VARY THE PACE

A wide, straight path puts the focus on the final destination at the far end. People tend to hurry down such a path, eager to reach their goal. In contrast, a narrow path that meanders through the landscape lends itself to a slower journey and encourages the traveler to stop along the way to notice details. Walking over stepping-stones requires more care; you need to watch your footing, and your rate of progress is slowed.

Paths also create visual effects in a landscape. A straight, narrow path that runs to the end of a short garden can make it feel larger. Paths that run diagonally across a narrow lot help make it seem wider. Snaking paths that disappear around bends or corners also promote a sense of spaciousness. In addition, paths are part of the bones (basic structure) of a landscape, enhancing the composition. Like hedges and specimen trees, paths add to the sense of design and order in the landscape. They are important structural features, especially during the winter months when eye-catching annuals have died and perennials have gone underground.

▼ *A gravel path* opens this otherwise inaccessible landscape to visitors who can experience the wetland garden while keeping their feet dry. The wooden boardwalk extends the path through an especially boggy section.

This straight brick path encourages strolling. The softly tumbling plants used as edging, and the slightly irregular brick pattern, make this path less formal than the path shown in the photo at the far left.

PATH SURFACES

The type of surface for the path affects its appearance as well as the experience of walking on it. Gravel makes a lovely crunching sound when you walk on it, and it's adaptable to both informal and formal settings. Some kinds of flagstone take on a beautiful sheen when they're wet. Wooden paths, especially those running through boggy areas, give you access to areas that otherwise might be out-of-bounds. A wooden surface has more spring to it than stone or brick. A bark or pine needle path through a woodland garden is in complete harmony with its surroundings. To make it more comfortable and convenient to cross a meadow, you can mow an informal path through the grasses and wildflowers.

Use Paving to Set a Tone. Paving choice also can convey messages. Consider changing the paving material from one section of the landscape to another. The difference will help set a new tone or mood. Even with your eyes closed you'll know you've entered a new part of the garden because the paving will feel and sound different. In some gardens, a crossroads in the path is signaled with a change of texture at the intersection.

Some of the most charming paths are a mixture of materials. At her famous garden at Barnsley House,

An informal mowed grass path leading through a wildflower meadow suits the back-to-nature look of this planting. Although the path appears casual, it is deliberately cut quite short to make it easier to cross.

English garden writer and designer Rosemary Verey has constructed a path from a combination of concrete paving and old bricks to set an informal tone within the geometric structure of her vegetable garden. In her famous laburnum walk, the path running through the tunnel of laburnum trees is a mixture of cobblestones and concrete slabs. In her book *Rosemary Verey's Making of a Garden*, Verey explains, "In winter the path made by David [her husband] with its unique pattern of stones is as important as the tracery of the laburnum branches."

Cost Considerations. A path paved with stone, concrete paving slabs, or brick is a major investment. While different materials are readily available at most garden centers, think carefully about the look that will best suit your garden; don't settle for second best because it is the easiest to find. Visualize the

A mixture of materials keeps Rosemary Verey's laburnum path informal. She used an unusual combination of cobblestones and concrete slabs.

Gravel path with open brick center pattern and brick edging is decorative but not as formal or expensive as a solid brick path. The edging contains the gravel so that it doesn't drift into the plants on either side of the path.

Loose-laid brick path gives Rosalind Creasy easy access to harvest her vegetables and herbs. The flat, smooth surface makes it safe to walk while holding scissors. The plants growing in the crevices complete the abundant cottage garden look.

Crevice plants soften the hard edges of these paving stones, breaking up the monotonous expanse of the flat walkway. Notice how some of the plants fit neatly in the cracks while others spill onto the path.

color and texture of the paving material, and how it will complement and blend with your house and garden. Spend the time to find what's right. The extra trouble will be worth it when you think about the lasting effect the path will have on your garden design.

Consider the less expensive alternative of creating a path with an open pattern of bricks. Fill the spaces with gravel or small stones, or plant the gaps with low-growing ground covers such as creeping thyme, thrift (*Armeria*), sweet alyssum, and sedums.

Think About Function. As you consider paving materials, don't overlook the practical function of a path. Some materials, such as wood and certain types of stones, become slippery when they are wet, creating a potential hazard. They would not be suitable materials for a front walkway. Gravel should be contained with proper edging or it will drift into the beds, creating problems. (See page 106.) Also avoid putting gravel at the bottom of a slope. Soil will wash down the slope into the gravel, spoiling the effect. If you will need to keep the path clear of snow, choose a solid surface that you can scrape and shovel without dislodging the paving material.

Paths are greatly appreciated in areas that tend to get muddy after a rain. Even a lawn is unpleasant to walk across if the grass is too wet. Consider putting stepping-stones across a well-traveled part of the lawn to reduce wear on the grass and to provide a dry spot to walk on when the grass is soaked.

This conveniently located path crosses the heavily used route to the gate. The stepping-stones protect the grass from excessive wear and tear while keeping people's feet dry.

Because one of the purposes of a path is to keep your feet dry, be sure the path slopes slightly so water won't puddle on it. In cases where the ground is wet for long periods, you may need to lay perforated drainage pipes under the path so that excess water is channeled away. (See Chapter 3, pages 77–78 for more information on installing drainage pipes.)

Practical Considerations. On a practical note, think of how the path will be used. If you plan to run a wheelbarrow or garden cart along the path, then it must be wide enough to accommodate that wheelbarrow. Generally 2 feet is the minimum width for a garden path, and three feet wide is better. The exception might be a winding track, like a deer path, through a wilder

▶ *The maintenance path* in Rosemary Verey's laburnum walk is only wide enough to accommodate one person. Compare this purely functional path to the wider, main walkway through the laburnum shown on page 96.

part of the garden. The minimum width for a path that allows two people to walk side by side, such as a front walkway, is 5 feet.

While many of your garden paths will be planned to enhance the design and structure of the garden, also think about the ergonomics involved. It is human nature to cut corners and to walk the shortest distance between two points. If the path is to create an unfolding garden experience, let it meander as you like. If it's more utilitarian, then design it so it is as easy as possible to use.

Maintenance Paths Give Access to Beds.

Maintenance paths within beds are important but often forgotten. Many gardeners fill their beds with so many plants that they leave themselves no way to get into the bed to work. Every time you walk through a bed, you compact the soil. A maintenance path needn't be fancy or wide; choose a material that is different from the mulch in the bed. Once you've put in maintenance paths, you can plant around them. You'll never again have to worry about compacting the soil or stepping on a tiny plant.

Lastly, don't clutter your garden with too many paths. The effect could be chaotic. Ultimately each garden path should take you to a worthy destination. As Hugh Johnson wrote in *The Principles of Gardening*, "... it is just as well if they [the garden paths] let you know when you have arrived by bringing you to a landmark: a seat or summer house or a view. Paths should live up to their promises."

Possible Materials for a Garden Path

Materials strongly affect the character of a path. Wood bark is perfect for woodland gardens. Flagstone is more structured, but still gives the landscape a country look. Terra-cotta tile is effective in establishing a sense of the Southwest. Crushed oyster shells also impart a strong regional flavor, and are one of the few ways to create a white path.

- Aggregate stone
- Bark (chipped or shredded)
- Brick or brick chips
- Ceramic tile
- Cobblestones
- Concrete paving blocks
- Crazy paving

- Fieldstone
- Flagstone
- Granite blocks
- Grass
- Gravel
- Interlocking pavers
- Marble
- Millstones

- Pebbles or cobbles set in mosaic pattern
- Pine needles
- Reconstituted stone
- Seashells (crushed)
- Terra-cotta tile
- Wood
- Wooden rounds

Grass

Tile

Flagstone

Oyster shells

Installing Paths

Whether your path surface is loose-laid brick or crushed quarry stone, a crazy pavement made of random-shaped flag- or field-stone, or a formal brick or stone path that is set with concrete and mortar, many of the steps for layout and building are the same. To estimate the amount of material you'll need for the path, measure the length and width, and then multiply the two numbers together to get the square feet of your path. For curved paths, it may help to run a string the length of the path, following the curves, and then measure the string. It's easy to work out the number of bricks needed if they are a standard size; however stone can be more difficult. Bring your measurements to the experts at the quarry, and let them work out the amount of stone you'll need.

Text continues on page 106 with "Edgings."

Some of the tools *that are required for installing stone or brick paths include (clockwise from bottom center): a tape measure, a level, a chisel, a brickset, and a mallet. You will also need a shovel to dig out the trench for the path.*

CUTTING BRICK OR STONE

To cut a brick, use a chisel or brickset to score along the desired break line on all four sides. Set the scored brick on sand. Place a brickset along the scored line with its bevel away from the side of the finished cut. Rap sharply on the end of the brickset handle with a hammer. To cut a piece of stone, after scoring it on the top and bottom, lay the stone across a support board, with the part to be removed hanging over the edge. Place a brickset on the score line and hit the chisel handle sharply with a hammer. Turn the stone over and repeat the process until the stone is cut. Wear safety glasses to protect your eyes from flying bits of brick, stone, or metal.

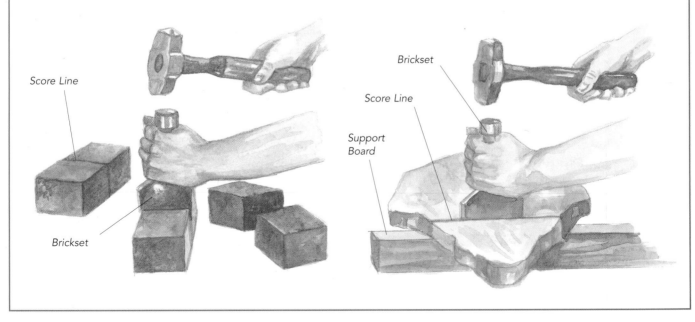

Score Line

Brickset

Brickset

Score Line

Support Board

How to Lay a Stepping-stone Path

*Difficulty Level: **Easy***

Stepping-stone paths are the simplest type of path to install; no heavy equipment or expertise is needed. The casual style brings to mind skipping from stone to stone to cross a stream. Whether the stones are round, square, or irregularly shaped (such as those shown here), the process is the same. Before you start, make sure you have enough stones to complete your path.

Tools and Materials: Shovel, tarp, long-handled knife, hand trowel, and a bucket of coarse builder's sand. Gloves and sturdy boots are recommended.

Step 1: Lay Out the Stones. *Lay the stones out, and walk their length, rearranging them as needed. Your feet should land squarely on the stones when you are taking normal strides.*

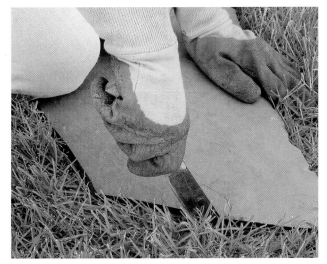

Step 2: Trace the Shape. *Cut around the edges of the stone with a long-handled sharp knife to remove the grass under the stone. Make sure you slice deep enough to get below the roots. Always wear gloves when using knives.*

Step 3: Remove the Grass. *Push a spade under the turf to lift it out; then set the turf on a tarp. If the turf doesn't lift out easily, slice around the edges again. Remember to bend your knees when you are lifting.*

Step 4: Level the Stones. *Fill the depression with builder's sand. Ultimately you want the stone flush with the ground, but because it will settle eventually, add sand until the stone sits slightly above the surface.*

How to Install a Loose-Laid Brick Path

Difficulty Level: *Moderate*

Many of the tools and techniques used to install a loose brick or mortared brick or stone path are the same. Combine the steps shown here with those shown on pages 104–105 to make a mortared brick path.

Tools and Materials: Shovel, wheelbarrow, metal rake, rubber mallet, string, level, landscape fabric or perforated plastic sheeting, stone dust, builder's sand, bricks or stones. The additional items needed for a cemented stone path (shown on pages 104–105) include: Circular saw with diamond-tipped blade, grout bag, masonite strips, rebar, concrete, water, and large sponge.

Step 1: Dig Out the Path. *Excavate the path to 7 inches. Line the path with perforated plastic sheeting to keep weeds down. In this picture, the deeper trench will bring water to a fountain that will be installed in the future.*

Step 2: Lay the Subbase. *Cover the plastic sheeting with a 4-inch layer of coarse ¾-inch gravel. Rake or walk on the gravel to make the surface as smooth as possible. The gravel provides a firm bed for the bricks.*

Step 3: Install a Retaining Edge. *Stretch string along the length of the path to keep the edges level and straight. Secure the edging with pegs that fit into slots built into the metal strips.*

Step 4: Create a Deeper Edge. *In spots where extra fill is required, such as on this slope, build a deeper edging out of pressure-treated lumber. Wedge the wooden edging into place with stakes hammered into the ground.*

Possible Brick Patterns

Running Bond

Basketweave

Herringbone

Diagonal Herringbone

Step 5: Add a Layer of Stone Dust. *Add a 1-inch layer of stone dust to the gravel subbase. Then draw a board across it. The stone dust creates a cushion on which the bricks rest.*

Step 6: Lay the Bricks. *Starting at the end of the path, lay the bricks. Place a spirit level over a row of bricks, and check both directions. Pound the bricks with a rubber mallet to set and level them.*

Step 7: Fill the Joints. *Sweep a medium-grade builder's sand over the surface of the bricks, moving the broom in different directions so that the bristles can work the sand into the narrow spaces between the bricks.*

Step 8: The Finished Walkway. *The finished, loose-laid path is traditional without looking rigid, making it ideal for inside the garden. However, for more-formal front walkways, choose brick and mortar.*

HOW TO INSTALL A CRAZY PAVEMENT PATH

Tools and Materials: See page 102.

Step 1: Dig Out the Path. *Excavate the path to 4 inches deep, and then stake masonite (hardboard) strips along the edges as a form for the concrete. Install a grid of rebar and pour the concrete to fill the trench.*

Step 2: Lay Out the Stone. *When the concrete has set, remove the hardboard. Position the stones, choosing pieces that fit together well. Don't cement the stones until you have worked out the pattern for a large section of the path.*

Step 3: Cut the Stone. *The pieces of a crazy path fit together like those of a jigsaw puzzle. However, you may occasionally need to cut a stone to make it fit properly. To cut stone, use a circular saw with a diamond-tipped blade.*

Step 4: Cement the Stones. *Lift the stones up one at a time, and put down a bed of mortar, using a cement trowel to smooth the mortar over the empty space. Then press the stone into the mortar, twisting it slightly to seat it firmly.*

Step 5: Level the Stones. *Place a level over several stones, and pound the newly positioned stone with a rubber mallet until it is level with the others. Move the level around to make sure the slab is level on all sides.*

Step 6: Mark a Clean Edge. *Stretch a string the length of a straight path, or run a hose along the curved sections of the walkway. Mark the edge of the path with a pencil.*

Step 7: Cut the Edge. *Cut a clean edge following the pencil line using a circular saw fitted with a diamond-tipped blade. Be sure to wear a dust mask and protective eyewear.*

Step 8: Fill in the Gaps. *Mix 1 part cement to 3 parts sand and enough water to make a thin batch of mortar. Apply the mixture with a grout bag. Finish by cleaning off the excess mortar with a wet sponge and water.*

The river-rock edging unites the "dry river bed" path with the loose stones and drought-tolerant plants growing alongside the path.

Edgings

Edgings are like the frame to a picture, drawing attention to the center and setting off the whole. They also serve a practical function, keeping soil, plants, or gravel within bounds. It isn't essential to edge beds and paths, but often the edge gives a finished look to the composition and makes the garden feel complete.

Use edging to unify your garden design. If you've used several different paving surfaces for paths and patios, link these elements together visually by edging them all with one material, such as brick or wood.

Edging with Plants. Don't overlook the possibility of edging with plants. Choose plants with a naturally compact form or those that respond well to pruning. Boxwood, lavender cotton (*Santolina*), and lavender are excellent plants for a formal, hedge-like edging. For a softer look, choose plants with a low, sprawling habit such as rock cress (*Aubrieta*), chives, alpine strawberries, or lady's mantle (*Alchemilla*). Good plant choices for edging shady paths include small hostas, lily turf (*Liriope*), or coral bells (*Heuchera*).

Many Edging Choices Available. An edging can be as simple as a mowing strip that allows you to mow right up against another surface, or as structured as bricks to define a path. A few edging choices—and how to install them—appear at right. Choose one that suits the path and that complements your landscape.

HOW TO INSTALL EDGING

Take the time to install edging carefully and properly. A hasty job may result in the edging heaving out of place and having to be reset. If the edging will run along a straight path or bed, tie string to stakes at each end of the path as a guideline for straight digging.

Plastic Edging. Install the edging after you have dug out the soil to form the route of the pathway and before you have put down the layers of landscape fabric, a loose stone foundation, and the material you plan to use as the top of the path. Lay the edging along the path route, and hammer the stakes through the bottom of the plastic strip to hold it down firmly. Set the edging strip no more than 1 inch above the level of the lawn adjoining the path so you can run the mower wheel along the path, cutting all the lawn right up to the edge and eliminating the need for hand trimming. (See Chapter 11, pages 230-231 for information on selecting grass height for a healthy lawn.)

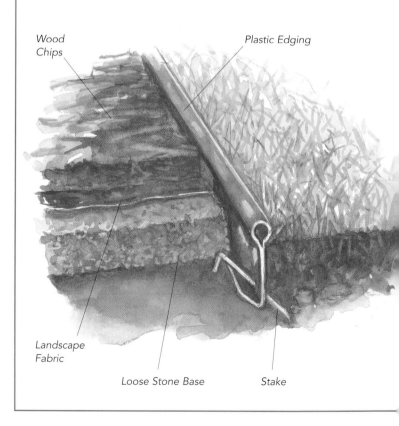

Wood Chips

Plastic Edging

Landscape Fabric

Loose Stone Base

Stake

Wooden Edging. Dig a trench along the path or bed deep enough so that the edging protrudes just 1 to 2 inches above the ground. Add sand to the trench to help level the edging, and then set each board in place. Pound 12-inch-long stakes into the ground every 3 to 4 feet to hold the boards in place. For extra stability, screw the stakes to the edging boards. Refill the rest of the trench.

Curved Wooden Edging. Make a series of saw cuts every 6 inches in ¾-inch- to 1-inch-thick wood over the length you wish to curve. Dig the trench as described above for wooden edging. Install the edging, using the cuts to help bend the wood to the desired curve. Pound in the stakes 1 foot or less apart to hold the curved wood in place. For extra stability, screw the stakes to the edging board. Refill the rest of the trench. For a gentle curve you may not need to cut the wood. Soak the lumber in water for a few days until it is pliable, and then install it while it's still wet.

Stone Edging with Mowing Strip. A mowing strip will save you hours of trimming. It's a flat edging that runs along the base of a wall, around beds, or alongside other edgings (such as bricks) that sit above ground level. The strip, which should be installed at or near ground level, helps to contain the lawn as well as provide a base for the lawn mower wheel. That way you can cut the grass right up to the edge. The strip needs to be just wide enough to support the wheel of the mower.

Dig a trench as wide as the vertical edging and horizontal mowing strip combined and 2 inches deeper than the bottom edge of the vertical edging. Spread 2 inches of sand in the bottom of the trench. Set the vertical edging pieces, making sure they're level and even with each other, and then continue to fill the rest of the trench with sand until the correct level is reached for the horizontal edging strip. Lay the horizontal strip pieces; then tap them to level them and to set them in place.

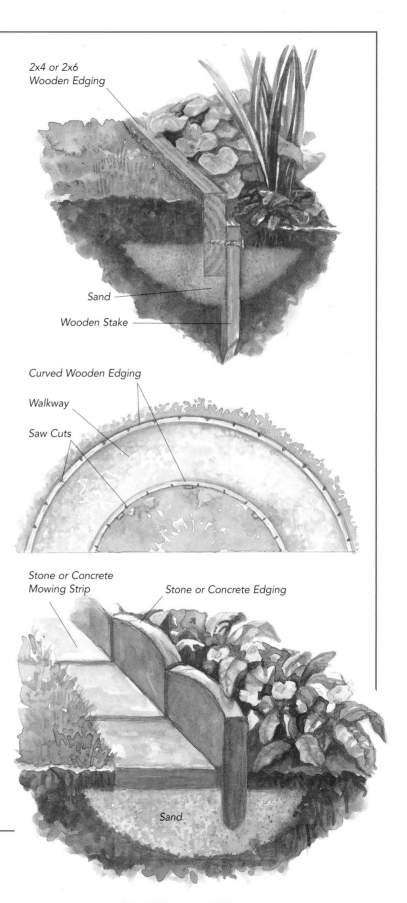

2x4 or 2x6 Wooden Edging

Sand

Wooden Stake

Curved Wooden Edging

Walkway

Saw Cuts

Stone or Concrete Mowing Strip

Stone or Concrete Edging

Sand

Garden Steps

A change in level in a garden adds interest and provides the opportunity for another garden design feature: a set of steps. The nature of those steps will depend on the physical situation as well as the aesthetics of your overall garden design. Remember that steps in the garden are different from steps indoors. Instead of designing outdoor steps to climb in as little space as possible, make the climb gradual (experts recommend a slight rise of 4 to 5 inches with a comfortably deep tread of 1 foot or more), with landings or a change of direction every 12 or more steps. In addition to making the steps less taxing to climb, a shallow rise makes it possible to run a wheelbarrow up and down the stairs; a ramp will help if you need to make frequent trips with a wheelbarrow.

STEPS ALTER THE PACE

Use your steps to help regulate how people move through the garden space. People tend to walk faster on steps with low risers and wide treads than they do on steps with high risers. Curved steps slow people down. If possible, make your steps wide enough for two people to walk abreast, which is at least 5 feet. Broad stairs look more inviting and elegant than a narrow set of steps.

Balance the Cost and the Look. Cost will surely be a factor in choosing the design and materials for your garden steps, but while considering budget, also bear in mind the look of the final result. Railroad ties or landscape timbers may be relatively inexpensive, but used in the wrong place they can spoil the look of a pretty garden. Steps near

Simple brick and railroad tie steps lead the way down a level and add interest to the lawn. Note that the steps are as wide as the path below the stairway, while the brick landing is slightly wider, which keeps the stairway safe.

the house should complement the architecture and style of the building and the style of the garden. Farther away from the house, especially if the garden becomes more informal, you can choose steps made out of less expensive materials such as logs.

Consider Safety. Regardless of the style of steps, keep safety and function in mind. As a general rule, the steps should be as wide as the path leading up to them. Uneven steps with risers that vary in height and treads of different depths are difficult and even dangerous to negotiate.

You may want to consider installing a handrail, even though most outdoor steps are not as steep as those built indoors. As an added safety and comfort feature, slope the tread ever so slightly so that water doesn't collect on it. If possible, make the tread of a nonslip material.

Stair Terminology

Tread: the horizontal surface of a step

Riser: the vertical face of a step

Nose: the front edge of the tread

Landing: resting place or turning point partway up a flight of steps. The depth of a landing should be an even multiple of the depth of the regular step treads.

Pitch: the angle of incline for the flight of steps. Experts recommend a pitch of no more than 40 degrees for safety and comfort outdoors.

HOW TO BUILD BRICK STEPS

Difficulty Level: Challenging

Find out whether your local building department has any codes for outdoor stairs. If you live in an area where the temperature drops below freezing, you will have to dig below the frost line. To determine how many steps you'll need on the slope, divide the vertical height of the slope by the planned height of your risers, allowing space for mortar, bricks, and the height of a paving slab tread on top. Once you've calculated the number of steps, work out the quantities of material you'll need to complete the project.

Tools and Materials: Shovel, wheelbarrow, level, cement trowel, water, crushed stone, concrete, framing wood, and bricks.

Step 1: Build a Wooden Frame. *The frame shapes the poured concrete foundation and is a temporary structure that will be removed once the concrete has set. Note that the frame has been anchored to the slope with temporary but sturdy stakes dug into the ground.*

Step 2: Fill the Frame with Concrete. *After pouring in the concrete, run a trowel over the surface to push large aggregate pieces into the mix and make the surface smooth. For this project, footings also have been created on either side of the stairs to support pillars.*

Step 3: Lay the Bricks. *Spread the mortar on the stairs and on the sides of the bricks. Place a brick, and tap it so that it is seated on approximately ½ inch of mortar. For the row beneath the top coping, use string as a guide to mark the angled cuts. Position the cut bricks in the mortar.*

Step 4: The Finished Stairs. *Because this slope is steep, the finished set of stairs has sides so that earth doesn't drift onto the steps. A pretty addition would be a billowing plant, such as catmint, edging down the sides of the stairs to soften the whole effect.*

CHAPTER 5

Patios, Decks, and Swimming Pools

Landscapes should be designed with people *and* plants in mind. You can enhance your outdoor living space by including useful and attractive amenities such as patios, decks, and swimming pools in your design. Add these features to your landscape, and you'll probably use and enjoy it more. After all, most people would prefer to dine under the stars surrounded by the sweet scent of the garden than indoors. On a hot night, a quick dip in your own swimming pool before bedtime is a refreshing luxury. This chapter gives you ideas and guidelines for planning and installing outdoor living and recreational spaces.

Designing Decks and Patios

Patios and decks increase the living space of your home. For a fraction of the cost of building an addition for your house, a new deck or patio can serve the same use as a new dining room, sitting room, or playroom. However, patios and decks are still costly. So plan carefully before you commit to such a project.

Your first decision is whether to add a wooden deck or a paved patio. Decks are ideal for sloping lots because they reclaim space that otherwise might go unused. In cases where the main floor of the house is several feet or more above ground level, a deck gives access to the outside. Level lots are ideal for patios.

Another consideration is location. If you plan to furnish the deck or patio with a table and chairs for outdoor dining, then choose a spot that's as close as possible to the kitchen. No matter how inviting the finished spot is, if you have to carry all of your dining paraphernalia a long way, you will not want to bother.

The conveniently located patio makes alfresco dining a pleasure. An umbrella that you can angle to follow the sun provides welcome shade.

Consider When You'll Use the Space. Also think about the time of day you will most likely use your outdoor space. For morning meals, an eastern-facing patio will catch the early sun. In the summer, a shady spot protected from the midday sun would be pleasant for lunch. A deck or patio facing west will stay warm longer in the evenings, but may be too hot on summer days. If you have the space and budget, consider the possibility of more than one patio to catch the light at different times of day. On a small property, a patio seating area at the far end of the lot draws the eye away from the house and encourages maximum use of the land.

Many Design Choices Exist. The design possibilities for decks and patios are almost limitless. Squares and rectangles are traditional; they are the easiest to construct because the lines are parallel and straight. If the patio is connected to a traditionally designed house, a geometric shape may be most suitable because it echoes the rectangular shape of the house. On the other hand, if you have a modern house full of unexpected curves and lines, you may want to try for shapes and lines that echo the outstanding features of the house. Consider ovals, circles, or other shapes for patios placed away from the house. To make it a delightful focal point and a desirable destination, furnish this distant patio attractively and comfortably. Plant around the patio to set off

▲ *A **swimming pool** and a place for comfortable outdoor dining transform your outdoor space into a personal recreational resort. While landscaping such as this is expensive, it extends the living space of your home dramatically and can cost about the same as adding extra rooms onto the house.*

▶ ***This spacious deck** allows plenty of room for relaxing, eating, and playing. Built out over a steep slope, the multi-level deck gives access to otherwise unusable land.*

Outdoor dining is comfortable and easy on a lath-covered patio. The small table, fresh flowers, and checked tablecloth make this spot near the house inviting, regardless of the season.

the space. Add containers full of plants to soften the paved area. If the patio is in a hot sunny spot, you may want to cover it with a lath roof.

In addition to shape, it is important to think about accessories that can complement your outdoor space. Raised planters incorporated into the design or built-in pools and fountains are among the many possibilities for making a patio more attractive. While you are in the planning stages, consider adding some of the following features to enhance both the appearance and the usefulness of the space.

INCORPORATE RAISED BEDS

Raised garden beds or planters are great assets in the garden. They add interest and variety to the design of a deck or patio, bringing plantings closer to eye level and breaking up a horizontal expanse. As an added bonus, plants growing in a raised bed are easier to tend; and the rim of the walls is a handy perch from which to work on the beds. Some people design raised beds to double as seating space on a deck or patio. If that is your plan, build the support walls to a comfortable height for sitting (standard bench seat height is between 15 and 18 inches) and make the rim wide enough to serve as a bench. If you fill the bed with sweet-smelling plants, the raised bed/garden seat will become a favorite place to sit outdoors.

Flowering plants cascade over the retaining wall, which gives a comforting sense of enclosure and privacy to this intimate garden. The crazy stone paving interplanted with a flowering ground cover softens the look and adds to the lushness of the verdant scene.

Beds as a Design Element. When you plan raised beds, think about how they will work with the overall design of your landscape and the deck or patio. If you run a raised bed along the edge of a deck or patio, it doubles as a low wall, helping to define the space. Perhaps you want a bed or planter to work as a partition, dividing a large space or creating a sheltered nook. If your patio has support posts for an arbor, consider building raised beds around the posts. Plant a vine in each bed, and train it to grow up the post. Excellent choices include wisteria, *Clematis montana* and sweet autumn clematis, honeysuckle, grapes, or star jasmine (*Trachelospermum jasminoides*). In frost-free climates, bougainvillea, *Stephanotis floribunda*, or Mandevilla 'Alice du Pont' are good choices.

Whether the raised bed serves as a low wall, garden seat, or both, its design should blend attractively with its

The raised beds *create an interesting pattern, while the different-colored paving distinguishes the path from the patio. The low-tiled wall is a comfortable height for sitting, and also works as a partition, dividing the space.*

Fragrant Plants for Patio Beds

Fragrant plants add a soothing dimension to your patio. Try creeping thyme between the paving stones; its pungent scent is released when the leaves are crushed underfoot. Or hang scented geraniums within easy reach of a favorite seat. Combine annuals and perennials for continuous fragrance on the patio.

FRAGRANT FLOWERS

Annuals

Amerboa moschata (formerly *Centaurea moschata*) (sweet sultan)
Ersimum cheiri (formerly *Cheiranthus cheiri*) (English wallflower)
Exacum affine (German violet)
Heliotropium arborescens (heliotrope)
Lathyrus odoratus (sweet pea)
Limnanthes douglasii (poached egg plant)
Lobularia maritima (sweet alyssum)
Matthiola incana (stock)
Nicotiana alata (flowering tobacco)
Primula (primrose)
Reseda odorata (mignonette)
Scabiosa atropurpurea (pincushion flower)

Perennials

Alyssum montanum, Zones 4–9
Convallaria majalis (lily-of-the-valley), Zones 3–9
Cosmos atrosanguineus (chocolate cosmos), Zones 7–9
Dianthus (carnations, pinks), zones vary with species
Erysimum helveticum, Zones 5–7
Hosta plantaginea (fragrant plantain lily or August lily), Zones 4–9
Iris graminea (Spuria iris), Zones 4–9
Iris unguicularis (Algerian or winter iris), Zones 8–10
Lavandula species (lavender), zones vary with species and variety
Meehania urtifolia, Zones 5–8
Phlox paniculata 'David' and other hybrids (perennial phlox), Zones 4–8
Viola odorata (sweet violet), Zones 4–8

PERENNIALS WITH AROMATIC FOILAGE

Achillea filipendulina (yarrow), Zones 3–9
Achillea millefolium (yarrow), Zones 3–9
Calamintha grandiflora (calamint), Zones 5–9
Dictamnus albus (gas plant), Zones 3–8
Nepeta x faassenii (catmint), Zones 4–8
Melissa officinalis (lemon balm), Zones 4–7
Mentha species (mint), zones vary with species
Ocimum basilicum (sweet basil), annual
Pelargonium x hortorum (geranium), Zones 9–10
Pelargonium species (scented geranium), Zones 9–10
Rosmarinus officinalis (rosemary), Zones 8–10
Salvia species (sage), zones vary with species
Tanacetum parthenium (feverfew), Zones 4–9
Thymus species (thyme), zones vary with species

Alyssum montanum

Convallaria majalis (lily-of-the-valley)

Thymus x citriodorus (lemon thyme)

surroundings. Build it out of materials that complement the house and patio or deck, and style the raised bed to be a decorative asset. In a formal setting, brick is probably your best option. Other possible building materials include stone, poured concrete, and wood. If the walls of the raised planter are solid, be sure to incorporate drainage holes in the sides near the bottom.

Scalloped-shaped planting beds that loop into the brick path highlight special plantings, such as the peppermint tree, and add an interesting pattern to the walkway. To have the best success growing plants in wells such as these, make sure the soil is of excellent quality.

USE DECORATIVE PLANTING HOLES

Instead of pouring a single concrete slab over an entire patio area, leave an open space with exposed earth as a ground-level planter. Here is an opportunity to plant a shade tree in the middle of the patio. If you don't need shade, consider a narrow, upright shrub to break the horizontal monotony and soften the expanse of hard surface. Be sure to pick a tree or shrub that won't drop leaves or berries and doesn't have roots that will crack and destroy the patio.

Choose Plants Suited to the Soil. Select a tree that is well adapted to your native soil, because its roots will extend far beyond any hole you can amend. Remember to make the open space large enough to accommodate the plant's mature size, and leave enough unpaved ground through which the roots can soak up water.

If you are paving your patio with flagstones or other paving slabs, consider removing a few squares to create planting pockets. Excavate the hole, and backfill it with enriched soil before you plant. Incorporate peat moss or compost into the improved soil to increase the soil's ability to retain water. Because the area around the planting spot will be paved, the plants' roots will have limited access to water, although the surrounding slabs will prevent evaporation and keep the roots cool.

Trees Suitable for Patios

Trees planted next to a patio or in a planter in the middle of the area provide welcome shade. Choose small, tidy specimens with noninvasive roots such as the following:

Acer griseum (paperbark maple), Zones 4–8
Acer palmatum (Japanese maple), Zones 6–8
Albizia julibrissin (mimosa), Zones 6–10
Betula (birch), zones vary with species
Carpinus betulus (European hornbeam),
    Zones 4–7
C. caroliniana (American hornbeam), Zones 2–9
Cercis canadensis (eastern redbud), Zones 5–9
Cercis occidentalis (California or western
    redbud), Zones 6–10
Chinonanthus retusus (Chinese fringe tree),
    Zones 6–10
Chinonanthus virginicus (fringe tree), Zones 5–9
Cornus florida (flowering dogwood), Zones 5–8
Cornus kousa (Kousa dogwood), Zones 5–8
Cornus x rutgersens (Stellar series), Zones 5–8
Crataegus laevigata (English hawthorn),
    Zones 5–8
Jacaranda mimosifolia (jacaranda), Zone 10

Useful Small Plants for Paving

Before you remove patio slabs, arrange the plants in their pots on the patio, and then stand back and analyze the effect. Try creating a checkerboard pattern of open spaces repeated throughout the patio, or choose a random design that leaves more paved space. Once you've settled on the pattern of planting spots, experiment with different planting arrangements. Try mass-planting each open space with one plant, or see how it looks when you place a large plant in the middle of each open quadrant and tiny ones at each corner.

Ajuga reptans (carpet bugleweed), Zones 3–9

Alchemilla alpina (alpine lady's mantle), Zones 3–7

Armeria maritima (thrift, sea pink), Zones 3–8

Brachycome iberidifolia (Swan River daisy), annual

Campanula carpatica (bellflower), Zones 3–10
    in West, 3–7 in East

Dianthus species and cultivars (pinks), zones vary with
    variety

Diascia rigescens, Zones 7–10

Erica species and cultivars (heaths and heathers), zones
    vary with variety

Helianthemum nummularium (sun rose), Zones 6–10

Juniperus (juniper), prostrate and dwarf cultivars, zones
    vary with variety

Lobelia erinus (edging lobelia), annual

Lobularia maritima (sweet alyssum), annual

Mazus reptans, Zones 5–8

Mentha pulegium (pennyroyal), Zones 6–10

Petunia x hybrida (common garden petunia), annual

Phlox subulata (moss pink creeping phlox), Zones 3–9

Portulaca grandiflora (portulaca), annual

Rosmarinus officinalis (rosemary), Zones 8–10

Salvia species (sage), zones vary with species and variety

Sedum (stonecrop), small species and cultivars, zones
    vary with species and variety

Soleirolia soleirolii (baby's tears), Zones 9–10

Stachys byzantina (lamb's ears), Zones 5–8

Thymophylla tenuiloba (formerly *Dyssodia tenuiloba*)
    (Dahlberg daisy), annual

Thymus species (thyme), zones vary with species

Viola tricolor (Johnny-jump-up), Zones 3–10

Stachys byzantina (lamb's ears) front, *Thymus* (creeping thyme) back center

Campanula carpatica (bellflower)

Petunia

WORK AROUND NATURAL FEATURES

If you have a beautiful mature tree growing in the space where you want your deck or patio, don't chop it down. Instead, build around the tree, leaving a gap for the trunk to continue to grow. The result is delightful; you have the sense of being in a treehouse and a chance to discover that tree trunks are surprisingly decorative. In addition, the trees impart an immediate sense of permanence and longevity to the new project. A large outcropping of stone is another natural feature around which you may want to build. Leaving these natural elements in place and working around them helps the patio or deck fit gracefully into its surroundings.

INCORPORATE CHANGES IN LEVEL

There are many practical and aesthetic reasons to design a patio or deck on different levels. On a flat property, establishing variation in levels relieves monotony and creates an interesting rhythm. On a steep slope, a series of platforms connected by steps or ramps can gradually move from one extreme level to another, spanning the slope as well as creating additional usable space.

Changes in level can also preserve a view. If you have a beautiful view from the house across the deck, railings can spoil it. Avoid the need for a railing that would block the view by building steps the width of the upper deck leading to a lower platform. Put the railing around the lower deck where it won't block the view from upstairs. If you don't have room for a two-level deck, step down the main body of your deck. If you incorporate two steps down from the house onto the deck, you'll retain the view from inside.

INCLUDE BUILT-IN SEATING AND STORAGE

You can save space and add to the interest of your deck or patio with built-in seating. Build benches into the railing of your deck (slant the rail outward for a more comfortable back support), or use benches instead of a railing. Add interest to a blank wall that adjoins the patio or deck by running a bench along its length. In addition to creating seating space, you can use the bench to display potted plants. Like raised planters, benches also can break up large expanses of paving and help define activity areas. If possible, arrange the seating so that people can look at each other. If you run benches down adjoining sides, you'll have a corner where people can turn toward each other to converse.

When the deck was built, a hole was left to accommodate the striking West Indian birch tree. The mature tree provides welcome shade, while its twisted form adds a sculptural element.

The stepped-down patio and path are unified by the paving squares and the retaining wall. The larger width of the patio (in the back) marks the space as a destination.

Add a bench and planter into your deck design to break up the horizontal space, as well as to provide more seating.

Many modern homes are short on storage space. Often the garage is barely large enough for the car, much less anything extra. You can alleviate this situation by building benches into your deck or patio that double as storage space. Instead of a bench seat resting on legs, build a weathertight storage box topped with a hinged lid. This chest becomes a great place to keep toys, outdoor sports equipment, chair cushions, or charcoal.

MAKE SOME SHADE

Another design option is to build an arbor or pergola along one side of the patio. In addition to being a striking decorative feature, an arbor or pergola adds interest by dividing up the space. Place it so that the support posts frame a view from the house and under the pergola into the garden. See Chapter 6, pages 145–147 for more information on arbors and pergolas.

In a hot climate, a lath or lattice-covered patio is a boon. The open roof creates a filtered light that, while the sun is shining, is neither too bright nor too dark. As the sun moves across the sky, there is an ever-changing striped pattern of sun and shade. Hang baskets of plants from the support posts and overhead beams to bring splashes of color to eye level, or train vining plants up the posts and across the top. Choose plants that need some light but won't tolerate direct sun to grow under the lath. Filtered light is ideal for fuchsias, begonias, ferns, *Brunsfelsia*, and impatiens. Save the sun lovers for around the edges.

ERECT A TRELLIS SCREEN FOR PRIVACY

As land grows more valuable and building lots get smaller, it is often difficult to find a private spot in your garden. In many cases, the most convenient location for your deck or patio may be in full view of the neighbors. Give yourself privacy with a trellis running the length of the exposed side. The open fretwork design of a trellis is less visually looming than a solid wall or fence. This screening also is effective to protect the space from prevailing wind or to create shade when the sun is low in the sky. A trellis also provides an opportunity for vertical gardening. Train flowering climbers up the trellis, and hang baskets on brackets attached to the support posts.

The easiest way to create a trellis screen is to purchase ready-made lattice panels and attach them to support posts installed in the ground. (See Chapter 6, page 141 for

Create some shade by planting a climbing vine in a tub or container at the base of a pillar. Here the vine softens the angular look of the pillar and scrambles across the top of the patio cover, creating a shady bower.

The trellis screens views of the surrounding houses, making a private patio. The vines growing on the curving trellis spread a little more every year, creating a verdant screen on top of the pretty lath pattern.

directions on installing fence posts.) The pattern in these panels is usually square or diamond. If you are feeling more ambitious or creative, you can make your own trellis pattern using lath or other strips of wood. By experimenting with spacing, angles, frequency of crossovers, and the width and length of your building materials, you can create thousands of different trellis patterns. Only your imagination and the amount of time you are willing to spend creating your masterpiece limit the possibilities.

INCORPORATE A WATER FEATURE

A water feature is an ideal accompaniment to a patio or deck. It is wonderfully soothing to contemplate the changing picture in a reflecting pond or to watch brightly colored fish gliding about. The sound of falling water can be musical. If space is a problem, consider a wall fountain. Some designs are self-contained and need only to be mounted on the wall. Another option is to install a narrow catch basin against the wall and then mount a fountain that drips into it. (See Chapter 7, pages 148–163 for more information on water features.)

Imagine soaking in a warm tub under the stars. If you surround an aboveground hot tub with a deck, it will look as elegant as the in-ground models.

A tiered fountain brings the music of falling water to a patio, and is a decorative, sculptural element in the design.

ADD A BARBECUE OR FIRE PIT

If you enjoy outdoor grilling, you may want to include a built-in barbecue in your design. Brick is probably the most common material. If you want it to blend with a stucco house, you could face a cinder-block barbecue with stucco. Think about plumbing your barbecue for gas.

A fire pit is another fun focal point for a deck or patio. You don't have to be a camper to build happy memories sitting around an open fire outside, toasting marshmallows. As a safety precaution, if you want a fire pit in a wooden deck, you would be wise to choose a gas-fueled one, in which the flames are controllable. Otherwise, you run the risk of setting the deck on fire.

A full-fledged barbecue is just what's needed on hot summer nights when no one wants to be in the kitchen. In the photo above, outdoor lighting and large patio spaces make this garden a magical place to entertain.

ADD LIGHTING

With proper lighting, you can extend the hours you spend on your deck or patio. Be sure to allow for GFCI (ground-fault circuit interrupter) electrical outlets near the deck or patio at the planning stage. Also consider lighting options. Include flood lighting or spotlighting (generally 120 volts) to illuminate the general area, as well as low-voltage accent lights that fit into tight spots such as under deck railings, steps, or benches. These low-voltage lights can be mounted horizontally, vertically, or on top of or under almost any surface where accent lighting is required. They are designed to direct light outward in a controlled pattern to provide brightness without glare.

Low-voltage lighting is safe and easy to install yourself. However, if you select 120-volt lights instead, hire an electrician to help you plan and install them. (See Chapter 3, pages 89–92 for more information on planning and installing outdoor lighting.)

Light fixtures designed to tuck into odd corners on decks and stairs increase safety at night as well as add to the beauty of your nighttime garden.

Choosing Paving or Construction Materials

The materials you choose for paving will depend on your budget and the style of your house and garden. For a deck, use rot-resistant wood such as red cedar, cypress, or redwood; or pressure-treated lumber, which resists decay. Wood is a comfortable surface to walk upon and is less expensive than paving stones. You might even want to surface a paved patio with wood for a comfortable, informal look that is warmer and prettier than concrete. Instead of running the boards in parallel lines, experiment on paper with different patterns for a more interesting surface design. (See page 122 for pattern ideas.)

The choice of materials available for patio paving is constantly expanding. Brick and flagstone are traditional, but you can also use interlocking concrete pavers cut to different patterns, poured concrete, exposed-aggregate concrete, and pebbles and river stones set in concrete. A wide array of tiles and paving slabs with pre-molded patterns such as cobbles, brick, or crazy paving is available.

You can combine different surfaces in a variety of ways. For example, you might border a concrete patio with brick, and create a cobblestone design in the center. If you decide on concrete paving, consider adding pigment. You can add the color to the dry concrete mix, to the wet material before it is poured, or during the floating stage when the concrete is stroked with a trowel to settle the aggregate under the surface and float the cement to the top. A variety of paints, waxes, and stains suitable for concrete is available; you can use these if you decide to make a change once the patio has been poured.

Possible Paving Materials

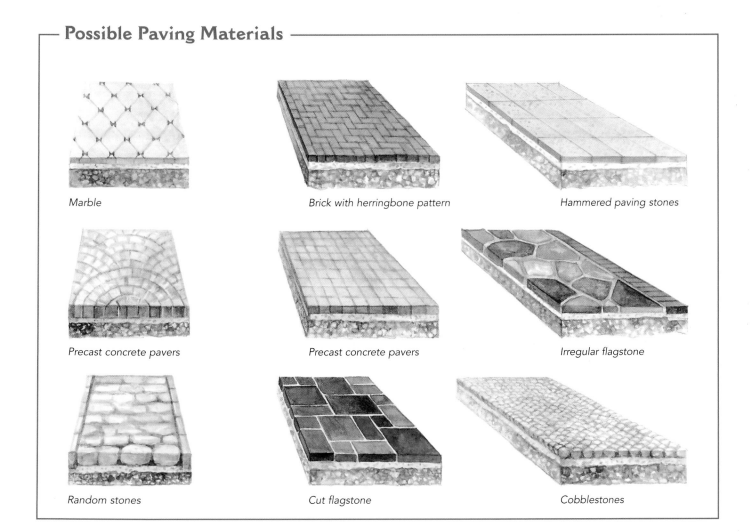

Marble

Brick with herringbone pattern

Hammered paving stones

Precast concrete pavers

Precast concrete pavers

Irregular flagstone

Random stones

Cut flagstone

Cobblestones

HOW TO INSTALL A PATIO

Difficulty Level: *Moderate*

The prices of paving materials will vary from region to region; *importing* stones and pavers can drive up the cost of your patio. Before making a final decision about the paving material you want, research all of the options, and then choose the one that best meets your design needs and budget. In the installation shown below, pre-cast blocks were used. The patio is loose-laid on a base of sand and gravel, thus much of the process is similar to installing a loose-laid brick path described in Chapter 4, pages 102–103.

Tools and Materials: Shovel, wheelbarrow, string, level, metal rake, tamper, rubber mallet, landscape fabric, gravel, stone dust, builder's sand, precast blocks, plastic edging, pegs, soil, plants, mulch.

Step 1: Build a Subbase. *Excavate the space down 6 inches. Lay down landscape fabric, gravel, a thin layer of stone dust, and 1¼-inch of builder's sand. Position the blocks, leaving 1/16- to 1/8-inch space between blocks.*

Step 2: Install the Edging. *Before you place the last row of blocks, lay plastic edging down. Fasten it by hammering pegs through the loops. This edge supports the inner row of blocks next to the planting row.*

Step 3: Level the Blocks. *Use a power tamper to level the blocks and seat them firmly on the subbase. Depending on the size of the job, you may also use a hand tamping tool or a rubber mallet.*

Step 4: Plant the Patio. *The finished patio features two crossed open rows of soil for planting. Position the plants close enough that they will eventually overlap. Note how the design uses different-colored blocks in the inside rows.*

Planning and Building a Deck

Before you begin to build a deck, take the time to draw up your plans and make a complete materials list, allowing 10 to 15 percent extra wood for wastage. Then price out the materials to make sure the project will come in within your budget.

The cost will vary with the type of wood you choose. Least expensive is green or brown pressure-treated lumber. However, treated wood is more likely to split than naturally rot-resistant woods, and it is not as attractive as untreated wood. Cedar and redwood are the two preferred choices for decks because they are strong and durable; both woods weather to a pleasing natural gray. However, while cedar and redwood are decay-resistant, they are vulnerable to rot in areas that remain warm and damp for extended periods. If your deck will be in a shady spot in a hot, humid climate, build with pressure-treated lumber.

The basic components of a deck are posts set into footings or piers, support beams and joists, the deck surface, and railings. You also may want to include stairs leading from a raised deck to another level or to the ground. Even a deck near ground level may benefit from a step or two to ease the transition from the platform to the ground. Lastly, be sure you check all the local building codes and obtain all the appropriate permits before you begin construction.

This expansive deck, with its changes in level and different shaped spaces, is an ideal outdoor recreation room, increasing the home living space dramatically and making the garden as welcoming and comfortable as the house.

Deck Anatomy

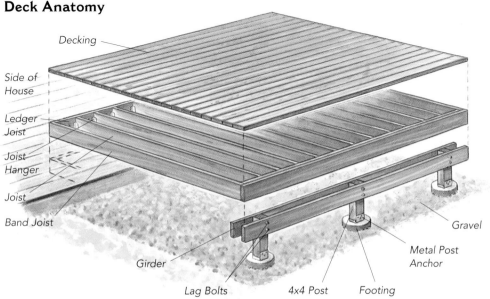

Decking

Side of House

Ledger

Joist

Joist Hanger

Joist

Band Joist

Girder

Lag Bolts

4x4 Post

Footing

Metal Post Anchor

Gravel

Before you start your deck, check local building-code requirements to establish the depth of footings and specifications for the proper concrete mix. Codes also specify that any deck higher than 30 inches off the ground must have railings and stairs. The code will also determine railing height and baluster spacing. Girder size and spans, joist size and spacing, and thickness of decking may vary slightly due to species of wood used and a particular locality's building codes. If you plan to design the deck yourself and do the required drawings, you may need an engineer's seal to certify that your drawings are technically and structurally correct.

Surface Patterns

The obvious and most common way of surfacing a deck is to run the boards either parallel or at right angles to your house. For more visual interest, run the boards on a diagonal, or consider creating a pattern such as herringbone, parquet (or checkerboard), or V-shape. For example, you could use a V-shape to draw the eye to an attractive garden feature or view in the distance. A diamond pattern brings the eye into the center of the space, creating a sense of being drawn together in intimacy.

Although they look complicated, the herringbone and parquet patterns actually are not much extra work because the boards are cut straight. With the herring-bone design, the boards can be run wild (or allowed to overhang the edge on the three sides of the deck not attached to the house) and cut off in a straight line once all of the boards are installed. The mitered (angle cut) herringbone, diamond, and V-shape patterns require more measuring and cutting, and as a result waste more time and lumber than a simpler design. You will need to allow about 30 to 35 percent for wastage.

If your deck has multiple levels or is divided into distinct spaces, you might want to use a different pattern in each area. In addition to the pleasing variety, you'll be sending a visual message that these spaces serve different purposes.

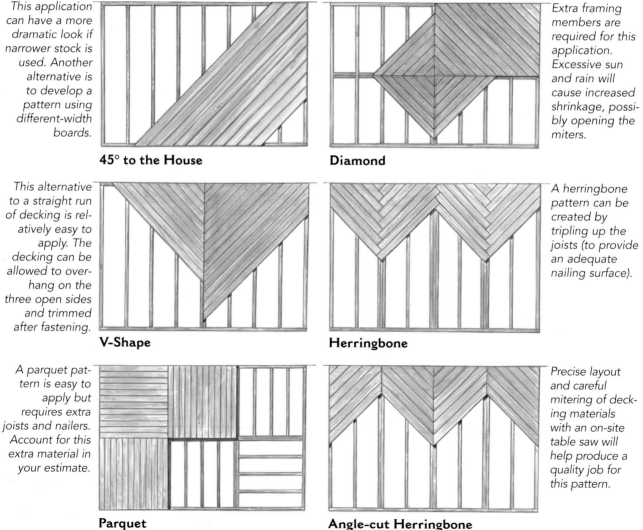

This application can have a more dramatic look if narrower stock is used. Another alternative is to develop a pattern using different-width boards.

45° to the House

Extra framing members are required for this application. Excessive sun and rain will cause increased shrinkage, possibly opening the miters.

Diamond

This alternative to a straight run of decking is relatively easy to apply. The decking can be allowed to overhang on the three open sides and trimmed after fastening.

V-Shape

A herringbone pattern can be created by tripling up the joists (to provide an adequate nailing surface).

Herringbone

A parquet pattern is easy to apply but requires extra joists and nailers. Account for this extra material in your estimate.

Parquet

Precise layout and careful mitering of decking materials with an on-site table saw will help produce a quality job for this pattern.

Angle-cut Herringbone

DECK RAILINGS

Most building codes require railings at least 3 feet high if your deck is more than 30 inches off the ground. To prevent a small child from slipping between the gaps, the spaces between the horizontal rails or vertical balusters must be no more than 4 inches. The requirements vary from community to community, so check with your local authorities before you commit your design to paper.

The railings can be horizontal or vertical. They can be spaced evenly or in an attractive pattern. You may want to insert a design into the railings such as a sailboat motif, a rising sun, or a pinwheel pattern. For a traditional look resembling an old-fashioned porch, insert milled balusters. For more privacy you may want to create a solid enclosure. You could create a diamond, lattice design, or angle vertical slats for an interesting visual effect.

Extend Deck Life. To extend the life of your deck, design it so that the vertical balustrades and posts are exposed to as little water as possible. Any piece of wood with its end grain exposed, such as the end of a post or baluster, is going to soak up water and be especially prone to rot. Avoid the problem by covering the end grains with a top cap. For example, instead of attaching the posts and balustrades to a horizontal top rail with their ends exposed, run the rail on top of the ends as a cap. A second-choice technique would be to cut all the exposed tops at a 45-degree angle so that water will run off. The bottom of each balustrade and post is best left open to the air so the end grain can dry quickly.

USE THE SPACE UNDER A DECK

On many properties the space under a raised deck is wasted. Because it is too dark and dry to grow plants there, the space is often ignored. You might consider leveling off some of that unused space for storing bulky items such as a riding lawn mower, extra pots, or bicycles.

Also consider camouflaging the space with lath, lattice, or trelliswork. The trellis gives an attractive, finished look to the deck; it also affords an opportunity for growing climbing plants. Lattice is a good choice for a screen or "skirt" because it covers the unsightly space but still allows for air circulation underneath. If you choose a solid skirt, leave a gap between each board so that the space can breathe. The skirting should stop an inch or two above the ground to protect it from rot. Another option is to plant evergreen shrubs around the deck.

Railing Styles

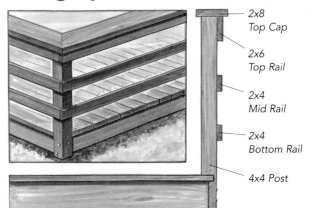

Horizontal Rails. Horizontal rails complement a house built on horizontal lines. They can be used only on low-to-the-ground decks, however.

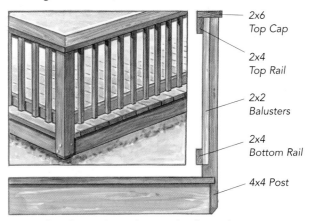

Vertical Rails. Traditional vertical rails can be square, round, or shaped with contours like the decorative spindles on an indoor staircase.

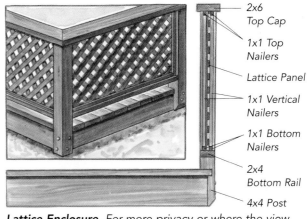

Lattice Enclosure. For more privacy or where the view below is not attractive, select a lattice design that allows air to circulate but also provides screening.

How to Build a Deck

Below are some of the main steps involved in building a deck, but space limitations prevented giving complete installation instructions. As with all of the other building projects described in this book, please consult with your town for the local building codes. Begin by measuring out the deck and ensuring it is straight with a chalk line and diagonal measurements. You will not need a continuous foundation under your deck as you would for indoor living space; a few well-anchored posts will do. Make sure the footings rest below the frost line. (The frost line

Step 1: Make the Post Supports. *Dig the posthole below the frost line. Insert the concrete tube form, and fill it with concrete. Insert the post anchoring hardware, and anchor in the post when the concrete has cured.*

Step 2: Install the Girder. *Support the girder with a post. Clamp a temporary block in place next to the post. The clamp and block hold the heavy girder until it is fully attached.*

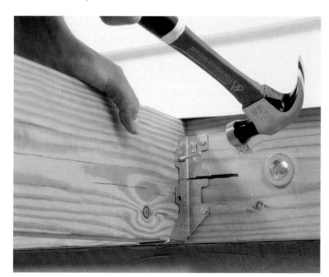

Step 3: Lay the Joists. *Attach the ledger to the house with lag screws. Set the joists with one end resting on the girder, the other in a joist hanger attached to the ledger. Continue until all the joists are in place.*

Step 4: Install the Decking. *Nail the decking across the joists, inserting a 12d nail between the boards as a spacer. Leave at least ⅛ inch between boards for drainage. The chisel is used to straighten out slightly curved boards.*

Difficulty Level: *Challenging*

varies depending on where you live; your local building department can give you the local frost-line depth.)

Tools and Materials: Lumber, joist hangers, post anchor hardware, L-brackets, galvanized fasteners, post-hole digger, level, hammer, combination square, measuring tape, chisel, circular saw, pencil, socket wrench, framing square, drill, clamps, ratchets, concrete tube form, concrete, water, chalk-line box, wheelbarrow, plumb bob. Optional: power hole digger.

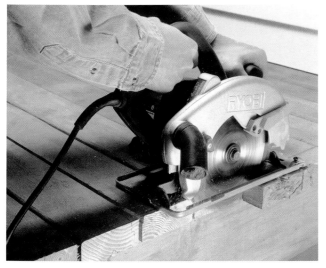

Step 5: Trim the Decking Edge. *When all the decking pieces have been installed and fastened, snap a chalk line to get a straight edge. Use a circular saw to trim off the ends of the 2x4s where they extend over the joists.*

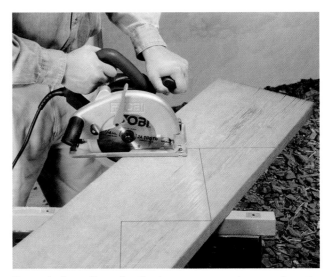

Step 6: Lay Out the Stringers. *A 7-inch rise with a 10-inch run is a good starting point for a comfortable stair. Make the plumb cut (where the stringer connects to the deck) and the horizontal cut (where the stringer rests on the landing).*

Step 7: Attach the Treads. *Align the tread with the pencil lines on the stringers, and then use L-brackets to connect them together. Screws (in predrilled holes) are less likely to cause splitting than nails.*

Step 8: Finishing Touches. *Use a router to put a finished rounded edge on the railing top cap. There are many railing styles from which to choose; the balusters shown here are vertical 2x2s.*

Landscaping Swimming Pools

For many homeowners, the ultimate landscape luxury is to have a swimming pool. In addition to being a recreational delight, your pool can be an asset to your overall landscape design, complementing the other features in your garden or the surrounding property.

A successful example of blending the swimming pool into the site is the Mushinsky property in Potomac, Maryland. The space for the swimming pool is the one sunny spot in a shady garden surrounded by forest. Allen Mushinksy, who is an architect, designed his pool to resemble a woodland pond. As an alternative to the standard rectangle or free-form shape, this pool has a unique, relaxed form that enhances the illusion that it is a natural pond. Instead of installing tropical blue tile to tint the water turquoise, Mushinsky painted the bottom black, giving it a sophisticated, mysterious look. And rather than use standard coping, he rimmed the pool with natural stone and added small planting beds right up against the pool to soften the expanse of surrounding paving. The strikingly beautiful pool is in complete harmony with its setting.

CHOOSING POOL DECKING

The paving around a pool is equally important as a design element and for safety. The minimum width for decking around a pool is 3 feet; if you want room to sunbathe or have space for a table and chairs, you'll need to make it wider. Look for a balance between enough paving for adequate living space and not so much that it becomes a vast wasteland.

The most common poolside decking is concrete because it is both economical and versatile. But if you would prefer a rough-textured finish, leave the aggregate exposed. In addition to being an attractive texture, an exposed-aggregate surface is less slippery than smooth concrete. Because people spend a lot of time barefoot near the pool, you'll want a fine, even-textured aggregate such as pea gravel that doesn't have a lot of sharp edges. For a unique look, landscape architect Pamela Burton incorporated flecks of black silica carbide into the concrete decking of the Malibu pool she designed. The sun reflects off these flecks, causing them to sparkle like diamonds.

Another option is to tint the concrete. Choose a color that will blend with other elements in your landscape as

This free-form swimming pool resembles a woodland pond in a clearing. With its black bottom and irregular shape, the Mushinsky pool is in complete harmony with its surroundings. The planting beds soften the decking.

The modernistic arbor adds a vertical element to the expanse of horizontal pool decking, and fits in perfectly with the contemporary home. Tropical plantings on the edge of the property add a lush effect.

well as give the deck surface a warmer feel. Tinted concrete also creates less glare—an important consideration where the summer sun is intense. Concrete can become burning hot when it is exposed to hours of direct sun. A more-expensive option is to have a special cooling surface troweled onto the concrete when your pool decking is installed.

Other possibilities for pool decking include wood, paving tiles, blocks, brick, flagstones, and granite. Your choice should be guided by budget, as well as how the material will blend with your overall landscape design. Brick and flagstone laid in symmetrical patterns tend to look formal, while flagstone laid in a crazy-quilt pattern and wood decking are more casual.

FENCING FOR POOLS

Most communities have regulations about fencing swimming pools to protect small children. Your pool contractor will know the local rules and can advise you on specific details. For information on building fences, see Chapter 6, page 141.

PLANTINGS AROUND POOLS

Plantings around a pool relieve the starkness of paving and add much-needed height to a predominantly horizontal landscape feature. Bear in mind, however, that swimming pools can create specific challenges for plants:

❧ *Poolside plants should be tidy.* Avoid plants that will drop leaves, petals, or fruit, as well as plants with tiny leaves that can clog the filter. Choose trees that don't have invasive or extensive roots, which can cause the decking to heave.

❧ *Choose chemical-tolerant plants.* It's attractive to have planting beds right next to the pool, with foliage drooping over the edge. However, these plants are likely to have chlorinated water splashed onto them. A good solution is to choose plants that are less sensitive to pool chemicals. Some of the many plants suitable to grow near swimming pools are ornamental grasses, treasure flower, daylilies, junipers, and Atlas cedars.

❧ *Use plants to hide unattractive maintenance equipment.* Tall ornamental grasses, such as *Miscanthsis sinensis*, make excellent screens, as do evergreen shrubs.

Poolside plants *should be tolerant of pool chemicals. Some of the plants used here include l. to r.:* Bougainvillea, Echium fastuosum *(viper's bugloss),* Jacaranda mimisofolia *and beech trees, and* Helichrysum.

❧ *Use low-maintenance plants.* When designing your poolside plantings, keep the beds as low-maintenance as possible so you can spend your time swimming rather than tending plants that require high care levels. Avoid plants such as roses, that often require a program of regular spraying to look their best; you wouldn't want those chemicals in the pool water.

❧ *Try potted plants instead of beds.* Invest in several tubs or urns that are large enough to hold a small tree or shrub. Fill several pots with a variety of flowering annuals to create colorful bouquets; then cluster them together to add weight and importance.

❧ *Exercise caution with fragrant plants.* Plants with fragrant foliage or flowers bring an added sensuous dimension to a poolside, but use caution with plants that attract bees. While bees are harmless to most people if left alone, some people are allergic to bee stings and others are just spooked by bees. You're better off avoiding the situation altogether.

❧ *Include drainage in the pool decking.* Whether you decide to include beds right up to the pool or place them around the periphery, make sure the decking has a good drainage system that will direct water away from the house and the beds.

CHAPTER 6

Walls, Fences, and Other Structures

Most gardens benefit from vertical elements such as walls, fences, arches, arbors, pergolas, and decorative freestanding plant supports. Walls and fences help define boundaries as well as enclose special spaces. Properly positioned, an arbor or arch is an eye-catching accent, adding visual drama to the scene and providing an attractive focal point or point of passage between two parts of the garden. A pergola transforms an ordinary path into a special, shaded, and sheltered passageway, while a freestanding plant support is like an exclamation point, drawing attention to itself and creating a pleasant focus.

As an added bonus, any one of these features provides an opportunity to grow and enjoy the wide range of climbing plants such clematis, wisteria, climbing roses, honeysuckle, trumpet vine, and jasmine. These vertical plants add a sense of lushness to the garden as they scramble up walls and over trellised arches or droop heavy panicles of flowers through the open fretwork ceiling of a pergola.

▶ ***The circular opening** of the outer gate and the matching curves of the inner gate combine to create a western version of a Japanese moon window. The resulting view through one "moon" to the other offers a fresh perspective on the garden and invites entry.*

Walls

Walls impart a sense of permanence to a garden. They also provide structure, define boundaries, give privacy, and create pleasing microclimates. If designed to hold back earth, as when a slope is carved into level terraces, they are called retaining walls. A wall facing south will absorb and then radiate heat, jump-starting nearby plants' growth in spring and extending the growing season well into autumn. Walls also deflect the wind, adding protection as well as warmth. Walls

***The stone wall** is softened by rosemary trailing over the top and across the bumpy face. The bright green baby's tears (Soleirolia) thrives in the narrow planting space at the base. The plants reaching toward each other give this very solid-looking wall an organic feel.*

Building a freestanding wall up to 3 feet tall is an appropriate do-it-yourself project. If you need a taller structure, it is best to turn to a professional. In addition to being a beautiful architectural feature, a wall must be designed for stability, and a freestanding wall must be able to remain upright in high winds. It takes experience and training to successfully construct a tall, strong wall.

MAINTAIN STRUCTURAL INTEGRITY

Issues to bear in mind for structural soundness include the ratio of wall thickness to height. Walls over 3 feet need to be reinforced with internal rods or support pilasters and are best left to professionals. The foundation must be substantial to keep the wall from shifting due to settling and frost heaving. The necessary width and depth of the foundation will depend on the stability of the soil, the frost line (with the foundation extending below the lowest depth to which the soil freezes), and the width of the wall. In stiff clay the foundation should be a minimum of 2 feet deep; in sand it should extend at least 3 feet into the soil. Generally the foundation should be twice as wide as the thickness of the wall.

make a wonderful backdrop to perennial borders; they have an advantage over hedges because plants don't have to compete for root space and nutrients as they do near a hedge. On the negative side, walls built on the south end of a garden may block the light, and on a windy site they can create strange wind patterns. Despite these potential drawbacks, a wall is a valuable garden feature.

*A **rustic split-rail fence** is easy to build and looks at home in a rural or casual setting. Here the bright flowers contrast beautifully with the weathered gray wood, adding a festive note. The informal garden and the rustic fence are a perfect country pair.*

Allow cooling breezes to flow into your garden by building a brick wall with a fretwork design. The effect is pretty and lacy, as well as practical. In hot, humid climates, good air circulation is important.

Decorative Features Add Stability. Many of the decorative features in the design of a wall, such as a varied brick pattern (called the bond), an attractive cap or coping, and regularly spaced thicker wall sections called pilasters or piles are, in fact, incorporated to improve the structural integrity of the wall. The cap keeps water out of the wall, preventing the problem of expansion and contraction caused by freezing and thawing water caught in the seams. Aware of the importance of a coping or cap, Thomas Jefferson had the message, "If you keep my hat on I will last forever," carved on a stone wall he built in southern Virginia.

Open Walls Look Lighter. Not all walls are solid. Screen walls, made either by alternating bricks with open spaces or by using screen blocks, have an open, fretwork design that is visually less domineering than a solid wall. They are popular in hot southern climates because they allow cooling breezes to flow into the garden. Open screen designs are usually set into a solid wall as a decorative element. They usually run between pilasters and begin several feet up from the ground atop a solid base of wall.

Whether you choose to build a wall yourself or hire an expert, be sure to check with your community's building inspector. You need to be in compliance with local ordinances regarding issues such as the height of the wall, type and depth of the foundation, and any internal reinforcing rods that may be required.

This low brick retaining wall doubles as an attractive raised planter. In addition to solving the problem of poor soil, a raised planter is easy to tend because you can sit on the edge of the wall, rather than having to work on your knees.

BRICK WALLS

Brick is a classic, though expensive, material for garden walls. The warm red earth tones of natural brick blend beautifully with architectural structures as well as with plants and surrounding soil. Brick adapts easily to many settings, and the standard-size blocks lend themselves to many design patterns and compositions. You can be as creative in designing a brick wall as you can working with children's Lego blocks.

If you decide to build a brick wall, first study photographs to see the wide scope of possibilities for wall detailing and design. This wall will be a major investment, and you want to make sure you are completely satisfied with the final product.

There are three grades of brick suitable for outdoor walls. The cheapest bricks, which are made for general-purpose building, are called commons. Because they have no finish, they are subject to weathering. The next grade is called facing brick because there is a weather-resistant finish on the sides, or faces. This provides some resistance to weathering if the brick is laid with the finished facing exposed. The top grade of brick is called engineering brick. These bricks are the hardest and most impervious to weathering. Within these categories you can find bricks of different sizes and colors.

BRICK-WALL CONSTRUCTION

In addition to selecting brick, you must decide on the arrangement of bricks in the wall, called the bond. The four standard choices are running bond, stack bond, Flemish bond, and English bond. The bond patterns in which perpendicular mortar joints are bridged by courses above and below are generally stronger. Hence the weakest bond is the stack bond, although it should be fine to use for a low wall no more than 3 feet tall. Flemish and English bond, which have periodic headers that bind the double row of bricks, or wythes, are the strongest of the group.

Running Bond

Stack Bond

Flemish Bond

English Bond

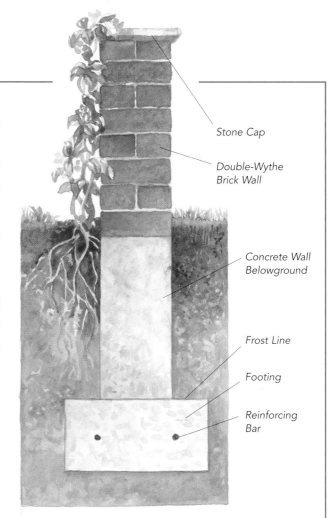

Stone Cap

Double-Wythe Brick Wall

Concrete Wall Belowground

Frost Line

Footing

Reinforcing Bar

To be stable, a masonry wall must be supported by footings that reach below the frost line. The brick wall you see is like the tip of an iceberg. The footing should be twice the width of the wall and nearly as tall.

Brick-Wall Terminology

Bat: A brick cut in half lengthwise.

Bed Joint: A horizontal masonry joint.

Bond: The arrangement of bricks in a wall that creates a pattern.

Collar Joint: The vertical joint between wythes.

Course: A horizontal row of bricks.

Footing: A concrete foundation to support walls.

Headers: Bricks turned horizontally to the stretcher courses.

Head Joint: A vertical masonry joint.

Jointing: The finish given to the mortar that exudes from each course of bricks.

Pointing: Repairing the joints of a wall.

Reinforcing Bar: A steel rod used to reinforce concrete, both horizontally and vertically.

Sailor: An upright brick with the broad face positioned out.

Soap: A brick halved in width.

Soldier: An upright brick with the narrow edge positioned out.

Split: A brick halved in height.

Stretchers: Bricks laid horizontally in the direction of the wall.

Wythe: A vertical tier of bricks in a wall.

How to Build a Concrete-Block-and-Stucco Wall

Difficulty Level: Moderate

Concrete-block walls are less expensive than brick, but equally solid. You can dress up block walls with a coat of stucco. Made with cement, lime, sand, and water, stucco is the same material you use indoors for plastering. You can use it in its natural color or add tints for a permanent pigment. In addition to improving the appearance of the wall, the finish blends nicely with the walls of stucco houses, thus marrying the architecture of the house and garden to promote a sense of unity and harmony. Estimate the number of blocks you will need by multiplying the number of units in the wall length by the number of courses in the wall height. Estimate 6 cubic feet of mortar for every 100 square feet of wall surface. For more information on stucco, see the sidebar at far right.

Tools and Materials: Concrete blocks, corner blocks, mortar, water, mixing hoe, wheelbarrow or mixing pan, wire reinforcement, reinforcing bar, string line, plumb bob, batter boards, brick hammer, brickset, trowel, level.

Step 1: Dig Trenches for the Footing. *Stretch a string between stakes to keep the trenches straight. Then lay rebar down the center of the straight-sided trenches. Raise the rebar off the ground with blocks, so it is in the middle of the poured concrete. Allow the concrete to cure.*

Step 3: Build the Wall. *Apply mortar to the surfaces where the blocks touch each other. Remember, the joints should be about ⅜ inch thick. Continue mortaring each course, running rebar horizontally between levels as well as vertically through some of the blocks for added stability.*

Step 4: Spread the First Layer of Stucco. *Apply a thin (⅜-inch) scratch coat of stucco with a trowel. To make the wall stronger, alternate the blocks in each course so that a joint doesn't run from top to bottom. Top the wall with bricks placed lengthwise; mortar the bricks in position.*

Step 2: Lay the First Row. *Mix the mortar and apply it to the blocks with a trowel. Erect the corners several rows high. Maintain ⅜-inch-thick mortar joints. Set the first row of blocks between the corners in a mortar bed. Use a guideline stretched between the corners, and level each block.*

Step 5: Apply the Stucco. *Just before the scratch coat of stucco has hardened, scratch the surface with a piece of ⅛-inch mesh or a stiff wire brush. Then apply the top coat of stucco in a ¼-inch layer using a trowel, smoothing it carefully so it is blemish-free.*

How to Stucco a Concrete-Block Wall

To add a stucco coating to concrete block or to an existing concrete block wall, first prepare the wall by painting on a concrete bonder. This material acts like glue, firmly bonding the stucco to the wall surface. Plan to apply at least two coats of stucco to the surface. The first, called a scratch coat, should be about ⅜ inch thick. Spread the scratch coat with a 12- or 14-inch-wide cement finisher's steel trowel. Begin at the bottom of the wall, and trowel on the stucco, spreading it upward with a smooth, curving action. Apply the second swath, slightly overlapping the first. Press the trowel firmly against the wall as you apply the stucco, so it creates a firm bond. When you've applied several swaths, go back and smooth the surface to make a uniform thickness.

Let the First Coat Dry. The second coat can be applied as soon as the first has set enough to support the additional weight. Depending on the weather, the first coat will be dry from 4 hours to 3 days after it is applied. Keep the scratch coat moist as it cures by gently spraying it with a hose as needed over 48 hours. After that, the stucco will have cured, and you can allow it to dry out.

Apply the Top Coat. Prepare the scratch coat surface by scoring it with hardware cloth, a stiff wire brush, or a piece of metal lath. Whichever tool you use, simply draw it across the surface to roughen it. This job should be done before the scratch coat hardens. Just before you apply the top coat of stucco, moisten the surface. To apply the top coat, use the same technique as you did for the scratch coat, but make the layer slightly thinner, about ¼ inch thick. Smooth the layer carefully so that there are no scratches or other surface defects.

The stucco must be kept moist for at least 48 hours to cure properly. Either spray the surface with water to keep it wet, or drape plastic over the stucco to keep in the moisture.

The flat-topped gray stone wall makes a beautiful backdrop for the colorful annuals planted against it. The narrow planting bed, about the same depth as the wall is high, is in pleasing proportion to the wall.

STONE WALLS

Stone walls are beautiful landscape features, especially if they are made from local stone that looks at home in its surroundings.

There are two types of stone used for building walls. *Rubble stone*, including fieldstone, is irregular in size and shape. *Ashlar* is stone that has been cut at the quarry to produce smooth, flat surfaces that stack easily.

The dry-laid stone walls that crisscross the New England countryside are made from local fieldstone that was picked out of the fields and put to good use. Walls made from quarried and cut ashlar stones are more formal looking and generally easier to build because the flat surfaces of the stones fit together easily. (See pages 135–37 for information on stone wall installation.)

Whether you buy rubble or ashlar stone, it will be sold by the cubic yard at quarries and stone suppliers. Because of the extreme weight, don't plan on bringing the stone home in your car; ask your supplier to deliver it.

Determine the Amount of Stone. To work out how much stone you need for a dry-laid or mortared wall, multiply the length times the height times the width of your wall in feet to determine the cubic feet. To translate the resulting number into cubic yards, divide by 27. Add about 10 percent to your order if you are working with ashlar stone to allow for breakage and waste. If you are planning a rubble wall, add at least 25 percent.

Retaining Walls

MASONRY RETAINING WALLS

Retaining walls have a double purpose. In addition to being ornamental, they hold back soil to convert a slope into level areas or terraces. For an introduction to using retaining walls in the landscape, see Chapter 3, pages 78–79 for information on "Terracing."

Brick and Concrete Retaining Walls. Retaining walls of brick, concrete block, or poured concrete are usually reinforced with steel rebar. Well-made mortared masonry walls tend to be the strongest of all the types of retaining walls. Opt for these materials if your wall will be taller than 4 feet or if you are retaining an especially steep slope with unstable soil. Before you begin building, check with local authorities. Many communities require that you hire a professional engineer to design any retaining wall more than 4 feet tall.

Brick Retaining Wall Anatomy

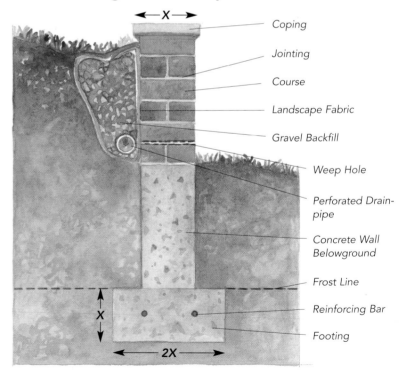

Retaining walls must be very strong to hold back the tons of soil pushing against them. Waterlogged soil is even heavier and more unstable, so be sure to provide drainage behind the wall to remove excess water.

To create a series of level terraces on a slope, use the soil from the base of the retaining wall as the backfill behind the wall, as seen in the top illustration. If you prefer one large, level space, cut the slope where you want the wall, and then use the excess soil to level the slope farther downhill, as shown in the bottom illustration.

Retaining walls constructed of brick or block must stand on a concrete footing to make them stable. Because retaining walls must be able to support the added weight of tons of soil, they must be even more stable than freestanding garden walls. As with garden walls, the footing of retaining walls should extend below the frost line where freezing is an issue. Footings should be the same thickness as the wall and twice as wide as they are thick. For example, a brick wall 8 inches wide should be built on a footing that is 8 inches thick and 16 inches wide. (See drawing above.) In cases where the frost line runs from several inches to several feet below ground level, you can save on expensive wall materials by building a belowground wall of concrete on top of the footing, and then building the retaining wall on top of the concrete wall at ground level.

Build in Drainage. To ensure proper drainage (important for the stability of the wall, as well as for plant health), lay a perforated drainpipe behind the wall at the original ground level. If the drainpipe holes are on only one side of the pipe, be sure they face downward. Make sure the pipe slopes at least ¼-inch per foot to ensure that it moves the water away from the wall instead of just collecting behind it. Surround the pipe with gravel

to keep soil out of the pipe, and then backfill. Another option is to insert drainpipes through the lower part of the retaining wall every 32 inches so water can flow out the front of the wall.

MORTARED STONE RETAINING WALLS

A mortared stone wall is no more durable than a dry-laid wall. (If it is properly built, a dry stone wall will endure for centuries.) However, mortared stone walls have a more formal look suitable for tailored gardens. A mortared wall also is preferable in situations where people are likely to disturb stones, perhaps by sitting or walking on the wall. A mortared stone wall can also be built with irregularly shaped stones, rather than those that fit snugly, because they'll be bonded together with mortar.

Footings are Required. Like brick walls, a mortared stone wall must stand on a footing with a depth equal to the thickness of the wall and a width twice the wall's thickness. Check with your local authorities on recommendations and regulations regarding the underground depth of the footing to accommodate frost lines.

Begin with the largest stones on the bottom course. The squarest stones are most suitable for the ends and corners of the wall, and the flattest stones are best on

This formal stone retaining wall is an attractive boundary for the patio. The wall blends beautifully with the flagstone paving, while the lush plantings of hosta, sweet woodruff, and other shade-loving plants soften the extensive stonework.

Dry-Laid Stone Retaining Wall Anatomy

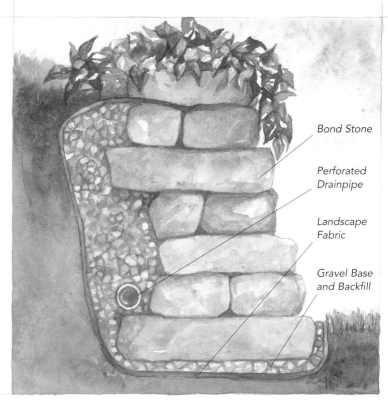

Bond Stone

Perforated Drainpipe

Landscape Fabric

Gravel Base and Backfill

A dry-laid stone retaining wall should lean slightly into the slope to give it stability. Use a large bond stone every few rows to help anchor the structure. The gravel backfill and perforated pipe help drain water away from the wall.

top. If your wall will be built with different-sized stones running in parallel rows, be sure to use bond stones that extend through the full thickness of the wall every few feet. Stagger the placement of the bond stones in each course so that they are never directly above one another.

DRY-LAID STONE RETAINING WALLS

Dry-laid stone walls are not mortared together. They look beautiful as retaining walls on a short slope or running across a hill to create terraces. However, since they are not strengthened by mortar, dry-laid stone retaining walls should not be more than about 3 feet tall. A 3-foot-tall dry-laid stone wall should be at least 2 feet thick at its base. While it does not require a concrete footing, a level layer of gravel underneath will improve drainage and reduce frost heaving. Dig an 8-inch trench, and fill it with 4 inches of gravel; then lay the stones on top of the gravel. If possible, choose indigenous stone. The resulting wall will be in better harmony with its surroundings.

Building a dry-laid stone wall is similar to solving a jigsaw puzzle because you need to choose stones that fit together nicely. The bottom row of the wall should have the largest stones. The wall should consist of two vertical stacks, or wythes, with large bond stones that extend into the side of the slope placed every several feet. (These serve the same purpose as the deadmen discussed in "Wood Retaining Walls," Chapter 3, page 78.) For extra wall stability, lay the stones so that they tip slightly into the slope at a rate of about 2 inches for every foot of wall height. If a sloping front bothers you, tilt the inside layer of the wall and build the outer layer so it stands vertically. In this instance, however, the footing must extend beyond the wall into the slope. As you build, backfill any space between the wall and the slope with gravel. As you work, add soil to pockets between the stones. If you want plants growing out of the wall, add them as you build. (See page 138.) Top the wall with a row of flat capstones to cover the entire thickness of the wall. Some stonemasons like to set the capstones in mortar to prevent moisture from seeping into the wall and to keep the stones from being knocked off.

HOW TO BUILD A DRY-LAID STONE RETAINING WALL

Difficulty Level: Challenging

Retaining walls must stand on a firm footing. Excavate a trench down about six inches and tamp the dirt leaving an undisturbed base on which to build the wall. Line the trench with landscape fabric. Put a few inches of gravel on top of the fabric, rake it level, and then lay the first course of stones on top of the gravel. To determine how much stone you will need, see page 134. For taller walls, or those holding back soil on a steep slope, you will need to add a drainage pipe as shown on the previous page. Wear goggles or protective eyewear.

Tools and Materials: Landscape fabric, gravel, stones, pick, shovel, rake, wheelbarrow, string, stakes, line level, brick hammer, cold chisel, safety glasses.

Step 1: Lay the First Course. *Dig the trench the width of the stone wall and about 6 inches deep. Lay the first course (or level of stones), choosing the largest stones for the outer edges. Fill in the middle area with the smaller stones.*

Step 2: Cut Stones to Fit. *Shape stones by chipping off the edges with your brick hammer. To split larger stones, set them flat on the ground, score a line with a cold chisel and hammer, and then place the chisel in the center of the scored line and strike it firmly with the hammer.*

Step 3: Fill the Gaps between Stones. *Chink large gaps in the wall with stone chips by hammering an appropriately sized chip into the space. When you reach the top layer of the wall, the stone chips also are useful to raise a stone slab to make it level with the string guide.*

Step 4: Complete the Top Course. *For structural stability, choose and place stones so that the vertical joints alternate between courses, rather than running in a straight line. While you want to keep the middle courses fairly level, the top course, where the string is set, is most important.*

How to Do a Stone-Wall Planting

Difficulty Level: *Easy*

A planted dry-laid stone wall is a beautiful garden feature. Although many homeowners plant the wall while it is being built, you can plant in crevices on the sides of the wall and in joints on the top of a finished wall.

Tools and Materials: Potting mix (free-draining and water-retentive soil such as 1 part topsoil, 1 part peat moss or well-rotted leaf mold, and 1 part grit or stone chippings), rooted cuttings or young plants in very small pots, trowel, spray bottle for misting

Step 1: Fill the Joints with Potting Mix. *Use a small trowel to work the potting mix into the joints between the stones. Pack in as much soil as you can, as this soil will be all the plant has to grow in.*

Step 2: Choose Shallow-Rooted Plants. *Heat- and drought-tolerant plants such as alyssum, creeping thyme, and Dianthus do best in wall conditions. Plants with spreading or cascading habits are particularly appealing.*

Step 3: Insert the Plant in the Crevice. *Position the plant so that the root ball makes good contact with the soil. Small, young plants will settle in best. Add stone chips to keep the potting mix from spilling out of the crevice.*

Step 4: Water the Newly-Planted Garden. *Use a spray mist bottle for this delicate job. Don't use a garden hose, or you'll risk washing out all the soil. As the plant's roots spread, they will anchor the soil.*

Fences

Erecting a fence is the quickest and generally easiest way to define the boundary of your property. To be a successful part of a landscape design, a fence should be planned to complement the architecture of your house, possibly even echoing a distinctive design feature. Also bear in mind the character of your neighborhood and region. Your fence may be beautiful in and of itself but look out of place in the neighborhood where you live. In addition to style, other considerations for making a fence harmonious with its surroundings include height, color, and material.

The fresh, white picket fence sets off this cottage garden profusion of orange and yellow lilies and daylilies, with red bee balm in the background, making a memorable garden vignette.

MANY DESIGN OPTIONS EXIST

With that in mind, the possibilities for fence designs are limitless. Traditional options include wrought iron, wooden pickets (or palings), stockade, split-rail, double- and triple-bar ranch fences, and even chain-link fences. Within those basic styles are an infinity of variations. For example, iron can be wrought in fanciful designs from modern clean-cut to the fancy curlicues of the Romanesque style. Picket points can take the form of arrows, fleurs-de-lis, or any other design. The pickets can be spaced in a variety of ways. Stockade fences can be closed- or open-board, or have angled paling boards. To add extra charm and interest, a solid wooden fence can be topped with a row of lattice. Chain link can be left bare or filled in with lath slats woven throughout the links.

A fence that complements the style of the house ties the landscape design together. Here the picket fence, which is painted to coordinate with the color of the stone house, looks absolutely right.

Function Dictates Style. The primary purpose of the fence will influence your design. For privacy you'll want a tall, solid fence. If the goal is to keep the dog contained, the fence can have open slats, but you'll have to think about whether the dog is likely to jump over a low fence or burrow underneath. Rabbits, woodchucks, and mice may also burrow under fences. To keep rabbits and woodchucks out, you'll need a wire mesh no larger than 1½ inches buried at least 6 inches under the soil. To exclude mice the mesh should be a fine ¼ inch, and the barrier should extend 1 foot below the soil. Deer can jump 8 feet straight into the air. To keep them out you

need a very tall fence or a fence combined with other deterrents. If the fence is to act as a windbreak or create a shady spot, you'll want a more solid design.

In addition to fencing the boundary of your property, you may want a fence to define a smaller space within your garden. In small gardens where there isn't room to plant a hedge behind a flower border, a fence creates an excellent backdrop for the flowers. You may be able to optimize your space by planting a border along both sides of the fence.

Include a Beginning and End. A fence should have a logical starting and ending point. A common mistake is to erect a fence to block an unwanted view without connecting it to any other feature in the garden. This approach tends to look jarring. Far better is to connect the fence at both ends to an architectural feature or to have the fence run full circle and connect to itself.

Like a chain, a fence is only as strong as its weakest component. If you are building a fence, be sure to choose strong posts and sink them properly into the ground. Erect fence posts the same way you would install posts to support a wooden retaining wall, as described on Chapter 3 page 78. If you're building a wooden fence, you will save money if you design the fence so you can use standard lengths of lumber. Otherwise you'll waste too much time measuring and cutting, and you'll end up with a lot of wasted wood.

Before you begin a do-it-yourself fencing project, check with local authorities for relevant codes and ordinances. Height and placement regulations (especially required setbacks from property lines) vary from community to community, and some residential neighborhoods have their own covenants.

Fence Anatomy

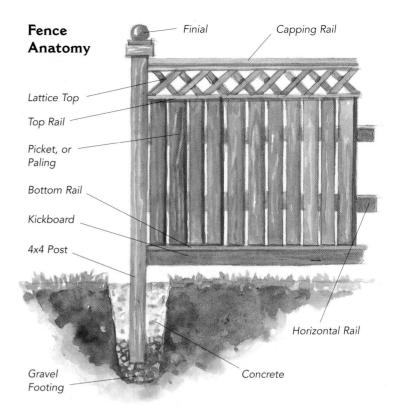

The main components of a board fence are pickets, horizontal rails, a top rail to protect the end grain of the pickets from moisture, the kickboard, and the support post.

Options for Fences on Slopes

A slope presents a special challenge for fence design as fence sections are generally straight and parallel to the ground. Three possible solutions include stepping the fence down the slope, allowing gaps to occur as the slope progresses downward; building the fence to follow the hillside so that the top of the fence is angled at the same degree as the slope; and custom-building the fence so each paling touches the ground, creating a wavey line across the fence top and bottom.

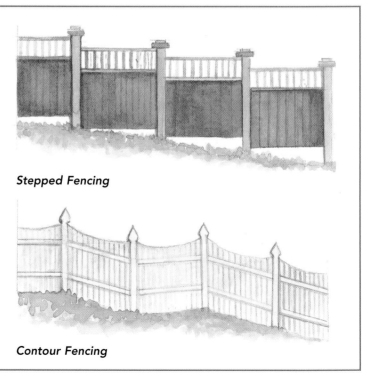

Stepped Fencing

Sloped Fencing

Contour Fencing

HOW TO INSTALL A FENCE

Difficulty Level: Moderate

The redwood picket fence illustrated below is based on photographs from 1881 and a few existing old pickets. This low fence marks the property line and contains children or pets without obstructing the view of the lovely Victorian house. To calculate the amount of materials, determine what it will take to build one fence bay (usually 8 feet from post to post). Then multiply that figure by the number of bays needed to complete the fence.

Tools and Materials: Stakes and string, posthole digger, 4x4 or 6x6 posts, level, concrete, lumber for top and bottom rails (lumber here is saw-textured, clear heart redwood, Douglas fir rails), aluminum-alloy or stainless-steel or double-hot-dipped-galvanized fasteners: 16d common nails for the frame, 8d or 10d box nails for the fence boards, 6d or 8d finish nails for the fine trim.

Step 1: Install the Posts. *Mark the course of the fence using stakes and string, and then mark the location for each post (usually 6 to 8 feet apart). Dig postholes three times the width of the posts and 1 foot below the frost line. Set the posts, check that they are plumb, and pour the concrete.*

Step 2: Build the Frame. *Measure and cut the top and bottom rails. Fasten the top rail in place, then the bottom rail. Top rails are butt-joined over the posts and mitered at the corners. Bottom rails can be toenailed, fastened using a block or metal brace, or inset into the post by cutting a dado or notch.*

Step 3: Nail in the Pickets. *Tack a string across several bays to mark the bottom fence line. Starting at the end, begin nailing up the fence palings. Every few feet, check the level of the vertical edge of the last board you've fastened, and adjust as needed. Mark the bottom edge of the fence to match the contour of the land. Trim as needed.*

Step 4: Finish the Fence. *Fasten the remaining pickets, and then build and hang a gate. (See page 143.) Install any necessary gate hardware. Remove any stakes or strings used as guides. This picket fence perfectly complements the style of the house and enhances the landscape. (A furniture company custom-cut these pickets.)*

Gates

The garden gate meets many needs, from practical to aesthetic to psychological. It is a place of romance—where else would an ardent suitor steal a kiss or wait for a late-night romantic tryst but by the garden gate?

On the purely practical side, a gate allows passage to and between a front and back garden. This functional aspect is closely tied to a gate's symbolic meaning. A locked, solid gate set in a high wall or fence provides a sense of privacy, enclosure, and security. A gate with an open design, even when set into a solid wall, has a welcoming air about it.

GATES CONCEAL SECRET GARDENS OR WELCOME VISITORS

An open gate beckons; a tall, solid gate adds mystery, suggesting the entrance to a secret garden. It can guide the eye to a focal point, or add charm, intimacy, drama, or panache.

Gates, even short ones that stand only 3 feet high, serve as important transition points from the garden to the outside world or from one part of the garden to another. They define boundaries while linking the two areas together.

Don't confine your gates to the perimeter of your property. Use them within your garden as well, to divide space visually and to mark the boundaries between different areas or garden rooms.

This decorative gate, embellished with a profusion of climbing roses, is a welcoming beginning to the garden experience. It suggests a garden inside that is designed and planted with style.

A lattice fence and gate provides privacy and security, at the same time allowing tantalizing glimpses into the garden. The pretty fretwork pattern is an added bonus.

Consider Function and Aesthetics. Gates can be adapted to many different settings. If you have a patio that leads to a lawn, for example, consider planting a low evergreen hedge to frame the edges of the patio, with a gate in the opening that leads to the lawn. The gated hedge performs two functions. First, it breaks up the horizontal monotony created by the patio spreading into the lawn. Second, it sets the patio apart as a special place for sitting and dining, with the gate providing access to the rest of the garden.

Make sure your gate is wide enough to wheel your garden wagon through. If it is the main access to your property, you may want it to be wide enough for two people to pass. Narrow gates, however, are appropriate for interior passages.

A STYLE OF GATE FOR EVERY LANDSCAPE

Gates come in an endless variety of styles and sizes. Massive wrought-iron gates mark the entrances to many large Victorian parks and private estates. Painted, slatted gates set in white picket fences tend to belong with small, intimate cottages or traditional country homes. The gate to a vegetable plot at the bottom of the garden might be rough-hewn, in keeping with an untreated wooden fence designed to keep out foraging wildlife.

Japanese moon gates have cutout circles symbolic of the full moon. These circles may be open or filled in with a fretted design of wood or iron to add visual interest and increase security.

Choose your gates to fit the style of your garden, but don't be afraid to have fun. Experiment with color, such as terra cotta to blend with a Spanish-style house. A light-colored gate is particularly effective against a dark backdrop of heavy foliage. Similarly, a dark-colored gate is striking when seen against the sky or silhouetted against a long view of fields or parkland. Try dark blue near water.

Manufactured or Custom-Made Gates. There are many sources for gates. Someone handy with tools can make a gate fairly easily. Good fencing companies usually offer a great range of gate styles and materials. Old wrought-iron gates are popular items in antique shops.

Whatever you decide for your garden gates, let them be more than functional. Allow the gates to convey the subliminal message you want for your garden, thus enhancing your environment both visually and emotionally.

Hanging a Gate

***Difficulty Level:** Moderate*

Gates are hung from posts, which are generally made of metal, brick, wood, or concrete. The diameter of the posts should be determined by the width of the gate. A gate 3 feet wide or smaller should be mounted on a 4x4 post sunk 1½ feet into the ground for stability. Gates 3 to 4 feet wide need the extra strength of a 6x6 post sunk 2 feet deep. There should be a 3-inch gap between the bottom of the gate and the ground to allow for easy opening and closing.

Allow the concrete to set completely before you hang the gate. Read thoroughly the instructions on the bag of concrete to know how much time is required.

Once the gate is hung and you've made any necessary adjustments so that it swings properly, install the latch. Use galvanized screws that are as long as possible without protruding from the opposite side.

To prevent the gate from swinging past its closed position and putting unnecessary strain on the hinges, attach a vertical strip of wood to the gate post to stop the gate when it closes.

Tools and Materials: Posthole digger, shovel, battens, nails, stakes, gravel, concrete, mixing hoe, mixing pan, gate, gate posts, gate hardware (latch, hinges), screws, drill/driver, hammer, level.

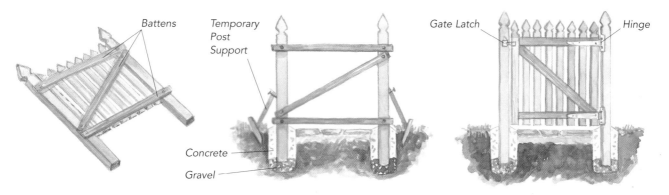

Battens   Temporary Post Support   Gate Latch   Hinge   Concrete   Gravel

Step 1: Space the Posts. *Lay the gate on the ground, and position the posts on each side, allowing enough space for the hinges and latch. Make sure the tops and bottoms of the posts are even. Nail temporary battens onto the posts as shown. (The bottom batten should be at the bottom of the gate.)*

Step 2: Set the Posts. *Dig postholes, and then set the posts on a bed of gravel, making sure the bottom batten is 3 inches off the ground and that the posts are plumb and level. Secure the posts with braces and stakes as temporary supports, and then fill the holes with concrete. Check again for plumb and level before the concrete sets.*

Step 3: Hang the Gate. *When the concrete has completely cured, remove the braces and battens, attach the hinges (with the gate attached) to the post, and then attach the latch. The job is easier if one person holds the gate in position while the other drills the screw holes and attaches the hardware.*

Trellises

Trellises were a key element in Renaissance gardens and continued in popularity through the eighteenth century. Trellises enjoyed a resurgence of popularity in the late-nineteenth century, but never to the extent of earlier times.

Trellises can lend an air of magic and mystery to a garden. Generally we think of trellises in terms of the prefabricated sheets of diamond- or square-grid lattice and the fan-shaped supports for training climbers, both of which are readily available at home and garden centers in both wood and plastic. Lacking a pattern book, most gardeners are unaware of the incredible variety of designs, patterns, and optical illusions that can be created with trellises.

USE TRELLISES TO DIVIDE SPACE OR PROVIDE PRIVACY

A trellis screen is a wonderfully airy way to achieve privacy or to partition off a space. The lath slats of lattice interrupt the view without totally obscuring it, creating the effect of a transparent curtain. Left bare, the pretty design of diamonds or squares makes an attractive effect. Covered in vines or decorated with hanging baskets, a trellis screen is enchanting.

This pergola, with its pointed, gothic arch has a ceremonial air. Festooned with climbing roses, it turns the passage from one part of the garden to another into a celebration.

Cover a Wall with a Trellis. The art of treillage, as the French call it, is not limited to screens. You can cover a bare wall or unattractive fence with a trellis pattern. Arrange the trellis pieces to create an optical illusion of an archway in the wall. Paint a realistic mural of the make-believe garden space beyond. Use a trellis for the walls of a gazebo to provide enclosure without being claustrophobic. Put a trellis screen with a pleasing, intricate pattern at the end of a walkway as a focal point.

Some Trellis Designs

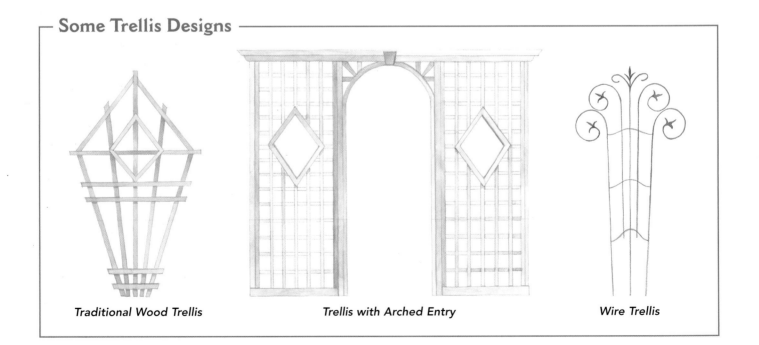

Traditional Wood Trellis　　　　*Trellis with Arched Entry*　　　　*Wire Trellis*

Arbors, Pergolas, and Arches

Far from being luxury items in the garden, arbors and pergolas can play a vital role in elevating the design and use of space from the ordinary to something special. The differences between an arbor and a pergola are somewhat technical, and you'll find people using the terms interchangeably. An arbor is a sheltered spot in which to sit. A pergola is generally a tunnel-like walkway or seating area created with columns or posts that support an open "roof" of beams or trelliswork. An arch (whether or not it has a curved top) is a structure through which you can walk. Usually all three structures are covered with vines.

DESIGNING WITH ARBORS AND PERGOLAS

Because they stand tall, they add drama and importance to the scenery, especially if the rest of the garden features are predominantly horizontal. Take advantage of the upright supports to indulge in vertical gardening, growing climbing vines—preferably ones that flower profusely—up and over the structure. In addition, an arbor or pergola creates a shady, private retreat with pleasing contrasts between light and shadow.

Use Arches and Pergolas to Create Transitions.

Arches, arbors, and pergolas are stylish ways to mark the transition from one part of the garden to another. Place an arch or arbor around the gate into the garden, or to mark the entrance from one garden room to another. Design the garden with reference to the arch or arbor so that it works like a picture window, framing a vista or a pretty vignette. Another idea is to nestle an arbor on the edge of the property to give the illusion that there is a passageway to another section. Place a bench beneath the arch for a protected, private place to sit. Design it so there is an appealing view from the arbor seat into the rest of the garden.

The English language is rich with synonyms for garden structures. Pergolas are also known as colonnades, galleries, piazzas, or porticos. Whatever you call them, these structures play a valuable role in the landscape design. In addition to being a walkway leading from one place to another, a pergola or gallery also can function as a garden wall, dividing two spaces. Instead of using a pergola as a walkway, you might place one across the far side of a patio so it serves as a partition, dividing the

This arch, with a striking pyramid top, marks the entrance to a charming garden room. It is crowned by the fragrant flowers of Japanese wisteria (Wisteria floribunda 'Issai').

The passage through this classic white pergola is sweetened by a profusion of pale pink roses. Set alongside the house, the pergola is a special place to sit, and frames the garden view from indoors.

paved space from the planted area beyond. In addition to being a handsome architectural feature, the vine-covered structure will provide a shady retreat where people can comfortably sit, and if the central support posts are spaced properly, they can frame the view into the rest of the garden.

INTEGRATE ARBORS INTO THE LANDSCAPE

Proper siting of an arbor or pergola is essential to its success in the design. All too often people plunk down an arbor in the middle of a lawn or garden space with no reference to the rest of the environment. Instead of being a beautiful feature, such an oddly placed structure is a curious anomaly, looking uncomfortably out of place.

Arches, arbors, and pergolas must be connected to the overall design. For example, a path should lead to an arch or arbor. Place an arbor on the edge of the property, and then enhance the illusion that it is leading to additional grounds by camouflaging the property boundary with shrubs. Be sure to have a path leading to the arbor to anchor its position and to encourage people to stroll over and enjoy the haven it provides.

Position Pergolas Over Paths. The best location for a pergola is over an important path. Ideally a pergola should not lead to a dead end. Even a small garden can have room for a pergola. Instead of running it down the center of the property, set it along the property line. Plant shade-loving plants under its protected canopy, and place a bench underneath to create a shady retreat. A vine-covered pergola gives much-valued privacy from the upper stories of adjacent houses.

Although a pergola often covers a straight walkway, there is no rule that says a pergola cannot cover a curving path. In such a case, the curve prompts curiosity.

Near the house it is wise to choose a design for your arbor or pergola that complements the design of the building. For a traditional-style house you may want to support your arbor or pergola with classical columns made of concrete, fiberglass, or stone. Augment a brick house with brick support posts. Cast-iron or aluminum posts could echo other wrought-iron features, such as a balcony, railing, or gate. Farther from the house, you can have more leeway.

Scale Pergolas to Garden Size. In a small garden, make a pergola less architecturally domineering by building the support posts and rafters out of thinner material such as metal or finer-cut lumber. In a large garden where you need the extra mass, opt for columns built of brick, stone, or substantial pieces of lumber.

Pergolas should always be somewhat higher than they are wide. A minimum width of about 5 feet allows two people to walk through the pergola abreast. The structure should be high enough to allow a tall adult to walk underneath comfortably. The upright support posts also need to be in proportion to the roof. If the supports are hefty, the overhead beams also should be substantial. How far apart you space the roof beams depends on the final effect you want. Wide spacing creates a skylight. Close spacing makes the pergola more tunnel-like.

Bear in mind that an arbor or pergola covered in vines must bear a lot of weight. The upright posts should be strong and properly rooted in a solid foundation, and the roof structure should be well constructed. (See page 141 for information on sinking posts.)

Pergola Construction Techniques

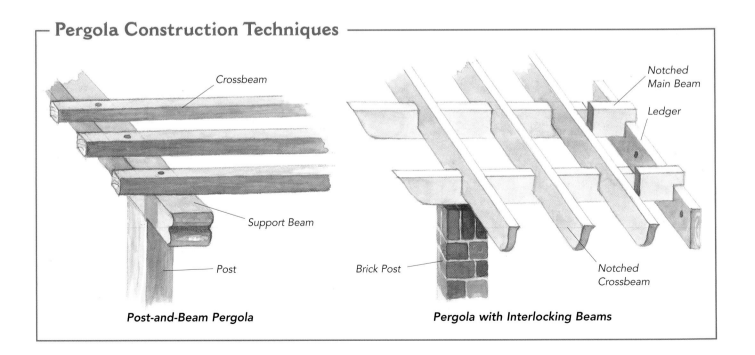

Post-and-Beam Pergola

Crossbeam

Support Beam

Post

Pergola with Interlocking Beams

Notched Main Beam

Ledger

Brick Post

Notched Crossbeam

Plants to Train on Arches, Arbors, and Pergolas

There are several different ways clinging vines manage to do just that. Some attach themselves to supports with tendrils. Others, called twining vines, wind themselves around uprights. Vines such as ivy attach themselves to walls and structures with aerial rootlets. A fourth type of vine doesn't cling at all; it depends on the hand of man to tie it to a support.

Aristolochia macrophylla (Dutchman's pipe),
   Zones 4–8
Bignonia capreolata (cross vine), Zones 6–9
Bougainvillea cultivars, Zone 10
Campsis radians (trumpet creeper), Zones 4–9
Clematis species and cultivars
   'Comtesse de Bouchard', Zones 4–9
   'Duchess of Albany', Zones 4–9
   'Ernest Markham', Zones 4–9
   'Gypsy Queen', Zones 4–9
   'Gravetye Beauty', Zones 4–9
   'Hagley Hybrid', Zones 4–9
   'Henryi', Zones 4–9
   'Horn of Plenty', Zones 4–9
   C. x jackmanii 'Superba', Zones 3–9
   C. montana, Zones 6–9
   C. tangutica 'Bill MacKenzie', Zones 5–7
   C. terniflora (sweet autumn clematis),
      Zones 5–9
Hydrangea petiolaris (climbing hydrangea),
   Zones 4–9, 4–10 in west
Lonicera species (honeysuckle), zones vary
   with species
Parthenocissus tricuspidata (Boston ivy),
   Zones 4–9
Rosa cultivars (climbing rose)
   'Alberic Barbier', Zones 4–10
   'Albertine', Zones 4–10
   'Blaze', Zones 4–10
   'Chaplin's Pink Companion', Zones 4–10
   'Felicite Perpetue', Zones 4–10
   R. filipes 'Kiftsgate', Zones 5–10
   'Mme. Gregoire Staechelin', Zones 4–10
   'New Dawn', Zones 4–10

   'Veilchenblau', Zones 4–10
Schizophragma hydrangeoides, (Japanese
   hydrangea vine), Zones 5–9
Trachelospermum jasminoides (star jasmine),
   Zones 8–10
Vitis coignetiae (crimson glory vine), Zones 6–9
Vitis vinifera 'Purpurea' (purpleleaf grape),
   Zones 6–9
Wisteria species (wisteria), Zones 5–10

Lonicera periclymenum 'Belgica' (honeysuckle)

Clematis x jackmanii 'Superba'

Wisteria sinensis (Chinese wisteria)

CHAPTER 7

Water Gardens

Since ancient times, gardeners have used pools, ponds, and fountains to add interest to their gardens. In fact, for centuries water was considered an essential feature for a garden. Elaborate water gardens graced Persian landscapes. The Italians mastered the art of garden features in the sixteenth century. Later, the French and then the English adapted the Italian model to fit their ideas of landscaping.

Water Gardens: Soothing and Cooling

Most of us don't have the space or financial means for the grand waterworks and features of the famous historic gardens. Nevertheless, a small pool, pond, or fountain is within nearly everyone's reach today and makes a welcome feature in the garden. Water is cooling, both physically and psychologically. Physically, water cools

◄ *The formal reflecting pool is a strong part of this landscape design, bisecting the manicured lawn and drawing the eye to the summer house in the back. The sparsely planted water lilies accent the pool without detracting from its elegant lines.*

and humidifies the air immediately around it, creating a beneficial microclimate for plants that require relief from the drying heat. Watching water, whether it is still or moving, tends to soothe the soul and refresh the spirit, as does hearing the sound of falling water. Wide, still pools are magical with their reflections, doubling the view of the garden. Falling water can be regulated to produce myriad sounds, from a soothing splash to a lively chatter.

MANY DESIGN OPPORTUNITIES EXIST

The design possibilities for water features in the garden can range from a miniature pond in a sealed barrel to a large reflecting pool filled with water lilies, fountains, and sculpture. A pond or pool may be free-form or geometric, formal or informal, naturalistic or stylized. The choices depend on your taste, your budget, and what works best with your house and garden. The goal is to create a design that will enhance and refresh the landscape.

Water Features for Small Gardens. Even in a small patio garden, you can find room for a little pool or a fountain. A variety of tub garden kits is now available from suppliers. To save space, build a fountain into a wall or mount one on a fence. If you have an enclosed courtyard patio, install a tiered, upright fountain in the middle as the centerpiece.

If your garden is next to a busy street, put in a fountain that produces a large amount of splashing water noise; the pleasing sounds will help to mask the noise of the traffic.

▲ *Water gardens add a soothing element* to the landscape. *The tranquil spot shown above combines the sound of falling water with a dark reflecting pool. The spring flowers brighten the shade.*

▶ *This dimunitive water garden* fits the scale of this town property well. The brick edging lends a country informality to the traditional rectangular shape. Flag iris and foxglove bloom along the edges.

Planning Your Pond or Pool

One of the most important decisions to make before you embark on a water-garden project is the location. If you plan to grow water lilies, choose a spot that gets at least four hours of direct sunlight a day. Find a spot away from trees, which create unwanted shade and dirty the water with their falling leaves. The decomposing leaves of some trees and shrubs, particularly holly, laurel, rhododendron, laburnum, poplar, horse chestnut, and willow, produce salts and gases that are toxic to fish. In addition, invasive tree roots can damage some pond linings, and cherries and plums are hosts to the water lily aphid.

Locate the Pond Where You'll Enjoy It. A pond or pool can be a big investment, so choose a location where you will see it often. Try to locate your pond so that sources of water and electricity are easily accessed. All electrical pond equipment must be grounded with ground-fault circuit interrupters (GFCIs). If you're planning a fountain, you want to be able to hear it from a spot where you frequently sit.

Next Decide on the Shape and Style. Other choices you face are the size, shape, and style of the pond or pool. With the exception of mini-pools housed in tubs

The large, free-form pond *shown here resembles a natural pond. Water lilies and pickerel weed are planted in pots below the surface. The shoreline is planted with large swaths of black-eyed Susans and variegated ornamental grass.*

or small rigid liners, the ideal planted pond should have a water surface of at least 40 square feet with a minimum depth of 18 inches in at least one area. For larger ponds, 2 to 2½ feet deep is better. Include a shelf about 10 inches wide and 9 to 12 inches below the water surface if you plan to grow plants that need their crowns under water. Such plants are called *marginal plants* because they grow along the margins or edges of water bodies; yellow flag (*Iris pseudacorus*) is one example.

Building Your Pond or Pool

Installing a garden pond or pool in most cases no longer requires you to mix concrete and have a sophisticated knowledge of masonry skills. Today homeowners can build a pond using either a lightweight, long-lasting synthetic liner or a rigid fiberglass shell. While either option still requires a lot of work to dig the hole and get the liner or shell fitted properly, doing so is much easier and requires less experience than the old method of mixing and spreading concrete.

Centrally located in the landscape, *this lush water feature blends well with the perennial garden next to it. The dry-laid path echoes the stone edging and ties the pool to the rest of the garden.*

FLEXIBLE LINERS

When the pond you plan is too large for a prefabricated rigid liner or the shape you want is not available, then you should opt for a flexible liner. A quality flexible liner costs about the same per square foot as a rigid liner. The tradeoff is that while you can build a pond with a custom shape, you will have wrinkles. However, once your pond is filled with water, the wrinkles should not be obvious.

Three different types of flexible liners are on the market today:

❧ *Polyethylene* should be used only for temporary pools. It tears easily and cracks after extended exposure to sunlight. Most brands will last two to three years if you install a double layer of 500-gauge sheeting. Some more-expensive brands guarantee a longer life span, but this material is far from permanent.

❧ *Polyvinyl chloride (PVC)* is the midprice option. Strong and stretchable, it has a life span of 10 to 15 years, making it much more durable than polyethylene but not as long lasting as synthetic rubber. An upgraded version, called PVCE, is guaranteed for 10 years.

❧ *Synthetic rubber sheeting* is the latest breakthrough in pond liner technology. Two types on the market are EPDM (ethylene propylene diene monomer) and butyl rubber. Both are durable, flexible materials safe for all aquatic life. Impervious to sunlight and frost and resistant to air pollution, the rubber's elasticity allows it to give when subjected to ice pressure and earth movement. This stretchable quality makes it better for lining ponds and pools than old-fashioned concrete, which would crack under stress. EPDM liners are 45 mil thick and a dark charcoal color. Butyl rubber liners are 30 mil thick with a flat black, slightly textured surface. Both last longer than any other liner after 20 years of field tests. Although synthetic rubber sheeting is much more expensive than PVC liners, it is a reasonable long-term investment if you want a pond that will last for decades.

Pond Anatomy

To figure out how much liner you will need, calculate the liner width by adding twice the maximum depth of the pool plus an additional 2 feet to the width. Use the same formula to calculate the length. So, for a pond 2 feet deep, 7 feet wide, and 15 feet long, the liner would be 4 feet plus 7 feet plus 2 feet (or 13 feet). The length would be 4 feet plus 15 feet plus 2 feet (or 21 feet).

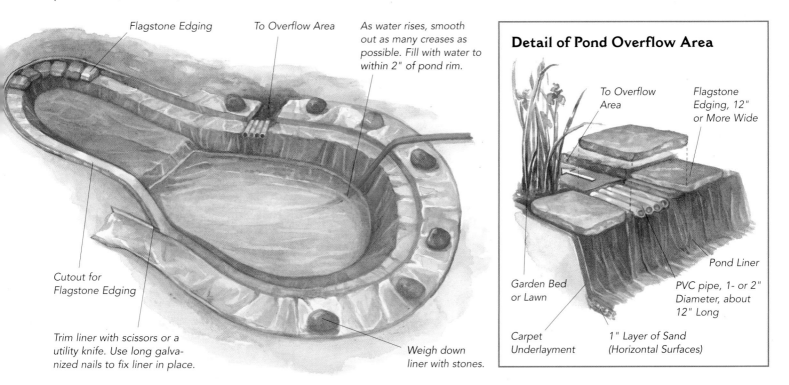

Flagstone Edging

To Overflow Area

As water rises, smooth out as many creases as possible. Fill with water to within 2" of pond rim.

Cutout for Flagstone Edging

Trim liner with scissors or a utility knife. Use long galvanized nails to fix liner in place.

Weigh down liner with stones.

Detail of Pond Overflow Area

To Overflow Area

Flagstone Edging, 12" or More Wide

Garden Bed or Lawn

Pond Liner

PVC pipe, 1- or 2" Diameter, about 12" Long

Carpet Underlayment

1" Layer of Sand (Horizontal Surfaces)

HOW TO INSTALL A FLEXIBLE-LINER POND

Difficulty Level: Moderate

Flexible pond liners give you greater choice of size and shape than rigid liners, but they must be installed more precisely. The surface must be level and free of stones, and sand, carpet underlayment, or other padding must be laid under the liner to keep it from being punctured. See a description of the different liners available on the previous page. Start by marking the shape of the pond with a hose. Then sprinkle lime along the hose as a guide. Excavate the hole for your pond. Add or remove dirt as necessary to keep it level.

Tools and Materials: Shovel, scissors, tape measure, level, lime, hose, flexible liner, carpet underlayment, sand, pump, PVC pipe, cinder blocks, flagstone edging.

Step 1: Prepare the Pond. *Outline the pond, and dig it to the desired depth. Measure the outside dimensions, and cut the liner to size. (See page 151.) Spread sand on the bottom, and place carpet underlayment on the walls.*

Step 2: Anchor the Liner. *Spread the liner across the hole, smoothing out as many wrinkles as possible. Make sure the liner extends several inches beyond the hole on all sides. Anchor the liner with concrete blocks.*

Step 3: Install the Recirculating Pump. *Position the pump on the bottom of the pond within reach of a GCFI electric outlet. Connect the pump to the fountain head with a length of PVC pipe.*

Step 4: Edge the Pond. *Lay the flagstones around the pond, leaving small planting pockets between the stones if desired. Brush sand between the stones, plant along the pond, and fill it with water.*

Rigid Liners

Prefabricated liner technology has come a long way. In the early days the less-expensive models had a short life span, ultimately cracking and leaking. In addition, most of them were too shallow for fish and plants to survive. The result was a mucky, algae-filled pool.

Today all of that has changed. It is now much easier to find a rigid liner with a surface area of at least 40 square feet and a proper depth of 18 inches. Many come with shelves for marginal plants, and some even have rims that dip below soil level on the outside edge designed to house bog plants. Before you buy, look for top-quality materials and design. The initial investment is quite large, so opt for the best to save yourself heartache and trouble later.

Fiberglass and reinforced plastic are the longest-lasting materials for rigid liners. Reinforced plastic liners usually come with a guarantee of 10 to 20 years. Fiberglass is virtually impervious to freezing, heaving, and degradation from the sun's ultraviolet rays. It is considered the best construction material for prefabricated ponds. Look for a guarantee of at least 20 years. In addition to being relatively easy to install as in-ground ponds, rigid liners are excellent to line small raised pools.

*A **preformed rigid pond liner** is installed using similar steps to the flexible pond liner. Rigid liners don't have to be dug as precisely as flexible liners, and there is less outside edge to hide.*

*An **irregularly shaped rigid pond liner** with rounded edges has a natural, less formal look. The stone edging and water plants, including peonies, iris and water lilies, disguise the lip of the liner.*

Elevating Your Pond or Pool

Like a raised bed, a raised pool has many benefits: The fish and plants are closer to eye level. And, small children are less likely to fall into a raised pool, although they should still be closely supervised. A raised pool is easier to maintain than an in-ground pond. You don't have to get down on your hands and knees to deadhead or weed. And if the pool needs to be drained for cleaning, it is easy to siphon out the water.

A raised pool can be a stunning feature on a patio, even providing extra seating if it is constructed with a wide edge. Another idea is to build a raised pool on a terraced slope, using the retaining wall as one side of the pool. Build the side walls of a durable material that complements other elements in your landscape, and make sure the pool is scaled to blend comfortably with the site.

*A **raised pond** brings fish into close view. The white brick pool blends well with the wall behind it, and the wall-mounted fountain makes the most of a small space.*

The whiskey-barrel tub garden shown above is planted with umbrella plants, water lilies, water hyacinths, and irises. A preformed, rigid liner rests on the lip of the barrel and contains the water.

Tub Gardens

Even a large tub or container has the potential to be a raised pond. Choose a completely sealed vessel. If you opt for a barrel that once contained wine, whiskey, or olives, line it with a flexible pond liner to seal out bacteria in the wood that could harm plants and fish.

Balance Number of Fish and Plants. A square yard of water surface is enough to plant, for example, one water lily, one Japanese arrowhead (mature height 3 feet), one pennywort, and one bunch of *Sagittaria sinensis* (an oxygenating grass). The water in a tub garden is likely to get much hotter than in a larger pond because of the small volume. As a result, sensitive fish such as goldfish and koi may not survive. If you want to include fish, opt for guppies or mosquito fish that can tolerate the heat and temperature fluctuations.

Setting Up Your Pond

In most communities the tap water is chlorinated. To avoid damaging water plants, give the chlorine a few days to outgas before you begin to add plants. Fish love to nibble at plant leaves and to nose about in their roots. If you wait four weeks after planting your pond before you introduce the fish, you'll give the plants a chance to establish themselves and allow time for the pond to settle into a healthy balance.

Check with your water district to find out whether chloramine (a combination of chlorine and ammonia) is being used. Aquatic plants can tolerate these additives to drinking water, but fish can't. Chloramine reducer is sold by most pond retailers. Wait 10 minutes after adding the reducer before you introduce fish, snails, and plants to your pond.

It's a good idea to test the pH of the water. The ideal pH for water-garden fish is close to neutral (7.0), but many aquatic plants do well in slightly acidic water (pH 5.5 to 6.5). Test kits are available in both garden centers and pet stores that sell fish. Ask your retailer for instructions on using the pH test kit.

Planting Your Pond or Pool

Plants perform both an ornamental and an ecological function in a water garden. When choosing plants for your water garden, you need to keep their ecological function in mind. For example, although they are not particularly attractive in their own right, you should include oxygenators, those plants that help starve out algae and contribute to a balanced environment. Try to include some plants that cover the water surface to create shade, which discourages algae growth and gives fish a respite from the hot sun. Aim to have about one-half to two-thirds of the water surface covered with plants.

A planted pool takes advantage of the sunny location. Some of the plants in this water garden include: water lilies, irises, and ornamental grasses. The pool is framed by a fence covered with vines.

Young, freshly planted water lilies will not cover enough surface area to shade the pond. In the meantime, many people introduce floating plants to give extra coverage until the water lilies are established. Floater plants do not grow in soil; instead they float on the surface and draw their nutrients from the water. Most floaters are beautiful as well as useful. Consider planting frogbit (*Hydrocharis morsusranae*), which looks like tiny water lilies, or water hyacinth (*Eichhornia crassipes*), which blooms in pale lavender spikes. Be aware, however, that water hyacinth is creating a major nuisance where it has escaped into waterways in Florida and California.

Frogbit is less invasive than water hyacinth, making it ideal for small ponds and pools. You may need to be ruthless about thinning the more prolific spreading floaters, especially once your water lilies and deep-water aquatic plants come into their own. Take care to keep all water plants, their trimmings, and fish away from natural bodies of water or ponds that overflow into streams so that you don't inadvertently introduce an alien plant nuisance or fish disease into the local water.

The final category of plants for a pool or pond garden is marginal plants, those that naturally grow near the edges or margins of water bodies. These need to be submerged in shallow water so that their roots are permanently underwater while their leaves and flowers emerge above the surface. These plants prefer shallow water, so place them on the underwater shelf around the edge of your pond. Grow them in baskets or pots so that you can divide and repot the plants easily. Avoid mixing different varieties in a single container. Some examples of marginal plants are water iris (*I. laevigata*) and pickerel weed (*Pontederia cordata*).

Creating a Balanced Pond Environment

To maximize the health of your pond and minimize the upkeep, you will want to establish an ecological balance. The experts at Van Ness Water Gardens in Upland, California, have developed a formula for building a pond that will stay beautiful naturally. For every square yard (9 square feet) of pond surface area, they recommend the following:

Twelve Water Snails. *Water snails glide along pond surfaces eating algae and plant material in various stages of decomposition.*

Two Fish. *Fish help the water garden environment by gobbling up pests such as aphids, flies, and mosquito larvae.*

One Water Lily. *Water lilies promote pond health by covering the surface. They prevent oxygen loss and evaporation, and provide shade for the fish.*

Two Oxygenating Plants. *These are underwater plants that absorb nutrients and carbon dioxide from fish waste and decaying materials, thus helping to starve out algae.*

One Bog Plant. *These water-loving plants are excellent for keeping a pond clean and clear of algae because they consume excess nitrogen and phosphates.*

Water Lilies and Lotuses

Water lilies (*Nymphaea* spp.) are the staple ornamentals of water gardens. They are divided into two categories: hardy and tropical water lilies. If your pond is big enough, you may want to stock a few of both types to extend the bloom time each day.

Lotuses (*Nelumbo nucifera*) are the kings of garden ponds. They are large plants. The bigger cultivars produce 6- to 8-inch diameter flowers that stand as tall as 5 feet above the water surface. These giants produce round, 18-inch leaves. They are aggressive growers that will take over an earth-bottom pond in just two to three years. Once established, they are nearly impossible to eradicate. It is safest to grow lotuses in containers in a pool with a liner.

Water lily (*Nymphaea* spp.) and lotus (*Nelumbo nucifera*)

HARDY WATER LILIES

A plant with a wide tolerance for climates, the hardy lily thrives in Zones 3–11. It will bloom as long as the water temperature is above 60°F and the air is above 70°F. In parts of the country with cold winters, water lilies will bloom from about late May into September, depending on how warm the days are. In frost-free climates where daytime temperatures remain in the 70s even in winter, hardy lilies will bloom nearly year-round, although blooms are less profuse during the colder months. In regions with frost, plants die down in the fall and then sprout new leaves in spring.

Hardy lilies bloom during daylight hours. Generally the flowers open around 9:00 A.M. and close in the afternoon between 3:00 and 5:00 P.M. The times depend on variables such as the hybrid, how sunny and warm the day is, and the age of the flower.

Hardy water lily (*N.* 'Perry's Fire Opal')

TROPICAL WATER LILIES

As the name suggests, tropical water lilies are frost tender. In zones 10–11, they grow as perennials and bloom all year. In colder climates they are grown as annuals and replaced each spring, or they are unearthed and overwintered away from freezing cold. (See page 161 for overwintering instructions.) Tropical lilies will begin blooming once they've experienced two to three weeks of 80°F temperatures. Because they need the warm temperatures to bloom, they generally do not perform well in the Pacific Northwest and other parts of the country with cool summers.

Tropical water lily (*N. colorata* 'Evelyn Randig')

There are two types of tropical water lilies: day-blooming and night-blooming varieties. Like the hardy lilies, day bloomers open their flowers in the morning and close in the mid- to late afternoon. Night bloomers open after sunset and stay on display until late morning or early afternoon the next day. Both types of tropical water lilies are fragrant. If you plant both day and night bloomers, you'll have flowers to enjoy 24 hours a day.

WATER LOTUSES

Although the lotus can overwinter in a climate as cold as Zone 4, it requires warm weather (above 90°F) for several weeks to bloom well. The bloom season lasts for six to eight weeks in areas with hot summers; each flower opens in the morning and closes in the afternoon. After three days the flower petals start to fall, leaving the distinctive cup-shaped seed pod that is so popular in dried-flower arrangements.

Lotuses are generally large plants. Some varieties such as 'Alba Grandiflora' produce 6- to 8-inch blossoms on stems 4 to 5 feet above the water surface, and 'Mrs. Perry D. Slocum' has leaves that are 18 inches across. But there are several cultivars that are suited to small container water gardens and small ponds. Smaller than the average lotus, 'Charles Thomas' produces fragrant lavender-pink flowers on stems that stand 3 to 4 feet above the water. This lotus adapts well to a small pond or a container.

Even smaller is the tulip lotus 'Shirokunshi', which produces white, tulip-shaped flowers on compact plants that grow only 18 to 24 inches above the water.

American lotus (N. lutea)

Lotus plants are aggressive growers. Never plant lotus directly in an earthen-bottom pond. Instead, plant them in pots and only in ponds with liners.

LOTUSES CAN BE INVASIVE

As with a flower bed or shrub border, it is easy to overplant a pond. Learn about the growth habits of the plants before you buy them, and allow room for them to multiply and grow to their full size. Frank and Maribe Varcolik learned about plants taking over a pond the hard way. Several years ago they planted six lotuses in their 1-acre, earth-bottom pond. Within a few years the lotus plants had multiplied so much that they took over the entire pond. The Varcoliks hosted a weeding party, inviting guests over for a meal in exchange for helping to pull out the excess plants, but enough remained to spread again. Finally they had to use a syringe to inject each stout, woody stem with an herbicide. That procedure set the plants back, but did not eradicate them. Their battle against the invasive lotus plants continues. If you have an earth-bottom pond, think twice before you introduce lotuses.

Even containers will not stop these vigorous spreaders from taking over the entire pond. To be safe, grow lotuses only in pots placed in ponds lined with plastic or rubber.

Take Care when Buying Budget Water Lilies.

Be aware that less-expensive water lilies are priced low because they are easy to propagate and, thus, invasive. Choose lilies that have a combined mature spread of no more than one-half to two-thirds of the water surface.

Newly Planted Water Gardens Take Patience.
A new water garden will not appear to flourish immediately. "It takes a while for a new water garden to become established," says Charles B. Thomas, of Lilypons Water Gardens, a mail-order water garden company in Buckeystown, Maryland. "Many gardeners become anxious after about four weeks because the plants begin to look a little less healthy than when they were purchased and because algae begins to develop. At this stage the presence of algae is a healthy sign, and by the sixth week all the plants should show signs of healthy growth," explains Thomas. The plants and fish may take a few weeks to acclimate but will soon recover and start to actively grow.

The appropriately planted pond's surface is covered about one-third with plants; two-thirds of the surface are open. Water lilies grow in the pond, astilbes are planted on the edge.

POTTING POND PLANTS

Choosing Containers. Unless you have a natural pond in your garden with earthen sides and bottom, you will want to grow all but your floating aquatic plants in containers. Choose plastic or pulp planters. Never use redwood because the wood will discolor the water. Water lilies do best in a large container, so they have room to grow and spread. The minimum size pot for water lilies is about 12 inches in diameter and 9 inches deep. In general, the larger the pot, the more robust your water plants will be.

When and How to Plant. The best time to plant is during the growing season between May and September. Line the pot with natural burlap to keep the soil from spilling out the drainage holes. Use natural burlap, not the synthetic material that is now available. Then fill the container with good-quality topsoil. Do not use potting mixes, compost, or peat. These materials are too light and won't stay put in the pot under water. Water well to saturate the soil, and then plant. Hardy lilies should be set at a 45-degree angle, with the tuber against the side of the pot and the crown just out of the soil. Tropical lilies and other plants should be placed in the center of the container.

Add a 1-inch layer of pea gravel or coarse aquarium gravel on the top of the soil to keep the fish from nosing about in the soil and disturbing the plant roots. The pebbles or pea gravel also will stop any light particles of soil from floating out of the pot.

Caring for Container-Grown Water Plants
Fertilize your aquatic plants regularly, as you would any container-grown plant. Look for fertilizer pellets specially formulated for water plants, and follow the directions on the label for frequency of feeding and recommended doses.

Different plants flourish at different water depths. If the plants are not labeled with their ideal depth, ask you retailer how to care for your water plants. For those that require a shallower depth than that of your pond, place the pots atop bricks arranged to bring the plants to the appropriate level. Young water lily plants may need to begin on several bricks and then be lowered as their stems grow taller.

Gravel

1- to 3-gal. container lined with burlap and filled with heavy garden soil.

Stocking Your Pond

Fish are not essential for the ecological balance of your pond, but they do make a garden water feature come alive. Their movement and flashes of color through the water are delightfully entertaining.

For just a few dollars, you can stock your pond with the little "feeder" goldfish from a pet store. Start with 10 goldfish for a 4×6-foot pond; they will grow and reproduce to the pond's capacity, eating any mosquitoes that venture near the water.

Or you can stock your pond with more expensive Japanese koi. As a general rule, allow about 1 square yard of pond surface for every koi. You can break that rule and have a somewhat denser population if you aerate the water with pumps.

Look for Healthy Fish. Make sure each fish is healthy before you introduce it to your pond. Signs of good health include an erect dorsal fin along the fish's back, bright eyes, no missing scales, and good energy. (Be suspicious if the fish is sluggish when the others are active.) Never purchase a fish with white spots on its body that look like salt grains. That is the symptom of ich, the most common disease of pond fish. Never release pet fish or water garden fish (or snails) into natural lakes or waterways, as they can spread diseases to native fish populations or even crowd out native fish.

Protect Fish from Predators. Fish in ponds and pools are vulnerable to natural predators. Cats are known for their taste for fish. Herons are even more pesky. They will eat an entire pond-full of koi in a matter of days. In regions where birds prey on the fish, either choose less-expensive fish or protect the pond with netting. One family in San Diego created a network of fine wire overhead in their garden. The wingspan of the heron is too large to get through the wire grid.

When you introduce store-bought fish or water snails into your pond, set the unopened plastic bag in the water, and leave it there for about 30 minutes so the water temperature in the bag reaches the same temperature as the pond water. Then open the bag and gently release the animals. This procedure will minimize the shock of a new environment for the fish. Don't feed fish for a few days after introducing them to the pond. They will probably spend their time hiding near the bottom of

This pond is stocked with water lilies, water hyacinth, one lotus, and a variety of fish. The margins are planted with grasses and canna. There is enough water surface free of plants that the fish have ample oxygen.

Fish survive in the winter if the water is deep enough and if you make a hole in the ice through which toxic gases can escape.

An overhead string grid protects koi from heron. The homeowners felt this netting was less noticeable than a barrier at the water level.

the pond, occasionally venturing out to explore their new home. They are best left alone to adjust.

While fish in an ecologically balanced pond will get enough nutrients from the plants and algae, it's all right to feed them a little additional food. Limit feeding sessions to once or twice a day, and remove any food that is uneaten after five minutes. If you are away on vacation, the fish will survive without your attention.

Maintaining Your Pond

SUMMER MAINTENANCE

While you are enjoying the beauty of your pond, keep an eye out for pests. They are much easier to control if you catch them early. One easy preventive method is to regularly hose the leaves of marginal plants with water to knock off insects.

Topping Off the Water Level. In the summer months, it's not uncommon for the water level to drop one-half inch or more in a week. It is safe to add small quantities of chlorinated water to maintain the water level. Chlorinated water is, however, damaging to plants and fish in large quantities. To replenish the level, place the hose where the added water won't come in direct contact with the fish, and let it run slowly for a few minutes. A sprinkler running for 10 minutes every other day is another excellent way to top off the water level. Don't let the water level get too low, or you risk hurting the fish and plants and damaging the pond liner.

Deadhead Plants. When the flowers of water plants fade, deadhead them to maintain the strength of the plants and to minimize the job of weeding seedlings.

AUTUMN CLEANUP

When the days cool down in autumn, start cleaning up the pond or pool. Skim off fallen leaves, so they don't sink to the bottom of the pond where they will rot. If you have deciduous trees on your property, consider placing a fine mesh net over the pond to keep out the falling leaves. Cut back the oxygenator plants, and trim off the dying leaves of the marginal plants. This process of tidying up is not just for aesthetics. Dead leaves provide a safe haven for overwintering pests.

Summer pond-maintenance is easy, as reflected by this statue of a man lounging near the water. Just don't let the water level drop, and keep an eye out for pests.

Winter pond maintenance: Set a pan of boiling water on the ice until it melts. Electric deicers are another easy option to keep the surface open.

WINTER CARE

In warm-climate zones where frost is nonexistent or rare, there are no special winter procedures to care for your pond. In cold climates, you need to protect the plants and fish.

Outdoor Fish and Plant Care. You can leave your plants in the pond as long as the roots of hardy water plants are below the ice line. However, if an ice sheet covers the pond for more than a few days, you risk killing the fish from an accumulation of trapped gases that are produced by decaying organic matter. To release the marsh gases, you could knock a hole in the ice with a hammer, but the shock waves may harm the fish. Instead, set a pan of hot water on the ice until it melts through, or use an electric pond deicer, which sits on the bottom of the pond throughout the winter and has a thermostat to turn it on and off as needed. The retailer from whom you purchased your plants and fish will be able to tell you how protect your fish and plants over the winter in your climate. Be sure to get detailed instructions before the weather turns cold.

Seasonal pest control. This attractive domed frame supports netting that keeps heron from getting at the fish.

Indoor Fish and Plant Care. In very cold climates where the pond may have more than 6 inches of ice or freeze completely, you need to remove the fish and plants. Keep the fish indoors in an aerated aquarium covered with screen. Store the water lilies in their pots, double bagged in clear trash bags. Seal the bags, label them, and keep the plants in a dark location that remains at 50° to 60°F. Keep the soil damp.

Cover the Pond for the Winter. Another option in cold climates is to build a frame to support a pond cover made from sheets of fiberglass. The cover should be kept over the pond every night during winter, even if the weather report promises warm temperatures. Use a pond deicer to keep the water temperature even. The reward for all your trouble during the winter is an earlier and faster start on plant growth in spring.

OVERWINTERING TROPICAL LILIES

*Difficulty Level: **Easy***

Tropical water lilies are often grown as annuals in cold climates. However, they are fairly costly, so it is worth your while to try to overwinter the bulbs. Because only repeated and prolonged freezing temperatures kill tropical lilies, wait until a month after the first killing frost to remove them from the water. Remove the plant from its pot, and wash away the soil. Leave the tubers to dry at room temperature for two days; then remove any remaining roots and foliage, and place the dried tubers in a jar of distilled water. Store the jar in a dark spot where the temperature stays between 50° and 60°F. Two months before you expect the pond water temperature to reach 70°F, remove the tubers from the jar and place them in a pan of water in a sunny window. Once they start to sprout, repot them in a 4-inch container submerged in 2 to 4 inches of water. As soon as the pond water temperature reaches 70°F, replant the tropical lily in its original container, and place it in the pond.

Tools and Materials: Sharp knife, jar with screw-on cover, distilled water, tap water, shallow pan.

Step 1: Remove the Tubers. *Remove the plant from the pot a month after the first killing frost.*

Step 2: Wash the Soil off the Tubers. *Allow the tubers to air-dry at room temperature for two days.*

Step 3: Trim the Tubers. *With a sharp knife, cut away any remaining foliage and roots.*

Step 4: Keep the Tubers Moist. *Put the tubers in a jar of distilled water. Cover and store in the dark.*

Step 5: Give them Light. *At the end of the winter, put the tubers in a sunny window.*

Step 6: Repot the Lily. *When the tubers sprout, plant them in a pot, and submerge it in water.*

When the danger of frost is over, clean the pump, and clear any debris from the water left over from the winter. Get ready to reacclimate fish and plants to the outside water.

SPRING CLEANING

Once the danger of freezing is past, remove your pond deicer, and check the wiring and mechanics of any electrical equipment, including pumps. Use a net to clean out dead leaves and rotting organic material from the pond bottom. Your pond may turn green in the spring because the algae starts growing sooner than your water plants. Once the other plants start growing, the green should vanish. If the pond or pool is still too green by early summer, consider using one of the algae control products available for ponds.

Reacclimate Fish to the Outdoors. If you brought your fish inside over the winter, you will have to reacclimate them slowly to the outdoor pond. Follow the same process that you used to initially introduce the fish to your pond. (See "Stocking Your Pond," page 159.) It should be warm enough to put your fish outside when the plants in the pond start to show new green growth.

Divide Overcrowded Plants. Spring or early summer is the ideal time to divide overcrowded plants and to put in new plants. (See Chapter 12, pages 263-65 for instructions on dividing perennials.) Also begin your monthly plant-feeding program with special fertilizer pellets formulated for underwater plants.

▶ *Two waterfalls* grace this naturalistic pond. Moss covers the ledge stones over which the water cascades into still water. Boulders hide the mechanical elements from view.

Fountains and Waterfalls

Fountains and waterfalls add a magical element to water gardens. A pattern of falling water that catches the sunlight and makes musical sounds is delightful and soothing to both the eye and ear.

FOUNTAINS

Natural rock formations, ceramic pots, and millstones drilled and piped for water are all possibilities for appealing fountains. You can select a fountainhead to make almost any imaginable pattern of falling water, including single sprays, multi-tiered sprays, whirling sprays, geysers, bells, fanned fishtails, flared trumpets, and multiple sprays resembling a dandelion seed head. In addition to the visual variations, each type of spray or jet makes a different sound and keeps the water moving.

Keep Fountains Away from Plants. Be aware that fountains are not compatible with water lilies and lotuses. The spray damages their leaves, and the plants prefer to grow in still water. Also be careful to keep floating plants out of range of the pump. If you want to combine plants and water play, you need a large pond with plants at one end and the fountain at the other.

WATERFALLS

Waterfalls also provide a wonderland of possibilities. Direct the water so that it trickles around stones or cascades over a smooth rock edge to create a ribbon of falling water. Another possibility is to create a slender stream of falling water, known in Asian landscape design as a "silver thread." You can purchase all the fountain and pump components separately, but the easiest approach is to buy a kit that includes all the necessary parts as well as instructions for installation and maintenance.

Bog Gardens

The edge of an informal pond is an ideal spot to plant a bog garden, filled with the special plants that require humus-rich soil that never completely dries out but also doesn't remain waterlogged.

CREATE A BOG

A bog garden is delightful beside a garden pond, forming a natural transition between the water garden and the dry land. If your land isn't naturally boggy, you can create the necessary conditions by excavating the soil 12 to 18 inches and then lining the hole with heavy plastic. Make a ½-inch drainage hole in the plastic about every 3 feet. Add a 2-inch layer of lime-free grit or gravel, and then refill the hole with good-quality loam composed of 3 parts topsoil, 3 parts peat moss, and 1 part ground limestone. The goal is to create a mixture that is water retentive but also free-draining. Disguise the edge of the plastic sheeting with a border of stones or pebbles. Water your bog garden as necessary to keep the soil moist. Be especially alert during long periods of hot, dry weather. You don't want the soil to become dry.

A bog garden in early summer. The bog is planted with water-loving marginal plants, which include ferns and grasses. Newly planted iris poke out of the ground in the left corner.

Plants for Bog Gardens

Acorus calamus (sweet flag), Zones 4–11
Acorus gramineus (dwarf sweet flag), Zones 4–11
Calla palustris (bog arum), Zones 3–8
Caltha palustris (marsh marigold), Zones 4–9
Canna cultivars (water canna), Zones 7–11
Carex pendula (weeping sedge), Zones 5–9
Crinum americanum (crinum lily), Zones 8–11
Eupatorium fistulosum (Joe Pye weed), Zones 3–8
Filipendula species (meadowsweet), zones vary with species
Hosta species and cultivars (plaintain lily), Zones 3–9
Hemerocallis cultivars (daylily), zones vary with cultivars
Iris *ensata* (Japanese iris), Zones 4–11
Iris *pseudacorus* (yellow flag), Zones 4–11

Iris *sibirica* (Siberian iris), Zones 3–8 in east, 9 in west
Iris versicolor (blue flag), Zones 3–8 in east, 9 in west
Lobelia cardinalis (cardinal flower), Zones 3–9
Pontederia cordata (pickerel weed), Zones 3–11
Primula japonica (Japanese primrose), Zones 5–8
Ranunculus lingua (greater spearwort), Zones 4–8
Sagittaria latifolia (arrowhead), Zones 5–10
Saururus cernuus (lizard's tail), Zones 4–9

Canna 'Endeavor' and C. 'Ra'

Pontederia cordata (pickeral weed)

CHAPTER 8

Garden Accents and Ornaments

Benches and Furniture

No landscape is complete without seating. A garden bench or seat is both a place to sit and an ornament. As an ornament it should be decorative, perhaps serving as a focal point. It should be made of materials that are attractive, durable, comfortable, and suited to the style of the garden.

COMFORT AND STYLE

When shopping for a seat, the best test of comfort is to actually sit down and see how it feels. Look for one that has the seat slanted slightly toward the back so that water runs off and you can recline. The seat should be deep enough to support your thighs and high enough that your feet rest flat on the ground. The back of the seat should support your back up to your shoulders. Chair arms are handy and add to the comfort. Make sure the seat is well made, with no protruding screws or nails that a can tear your skin or clothing.

Site a Bench Where It is Inviting. Siting a seat or bench is critical. Put one in an herb garden or near fragrant flowers so you can enjoy their wonderful scents and the busy activity of the bees. Let a seat be the destination at the end of a long walk; guests will appreciate the chance to rest. Of course, a stunning view demands a bench or seat so that visitors can linger comfortably and contemplate the scene. A secret garden also needs to include a place to sit. Think about how the furniture placement will enhance the garden as well as how the position will entice people to sit there.

Wicker seat

Tables and Chairs Add the Element of Dining. Remember to include tables and chairs in your plans. A well-chosen set adds a wonderful element to the garden. Whether it's large enough to serve a meal for several people or a cozy table for two, a table extends the time you can spend just enjoying your landscape.

Regional Furniture Enhances the Landscape. Different regions of the country are known for specific styles of furniture. The Adirondack chair is indigenous to the mountains of New York, and bentwood chairs are often found in rural mountain areas.

In an informal garden you can make a charming seat from a slab of stone or a sliced tree trunk laid horizontally. Graceful benches made of wrought iron, untreated teak that weathers to a beautiful silvery gray, or carved stone are beautiful in formal settings. Painted furniture can add a pleasing dimension to the garden, but consider how the color will look in its setting.

Bentwood table and chairs

Painted Adirondack chair

Wrought-iron furniture

Formal wooden bench

Gazebos and Follies

Gazebos are enjoying renewed popularity as homeowners appreciate their valuable contribution to a pleasing landscape design, but gazebos are nothing new. The basic idea dates back 5,000 years to the Egyptians, who built them for their royal gardens. The Greeks also used gazebos. Paintings dating back to 1400 BC were found in Greek tombs. In one painting, four gazebos overlook large pools. The ancient Persians built gazebos for their ornamental gardens, often at the union of intersecting waterways.

GAZEBO WITH A VIEW

Fifteenth-century English landowners built their gazebos on top of garden walls. From these lofty perches they got admirable views of both the formal gardens below and the surrounding countryside. In the early 1700s a few wealthy Virginians appreciated gazebos as shady retreats from the hot summer sun. Thomas Jefferson had a gazebo built on the edge of his terraced vegetable garden, overlooking both the garden and a panoramic view of the tree-covered mountains around his property. The windows were paned so that he could sit in comfort year-round to supervise the cultivation of his garden and to enjoy his "sea view," as he called the undulating vista of trees and hills.

Gazebos Provide a Sheltered Place to Relax.

In addition to being an attractive focal point, a gazebo is a sheltered spot in which to relax and enjoy the garden. The word gazebo is derived from the English "gaze about." Situate one where the view of the garden or surroundings is especially pretty. If your garden is small, consider installing a gazebo with a solid back wall that can abut one of the boundaries of your property. The 180-degree vantage will make the garden seem bigger. If biting insects are a problem, add screening to the sides. If you go to the trouble and expense of installing a gazebo, you want it to be a comfortable place.

Gazebos Are Affordable to Many Homeowners.

Today gazebos are available in a great range of prices, including less-expensive kits, which are affordable to most homeowners. On the high end, you can have a gazebo custom-made with luxury features, including running water and electricity. An attractive, well-placed gazebo is worth the cost, adding immeasurably to the beauty and usefulness of the garden. In addition to being a special place for contemplating a view and meditating, a gazebo is a wonderful place to entertain. Furnish the space with a table and a few chairs. Your gazebo will become a favorite place to enjoy sipping drinks and dining outdoors.

FOLLIES—PURELY ORNAMENTAL

"Folly" is the term given to any structure in a garden that serves no real purpose except to look interesting. On old estates, follies often took the form of a Greek-style "temple" or a stone tower built on a hill where it could be seen from afar and serve as a goal for long walks. Other favorite motifs in country estate gardens were fake ruins and grottoes inspired by trips to Italy.

Woodland gazebo

Bandstand-style gazebo

Two-story gazebo/"treehouse"

Ornamental garden folly

Classic summer house

Bridges

Bridges are particularly satisfying garden ornaments. Even if you don't have a pond in your garden, there may be a place for a bridge. Consider placing a bridge to cross a drainage swale or a dip in the landscape.

A BRIDGE FOR A JOURNEY

In addition to being visually arresting, a bridge can mark the passage from one part of the garden to another. Crossing it is like a rite of passage. Just be sure the bridge leads to someplace worth going. It's disappointing to come to the end of a pleasant journey only to realize you've arrived nowhere. A well-designed bridge is a satisfying, delightful addition to a garden, providing both a picturesque focal point and an appealing destination.

Whatever landscape structure you are planning, check with your local building authority. Some towns require building permits for any structure, even if it is a kit. If you don't comply with your town's requirements, it can force you to take down anything you erect.

Match Bridge Style and Landscape. The style and size of your bridge will depend on the setting and the overall style of the landscape. A bridge spanning a narrow swale or "river bed" of dry stones might be quite simple: perhaps a large, flat slab of stone or massive planks of wood that fit into the bank, joining both sides. Even more rustic looking are bridges with the side railings built of unmilled logs. They look charming in a wild woodland setting.

Moon Bridges Bring Style and Serenity. A high arching moon bridge typical of Japanese gardens is a striking feature that inevitably draws visitors. The semicircular bridge and its reflection in the water below form a circle-like feature, symbolic of the moon and perfection. Japanese Zen gardens often incorporate zigzag bridges and stepping stones that are not connected to the land to foil evil spirits that may want to cross the water.

For a more Western look, choose a bridge with a less extreme arc. The individuality of these bridges is often expressed in unusual designs for the side railings or banisters. Some are starkly simple, others have a lacy pattern of fretwork.

Wood-and-brick bridge

Painted Bridges Make an Individual Statement. A bridge is a wonderful opportunity to introduce an unexpected bold color into the landscape. Wooden bridges in Japanese-style gardens are often painted a distinctive reddish-orange color. Claude Monet chose a bluish-green paint for the beautiful wisteria-covered bridge that spans his water garden. He left the wooden floor of the bridge unpainted. In addition to being practical (constant foot traffic would quickly wear off the paint), the natural wood provides a pleasing contrast to the painted parts, which seem to float in the air above the water.

Whatever the design and color you choose for your bridge, make sure it is structurally sound. Bridges have a "come hither" aspect to them, and people want to cross them. It wouldn't do if the bridge couldn't take heavy foot traffic. If the bridge spans water, provide side railings for added protection and as an arm rest for people who want to lean over the edge.

Kits Lower the Cost. As the demand for garden ornaments and accents increases, many mail-order companies have begun offering bridge kits for sale. These kits come with all the wood and hardware required, as well as instructions for putting them together. Handy homeowners may be able to create their own bridge design or make a drawing of an existing bridge that they can reproduce in their workshop.

Gently arching bridge

Cobblestone-and-brick bridge

Wooden plank bridge with railings

Japanese-style bridge

Sculpture and Topiary

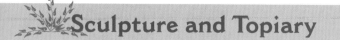

Gardens and sculpture belong together. Well-placed sculpture can serve several functions in the landscape. It can provide a focal point, add a touch of whimsy, or fill a niche in a hedge or wall.

SCALE SCULPTURE TO LANDSCAPE

Choosing the right sculpture for the right place in the landscape is the key. First, the sculpture should be in scale with its surroundings. A small ornament set by itself in a large space will be dwarfed. However, this same piece of sculpture becomes a treasured detail when it is tucked into a small gap between two stones. In contrast, a large sculpture needs a place of importance. Use one as the focal point at the end of a long pathway.

Use Natural Items with Sculptural Shapes.
Don't overlook the possibility of natural items that have a sculptural quality to them. Large seashells make pretty garden ornaments, and a piece of driftwood may deserve a place of honor in a garden as arresting as a finely wrought abstract sculpture. In Chinese gardens, rocks weathered into appealing shapes are often used as pieces of sculpture.

The increased demand for garden ornaments has encouraged garden centers and mail-order catalog companies to stock a large selection of inexpensive sculpture for the garden. If you intend to tuck the piece into a quiet corner, it may not matter if the cement seams show. Also, you can "antique" newly purchased cement sculpture by painting it with diluted buttermilk; in a shady location, it will quickly become covered with moss.

TOPIARY SCULPTURE

Topiary, the art of pruning plants into geometric or fanciful shapes, creates living sculpture for your garden. Topiary is much less expensive than many sculptures, yet it serves the same design function in the landscape.

Pick Plants that Match the Topiary Shape.
To make the job of creating and maintaining your topiary easier, choose a plant whose natural growth habit is compatible with the shape you want to create. Generally topiaries are created from slow-growing plants, such as boxwood and yew. A slow-growing topiary will need less-frequent pruning once it's established. A shortcut to the traditional pruned topiary is to create one by growing a vine over a wire form. Choose a fine-leafed, vigorously growing vine such as a small-leafed ivy cultivar or creeping fig (*Ficus pumila*). Topiaries trained on forms are well-suited for containers. Put a monumental form in a large container to create a dramatic garden accent, or plant a small form in a pot that will fit comfortably on a tabletop to create a striking centerpiece.

SPECIMEN PLANTS AS SCULPTURE

Sometimes a single plant stands out as a dramatic garden accent because of its size, color, or form. When properly positioned in the landscape, one of these plants can play the same design role as a piece of sculpture. Colorado blue spruce (*Picea pungens* f. *glauca*), with its perfect conical form, makes a striking landscape accent. Likewise, a single stand of pampas grass (*Cortaderia selloana*) or maiden grass (*Miscanthus sinensis*) has lovely sculptural qualities and deserves a place in the spotlight.

Some cultivars of Japanese maple (*Acer palmatum*), with its twisted, contorted branches, are often effectively grown as a single accent. The fascinating branch structure is particularly evident and pleasing in winter when it stands out in stark silhouette.

Flying horse on green clouds

Buddha in water garden

Topiary shrubs

Classic stone sculpture

'Taihaku' cherry tree

Maiden grass (Miscanthus sinensis)

Containers for Plants

People have been gardening in containers at least since King Nebuchadnezzar built the Hanging Gardens of Babylon in 600 BC. While most people do not attempt container gardening on the massive scale achieved by Nebuchadnezzar, containers still play an important role in enhancing a garden. There are many advantages to container gardening.

Container Gardens are Versatile.
Container gardens can be moved when they are past their prime. You can grow tropical plants in containers by keeping them outside in the summer and moving them indoors to overwinter where winters are harsh. If your soil is alkaline, you can grow acid-loving plants in pots. Containers add color and excitement to patios. Cluster a group of containers to create a pleasing composition of shapes, sizes, and colors. Attach baskets of cascading plants to pergolas, arbors, and eaves to bring color up high.

DESIGNING WITH CONTAINERS

Choose your containers with the same care as you would a sculpture or any other garden ornament. In addition to finding pots that complement your garden style, think about which plants to put in them.

Match Plants to Containers. Showy plants such as palms, *Dracaena*, and shrubs pruned as standards look best in traditionally designed planters such as classic urns or white planter boxes. Rustic barrels or half barrels are inexpensive and unpretentious containers in an informal setting.

Try Unusual Containers. Fill an old wheelbarrow with potted plants, or give new life to a leaky metal watering can by turning it into a planter. Or plant an old shoe with shallow-rooted succulents.

Use your imagination and have fun. Whatever container you use, however, make sure it has drainage holes in the bottom. Unless you're growing bog plants, they'll be short-lived if their roots are sitting permanently in water.

Decorative old wagon

MAINTAINING CONTAINER PLANTS

Plants growing in containers need special care. Small containers dry out quickly and need frequent watering. In dry climates or on windy days some containers should be watered at least once, if not twice, daily. However, frequent watering leaches out soil nutrients, so container-grown plants should be fertilized regularly.

Use Light, Well-Draining Soil. The soil in containers should be light and nutritious. Soil collected from the garden is too heavy. But soilless container mixes are often so light they dry out quickly. As a compromise, combine 2 parts potting mix with 1 part compost. The compost will give more body to the mix, as well as provide important nutrients.

Choice of Fertilizer Depends on What's Growing. The type and frequency of fertilizing depends on what's growing in the container. Some experts recommend fertilizing with half-strength fish emulsion every time you water. This makes it easier to remember when you last fed the plants. Or fertilize your plants with organic slow-release fertilizer pellets every 4 to 6 weeks. Mix the pellets with the potting mix at planting time; a good dose should feed annuals for the entire season.

Tips for Containers and Hanging Baskets

◙ To keep down the weight of containers filled with soil, fill the lower half of large pots with foam peanuts, perlite, or any other lightweight material that will not compact over time. Put potting mix in the remaining space, and plant as usual.

◙ To keep up with the heavy feeding most container-grown plants need, add compost to the planting mix or add liquid seaweed or a fish emulsion/liquid seaweed combination to the water every few weeks to ensure a well-balanced supply of all essential micronutrients.

◙ To remoisten peat moss if it becomes dry, fill a tub with water and add a drop of liquid detergent to help the water stick to the peat moss. Set the basket in the water, and leave it for several hours until the potting soil and peat moss mix is saturated with water.

◙ Pinch off dead blossoms regularly to keep container plants bushy and full of flowers.

◙ Cluster your pots together in a sheltered spot if you will be away for several days. The plants will need watering less frequently, and it will be easier to water if the containers are all in one place.

◙ To automatically water containers, bury one end of a long wick (such as those sold with oil-fueled lanterns) near the plant's roots. Insert the other end in a bucket of water. The wick will gradually soak up the water and provide a slow, continuous source of water for the plant.

◙ If a plant is root-bound, prune the roots by cutting back the outer edges of the root ball instead of transplanting it to a larger container. Then repot it in the same container with fresh soil.

◙ Consider watering many containers with an automatic drip irrigation system; install a line to each container.

◙ To reduce moisture loss, top the soil in your containers with mulch.

Hanging moss basket

Stone container

Ceramic urn with rose

PLANTING A WIRE HANGING BASKET

Difficulty Level: Easy

The advantage of a wire hanging basket is that plants can grow out the sides and bottom as well as the top, so the underside looks pretty when viewed from below. Planting a wire basket is an easy, fun garden project. To get the most effect for the longest time, plant the basket as soon as the danger of frost is past.

Tools and Materials: Wire basket, long-fibered sphagnum moss, potting soil, perlite, peat moss, and plants.

Step 1: Line Basket with Moist Sphagnum Moss.
Soak the moss until it is saturated with water, and then wring it out so it is damp, not soggy. Stuff handfuls of damp moss between the basket wires to create a bowl for the potting soil.

Step 2: Add Potting Soil, Perlite, and Peat Moss.
Fill the basket with a mixture of 2 parts potting soil, 1 part perlite, and 1 part peat moss. The perlite will reduce the weight, and the peat moss will increase water retention.

Step 3: Push the Rootballs through the Moss. *Use your fingers to open a space in the moss and soil large enough for the plant's rootball. Insert the rootball into the space so that the plant crown is at soil level. Firm the dislodged moss and soil back into place.*

Step 4: Finish Planting, and Water the Basket.
Continue planting around the sides, and then add a few plants to the top of the container. Water well. A hanging basket generally needs to be watered at least once a day. Fertilize as needed to keep plants blooming.

PLANTING A STRAWBERRY POT

Difficulty Level: Easy

Strawberry pots are wonderful containers for more than just strawberry plants. Any shallow-rooted plant that isn't too big on top is well suited to these eye-catching containers. Choose plants that will trail over the edge of each cup, such as creeping thyme or Johnny-jump-ups.

Tools and Materials: Strawberry pot, PVC pipe, perlite, drill, hacksaw, marking pen, potting soil, plants.

Step 1: Mark the PVC Pipe. *Center a 2- to 4-inch diameter PVC pipe in the strawberry pot over the drainage hole, and mark the pipe at the top of the pot and at each pocket. Drill ½-inch holes in the pipe at each spot marked for the pocket locations. Use a hacksaw to cut the pipe so that it stands about 4 inches below the rim of the pot.*

Step 2: Fill the Pipe with Perlite. *Put the pipe in the pot, making sure the drilled holes line up with each pocket, and fill the pipe with perlite. The perlite is lighter than potting soil and helps the water percolate down the center of the pot and out each drainage hole to the plant's root systems. Add potting soil until it reaches the level of the bottom pocket.*

Step 3: Position the Plants. *Insert the plant rootball through the pocket so it is lying on the soil. When buried, including any soil in the pocket, the plant should be at the same depth it was in its original container. Add soil to the next level, and continue planting. Tuck a little sphagnum moss around each plant in a pocket to stop soil from splashing out when you water.*

Step 4: Water the Strawberry Pot. *Water thoroughly, filling the space between the soil level and the pot rim with water. Let it soak in, and fill again. Repeat until water starts to flow out the drainage hole in the bottom of the pot. These tall, narrow pots need a large volume of water to filter through all the plant layers.*

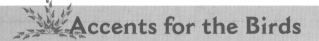

Accents for the Birds

As soon as you add plants to the landscape, you have made it attractive to birds, which bring life, color, and music to the garden. Many people seek to fill their gardens with birds by adding accents.

BEAUTIFUL, BENEFICIAL BIRDS

Gardeners have been attracting birds to their landscapes at least since Roman times, but it is only fairly recently that the motive has been sheer pleasure. In the past, the birds were lured as a food source or to catch insects.

The eighteenth-century residents of Williamsburg, Virginia, put great importance on attracting birds to their town. Researchers at Colonial Williamsburg have found many references to "Martin Pots," or bird bottles, in both shop and home inventories. The bird bottles were used as nesting houses to attract martins, which were valued because they ate mosquitoes and other flying insects. The copies of the original bottles sold today are equally effective and add an old-fashioned accent to the garden.

Birds—Natural Pest Control. Even today birds are appreciated for the part they play in providing a beneficial balance in the garden. In North Carolina researchers noticed that sparrows and goldfinches ate a million grain aphids a day while feeding on 100 acres of grain fields. Wrens will feed each of their fledglings as many as 500 insects in an afternoon, and redstarts feed their young a minimum of 1,200 bugs daily. A brown thrasher eats thousands of insects a day. Of course, as any home gardener knows, birds alone don't control insects. However, they are part of the complex ecosystem and play an important role in the balance.

BIRD ACCESSORIES FOR THE GARDEN

Attractive bird feeders, birdbaths, and birdhouses make charming garden accents. A birdbath on a pedestal is a classic ornament in the center of a formal garden, but it is equally attractive in the midst of an informal flower garden or to break the monotony of a horizontal stretch of lawn or other ground cover. A hollowed out stone resembling an Indian metate for grinding corn or grain looks great resting directly on the ground and makes a beautiful, naturalistic birdbath. Put one where you can watch the antics of the birds splashing in the water.

Elevated bird feeder

Birdhouses for Every Taste and Budget.
Birdhouses come in a range of prices and styles, from simple woodworking kits to elaborate mansions made by craftsmen that can cost hundreds of dollars. Yet even an inexpensive birdhouse, especially if it has a peaked roof, looks charming hanging from a tree branch or tucked into a tree crotch. The more sophisticated styles are excellent as a focal point or at the end of a path, where they play the same design role as a statue.

Keep function in mind as well as aesthetics when choosing a birdhouse. Any birdhouse should have ventilation and be able to drain. Many also have a door that opens to ease cleanup between nests.

Watch the Activity at Feeders. Bird feeders can be as simple as the plastic cylinders filled with sugar water for hummingbirds or as elaborate as structures resembling miniature gazebos. Position a feeder where you can enjoy watching the birds, but keep the same design goals in mind as for a birdbath or birdhouse. Remember that spilled birdseed will sprout, creating a potentially weedy irritant.

Birchbark birdhouse

Traditional birdbath

Indian metate birdbath

Black-chinned Hummingbird   Bohemian Waxwing

Dovecote birdhouse

Sundials and Other Accents

Sundials, which are enjoying a renaissance in this country, speak of a simpler age when life was less frenetic. Many carry sweet mottoes such as "Grow old along with me, the best is yet to be." Others are more cautionary, forcing us to face our mortality: "*Me ortum vides forsan non occasum.*" [You have seen me rise but may not see me set.]

The sundial is believed to be the oldest device for measuring time, dating back to about 2000 BC. Before the invention of clocks, sundials were one of the primary ways for keeping track of the time.

Sundials Remind Us to Savor the Moment. Our word "dial" comes from the Latin *dies*, or day: the sundial marks the 12 divisions of the day according to the sun's placement in the sky. People have long felt the pressure of time. The Roman comic poet and dramatist Titus Maccius Plautus (about 254–184 BC) wrote, lamenting, about "The wretch who first … set a sundial in the marketplace to chop my day to pieces." Today, however, sundials make us think of a simpler time and remind us to savor the moment.

Most gardeners today see sundials as more decorative than functional. Several gardening mail-order catalogs feature sundials, and garden centers that maintain a good stock of garden ornaments, as well as specialty gift shops, usually carry some. Look for old ones at antique shops and flea markets. Mass-produced sundials generally are fairly inexpensive; antique or limited-edition sundials are, of course, more costly.

Endless Design Possibilities. There are limitless possibilities for placing a sundial in a garden. Before placing one, however, think about the potential design benefits. Also, choose a spot that gets sun most of the day. Otherwise it serves no purpose.

Point Vertical Sundials Due South. A vertical sundial makes a lovely focal point on a bare wall, breaking up the blank expanse. For the sundial to keep accurate time, however, the wall must face due south. While you're focused on the wall, consider growing a vine or espaliered plant on either side of the sundial to further break the monotony. If the ground along the wall is paved, consider a pair of large potted trees or shrubs to flank the sundial, adding to its interest and drawing the eye to the central focal point.

Sundial on a Pedestal. In a garden where most of the vegetation is low—creating a horizontal effect—consider placing a sundial on a pedestal to add height to the design. Put one in the center of your lawn to add unexpected interest, or at the end of a path to lure strollers to walk its length.

Many sundials come with matching pedestals, or you can create your own. Depending on your garden style, you may want to build a pedestal of bricks, use a piling or landscape tie, mold one out of cement, or simply stack up a column of upended clay pots.

Sundials in Formal and Informal Settings. A sundial or other tall ornament is the traditional focal point to symmetrical formal gardens as well as to a formally laid out herb garden, but it is equally at home in an informal, cottage-style garden surrounded by bouquets of flowers jostling each other for position.

Sundial as focal point

Country garden with sundial

Sundial on pedestal in lavender

Millstone base for sundial

CHOOSE ORNAMENTS THAT PLEASE YOU

A beautiful well-designed landscape full of thriving, living things, should impart a sense of *joie de vivre*, or buoyant enjoyment of life. It should reflect its owner's personality and sense of humor.

Humor in the Landscape. A touch of levity adds to the pleasure of a garden. Even in a formal landscape, there is room for a subtle, sophisticated joke—or some broad humor.

A childlike enthusiasm is often a factor in successful whimsy. Treehouses, in addition to being wonderful places for children to play, suggest a gardener who remembers the wonders of climbing trees for a bird's-eye view of the territory. Garden animal sculptures can be elevated to whimsy with careful placement. For example, concrete stalking cat sculptures with marble eyes are readily available and inexpensive. Stuck in plain view, these cats lack subtlety. But try placing one where it is partially hidden by arching shrubbery or cascading plants. Now you have a creature of the jungle on the prowl, glimpsed but not completely seen.

Be True to Yourself. Don't be daunted by the views of others. Be true to yourself, and express your own personality and sense of humor. With some thought and creativity, you can create a whimsical vignette or two in your garden that will lift your heart and tickle your funny bone.

PART THREE

Planting and Growing

You have done the preparation and set the stage. Now, it's time to bring on the plants—the real stars of this performance. Take time to enjoy the process as well as the finished product.

Chapter 9: Redecorating the Established Landscape *explains how to make the most of your existing, mature plants. Deciding what is worth keeping, moving large plants, and knowing how and when to prune are described.*

Chapter 10: Choosing and Planting Trees and Shrubs *guides you through the choices of trees and shrubs available. You will learn how to buy, plant, and care for them.*

Chapter 11: Lawns, Ground Covers, and Ornamental Grasses *teaches you how to start a new lawn, fix an old one, and use ground covers and ornamental grasses as alternatives to turf lawns.*

Chapter 12: Flowers in the Landscape *provides the icing on the cake. You will get design tips and planting and growing suggestions for perennials, annuals, and bulbs.*

Chapter 13: Vegetables and Herbs *shows how the edible garden can be ornamental; also how to plant and maintain crops, and how much to expect from each at harvest time.*

Chapter 14: Managing Pests and Diseases *explains a necessary component of any garden maintenance plan. Organic solutions are presented.*

CHAPTER 9

Redecorating the Established Landscape

There are many reasons to redo a landscape design. A landscape is a living thing and thus is constantly changing. What was once a beautiful design, perfectly in scale, eventually may overgrow its bounds. In addition, short-lived trees and shrubs such as Leyland cypress eventually begin to decline. These may need to be replaced. Although longer-lived specimens such as boxwood or beech trees usually grow slowly, they too one day reach the point where they block light and take up too much space. When these mature trees and shrubs crowd each other, obstruct windows, create dense shade, or encroach upon space intended for pathways, they need to be taken in hand.

◄ *The dark, established evergreens* are softened by the pale, airy bamboo growing behind them. Bamboo is a quick-growing plant that makes an excellent screen; however, certain species can be aggressively invasive.

Lifestyles Inspire New Gardens

Families and lifestyles change as well independently of landscapes. When children are young, it's valuable to have an area devoted to play space for them with features such as a swing set, a sandbox, and perhaps a treehouse. Eventually the children will outgrow those amenities, and you may want to rethink your design. Many people can't wait to retire, so they will have more time to devote to gardening. Shortly after the last day of work, they begin converting lawn to flower beds and opening up unused land so that they can garden to their hearts' content.

Tastes change as well. Both in North America and Europe, *au courant* gardeners are moving away from traditionally planted beds and borders and toward using plants such as ornamental grasses in unexpected ways. As a homeowner, you may simply want to try something new and different.

▲ *Mature plants, such as these beautiful dwarf conifers, are an asset in any garden. If you don't like where a tree or shrub is growing, consider moving it. The established plants shown here provide structure and permanence to a young spring garden.*

EXISTING PLANTS ARE AN ASSET

Whatever the reason for making major changes to your landscape design, remember that your existing plants are rich assets. Mature plants give a new landscape a more established look. In addition, you'll save hundreds of dollars if you can incorporate some of the plants you already have into your new landscape design.

Before you uproot and remove your old plantings, take time to decide whether each plant is worth saving. Bear in mind that many plants, even well-established ones, often can be successfully transplanted. Trees and shrubs that have grown too dense can be thinned. With a little care and nurturing, a plant that's currently a liability can be transformed into a treasure.

Save Only the Healthy Plants. When deciding whether a plant is worth saving, check whether it is healthy. Unless the plant is a rare specimen or you have an important use for it in your new design, there is little point in trying to save a failing plant. Fast-growing trees and shrubs with short life spans (20 to 30 years), may show signs of poor health that are simply the result of old age. If you are not sure why the plant isn't doing well, check with the staff of a nursery you trust.

Some thinning and trimming will maintain the plants' forms in this lush garden and prevent them from getting out of hand. The many strong design elements here will remain aesthetically appealing if the plants are given some routine maintenance.

Pruning Basics

How you prune will determine the future growth patterns of your trees and shrubs. If you want a full and bushy shrub (or perennial, for that matter), give it that message by shearing or pinching. Botanists have found that there is a concentration of growth hormone in the tips (*apexes or apices*) of growing plants. They've dubbed this phenomenon *apical dominance*. The net result is that when you pinch back a plant or shear it, you redirect the growth hormone to the growing buds below the cut. Every time you cut or pinch off the end of a branch, the plant sends out two shoots from each bud. The result is that every pinched or sheared branch will develop two or three new lateral branches, ultimately doubling the plant's fullness.

You can pinch back just about any plant, but not all tolerate shearing. For example, you would seriously damage a rhododendron if you sheared it, although there is no problem with shearing azaleas. Forsythia, with its lovely, loose shape, is a good example of a shrub that is spoiled by shearing. Generally shearing should be reserved for hedges and to shape formal evergreens.

PRUNING FOR FULLNESS

When you are pruning to make a plant bushier, always cut back to a growth bud. To find the buds, look for a swelling or projection along the stem or branch. The large, easily visible buds are actively waiting to grow. In addition, there are smaller, dormant buds that will sprout if you cut off the branch just above them. Make the cut at a 45-degree angle with the low end of the cut opposite the bud and even with it. If you cut too sharp an angle, or too high above the bud, the cut tip will die back rather than stimulating fresh growth. If you cut too close to the bud, you'll damage it. Cut to a bud that faces the outside of the stem or plant to encourage the shrub to grow in an open shape. Branches that grow inward, crisscrossing over and under each other, make a less attractive shrub and reduce the air circulation inside the plant.

BASIC PRUNING TECHNIQUES

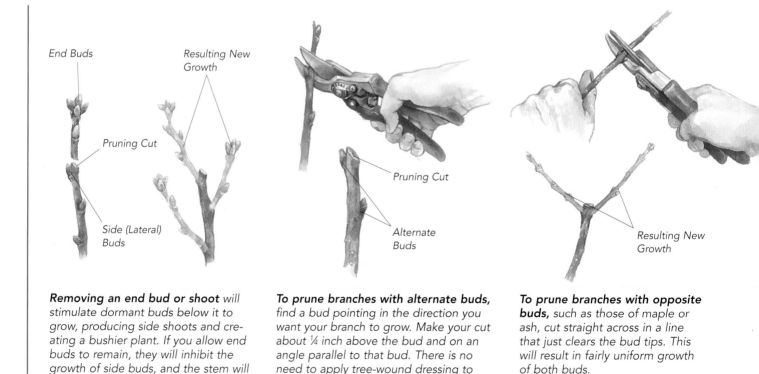

Removing an end bud or shoot will stimulate dormant buds below it to grow, producing side shoots and creating a bushier plant. If you allow end buds to remain, they will inhibit the growth of side buds, and the stem will grow mainly from the tip.

To prune branches with alternate buds, find a bud pointing in the direction you want your branch to grow. Make your cut about ¼ inch above the bud and on an angle parallel to that bud. There is no need to apply tree-wound dressing to cuts, whether large or small.

To prune branches with opposite buds, such as those of maple or ash, cut straight across in a line that just clears the bud tips. This will result in fairly uniform growth of both buds.

Prune Summer-Flowering Shrubs in Late Winter.

Summer-flowering shrubs such as glossy abelia (*Abelia x grandiflora*), broom (*Cytisus* species), butterfly bush (*Buddleia* species except for *B. alternifolia*), rose of Sharon (*Hibiscus syriacus*), peegee hydrangea (*Hydrangea paniculata* 'Grandiflora'), and shrubby cinquefoil (*Potentilla fruticosa*) bloom on new growth. You can create a bushier plant and increase the number of flowers if you prune these shrubs in late winter or early spring before the plant has started to actively grow. Cut each branch back to a growth bud. Every branch you prune should produce at least two new shoots, doubling the shrub's blossom potential. Because you prune these shrubs before the buds emerge, there is no danger you will cut off a flower bud.

The summer-blooming butterfly bush (Buddleia davidii) *will produce more flowers if you trim the bush back in early spring. Cut the shrub back to a framework of permanent branches, cutting at strong buds or where vigorous shoots are developing.*

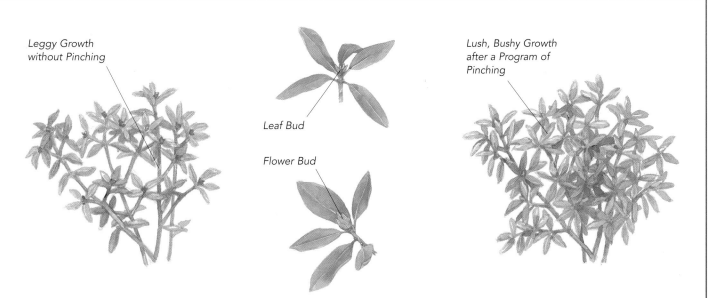

Leggy Growth without Pinching

Leaf Bud

Flower Bud

Lush, Bushy Growth after a Program of Pinching

When pinching back broad-leaved evergreens on plants such as rhododendrons, you can avoid leggy growth (shown at left), stimulate lush branching growth (shown at right), and control plant size by pinching back end buds of new branches. In a phenomenon known as apical dominance, these end buds control hormonal flow and inhibit growth of dormant side buds. Pinching (removal) of end buds sends chemical signals that stimulate the growth of side buds. **Caution:** avoid mistakenly pinching off the bigger, fatter flower buds.

Lilacs flower more profusely if they are pruned annually just after they finish blooming. The common lilac (Syringa vulgaris) can be renovated by cutting it back hard.

Wait Until Flowers Finish for Spring Bloomers.

Wait to prune spring-blooming shrubs such as lilacs until they are flowering (use the cuttings for flower arrangements indoors) or until after the blooms are spent. Most of these shrubs set flower buds on year-old wood, so an early spring trimming will cut off this year's blossoms. The pruning you do in early summer on spring-flowering shrubs will stimulate more flowers the following spring. *To avoid the risk of cutting off next year's buds just as they are being set, prune within a month after the shrub stops flowering.*

Prune Nonflowering Plants Any Time.

Nonflowering trees and shrubs can be pruned at any time, but again you have an opportunity to communicate a definite message to the plant by when you prune.

❧ *To improve health, prune in the winter.* If you want to increase the plant's vigor, prune when the plant is dormant (in the winter).

❧ *To slow down growth, prune in the active growth season.* If you want to slow growth on a tree or shrub that's quickly outgrowing its allotted space, cut it back when it is actively growing.

❧ *To open up a tree's form, remove the inside branches.* In cases where branches cross over each other or are too dense, you may wish to open up the form of a tree or shrub by removing inside lateral branches. Instead of cutting from the tip back to a growth bud, remove the branch at its growing source, either the tree trunk or the primary branch. The message you deliver to the plant is clear: don't send out extra shoots, there are enough here already. Step back to assess what cuts will yield a pleasing shape. This type of pruning can enhance the form of a tree as well as improve the tree's health, as it lets light and air into the interior of the plant.

❧ *When pruning to a growing source, do not cut it flush with the trunk.* If you do, you'll create a wound larger than necessary and increase the risk of disease entering the tree or shrub. Instead, make the cut on the branch side of the slight swelling where the branch meets the trunk but as close to the swelling, also known as the collar or saddle, as possible. A dying stub of wood that is too long is susceptible to disease.

YEARLY MAINTENANCE PRUNING

Not all trees and shrubs need pruning every year. However, you should inspect your woody ornamentals once a year to see whether they need to be pruned.

Remove Dead or Diseased Wood.

Look for dead and diseased wood, and remove any you find. In addition to being unsightly, the problem that killed a branch could spread to the rest of the plant if you don't cut it out. To prevent the spread of infectious diseases through your pruning tools, disinfect the tools by dipping them between each cut in rubbing alcohol. In the spring, prune away any branches or wood killed over the winter.

Regular Pruning Keeps the Job Manageable.

It's much easier to keep a tree or shrub at a maintainable size if you prune it back once a year rather than once every five years or so. In addition to the job being less work, you'll make life much easier on the plant if you remove just a little foliage every year rather than a large amount all at once. In addition, you can more easily influence the shape of the tree or shrub if you prune annually. If you see a garden full of beautifully shaped trees and shrubs, the odds are they are pruned at least once a year.

The thinned canopy of this pine tree makes a pretty, lacy pattern against the sky. The extra space or portholes between branches also allows the wind to blow through unobstructed—a useful attribute in this ocean-facing west-coast garden.

MAINTENANCE OF ESTABLISHED TREES AND SHRUBS

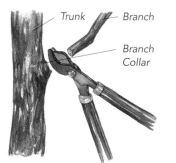

Trunk Branch

Branch Collar

When removing an entire branch, cut just outside the slightly thickened area, called the branch collar, where the branch grows from the trunk.

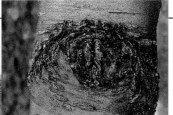

Proper pruning cuts just beyond the collar on this kwanzan cherry resulted in the nicely healing wound shown at left and the almost completely healed wound on another branch, shown above.

These rubbing limbs will eventually abrade the bark on one or both limbs, leaving exposed wood open to pests and diseases. Remove the weaker limb or the one facing inward.

Improper pruning results are shown in both pictures. Above: Careless lopping left a small, protruding chunk of wood, which won't heal as quickly as the surrounding edges. Right: A single top-to-bottom cut resulted in torn bark that gives diseases and pests access to the tree.

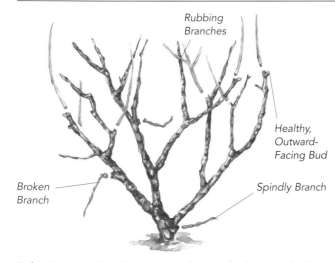

Rubbing Branches

Healthy, Outward-Facing Bud

Broken Branch

Spindly Branch

Selective Pruning. Remove weak, spindly, bent, or broken shoots (red). Where two branches rub on each other, remove the weaker or the one that's pointing inward (orange). Cut back long shoots to a healthy, outward-facing bud (blue).

Severe Pruning. In late winter or early spring, before new growth starts, cut all the stems of the shrub back close to the ground.

Tools for Pruning

Pruning tools should be an extension of your hand; look for tools that feel comfortable and are easy to use. Clean your tools after each use, and oil the blades and joints before putting them away for the winter. Above all, a sharp blade is the key to making clean cuts. Sharpen the blades yourself or bring them to a professional.

Bypass Pruner

Anvil Pruner

Pruning Knives. *Pruning knives are useful for smoothing rough edges on a cut. This step is important because rough and torn cuts are more susceptible to insect and disease invasion.*

Hand Pruners or Secateurs. *This tool is designed to cut through branches as thick as ½ to ¾ inch in diameter. There are two kinds of hand pruners: bypass and anvil.* **The bypass pruner** *has two sharpened blades that overlap when they cut, like scissors. When the blades are sharp, bypass pruners give a good, clean cut. If the blades are blunt, they tend to twist and make an undesirable tearing cut. Besides being unsightly, a ragged cut leaves the damaged wood more prone to pests and diseases.* **The anvil style pruner** *has one cutting blade, which closes on a plate, or anvil, made of softer metal. Anvil pruners are generally lighter than the bypass type and are easier to use, but the anvil prevents a close cut and may crush the bark.*

Bypass Lopper

Ratcheted Anvil Lopper

Loppers. *The long handles on loppers give extra reach and extra leverage so they can cut through wood up to 1¼ inches thick. Heavy-duty models can cut through 1¾-inch stems. Loppers are available with both bypass and anvil-style blades. The ratcheted lopper cuts thicker branches and takes the strain off your hands.*

Pointed Bow Saw

Bow Saws. *The narrow blade allows a bow saw to cut more quickly than other saws, but the arched back makes it too wide to fit into tight tree notches or between dense shrub branches.*

D-shaped Bow Saw

Extension Saw. This curved pruning saw is attached to a long pole, allowing you to work on branches that would otherwise be out of reach.

Pruning Saw. Pruning saws are designed with teeth that angle back (rather than the straight teeth of a carpentry saw), making it possible to cut green wood without binding. The small, curved pruning saws are useful for pruning branches up to 2 inches in diameter that are too close for a larger, wide-blade saw or bow saw to fit between.

Hedge Clippers. The long, scissor-like blades of hedge clippers are designed for trimming and shaping hedges and bushes.

Electric Shears. These are less expensive and weigh less than gas-powered shears, but the length of the cord limits the range. To prevent accidentally cutting the cord, tape a plastic pipe around the 2 feet of cord nearest the clippers as protection. If you don't want to be restricted by a cord, try rechargeable, battery-powered electric clippers.

Chain Saws. Designed for cutting down trees, removing large tree branches, and cutting up firewood, chain saws can be gasoline-powered, electric, or even hydraulically powered. A chain saw is one of the most dangerous power tools in common use, particularly in the hands of inexperienced, fatigued, or careless people. The prime single hazard—kickback—can occur when the chain operating around the nose of the bar unexpectedly hits resistance, such as an unnoticed limb or other obstruction. To avoid kickback, always hold the saw by both handles with a firm, opposable-thumb grip. Study the manufacturer's owner's manual and heed all of its safety instructions. Unless you have professional experience, do not attempt to climb a tree with a chain saw. As an amateur, use a chain saw only when your balance and footing are secure. Even then, exercise extreme caution.

Reciprocating Saw. The single blade on reciprocating saws is more suited to pruning than the spinning blade of chain saws. Reciprocating saws are especially useful when you need to cut near ground level about a third of the stems in a row of shrub hedges, such as lilacs. Always use the same caution recommended for chain saws.

Safety Note: For all electric tools, be sure your extension cord meets manufacturer's specifications and that it is protected by a ground-fault circuit interrupter (GFCI).

Restoring Old Shrubs

Unless the plant has reached the end of its natural life span, most old but healthy shrubs can be made new again or at least brought back into scale with the rest of the garden. However, shrub renovation is not for the faint of heart. It requires severe pruning, in some cases cutting the plant right back to the ground or to a few bare stubs. It also requires patience. It can take several years to restore a tired, overgrown old shrub to a youthful thing of beauty. When successful, however, the risk is well worth the patience and effort. You'll enjoy the benefit of having a beautiful, well-established shrub.

If you severely prune back old, tired-looking shrubs, they will generate fresh new growth, giving them a new lease on life. Spirea japonica 'Little Princess' (shown here) will rebloom if the spent flowers are sheared off the plant.

PROPAGATE SHRUBS BEFORE PRUNING

Just as there are risks when a doctor performs major surgery on a human, there is the possibility that the shrub you try to renovate will not survive. If you plan to work on an unusual or hard-to-replace specimen, propagate new plants as a precaution. To improve the chances of renovated shrubs making a good recovery, feed and water them well during the following growing season. Ideally, flowering shrubs should be fed twice a year—in the spring and autumn.

Take Softwood Cuttings in Spring. Softwood cuttings are taken in late spring before the new growth has fully hardened. Softwood is pliable because lignan, the substance that stiffens woody stems, has not yet developed. Cut off the new growth tips of branches, cutting pieces a minimum of 3 to 4 inches long. If the parent plant is large or if you are pruning away large sections, the cuttings can be as long as 2 feet. Remove the lower leaves from each cutting to expose a length of bare stem. Bury the stems of short cuttings 1 to 2 inches deep in a mix of perlite and vermiculite. Insert taller cuttings deeper into the pot so they stand on their own.

Trees and shrubs that root well from softwood cuttings taken in late spring include barberry, butterfly bush, flowering quince, *Deutzia*, forsythia, bush honeysuckle, mock orange, Japanese pieris, shrubby cinquefoil, and viburnum.

Summer is the Time for Semiripe Cuttings.
Semiripe cuttings are taken a few weeks later in early summer. They should be rooted using the same procedure as for softwood cuttings. Good candidates for semiripe cuttings are camellia, cotoneaster, daphne, hydrangea, mahonia, privet, pyracantha, spirea, and weigela.

Take Hardwood Cuttings in Autumn. Hardwood cuttings are taken at the end of the growing season when the wood has developed lignan and is no longer flexible. In parts of the country where the ground freezes, take the cuttings in early winter, and store them buried in slightly damp sand, wood shavings, or vermiculite. They should be kept moist and between 32° to 40°F. After the ground has thawed, you can place the stored cuttings directly into the ground or into pots or beds with prepared soil. In warm climates you can take hardwood cuttings in autumn. Hardwood cuttings should be pencil-thick and 5 to 8 inches long. Candidates for hardwood cuttings taken in autumn include boxwood, false cypress, juniper, and yew. Forsythia, gardenia, honey locust, aspen, cottonwood, spruce, and arborvitae respond better if their cuttings are taken in winter. (See page 192 on how to take a hardwood cutting.)

PROPAGATING WITH SOFTWOOD AND SEMIRIPE CUTTINGS

Difficulty Level: Easy

Propagating new plants by rooting cuttings is strongly recommended before you transplant or severely prune a mature tree or shrub that may not survive the process. Growing new plants from softwood and semiripe cuttings is an inexpensive way of reproducing shrubs, especially if you want many plants for a hedge or to fill a large space.

Tools and Materials: Pruners or secateurs, rooting hormone, soilless rooting medium (half perlite, half vermiculite), pot, plastic wrap.

Step 1: Cut Off the New Growth Tips. *Softwood cuttings are taken in late spring; semiripe cuttings in early summer. Each cutting should be 3 to 4 inches long. Remove the lower leaves, keeping just a few at the tip of the cutting.*

Step 2: Dip the Cutting in Rooting Hormone. *To keep the powder in the storage container fresh, pour out a small amount of powder, use what you need, and throw away the leftover.*

Step 3: Plant the Cutting. *Bury the stem of each cutting in the pre-moistened medium, with just the leafy top section sticking out of the medium. At this stage the cuttings do not need a lot of growing room; you can fit several into one pot. Water well, making sure the soil is saturated.*

Step 4: Keep the Cutting Moist and Warm. *To ensure consistent moisture, cover the pot with a clear plastic bag, The cuttings will root more successfully if you keep the soil mix evenly moist and warm. Look for a place, such as the top of the refrigerator or dryer where the cuttings will remain warm and get plenty of light.*

PROPAGATING WITH HARDWOOD CUTTINGS

*Difficulty Level: **Easy***

The process of taking hardwood cuttings is another way to propagate woody plants. It is quite similar to taking softwood or semiripe cuttings. The difference between the methods is when the cuttings are taken. Hardwood is older; cuttings are taken at the end of the growing season, after lignan has developed in the wood.

Tools and Materials: Pruners or secateurs, rooting hormone, pot, rooting medium (sand, wood shavings, or vermiculite).

Step 1: Make the Cut. *Cut the section at an angle just below a leaf node. Roots develop out of the cut, and the angle provides more surface area for more roots. Make sure there are at least three leaf nodes along the stem of the cutting. Remove all the leaves.*

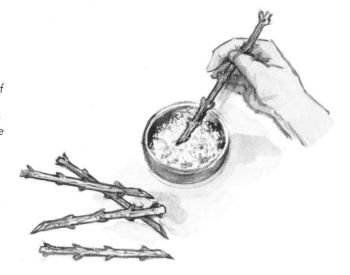

Step 2: Dip the Bottom End in Rooting Hormone. *Rooting hormone powder will boost your rate of success. To remember which is the top end and which is the bottom, cut the bottom at an angle, the top straight across.*

Step 3: Plant the Cuttings. *Several cuttings can fit into one pot. Be sure to put the bottom end (cut at an angle) into the rooting medium. Bury most of the cutting; roots will develop from each growing node.*

Step 4: Check Whether the Cutting Has Grown Roots. *Signs of successful rooting include new leaves sprouting on the stem and resistance if you tug gently on the cutting. Do not disturb the roots by pulling too hard.*

REJUVENATING OLD DECIDUOUS FLOWERING SHRUBS

You can increase the production of blooms and improve the form of shrubs by pruning. The best time to prune flowering shrubs varies with the type of plant. If you don't know when to work on a specific shrub, contact the local Cooperative Extension Service. Most plants respond best to severe pruning in late winter when the plants are primed to begin sending out new growth.

Prune Deciduous Shrubs over Three Years. Some plants, such as red-twig dogwood (*Cornus alba*), can be cut completely down to the ground all at once. However, a safer way to restore deciduous shrubs is to cut one third of the branches down to the ground or the main stem the first year, another third the second year, and the final third the last year. Remove the oldest and least desirable stems first, but also try to remove stems from all sides of the shrub so that you maintain a balanced form. In the second and third years, also remove new growth that is weak or that will spoil the shrub's form and balance.

To reduce the size of an overgrown shrub, cut the oldest stems right down to the ground, and remove all dead branches. Be sure to leave enough stems to provide energy to the plant. No tree or shrub will be able to survive without enough stems to produce chlorophyl. Then trim back the remaining stems to just below the ideal height you have in mind. Once the pruning wounds are healed, establish a maintenance pruning routine to keep the shrub in shape. (See pages 186–87 for information on annual maintenance.)

If shrubs such as flowering quince (*Chaenomeles* species) and shrub roses grow leggy, with branches arching to the ground, cut back the branches from their tips, at the same time thinning out the older, thick, woody ones.

Prune Shrubs Gradually in Colder Regions. In northern climates or for plants you don't want to put at any risk, rejuvenate the shrub by cutting back one-third of the branches at a time, spreading the operation over three years. Choose the longest, most unproductive branches first, and cut them back to their source.

ARBORIZING OVERGROWN SHRUBS

Difficulty Level: Easy

Overgrown shrubs can also be renovated by *arborizing* them, or pruning them to look like trees. This technique is especially effective with single-stemmed shrubs such as camellias and multi-stemmed shrubs with a prominent major stem, such as hollies. To arborize, choose a large and healthy stem as the primary trunk, removing smaller vertical stems and cutting back the lower horizontal branches to the main trunk. These shrubs are especially effective in small gardens where a full-size tree would take up too much space. To cover the newly exposed bare earth, underplant the pruned shrub with a shade-loving ground cover or with shallow-rooted annuals.

Tools and Materials: Pruners, loppers, or pruning saw, depending on the thickness of the lower branches.

Step 1: Prune the Lower Branches. *Start removing branches from the bottom, cutting them back to the main trunk. Step back to check your work after removing a row or two, so you don't cut off too many branches.*

Step 2: Complete the Arborization. *Continue cutting until the plant is the shape you want. Instead of a large shrub, the holly now resembles a small tree. There is now plenty of room to grow shallow-rooted plants underneath that appreciate the shade the holly provides.*

Renovating Broad-Leaved Evergreen Shrubs

RADICAL PRUNING IS RECOMMENDED IN WARM CLIMATES

In warm southern climates, shrubs such as rhododendrons, azaleas, and mountain laurels can be renewed by cutting them back to the ground. Old boxwood, which can live for hundreds of years, also has a good chance of surviving when pruned in this drastic fashion.

❧ *Heavy Feeding Prior to Surgery Lessens Stress.* The plant's chances for survival are improved if you feed it with a heavy dose of cottonseed meal and manure (or a high-nitrogen fertilizer formulated for acid-loving plants) at least a year before the radical surgery. Keep the plants well fed and watered after the surgery.

❧ *Prune in Early Spring for Best Results.* Whether you cut the plant down to the ground or remove the old growth in stages, do the job in late winter or early spring when the plant is bursting to send out new shoots.

RENOVATING FORMAL HEDGES

Some of the best hedging plants include boxwood, holly, hornbeam, privet, and yew because they grow slowly and are long-lived. If you have an overgrown hedge comprising any of these plants, it is well worth your time and trouble to restore it. While the hedge will look odd for several years while the restoration is going on, you'll have an attractive hedge again much sooner than if you start over with young plants.

❧ *Late Winter: Cut Down to the Desired Height.* Begin in late winter by cutting the top back to the height you want. Don't be afraid to cut back to bare branches. Any of the above-mentioned plants will send out new shoots, even from thick bare branches.

❧ *Prune One Side of the Hedge to the Main Stem.* Next, severely prune just one side of the hedge, cutting it back to the main stem or stems. Leave the other side untouched. (See page 195 top right.) Feed the pruned plant with a balanced fertilizer, and top-dress with compost or aged manure that will slowly release additional nutrients into the soil. Severe pruning makes the shrub more susceptible to drought stress. Water the hedge

This neatly trimmed formal boxwood hedge *makes a beautiful frame to the perennials growing inside, and provides a pleasing structure to the garden as a whole. Overgrown boxwood hedges can be brought back into scale with severe pruning.*

deeply if the weather gets dry, and add a thick layer of mulch to help maintain even moisture.

❧ *After One Side has Recovered, Cut the Other Side.* Wait until the pruned side of the hedge is showing vigorous growth before you cut back the other side. You may need to wait two or three years to ensure that the plant is strong enough to take another shock. Once you think the hedge is ready, cut back the second side, following the same procedure as you did for the first.

When the hedge is in shape, prune it so that the sides flare out slightly at the bottom. That way the entire surface will be exposed to light, ensuring a healthier, leafier hedge. When hedges are pruned in a wedge shape with the top wider than the bottom, the upper branches shade the lower portion of the hedge, preventing the foliage from growing properly.

Maintenance Pruning

Set up a pruning guide. *For accurate pruning on a formal hedge, it is helpful to tie string guides that have been set and leveled at the desired final height and width. Be sure to keep the electrical cord away from the blades of the hedge clipper.*

Renewing an Old Hedge

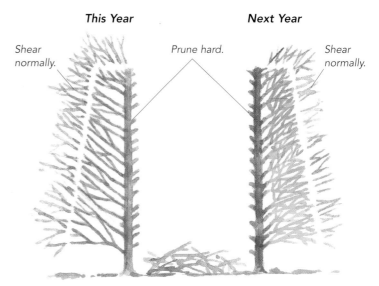

This Year *Next Year*

Shear normally. Prune hard. Shear normally.

Prune one side per year. *To avoid shocking a severely-pruned hedge to death, trim back one side the first year, and wait a year or two until the pruned side has started growing properly again before you cut back the opposite side.*

HOW TO MAINTAIN A HEDGE

*Difficulty Level: **Easy***

Fast-growing shrubs, such as the Euonymus 'Manhattan' shown here, will need pruning three or four times a year. Slower-growing plant materials, such as boxwood or yew, take longer to establish themselves as hedges but subsequently need pruning much less often.

   Tools and Materials: Electric or gas-powered hedge trimmer (or hand trimmer), rake, wheelbarrow.

Step 1: Prune the Sides. *Trim hedge sides slightly wider at the bottom than the top to allow light to reach the entire surface. Use an even, sweeping motion with the power clippers to cut a smooth, level top surface.*

Step 2: Finish Shaping the Hedge. *To achieve a crisp, clean finish on a shaggy hedge and to maintain the desired finished size, don't be afraid to cut back the new growth by several inches—or even a foot or more.*

Thinning Trees with Dense Canopies

A dense tree canopy creates heavy shade for the garden beneath it. Dense canopies are an even more serious problem in brittle trees such as Bradford pear. Branches of these trees are prone to snap off in high winds unless the tree is pruned to create "portholes" that allow the wind to pass through without resistance.

The goal here is to thin the canopy of the overgrown tree to create a beautiful, lacy effect that enhances the form of the tree and shows off its interesting structure.

HOW TO THIN TREE CANOPIES

If you plan to thin small- to medium-size trees yourself, first study the tree to determine which branches you want to keep and which should be removed.

Remove Excess Branches. Take away branches that cross over each other, rub against each other, or grow toward the inside of the tree. Remove any weak stems that sprout along a main branch. Limbs that have deep, narrow crotches tend to be weaker and more likely to break off. Remove them along with any branches that compete with the tree's central leader.

Work from the Inside Out. Start at the bottom of the tree, and work from the inside out, gradually working up the tree. If the tree is still small enough to prune from a small ladder, make a mental note of several

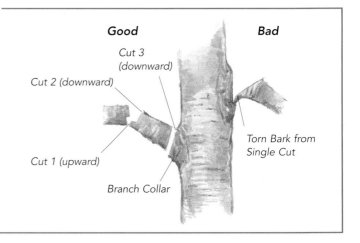

Create portholes to reduce wind resistance. The beautiful Bradford pear has many crossing branches (inset) that are prone to break in heavy winds. Protect such trees by thinning out excess wood and branches, creating portholes to reduce wind resistance.

needed cuts before climbing the ladder. Then descend to plan the next series, or follow advice from the ground by a trusted family member stationed safely away from falling, bouncing limbs.

MAKE A PRUNING CUT IN THREE STAGES

Large tree limbs should be cut in three stages to prevent the heavy branch from tearing loose when it is nearly severed. Make the first cut a few inches away from the joint with the tree trunk, sawing halfway through the branch from underneath. Make the second cut from the top, severing the branch. The final cut should be on the branch side of the ridge or collar that connects the branch to the tree, removing the short remaining stub. If you cut too close to the tree, you'll create a large wound that is more vulnerable to pests and diseases. If you leave a long stub, the dying wood may also harbor damaging pests.

Good   Bad

Cut 3 (downward)

Cut 2 (downward)

Cut 1 (upward)

Torn Bark from Single Cut

Branch Collar

The branches of this white ash could snap off under the weight of the heavy, wet snow. Keep trees pruned, removing weak, brittle branches, and when possible, dislodge heavy layers of snow and ice.

HIRE AN ARBORIST TO PRUNE LARGE TREES

A large tree generally needs to be pruned by professional arborists, who have the proper equipment for getting several stories off the ground to reach the treetop. Research to find a company that has the experience to thin the tree properly. Hire an insured, certified arborist, and be on hand to guide the work from a safe distance. Avoid uninsured "tree removers." Some of these unskilled people may even want to climb with spikes, which are mainly used on trees that will be completely removed. Those long steel spikes pock trees with holes and shatter bark, leaving them vulnerable to pests and diseases.

Get Bids from Several People. Obtain estimates from several arborists, bearing in mind that the cheapest price isn't necessarily the best deal. Low bidders may lack the skill and experience, and can potentially butcher a tree. It can take years for a badly pruned tree to regain good form. Worse yet, it may never fully recover. Ask for references, and call them. Your trees are valuable. You want an arborist who understands the natural form of the tree and knows how to enhance it.

If you have the skills, tools, and safety gear for climbing into larger trees and decide to prune the trees yourself, proceed with caution. Always attach your safety belt to a limb above the intended cut before cutting, and plan cuts so that branches can't swing or bounce back toward you. Always cordon off the fall zone with brightly colored tape, and keep children out.

Transplanting Large Shrubs and Trees

An amazing number of mature trees and shrubs will survive when transplanted, except for plants with deep taproots. If you have an old tree or shrub that's beautiful and healthy but in the wrong place for your renovated design, consider moving it rather than getting rid of it. The best candidates to transplant are those that have been growing in isolation so that their roots are not intertwined with their neighbor's.

You may need professional help and equipment to unearth and move large root balls and top growth. But you should be able to transplant any plant that you and one or two other people together can lift, either with your hands or using levers, dollies, and other tools to balance the weight.

Although most trees and shrubs can be moved at any time, in cold climates the best time is in early spring or in autumn when the weather is cool. In tropical and semitropical climates, opt for spring after the soil has warmed. In either case, at those times of year the plants will be less harmed by the inevitable loss of roots.

PRUNE ROOTS IN ADVANCE OF TRANSPLANTING

It's a good idea to prepare a large plant for moving by pruning its roots several months or even a year before you dig it up. Cut the roots around the tree or shrub with a spade, sinking the spade into the soil the full length of its blade. If possible, make the circle at least ten times the diameter of the plant's trunk at ground level, or dig around the plant at the drip line (the outer edge of the plant's canopy). The plant will grow new feeder roots where you cut the roots with the spade. When you're ready to move it, dig outside the original cut circle so the new feeder roots are included in the root ball.

Prepruning the roots of a plant marked for moving will enhance its chances of survival. However, if you haven't planned ahead and you're eager to move forward on your renovation plans, you can risk moving the plant without prepruning the roots. There is more of a chance that you will lose the plant, but if you dig up most of the rootball and keep the new transplant well watered the first year or two, it should survive the move whether the roots are pruned or not.

HOW TO TRANSPLANT A LARGE SHRUB

A few days before you dig up the plant, water it thoroughly to fortify it against the impending stress. Moist soil also will be easier to dig and will cling to the plant's roots to maintain a firm root ball. Prepare the new planting hole before you unearth the plant. Estimate the size of the root ball so the hole is an adequate size, and then dig the hole as deep as the root ball and twice as wide. Former wisdom suggested digging a deep hole and backfilling with amended soil. However, recent research has found that plants do better in a shallower hole because the backfilled soil often settles, allowing the plant to sink too deep into the ground, thus suffocating it. You may have to adjust the size of the hole once the plant is next to it and you see the actual requirements,

Step 1: Dig Out the Root Ball. *At about the drip line, cut around the root ball with a shovel, prying back as you go to wedge the shovel underneath the plant. Make your way around the shrub, loosening, cutting, and pulling to dislodge it.*

Step 2: Pull Out the Shrub. *Once the root ball is adequately loosened, pull on it to remove the shrub from the ground. (You'll need to work the shovel underneath it to cut the roots.) Sometimes it helps to rock the plant back and forth to further loosen it.*

Step 3: Move the Shrub to Its New Location. *Large shrubs with substantial root balls are heavy. If you have a dolly, balance the plant on that for easy transport. Otherwise, put the plant on a tarpaulin, and get assistance to carry or drag it to its new spot.*

Step 4: Fill the Planting Hole with Water. *You'll ensure a moist environment for the roots if you fill the hole with water before you plant. Wait for the water to disperse before you set the plant in the hole. Clay soil will absorb water more slowly than sandy soil.*

but the sooner you can get the plant back into the ground, the less stressful the operation will be to it.

If the soil around the roots is light so that it crumbles and falls away rather than holding together in a ball, dig a trench around the roots, and then encircle them with chicken wire fastened together at the ends to hold the soil in place. A large root ball will be very heavy. If it's too heavy to lift, drag it onto a sturdy tarpaulin or roll it onto a dolly. Then you and as many helpers as necessary can drag the tree or shrub to its new location.

Tools and Materials: Shovel, gloves, dolly or tarpaulin, source of water.

Step 5: Maneuver the Plant to the Hole. *While waiting for the water to soak in, bring the plant close to the hole. Gauge the size of the hole and root ball to make sure the plant will fit. If necessary, enlarge the hole, or backfill it if it is too deep.*

Step 6: Position the Plant in the Hole. *Set the plant in the hole, making sure it is standing straight and facing the way you prefer. Also make sure that the shrub is level with its former planting depth. In heavy clay soil, set the plant high—an inch or two above the old soil level.*

Step 7: Create a Berm around the Plant. *To ensure that water soaks into the soil and deep into the root ball rather than running off, create a berm or moat around the plant's drip line, using leftover soil dug from the hole. A berm is particularly important where the native soil is clay.*

Step 8: Water Well. *Fill the basin with water, wait for it to soak in, and then water again. During the first year while the transplant is getting established, keep the soil moist. Mulch around the plant to reduce weeds and maintain moisture.*

CHAPTER 10

Choosing and Planting Trees and Shrubs

Like a fine face, a beautiful garden must have good bone structure. The "bones" are the year-round features: paths, steps, hedges, walls, fences, and other permanent elements that provide structure and a sense of unity. The other major components of a garden's bones are trees and shrubs.

In old, established gardens, you may need to remove or rejuvenate overgrown trees and shrubs to reclaim the original structure of the garden. (See Chapter 9, pages 182–99, for information on renovating an older garden.) If you are starting from scratch, you should plan the trees and shrubs that will define the structure of the landscape before you begin thinking of details such as ground covers, perennials, and annuals. Choose trees and shrubs that will help define spaces, provide focal points, or serve as a background foil to other plantings.

HIGHLIGHT PLANTS WITH UNUSUAL SHAPES

Don't overlook the importance of key plants with a bold or unusual shape. A tree or shrub that naturally grows in a striking form, such as the pagoda dogwood (*Cornus alternifolia*), or a spectacular specimen tree, such as a monumental chestnut or beech tree, makes a fascinating focal point, giving structure and visual direction to the overall design. If your property already has a significant, established tree, try to design your landscape to emphasize that asset. A pragmatic thinker may believe it's a waste of time and money to plant a tree that won't come into its full beauty until he or she is long gone. While understandable, that attitude is unfortunate because American gardens are not being planted with the spectacular but slow-growing trees that take years to mature.

The traditionally clipped boxwood hedges form the bones of this classically formal landscape. The low hedge serves as an evergreen focal point of the garden but does not obscure the view of the manicured lawn beyond.

The distinctive shape of the weeping 'Higan' cherry makes it a striking specimen tree. It is equally ornamental in the spring as shown here or in the winter when the trunk and branches take on a sculptural quality.

Selecting Trees and Shrubs

Trees and shrubs have the potential to be the greatest asset in your garden, or the greatest liability if you do not choose the right ones. Spend the time to determine which plants will do well in your climate, including the specific soil, water, and light conditions on your property. Most climate zone maps indicate a plant's tolerance to cold. The American Horticultural Society recently introduced a map and rating system that records heat tolerance as well. (See the Introduction, page 15, for the American Horticultural Society Plant Heat-Zone Map.) If you live in a region with hot, humid summers, make sure the trees you select are able to endure the extreme heat and humidity.

DETERMINE THE PLANT'S PURPOSE

If you want to plant a tree or shrub as a focal point in the center of a lawn, you can choose a large spreading specimen that will become ever more spectacular as it grows. But if you want to plant a tree along a driveway or patio, don't choose one with invasive roots. For example, weeping willow roots search insistently for water, even boring through pipes, and can heave up a concrete walkway or crack a house foundation. For a patio tree, you want one that will provide shade as well as visual interest such as pretty flowers, fruit, foliage, and/or bark. Stay away from messy trees that shed regularly or drop sticky fruit or sap, creating the need for frequent cleanup on paved surfaces.

▼ *This hedge adds height and encloses the path* in this country landscape. The unusual choice of clipped Fagus (beech) adds personality and a bold use of color to this very individual garden.

Focal Point or Boundary Marker. Plant an avenue of trees to create a vista in your garden. Line your driveway with flowering trees such as crab apples for a spectacular "welcome home" in spring when the blossoms are open and a cool, shady drive in the summer. Add interest to an expanse of lawn with a grove of trees. Place a bench among the trees, and you'll have a special shaded seat.

Trees and shrubs are excellent for providing mass in your landscape. Include shrubs and even small trees in flower borders to provide interest in winter and to anchor the design. Border a bed with a low-growing shrub such as dwarf boxwood or *Santolina* to frame and give definition to the plantings. Line a path with scented shrubs such lavender or plant a bulky shrub at the curve of a winding path to obscure the view around a corner.

Screen a View, and Lower Heating Costs. Trees can be useful to screen an unattractive view, lower noise levels, cut the wind, and provide shade. A deciduous tree planted near the house, especially on the south side, can save heating and cooling costs. Likewise, a row of trees planted in the path of prevailing winds can deflect the icy gusts, thus helping to cut down on heating costs.

▲ *The focal point of this path* is the bright orange Japanese maple tree in the distance. Notice how the yellow flowering tree frames the path and points the way to the exclamation point in the distance.

▶ *These trees screen the view* of the house beyond. Although the shrubs in the foreground are not fully grown, they will grow into a continuous line and provide an understory for the larger trees.

Plants for Seasonal Interest

Plant trees and shrubs for seasonal interest such as spectacular autumn color, spring or summer flowers, or a compelling silhouette in winter. Choose a shrub for its fragrant flowers or foliage. Place a sweet smelling shrub under a window, or beside a patio or outdoor seating area so you can enjoy the scent. Some trees, such as the crabapple or dogwood, shine in more than one season. Look for these plants to take the spotlight throughout the year.

Viburnum is another delightful plant that gives good value for the space it uses. This is a large plant family with species such as V. lentago that is hardy down to Zone 2, to more tender specimen that need Zone 8 or warmer. Among the excellent choices for the home garden is the doublefile viburnun (*V. plicatum f. tomentosum*). In spring it is covered in white, lacecap-like flowers. The crinkled leaves (the Latin name *plicatum* refers to the leaf's pleated look) are a joy throughout the summer, and then in autumn bright red fruit lights up the shrub.

◀ *The fall colors* of Cornus stolonifera (red 'Ozier' dogwood). The clusters of white berries stand out crisply against the orange and yellow foliage.

For tight spaces, consider *Viburnum dilatatum* 'Catskill', a compact shrub that takes at least 15 years to reach a height of 5 feet with an 8-foot spread. The dark-green foliage takes on shades of red and yellow in fall. Abundant dark red fruit persists until midwinter. Viburnum 'Conoy' grows about as big as 'Catskill.' Its glossy, evergreen foliage is the perfect backdrop to the creamy white flowers in the spring and the brilliant red berries in autumn.

Winter Interest in the Garden

Winter is the best season to evaluate your landscape. In spring and summer, lush foliage and lavish floral displays can disguise many design problems. But once the foliage falls and the flowers fade, the true structure of the garden is clearly visible.

Evergreen trees are an obvious choice for maintaining color and interest in the fall and winter garden. The Colorado blue spruce (*Picea pungens* 'Glauca') is a wonderful choice both for its almost-perfect Christmas tree form and its silvery blue color. The golden yellow foliage of *Chamaecyparis lawsoniana* 'Lutea', brings a sense of sunshine into even the drabbest winter day. Evergreen hedges are real assets in the winter garden.

Deciduous Trees with Strong Silhouettes. Good possibilities include Japanese maple (*Acer palmatum*), with its marvelous twisting branches, and Harry Lauder's walking stick (*Corylus avellana* 'Contorta'). Another twisted wonder is the willow *Salix matsudana* 'Tortuosa'.

Berry-Bearing Plants. Berry-bearing shrubs and trees are a delight in a winter landscape. Hollies, *Nandina*, *Cotoneaster*, and *Pyracantha* all hold their berries into winter. Also look for *Viburnum dilatatum* 'Erie'. In addition to their visual appeal, berry-laden trees and shrubs attract birds.

Colorful Bark. Many deciduous trees and shrubs have colorful bark that stands out dramatically in a winter landscape. One excellent choice for beautiful bark is the red twig dogwood (*Cornus alba*), a small, multi-stemmed shrub with striking red twigs. Another interesting dogwood member is the golden-twig dogwood (*Cornus stolonifera* 'Flaviramea'), which has bright yellow winter shoots.

Birch trees are lovely in the winter landscape. There is a choice of bark colors from dark gray to silvery gold to the classic white. Some varieties of crape myrtle (*Lagerstroemia indica*) have beautiful bark streaked with green, gold, and pink. Moosewood or striped maple (*Acer pensylvanicum*) has green- and white-striped bark; *A. pensylvanicum* 'Erythrocladum' has coral red bark striped with silvery white.

Peeling Bark. Trees with peeling bark are another interesting phenomenon. Look for the paperbark maple (*A. griseum*), which peels off thin flakes of orange brown bark, and Heritage river birch (*Betula nigra* 'Heritage'), which exfoliates at an early age and peels off beautiful flakes of salmon white and orange brown-bark.

Chamaecyparis 'Aurea nana' (Japanese false cypress), center

Nandina (heavenly bamboo)

Bark of *Betula papyrifera* (birch)

Noteworthy Trees and Shrubs for the Landscape

Too often a young tree or shrub is planted close to a building or fence with no allowance made for its growth over time. The ultimate size of a tree depends on many variables, including the quality of the soil, average temperatures, and the potential of each individual specimen. Some of the plants listed here may technically be shrubs, but because of their mature height, they are listed as trees.

SMALL TREES (UP TO 30 FEET TALL)

Acer japonicum (Japanese maple), Zones 6–9
   A. tataricum ssp. *ginnala* (Amur maple), Zones 3–7
Amelanchier laevis (Allegheny serviceberry), Zones 4–9
Arbutus unedo (strawberry tree), Zones 7–9
Cercis canadensis (eastern redbud), Zones 4–9
Chionanthus retusus (Chinese fringe tree), Zones 6–8
Cornus florida (flowering dogwood), Zones 5–9
Franklinia alatamaha (Franklin tree), Zones 5–8 or 9
Magnolia x soulangiana (saucer magnolia), Zones 5–9
Magnolia stellata (star magnolia), Zones 4–8
Malus sp. (flowering crab apple), zones vary with species
Oxydendrum arboreum (sourwood), Zones 5–9
Prunus x blireana (flowering plum), Zones 5–8
Styrax japonicum (Japanese snowbell), Zones 5–9

MEDIUM TO LARGE TREES (30 FEET AND TALLER)

Acer rubrum (red maple), Zones 3–9
Acer saccharinum (silver maple), Zones 3–9
Albizia julibrissin (silk tree or mimosa), Zones 6–10
Cercidiphyllum japonicum (Katsura tree), Zones 4–8
Fraxinus pennsylvanica (green ash), Zones 3–9
Ginkgo biloba (ginkgo, maidenhair tree), Zones 4–9
Gleditsia triacanthos (honey locust), Zones 4–9
Gymnocladus dioica (Kentucky coffee tree), Zones 4–9
Halesia tetraptera (Carolina silver bell), Zones 5–9
Koelreuteria paniculata (varnish tree), Zones 5–9
Lagerstroemia indica (crape myrtle), Zones 7–9
Nyssa sylvatica (sour gum), Zones 4–9
Parrotia persica (Persian ironwood), Zones 5–8
Sophora japonica (pagoda tree), Zones 4–9
Stewartia pseudocamellia, Zones 5–8
Tilia cordata (littleleaf linden), Zones 4–7
Zelkova serrata (Japanese zelkova), Zones 5–9

Malus sylvestris (flowering crab apple)

Acer japonicum (Japanese maple)

Lagerstroemia indica (crape myrtle) with Spanish moss

SHRUBS WITH ATTRACTIVE FLOWERS

Camellia japonica, and *C. sasanqua*, Zones 7–10
Chaenomeles (flowering quince), Zones 5–9
Cytisus x praecox (Warminster broom), Zones 7–9
Daphne cneorum (garland flower), Zones 4–9
Deutzia gracilis, Zones 4–9
Hamamelis x intermedia (witch hazel), Zones 5–9
Hydrangea macrophylla, Zones 6–10
Hypericum sp. (St.-John's-wort), zones vary with species
Kalmia latifolia (mountain laurel), Zones 4–9
Kerria japonica (Japanese rose or kerria), Zones 4–9
Lagerstroemia indica (crape myrtle), Zones 7–9
Philadelphus species and cultivars (sweet mock orange), Zones 4–8
Pieris japonica (Japanese andromeda), Zones 6–8
Potentilla fruticosa (shrubby cinquefoil), Zones 2–7
Prunus triloba (flowering almond), Zones 3–8
Spiraea japonica (Japanese spirea), Zones 4–8
Viburnum species (viburnum), zones vary with species
Weigela florida (weigela), Zones 5–9

SHRUBS WITH ATTRACTIVE BERRIES

Berberis darwinii, Zones 8–10
Berberis wilsoniae (Wilson barberry), Zones 7–10
Callicarpa americana (beautyberry), Zones 7–10
Callicarpa bodinieri (beautyberry), Zones 6–8, good to Zone 10 in West
Cotoneaster lucidus (hedge cotoneaster), Zones 4–7
Cotoneaster salicifolius (willowleaf cotoneaster), Zones 6–8 in the East; 6–10 in the West.
Euonymus alata (burning bush), Zones 4–9
Ilex species (holly), zones vary with species
Mahonia aquifolium (Oregon grape), Zones 5–9
Mahonia bealei, Zones 7–9
Nandina domestica (heavenly bamboo), Zones 7–10
Photinia serratifolia (Chinese photinia), Zones 7–9 in the East; 7–10 in the West
Pyracantha coccinea (scarlet firethorn), Zones 6–9
Rhus typhina (staghorn sumac), Zones 4–8
Viburnum species (viburnum), zones vary with species

Chaenomeles (flowering quince)

Hypericum in summer

Cotoneaster lacteus (cotoneaster) in fall

Pyracantha (firethorn) in winter

▲ *The compact spirea shrub* *makes an effective hedge to separate two properties. It attractively marks the boundary without walling in the house.*

◄ *Slow-growing boxwood* (Buxus) *interplanted with columnar yew* (Taxus) *is a classic combination for a long-lived, low-maintenance hedge.*

Hedges

Hedges are invaluable in the landscape to screen unwanted views or high winds, to define garden spaces, to frame vistas, and to serve as a backdrop to borders or decorative elements such as sculpture. Traditionally we think of a hedge as a neatly pruned row of one species of plant. While that approach creates a tidy, uniform look that is ideal for formal settings, there is no rule against combining different shrubs with a variety of leaf colors and textures to create a hedge with a tapestry effect. You can either shear the plants for a tailored look or allow the shrubs to billow in their natural form for a soft, informal backdrop.

SLOW-GROWING PLANTS LIVE LONGER

The natural inclination when choosing a tree or shrub for a hedge is to choose a plant that will grow as fast as possible. While the quick results are gratifying, the downside is that faster growing plants tend to be shorter-lived. Slow-growing yew and boxwood, which can survive for hundreds of years, are the traditional shrubs used for hedges because they live so long. For this reason, boxwoods need only occasional pruning to

A mixed-planting hedge is a garden in itself. Some of the shrubs shown here include roses, forsythia, andromeda, peony, and yew.

keep them within bounds. As you consider all the wonderful plants available for creating hedges, weigh the pros and cons of the faster-growing hedging plants versus slower-growing plants with greater longevity.

Conifers for Hedges

With regular pruning, some of these plants can be kept the size of medium to large shrubs.

Cephalotaxus fortunei (Chinese plum yew), Zones 7–9, slow growing

Chamaecyparis lawsoniana (Lawson false cypress or Port Orford cedar), Zones 5–9, medium growth rate

C. x Cupressocyparis leylandii (Leyland cypress), Zones 6–10, very fast growing

Cupressus macrocarpa (Monterey cypress), Zones 7–9, growth rate varies with cultivars

Juniperus chinensis (Chinese juniper), Zones 4–10, slow to medium growth rate

Juniperus scopulorum (Rocky Mountain juniper), Zones 4–10, slow-growing

Podocarpus macrophylla (southern yew), Zones 7–10, slow growing

Pseudotsuga menziesii (Douglas fir), Zones 4–7, medium growth rate

Taxus baccata (English yew), Zones 5–8 in the East; 5–10 in the West, slow growing

Thuja plicata (western red cedar), Zones 6–7, growth varies with cultivars

Tsuga canadensis (Canada hemlock), Zones 4–7, medium growth rate

Chamaecyparis (false cedar), center

Podocarpus macrophyllus (Southern yew)

HEDGEROWS: UNDERUSED

Another option for a living wall that is too seldom exercised in American gardens is a hedgerow. These are the mixed plantings of trees and shrubs that line the country roads and divide the fields in rural England and parts of Europe. In addition to being a fascinating combination of plants, hedgerows are wonderful habitats for a variety of birds, small animals, and other wildlife; they provide food, shelter, and protected travel routes.

There are two approaches to planting a hedgerow. The first is to select the trees, shrubs, and vines you want and plant them in a random mixture. Space them half the distance recommended by the supplier. Once the plants have reached the height and width you want, shear them periodically to maintain the shape. Don't be shy about cutting back the trees. They will adapt and grow appropriately for a hedge.

PLANTING A HEDGE OR HEDGEROW

Planting a hedge or hedgerow takes a little more care than simply putting in one or two plants at random because you want the plants to follow the line of the hedge and to be spaced properly.

To work out the number of plants you need, first find out the expected mature width of the shrub. In theory you should then simply divide the length of the hedge by the projected width of each plant to find out how many plants to buy. However, you can't count on a plant ever growing to its optimal size. If soil, light, or moisture conditions are not ideal, the shrub may take years to fulfill its potential—or it may never reach it. Because you definitely want the plants to touch and even overlap to make an unbroken hedge, reduce the average expected width of each plant by about one third, and then do the division. For example, Japanese holly (*Ilex crenata*) is listed as having a spread of 10 feet at maturity. Figure on planting a maximum of 7 feet apart—and closer if you want a fully closed-in hedge more quickly. Divide the length of the hedge by 7 to get the number of plants needed. If your holly hedge will be 100 feet long, then you would need 14 or 15 plants. Because holly is such a slow growing plant, you might want to add another 3 to 5 plants to shorten the gaps. In that case, plant 20 hollies 5 feet apart. Commercial landscapers typically plant shrubs much closer together than necessary to get a filled-in hedge more quickly. As a homeowner, you probably want to compromise between using a minimum number of plants and jamming them in tightly for an instant effect.

Plow-and-Perch Method: Leave Planting to the Birds.

The second technique is rather fun because it leaves a lot to chance and nature. Called the *plow-and-perch* method, you create conditions that encourage the birds to "plant" the hedgerow for you. In summer or early autumn, till the line where you want your hedgerow to grow, making the soil receptive to seeds. Rent or borrow a large, heavy-duty rototiller that can cut through sod with ease. Mount posts at 15 foot intervals along the line, and attach a double row of strong string or wire between the posts. Seed- and fruit-eating birds will perch along the line, distributing plant seeds with their droppings. There are several advantages to the plow-perch method of planting a hedgerow:

🐦 *Less work.* It requires less trouble and less expense than seeking out and purchasing plants suitable for a hedgerow.

Mature lilacs create a windscreen *between a field and the road. When allowed to grow without pruning, these shrubs eventually reach the height of small trees.*

A hedgerow-like planting of lavender, roses, firethorn, and barberry has the casual appearance of something the birds might have seeded with some help from the wind.

🐦 *Birds will do the job.* The seeds sown are of plants definitely favored by local birds.

🐦 *Plants will thrive in local conditions.* The plants are well suited to the area where they will be growing.

🐦 *Transplant shock eliminated.* These seed-grown species should mature as quickly as those planted from rootstocks because they won't undergo transplant shock.

How to Plant a Hedge

Difficulty Level: Easy

First mark out the line where you want the hedge. If you are making a curved hedge, use a hose to mark out the line you want, and leave it in place until you are ready to dig. Once you have your plants, position them along the line, making the spaces between each as even as possible. Remember to allow growing space for the plants at each end; set these half the spacing distance in from the desired end of your hedge. Follow the appropriate directions for bare-root, balled-and-burlapped, or container-grown plants. (See Chapter 10, pages 211–213.) Mulch along the row with an organic material such as straw, shredded bark, or shredded leaves. The mulch should be 4 to 6 inches deep to be the most effective in minimizing evaporation and smothering weeds.

Tools and Materials: Hose, string, tape measure, stakes, shovel, tarp, plants, mulch, water.

Step 1: Mark the Hedge Line. *Run string between stakes along the hedge line. Either dig a trench beneath the string or position the plants precisely using a tape measure. Dig a hole for each plant, putting the soil on a tarp.*

Step 2: Plant Each Shrub. *Break up the root ball with your fingers. Position the plant straight in the hole, and backfill until the crown of the plant is at the same depth as it was growing in the pot.*

Step 3: Water and Mulch. *Water each plant thoroughly as you dig it in. Allow the water to disperse in the hole, and water again. Apply an organic mulch around each plant and between plants along the row.*

Step 4: Finish the Planting. *Check again that the plants are in a straight line. Dig new holes if necessary, and replant any shrubs that are out of line. Pull up the stakes and string, and fold up the tarp.*

Buying Healthy Stock

Once you've decided on the trees or shrubs that will best suit your purpose in the garden, it's time to make the purchase. Contrary to what instinct may tell you, the largest plant is not necessarily the best. The larger the specimen, the more transplant shock it will experience. In the case of big trees and shrubs, it can take two or three years from the time of planting before the plant will begin to grow vigorously. A small tree or shrub will usually adapt in one season. The result is that in just a few years, a smaller, less expensive tree will catch up in size to a larger one. Save money by purchasing small plants, and give yourself the pleasure of watching your garden grow.

Unless you want to nurse a sick plant back to health, pass by any plant that isn't thriving. Trees and shrubs are major investments, so it is worth paying a little extra to get top-quality plants. Shop only from the most reputable nurseries and mail-order catalogs, and check for a guarantee.

Stay Away from Injured Bark. Inspect the bark of trees for signs of injury or mistreatment. A strong tree should be able to stand on its own without staking. If you see sunburn damage—indicated by split, flattened, or unusually dull-colored bark—find a different tree. Also look for signs of pests and diseases. In addition to getting a weakened plant, you risk introducing the problem into your own garden.

EXAMINE PLANTS CAREFULLY

Before you purchase a woody plant, take the time to carefully inspect the condition of its root system or rootball. Container and balled-and-burlapped plants should show evidence of regular watering. Bare-root plants should be kept damp. If you are considering a container-grown plant, slide the plant out of its pot. Look for symmetrical roots that are white and plump, not dried out. Cut away the twine, basket wire, and burlap on balled-and-burlapped plants after placing the plant in the hole.

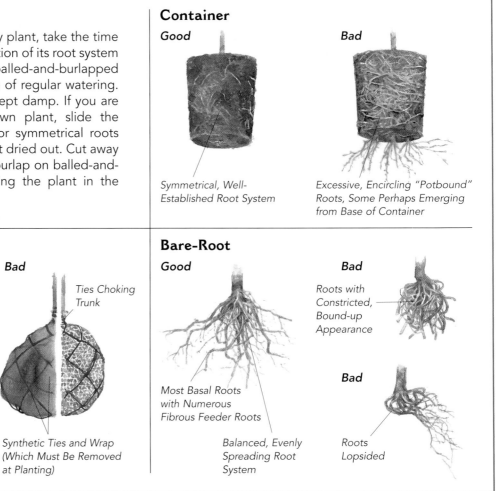

Container

Good

Bad

Symmetrical, Well-Established Root System

Excessive, Encircling "Potbound" Roots, Some Perhaps Emerging from Base of Container

Balled-and Burlapped

Good

Bad

Ties and Burlap of Natural Material

Ties Not Choking Trunk

Ties Choking Trunk

Heavy-Duty Metal Cage (Which Should Not Be So Tight that It Cuts into Rootball)

Synthetic Ties and Wrap (Which Must Be Removed at Planting)

Bare-Root

Good

Bad

Bad

Roots with Constricted, Bound-up Appearance

Most Basal Roots with Numerous Fibrous Feeder Roots

Balanced, Evenly Spreading Root System

Roots Lopsided

Planting Trees and Shrubs

The rules for planting trees and shrubs have changed. Today, instead of recommending a planting hole twice the width and depth of the rootball, experts suggest digging a hole just big enough to hold the plant. That way the soil won't settle.

Evidence suggests that trees and shrubs grow better if they are planted directly into the native soil rather than into amended soil. Ultimately you want the tree's roots to extend well beyond the original hole. If the soil in the hole is much richer than the surrounding native soil, the roots will avoid growing beyond that luxurious environment. The result is that they become rootbound in their own hole. These facts make it all the more important to choose trees and shrubs that are suited to the native soil. You'll experience nothing but frustration if you select a tree or shrub that prefers sandy soil and plant it in clay, or plant a shrub that needs acidic soil (a low pH) in alkaline soil. If your soil is heavy, plant trees and shrubs about 2 inches above the level it grew in the nursery field. Look for the soil-line stain on the trunk for a guide.

PRUNING AT PLANTING TIME

The conventional wisdom used to dictate pruning back trees at planting time to create a balance between roots and foliage. More recent evidence shows that the extra foliage produces hormones that encourage root regeneration. If there are any branches that are broken, remove them; leave the rest alone.

PLANTING BARE-ROOT STOCK

Difficulty Level: Easy

Many deciduous trees and shrubs are available in early spring as bare-root stock. This is an economical way to buy plants because they are lighter and less bulky for nurseries to ship. If you don't have time to plant them in their proper place, plant them temporarily in a shady, wind-protected location with the trunk tilted on a sharp diagonal to discourage rooting. (This technique is called *heeling in*.) Bare-root trees and shrubs are still dormant. Until they start sprouting, water only if the soil becomes dry. Once the active growing season begins, water as you would any new plant. (See page 215 for information on watering.)

Tools and Materials: Shovel, tarp to pile the soil on, ruler, water source, plant, mulch.

Crown 2" above Ground Level

Step 1: Check the Depth. *Place the roots on a cone of undisturbed soil. Lay a shovel across the hole, and make sure the crown is 2 inches above ground level.*

Step 2: Fill the Hole. *After removing any broken roots, use your hands to pack soil in and around the roots, firming the soil as you go to eliminate air pockets.*

Step 3: Finish Planting. *When the hole is half full of soil, water well. After the water seeps down, add the remaining soil and create a moat. Tamp the soil down with your foot. Apply several inches of mulch around the tree or shrub.*

PLANTING BALLED-AND-BURLAPPED STOCK

*Difficulty Level: **Easy***

Trees that are grown at the nursery are often balled and burlapped after they are dug from the ground. This means that the roots are enclosed in a ball of original soil and the ball is wrapped in burlap and tied together.

Like any newly planted tree or shrub, balled-and-burlapped plants need extra care their first year or so. Be especially careful with watering. Many balled-and-burlapped plants are field-grown in heavy clay soil, which absorbs water slowly. If your native soil is lighter, it will take in water much more quickly. When you water, make sure the rootball is getting properly saturated. If in doubt about whether you have watered enough, gently insert a dry wooden stick, such as a paint stirrer, into the soil. Pull it out after an hour or so. If the soil is moist enough, the stick will have absorbed the moisture and will have become slightly darker.

Tools and Materials: Shovel, hose, tarp, scissors (or wire clippers if the rootball is contained in a cage).

Step 1: Dig the Hole. *Remove enough soil to make a hole that is about the same depth as the rootball and twice as wide. Put the soil on the tarp. The bottom of the hole should be covered with firm, undisturbed soil.*

Step 2: Check the Hole. *Hold the plant at the base of the trunk, and place it in the hole to check the depth, making sure the crown is slightly above ground level. Add water until it pools in the bottom of the hole.*

Step 3: Remove the Burlap. *Untie the wrapping, or cut the cage off, and remove the burlap from the plant. Fill the hole with soil from the tarp, and tamp it down with your foot to eliminate air holes and stabilize the plant.*

Step 4: Water and Mulch. *Build a shallow moat around the trunk. Fill the moat with water, and let it dissipate. Put several inches of mulch around the trunk, but do not pack the mulch right up against the trunk.*

PLANTING CONTAINER-GROWN STOCK

*Difficulty Level: **Easy***

To get the plant off to a good start, loosen up its roots when you take it out of the container. Untangle any roots that are growing in circles around the bottom of the pot. Dig the planting hole to accommodate the roots stretched out to their full length. (You can dig special trenches to accommodate one or two extra long roots.) Place the soil from the hole on a tarp. Don't be shy about pruning, tearing, and cutting the roots. This seemingly rough handling will stimulate the plant to grow important new feeder roots.

Tools and Materials: Knife, sharp scissors, shovel, bucket of water or hose, tarp.

Step 1: Remove the Plant. *Water the plant; then lay the pot on its side and slide the plant out. If the plant doesn't come out easily, tap the sides of the container or cut open the pot.*

Note: This potbound plant needs emergency surgery. The goal is to break up the rootball as shown in the next photo.

Step 2: Break Up the Rootball. *Make several vertical cuts deep into the soil mass, and firmly tease the roots outward by hand. Thick, heavily tangled roots require more and deeper cuts.*

Step 3: Check the Depth. *Lay a shovel across the hole. With the roots resting on undisturbed soil, the crown should be 2 inches above ground level. If necessary, build up the soil under the root mass.*

Step 4: Plant the Shrub. *Return half of the soil on the tarp to the hole, and gently tamp it down with your foot to stabilize the plant and eliminate air holes in the soil.*

Step 5: Water. *Pour enough water into the half-filled hole so that it pools. Wait for the water to dissipate; then fill the hole with the remainder of the soil.*

Step 6: Create a Moat. *Using the shovel, build a shallow, moat-like depression around the trunk. Add more water, and let that settle. Note that the trunk's crown remains above ground level.*

STAKING

It is best not to stake a young tree. However, young trees whose tops are large in proportion to their root-balls may need extra support until the root system develops. Trees that have been previously grown with stakes in nursery fields also may need extra support until they are established.

There are lots of materials available for tying trees, including elastic webbing and stiff wire covered with pieces of old garden hose. Whichever you use, make sure it contacts the tree with a broad surface to minimize rubbing. Wrap the tie around the tree trunk so that it forms a loose loop, and attach it firmly to the stake. Wrap a second tie around the trunk, and attach it to the second stake. Tie the tree loosely to avoid girdling as the trunk grows and to allow it some movement between the two stakes.

You should be able to unstake a tree at the end of the first growing season. Untie deciduous trees after their leaves have fallen to see whether they can stand on their own. Wait until just before new growth begins in spring to unstake evergreen trees. If a tree still needs support, restake it and try again after the second growing season.

Very large trees may need anchoring until the roots grow into the parent soil. You can create a tripod support by attaching three guy wires that radiate out at approximately equal distance from the tree. Guys with springs for flexibility speed the ability of the tree to stand alone. The springs should have stops to give positive support in strong winds but provide flexibility in gentler winds.

HOW TO STAKE YOUNG TREES

Plan to make the stakes as short as possible. Otherwise, when it sways in the wind, the tree trunk may be damaged by rubbing against the edges of the top of the stakes. If you are just anchoring the roots in place, 36-inch stakes will suffice. Drive stakes into the ground about 18 inches deep. To find the proper height for stakes used to support tall, weak trunks, hold the trunk in one hand, pull the canopy gently so that the trunk is bent, and then release it. The point where the trunk returns to upright when the top is released is where it should be tied. Always use at least two stakes per tree. Be sure to position the stakes just outside the rootball; you won't damage the roots, and the firm soil will give better support.

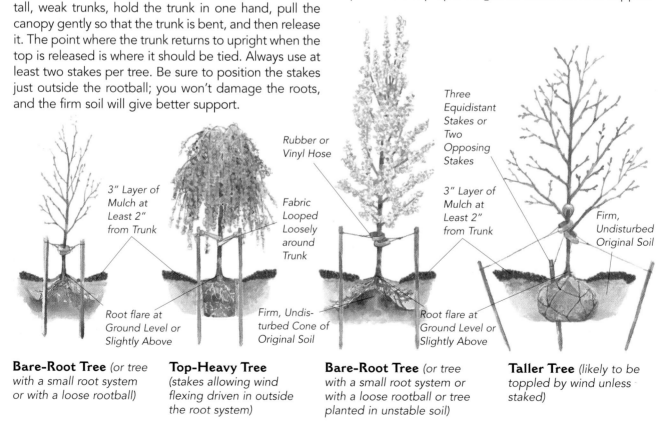

3" Layer of Mulch at Least 2" from Trunk

Rubber or Vinyl Hose

Fabric Looped Loosely around Trunk

Three Equidistant Stakes or Two Opposing Stakes

3" Layer of Mulch at Least 2" from Trunk

Firm, Undisturbed Original Soil

Root flare at Ground Level or Slightly Above

Firm, Undisturbed Cone of Original Soil

Root flare at Ground Level or Slightly Above

Bare-Root Tree (or tree with a small root system or with a loose rootball)

Top-Heavy Tree (stakes allowing wind flexing driven in outside the root system)

Bare-Root Tree (or tree with a small root system or with a loose rootball or tree planted in unstable soil)

Taller Tree (likely to be toppled by wind unless staked)

Caring for Newly Planted Trees and Shrubs

Trees and shrubs require little care once they are established. However, a bit of extra care while they are young will help them grow strong.

WATERING

Newly planted trees and shrubs need to be watered more frequently than established plants. How often plants should be watered and for how long will depend on many factors, including the water requirements of the specific plant, local rainfall, local temperatures, and the type of soil. To check whether the soil is dry, burrow an inch or two into the soil with your finger. If the soil feels dry, it's time to water. It won't take long, however, for you to get a sense of how frequently new trees and shrubs need watering based on the specific conditions in your garden.

If your soil is sandy, you'll need to water more often but for a shorter time. Clay soil remains moist much longer than sandy soil, but the water is prone to run off before it soaks in. If you are watering plants in heavy soil, let the hose run slowly for a longer time.

Shallow watering is damaging to trees and shrubs, encouraging them to grow shallow roots. Water deeply to stimulate growth of deep roots, which increase a plant's ability to absorb nutrients and tolerate dry spells. To ensure that the water goes deep into the ground, build a berm about 6 inches high around the drip line (the farthest reach of branches) of the tree or shrub to create a basin for the plant. When you water, simply fill the basin.

MULCHING

Mulch newly planted trees and shrubs to slow the growth of weeds, hold in soil moisture, and keep the roots cool. Organic materials, such as dried grass clippings, straw, shredded leaves, cocoa bean hulls, and shredded bark, improve the soil while they keep weeds under control. If you mulch with fresh grass clippings, spread the grass in thin layers and gradually top up to the recommended 4 to 6 inches as each new layer of grass dries out. Otherwise you'll end up with a slimy mess of rotted grass. Pile organic mulch 4 to 6 inches deep and 4 to 6 inches away from the trunk.

FERTILIZING

Young plants benefit from a nutritional boost. Your best option is to topdress yearly with compost or aged manure. In addition to providing a slow, constant source of many nutrients, compost and aged manure improve the soil's structure. If you are using commercially prepared chemical fertilizers, the best time to feed is in the spring and early fall. Follow the directions on the package for the amount to give each plant.

PLANTS THRIVE WITH PROPER CARE

Trees and shrubs form the backbone of your landscape, as mentioned at the beginning of this chapter. If you've chosen the plants wisely and give them extra care early on, they will reward you with nearly maintenance-free lives. While it is not impossible to move established trees and shrubs, it is not as easy to move a tree as it is to rearrange your perennial border. So take the time now to prepare the site, buy healthy stock, water, and fertilize to get your new plants well established. Years from now, when you are enjoying the stately presence of a mature tree or shrub in your landscape, you will be glad you gave the plant the extra attention it needed when it was new.

Inorganic mulches (counterclockwise from upper left) include gray granite (A), yellow beach pebbles (B), crushed red brick (C), crushed marble (D), light brown lava (E), red lava (F), and "jade" beach stones (G). The organic mulches include aged hardwood chips (H), fresh hardwood chips (I), red-dyed shredded cedar (J), shredded cedar (K), western pine-bark nuggets (L), shredded pine bark (M), shredded hemlock (N), pine needles (O), and shredded cypress (P).

CHAPTER 11

Lawns, Ground Covers, and Ornamental Grasses

Lawns and ground covers set the stage for the garden. Sweeping oceans of lawn give a sense of space to a property. Ground covers add a lush presence and a sense of depth and richness. Within the wide range of plants suitable for ground covers, many can adapt to difficult growing situations, such as dry shade, while providing a pleasing alternative to bare ground. Ornamental grasses are another diverse family of plants that can perform a host of landscape functions. There are tiny grasses ideal for bordering a pathway or bed, midsize ones to enhance a perennial border, and large varieties that work well as dramatic specimens.

This chapter is full of design ideas to get the most out of lawns, ground covers, and ornamental grasses in your garden. In addition, you'll find valuable information for caring for the plants and preventing pests and diseases. With care and planning, your garden floor can be an outstanding feature, laying the foundation for the rest of the landscape.

A healthy, well-manicured lawn is a pleasure to behold. While island beds and trees growing in the lawn make the job of mowing more time-consuming, they break the horizontal monotony of extensive grass.

Lawns

In many home landscapes, the lawn is there by default to cover bare ground rather than to provide an accent as a deliberately designed landscape feature. To really make the most of your lawn, put some thought into its design so that it becomes an emerald jewel in your garden. You might, for example, surround a small lawn with beds of scented flowers and shrubs to create an intimate, fragrant spot. You can use a lawn to provide horizontal relief in a garden with lots of vertical elements, or as a link between different parts of the garden. When you are

planning your landscape, think of the role you want the lawn to play in the overall look of the garden, and consider how your family will use it.

CHOOSING THE RIGHT GRASS
The ideal lawn grass is fine-textured and a deep, rich green. It should grow in a dense mat to keep out weeds. It should also send its roots deep into the soil to grow vigorously and to withstand drought. However, there is no one all-purpose grass that does well throughout the

Low-maintenance ornamental grasses are a good solution for steep slopes that are hard to care for. Here the tall pampas grass plumes glow in the evening sun while shorter grasses fill in the spaces in front.

A stunning ground cover, the brightly-colored ice plant makes an attractive carpet of color. Both heat and drought-tolerant, a ground cover of ice plant is an easy-care option in the garden.

country and meets all different needs. You should research the best lawn grasses for your area just as you would study which trees, shrubs, and perennials are the best to plant.

Cool- and Warm-Season Grasses. There are more than 40 different kinds of grass for home gardens. They are divided into two main categories: cool-season and warm-season. Cool-season grasses are appropriate for regions where temperatures go below freezing during the winter months. They grow best in spring and fall, going dormant in winter and during spells of hot, dry summer weather. Warm-season grasses are ideal for the mild climates of the southern third of the country; they require less water than most cool-season grasses. They go dormant and turn brown in winter, so many gardeners overseed them with annual ryegrass or fescue for winter color in the lawn. In addition to climate, consider the amount of sun the area gets, the foot traffic the grass is likely to experience, the soil quality, and the amount of water available.

Turf Grasses Bred for Shady Conditions

Following is a list of cool- and warm-season grasses that tolerate shade. Recommended cultivars are listed after the hardiness zones.

COOL-SEASON TURF GRASSES

Fine fescue (Chewings, *Festuca rubra* variety *commutata*; creeping red, *F. rubra* variety *rubra*; and Hard fescue, *F. longifolia*), Zones 1–6, 'Aurora', 'Jamestown II', 'Reliant', 'Scaldis', 'SR3100', 'SR5000', SR5100'

Kentucky bluegrass (*Poa pratensis*), Zones 1–6, 'A34', 'Georgetown', 'Glade'

Perennial ryegrass (*Lolium perenne*), Zones 4–6, 'Advent', 'APM', 'Express', 'Fiesta II', 'Manhattan II', 'Palmer II', 'SR4000', 'SR4100', 'SR4200'

Tall fescue (*Festuca elatior*), Zones 5–7, 'Apache', 'Arid', 'Bonanza II', 'Duster', 'Mustang', 'Pixie', 'Rebel Jr.', 'SR8200', 'Tomahawk'

WARM-SEASON TURF GRASSES

Bahiagrass (*Paspalum notatum*), Zones 9–11, 'Argentine', 'Pensacola'

Centipedegrass (*Eremochloa ophiuroides*), Zones 8–9, common, 'Oaklawn', 'Tennessee Hardy', Centennial'

St. Augustinegrass (*Stenotaphrum secundatum*), Zones 9–11, common, 'Bitterblue', 'Floralawn', 'Floratine', 'Raleigh'

Zoysia (*Zoysia* species), Zones 8–9, 'Belair'

Kentucky bluegrass (*Poa pratensis*)

Perennial ryegrass (*Lolium perenne*)

Tall fescue (*Festuca elatior*)

Bahiagrass (*Paspalum notatum*)

Centipedegrass (*Eremochloa ophiuroides*)

Zoysiagrass (*Zoysia*)

An enclosed grass lawn is set in the center of an encircling border of perennials, annuals, and shrubs. This small lawn has a beautifully manicured edge clean cut with a straight-edge spade or edging tool.

Grass is a Sun-Loving Plant. In the wild you find grass growing in open meadows where sunlight is plentiful. There are a few varieties bred to grow in some shade, but even these require at least a few hours of daily sunlight and do even better if the shade is relatively bright. (See page 218.) To reduce the amount of shade for lawns, you can prune lower tree branches (or limb them up) to allow more light to reach the ground. (See Chapter 2, page 56 for information on limbing up trees.)

Some Grasses Tolerate Heavy Foot Traffic. If you have children who will be running and playing on the lawn, select a sturdy variety such as perennial rye, tall fescue, Bermudagrass, Bahiagrass, or zoysia. Lawns growing in seaside gardens need to be salt tolerant. In northern climates the cool-season fescues tolerate salty air; try St. Augustinegrass in southern regions.

Heavy foot traffic has worn bare spots in the patch of sparse grass shown to the left. Dense turf crowds out weeds and withstands traffic better.

GRASSES FOR DIFFICULT SOIL CONDITIONS

Other grasses are well suited to difficult soil conditions. Bahiagrass is adapted to southern coastal areas and will grow in sandy, infertile soil. Buffalograss is suited to the heavy clay soils found in western Louisiana, north-central Texas, eastern Colorado, western Kansas, Nebraska, and Oklahoma. In addition, it is extremely drought tolerant, surviving on as little as 12 inches of rain a year. It also requires minimal mowing because its natural height is only 3 to 4 inches. For acidic soil, plant Canada bluegrass, chewings fescue, or hard fescue. Perennial ryegrass, wheatgrass, and Bermudagrass all adapt to alkaline soil conditions.

Some of the grasses, such as Bermudagrass, are invasive, spreading horizontally in an aggressive manner. If you have flower beds or a shrub border next to a lawn that includes Bermudagrass, plan to use a sturdy metal or plastic edging to help keep the spreading grass in the lawn and out of the beds.

Text continues on page 224.

Buffalograss (left) thrives in hot, dry climates and only occasionally needs watering or mowing. Bermudagrass (right) also tolerates sun, heat and drought. However, it is invasive and needs frequent edging.

PREPARING THE SOIL FOR A LAWN

Before planting a new lawn, send soil samples to a laboratory for an analysis of its components. (See Chapter 3, pages 67–69 for detailed information on soil tests.) The results will tell you whether you need to add any fertilizer, lime, gypsum, or sulfur to the soil before you plant. While you are waiting for the results, clean up the area, removing any debris, stones, stumps, or leftover building materials.

Amend the Soil. Using the results of your soil analysis as a guide, add whatever amendments are necessary to make the soil a suitable host for the grass seed. If you are committed to using a minimum of chemicals to keep your lawn free of weeds and robust, spend time and money now building the soil before you plant. Grass growing in deep, rich soil will be less vulnerable to pests and diseases, and less likely to need chemical treatments to solve those problems. It will grow vigorously, choking out weeds before they get a foothold, thus eliminating the need for chemical weed killers. Top-quality soil is the foundation of organic gardening; it will also make nonorganic lawns grow better and look better.

When you amend the soil, add a fertilizer high in phosphorus (such as 15-30-15) at a rate of 2 to 3 pounds per 1,000 square feet to help the new lawn establish a good root system. Till the soil to a depth of 4 to 6 inches to incorporate the amendments and to make it easier for the new roots to penetrate.

Eliminate the Weeds. After you've prepared the soil, you should eliminate the weeds and weed seed already present in the soil. A month before you plan to sow the grass seed, water the area regularly to encourage any seeds present to sprout. When they begin to grow, dislodge them with gentle tilling. Don't till too deeply, or you'll bring new weed seeds to the surface. While this step delays getting the lawn started by four weeks, it will make a major difference in successfully establishing a weed-free lawn. You can skip this step if you are laying sod; weed seeds won't sprout under the thick mats.

Grade the Site. If necessary, grade the site. Mowing steep slopes is difficult. In hilly situations where you don't want to grade, consider planting a low-maintenance ground cover over the slope rather than grass. Small dips and hummocks are also hard to mow; level these before planting to minimize scalping bumps with the lawn mower. Rake the area to smooth the soil and to remove any extra rocks and debris that were unearthed by the tiller. At the same time, fill in any low spots where water might pool, and create a pleasing, smooth surface. Finally, broadcast the seed, lay the sod, or plant the sprigs or plugs.

Tools and Materials: Wide metal landscape rake, rototiller or shovel, high-phosphorous fertilizer/and or soil amendments, hose or sprinkler, grass seed, sod, plugs, or sprigs.

Step 1: Work in Amendments. *Till fertilizer, lime, and organic matter or other soil amendments into the soil. Follow the recommendations from the soil test for amounts and types of amendments needed.*

Step 2: Water the Area. *Mist the area to be planted with a fine spray, and look for where puddles form. After the ground dries, fill any areas that puddled with soil taken from high spots.*

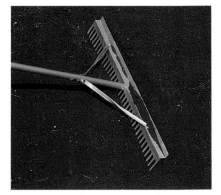

Step 3: Make Minor Grade Adjustments. *A wide metal landscape rake is the ideal tool to level the surface and remove any loose stones. A smooth lawn is easier to maintain than one with bumps.*

Purchasing Seed

Inexpensive or budget-priced seed is likely to have a low germination rate and contain a high proportion of weed seeds and inert matter or filler. Because these "cheap" packages contain so little that will actually grow, the real cost per pound often is higher than more expensive seed.

Read the package label carefully. Be sure that the seed is dated for the current year, and look for a guarantee of at least 85 percent germination and no more than 0.5 percent weed seeds. Make sure the label specifically states *no noxious weed seed.* Also look for a low percentage of annual grasses—no more than 3 to 5 percent. While annual rye is useful for overseeding warm-season lawns for winter green, it is not appropriate in a permanent lawn mixture because it dies after one season.

Today's grass has been bred for better long-term performance, disease resistance, deeper roots, and general attractive appearance. Look for trade or variety names rather than the generic name, such as Kentucky bluegrass. Don't buy the seed labeled VNS, which means *Variety Not Stated.* For cool-season grasses, look for a mixture that has been blended to meet specific growing requirements such as sun or shade, wet or dry, rich or poor soil, heavy or light traffic. According to The Lawn Institute (Marietta, Georgia), warm-season grasses should not be mixed. Most spread by stolons, and therefore instead of blending into a pleasing whole, they tend

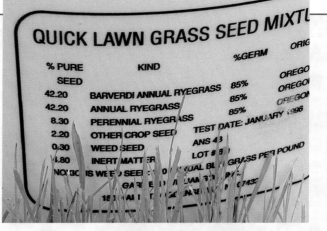

Grass seed package labels are required by law to provide information about seed content including germination rates, the date the seeds were tested, and percentage of different types of seed in the blend.

to form patches of distinct varieties. The Lawn Institute recommends choosing one particular turf grass among the warm-season grasses, one that will best adapt to your geographic area and particular lawn conditions.

If you are planting fescue or perennial rye, choose a seed mixture that contains at least 50 percent endophyte-enhanced seed. This seed is treated with fungi that kill many insects, including chinch bugs, billbugs, armyworms, aphids, and sod webworms. Unfortunately, endophytes do not attack grubs or Japanese beetles. The fungi survive only about 9 months, so be sure the seed is fresh.

Chinch bug

Sod webworm

Japanese beetle grub

HOW MUCH SEED TO USE FOR NEW LAWNS

Seed Type	Kentucky Bluegrass	Tall Fescue	Perennial Ryegrass	Fine Fescue
Pounds per 1,000 square feet	2–3	5–7	4–6	4

Note: Setter spreadings may vary with type and model of spreader. Consult your owner's manual for exact settings. Apply 50 percent more seed if you are attempting to sow a new lawn in the spring.

SOWING SEED

Difficulty Level: *Easy*

In addition to being less expensive than sod or even plugs and sprigs, seed provides a better choice of new high-quality cultivars. You can choose the grass type that will do best in your specific garden. However, it takes about a month for a newly seeded lawn to fill in, and several months for it to be durable enough for heavy use. In the meantime, there is a risk that the seed will wash away or be eaten by birds and that weeds will grow along with the grass.

Warm-season grasses germinate best when the soil is warm, between 70° and 90°F. To ensure a speedy and high rate of germination, wait to sow grass seed until late spring or early summer. Don't wait too long, however, or you'll risk giving the newly sown grass too short a growing season.

Late summer or early autumn, when the weather is cooling, is ideal for sowing (or overseeding) cool-season lawns. Cooler temperatures stimulate the germination process, and the autumn rains will relieve you of some of the watering chores. In northern climates, some people overseed their cool-season lawns in spring to fill in bare or thin patches and to improve the overall vigor of the lawn. Although possible, success is harder to achieve at that time of year. You must water faithfully until the grass is well-rooted and hope that the weather stays cool long enough so that summer heat doesn't damage young, tender roots.

Scatter the grass seed evenly over the soil. If you spread by hand, walk in one direction first, then walk perpendicular across the lawn to ensure full coverage. If you use a spreader, set it to release the grass seed at the rate recommended on the package label.

Once the seed is spread, rake lightly over the surface to scratch it into the soil, but don't bury it too deeply. All you really want to do is make good contact between the seed and the soil. Then lightly spread organic mulch, such as compost or straw, over the area to help keep the seed moist. Use a fine water spray to thoroughly moisten both grass seed and ground. Grass seed must continually be kept moist until it has germinated. If the weather is hot and dry the first week, you may need to water as frequently as three times a day. Once the roots start growing, you can back off to daily watering until the lawn looks strong.

Rope off the seeded area to discourage people and animals from walking across. If seed-eating birds are a problem, try tying strips of torn sheets or rags on the rope at regular intervals. They'll frighten the birds when they flap in the breeze. Don't mow a newly seeded lawn for at least four to six weeks. If you mow any sooner, you'll risk tearing up the shallow-rooted grass plants.

Tools and Materials: Measuring tape, spreader, rake, hose with misting nozzle or sprinkler, grass seed, organic mulch.

Step 1: Spread the Seed. *Aim for coverage of between 15 to 20 seeds per square inch after you've crossed the lawn twice with the spreader.*

Step 2: Rake the Seeded Surface. *Rake lightly to mix the seed into the top ⅛ inch of soil. The raking can also disperse seed that was spread too thickly.*

Step 3: Nurture the Young Plants. *Keep newly sprouted grass moist, watering twice a day if there is no rain. Maintain this level of moisture until the plants are 2 inches tall.*

OVERSEEDING A BARE PATCH

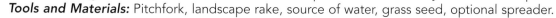

*Difficulty Level: **Easy***

Lawns occasionally develop bare patches, which should be repaired so that they do not detract from the look of the rest of the lawn. Bare spots can easily be fixed by overseeding, a process similar to seeding, except in a smaller area. In the North, the best time to overseed is in late summer and early fall; in the South the recommended time is spring or early summer. Before you begin, choose an appropriate seed as discussed on pages 216–19. First roughen the surface with the rake. Then spread the seed with your hand or a spreader.

Tools and Materials: Pitchfork, landscape rake, source of water, grass seed, optional spreader.

Step 1: Loosen the Soil. *To repair a bare patch of lawn, use a pitchfork to loosen the soil in the bare spot to a depth of 6 to 8 inches.*

Step 2: Level the Soil. *Drag the flat end of a landscape rake over the patch to level the planting surface and remove all debris.*

Step 3: Spread the Seed. *With your hand, evenly spread a mixture of seed, fertilizer, and soil over the affected area.*

Step 4: Tamp the Seeds Down. *Use the flat end of the rake to tamp the seeds into the soil, or roll with a one-third full roller.*

Plant grass sprigs so that the top one-quarter of each plant is exposed. Grass sprigs can be broadcast at a rate of 5 to 10 bushels per 1,000 square feet or planted in furrows 1 to 2 inches deep.

HOW TO PLANT PLUGS AND SPRIGS

An inexpensive alternative to sod is sprigs or plugs of grass. Warm-season grasses that spread readily—Bermuda, centipede, St. Augustine, and zoysia—are available as sprigs and plugs. Plugs are small strips or cubes of sod. Sprigs are individual grass plants or runners. Generally the plugs are sold in trays or flats of 12 or 24. Sprigs are usually sold by the bushel. In most cases you should plan for 4 to 5 bushels of grass sprigs per 1,000 square feet of lawn.

Plant the plugs or sprigs as you would any small plant, spacing them at recommended intervals. Bermudagrass plugs should be put in 4 to 12 inches apart. Centipedegrass, St. Augustinegrass, and zoysiagrass plugs all can be planted 6 to 12 inches apart. To save money, put them a little farther apart; for quicker coverage, put them closer together.

Grass plugs can be planted in furrows 6 to 12 inches apart or in individual holes. You can make your own plugs from unwanted areas of turf. Use a golf-green cup cutter for circular plugs or a sharp knife to cut square plugs.

LAYING SOD

Sod is strips of growing lawn that have been cut out of the ground. Although more expensive than sowing a lawn from seed or plugs, sod provides instant coverage. When you order sod, have it delivered when it can be laid immediately. Even a few hours in the sun can damage the grass.

First, moisten the ground where you plan to put the sod. Then lay the sod, butting ends of adjoining strips together but not overlapping them. Work from the sodded area to the open soil. To protect the already-

Step 1: Cut the Sod into Pieces. *Use a sharp trowel to cut sod to fit at butt joints (shown above) or when cutting against a straightedge. You may also use the trowel to level any irregularities in the soil.*

Step 4: Cut the Last Piece to Fit. *After you have laid sod to the opposite side of the area you're working in, cut the next-to-last piece to fit. Before cutting, roll out the sod for a test fit.*

laid sod from excess foot traffic, place a plywood sheet over the surface while you are working.

Tamp down the soil to ensure that the roots make good contact with the soil, and then water thoroughly. The traditional way to tamp sod is to roll a water-filled roller over it.

Water within 30 minutes of laying the sod. Irrigate daily for the first ten days; then back off to every second or third day until the new roots are well devel-oped. It should take from two to four weeks for the sod to become properly established. After that, water slowly and deeply so that the water penetrates at least 6 inches into the soil. This method will encourage a deep root system that is more drought-tolerant than shallow-rooted grass. (See "Watering," on page 230 to determine how long to water for best results.)

Tools and Materials: Hose or sprinkler, plywood board, trowel, roller, rake, optional edger.

Step 2: Lay the Sod. *It's important to have full strips at the perimeter; narrow strips dry out faster than wide ones. As you lay the sod, keep all joints as tight as possible, but avoid overlapping or stretching the sod.*

Step 3: Fit Sections Together. *When fitting two pieces of sod at an odd angle, lay one piece over the other, and cut through both at once. Then lift the top piece, and remove the waste underneath.*

Step 5: Roll the New Sod Lawn. *If necessary, use an edger to trim between the edge of the sod and the bed. Then use a water-filled roller to eliminate air pockets and ensure that the roots make good contact with the soil.*

Step 6: Clean Up Any Remaining Soil. *Fill the joints between strips with fine soil. Use a small, flexible rake to work any excess soil into the cracks between pieces of sod. Always stand on the board to protect planted areas.*

Restoring a Lawn

Over the years a lawn may begin to look ragged, especially if it isn't cared for properly. If more than half your lawn is full of weeds, has large worn-out or bare spots, or is rough and bumpy, consider replanting the entire area. Strip off the existing grass with a spade, working the blade in horizontal thrusts to cut through the roots. If the lawn is extensive, it may be more efficient to rent a sod-cutting machine. When the old grass is removed, prepare the soil as described on page 220, and replant.

In most cases you can renovate an existing lawn, rather than starting over. The best time of year to renovate a lawn is autumn or spring, when cooler weather and more frequent rains will promote regeneration.

The first step is to determine the source of the problem. Patchy, yellowed lawns are frequently the result of thatch buildup or soil compaction. Thatch is a light brown layer of grass debris that builds up just above the soil surface. Eventually it forms a dense mat that stops water and fertilizer from penetrating the soil. As a result, the lawn languishes. Compacted soil, caused from heavy traffic (especially when the soil is very wet) also keeps water and oxygen from penetrating the soil, starving and suffocating the grass roots. Cut out a 3-inch section of lawn, and study the cross section. If the thatch is more than ½ inch thick or the soil is compacted, you'll need to take remedial action. Both dethatching and aerating are best done before you spread any seed, fertilizer, or amendments.

DETHATCHING

Difficulty Level: Easy

Thatch is an accumulation of grass stems, stolons, rhizomes, roots, and leaves in the lawn that have not decomposed. It is more common in lawns with grasses that have stoloniferous roots running above ground such as bent grass, Bermudagrass, St. Augustinegrass, and zoysiagrass. Overfertilized grasses (especially those treated with concentrated, fast-acting synthetic fertilizers) are also more prone to develop thatch. Proper mowing (cutting off no more than one-third of the grass at one time) and fertilizing (not giving the lawn too much nitrogen, or using a slow-release formula) will help reduce the likelihood of thatch buildup. Also, aerate the lawn at least once a year. (See next page.) For lawns that develop thick thatch no matter what you do, experts recommend dethatching every three to five years. Topdressing with organic matter (ideally compost, which supplies organisms that break down thatch) is the best way to reduce thatch in the long run. Dethatching doesn't do anything to improve the soil or prevent future thatch buildup.

You may want to rent a power rake to remove the thatch and weeds. Set the blades to penetrate the thatch layer plus the top ¼ inch of soil. Run the machine back and forth in rows going in one direction, and then repeat the process, covering the ground from another angle. Water the lawn throughly to stimulate fresh growth. If you are seeding, keep the grass seed moist until it sprouts.

Tools and Materials: Lawn mower, shovel, power rake, aerator machine or shoes, water source.

Step 1: Analyze the Severity of the Problem. *Dig up some lawn. Short roots, such as these, can result from excess thatch buildup.*

Step 2: Measure the Thatch. *Roll back the grass. Thatch of more than ½ inch thick hinders water and amendments from reaching roots.*

Step 3: Power Rake the Lawn. *Some grasses naturally produce more thatch. A healthy population of earthworms breaks down thatch.*

AERATING

There are special forks and shoes with prongs designed to penetrate the ground to aerate the grass. While wearing the shoes, walk around the lawn, punching holes as you step. The forks and shoes that remove plugs are fine for a small lawn, but the most efficient and effective way to do the job on a large lawn is to use an aerating machine. Look for the kind that actually lifts out the cores of soil. These machines are available at outdoor equipment rental stores. Crisscross over the lawn in different directions to thoroughly work the space. Lawns growing in heavy clay soil will need aerating more often than those growing in sandy soil or loam. Aerating lawns growing in clay soils when they're wet will cause compaction rather than improvement.

A manual aerator does the job well, but slowly. Step down on the aerator every few inches as you walk across the lawn. Special aerating shoes with prongs are easier to use.

▲ *An aerating machine* (above) is the best way to do the job. Long, slim corers (top right) scoop out plugs of the soil's top layer (shown on the bottom right) and deposit them on the surface, where they eventually break down to feed the grass.

REPLANTING

Begin by mowing the lawn as close to the ground as possible. Then use a dethatching machine or power rake (available from equipment rental stores) to break up the grass. Run the machine back and forth in rows going in one direction; then repeat, covering the same territory from a different angle. Continue passing over the area until the grass is well broken up and the soil surface is exposed between the remaining grass plants. Rake off the excess debris.

If a soil test recommends lime or sulfur to adjust soil pH, spread it over the lawn now. If you aren't using lime, you can fertilize now. Don't spread fertilizer at the same time that you spread lime, or a chemical reaction will cause the nitrogen to evaporate; wait a few weeks. Wait until after you seed to spread topdressings of compost or aged manure.

Select a blend or mixture of named, improved varieties of lawn seed. Look for ones that match your growing conditions (sun, shade, or high-traffic). Insect and disease resistance, stress tolerances and sufficient vigor to crowd out weeds are other factors to consider. Because you are going to all this trouble, you want to be sure to plant a seed variety that you know is an improvement over the common older varieties. Sow the seed using a drop or broadcast spreader. You can plug grasses that spread with runners (St. Augustine, zoysia, Bermuda, and buffalo) directly into the renovated lawn. Water the newly seeded lawn frequently to keep the seed moist but not overly wet until it sprouts.

If you are overseeding a warm-season lawn with annual rye for a green winter lawn, simply mow the existing lawn as short as possible, rake off clippings and thatch, spread the seed, and water to keep the seed continuously moist until it sprouts. This shorter technique also works for areas of lawn that are a bit thin but not too weedy. (See "Overseeding a Bare Patch," on page 223.)

Lawn Maintenance

Grass is probably the highest-maintenance plant in a garden. It requires weekly mowing during the growing season, edging, trimming, fertilizing, and watering. Nevertheless, by following a few basic principles for a care regimen, you can grow a healthy, beautiful lawn.

FEEDING AND WEEDING

Poor soil leaves a lawn looking thin and weedy. Too much fertilizer also causes problems, making the lawn prone to thatch buildup as well as insects and disease. The ideal for the health of your lawn and your budget is to use the minimum amount of fertilizer necessary to keep the grass looking healthy and green.

Your goal is to provide enough nutrients to encourage a strong root system that will support healthy top growth. The best way to fertilize a lawn is to use slow-release nitrogen. Homeowners who spread quick-release nitrogen in large quantities on their lawn for an instant rich, green effect do more damage than good. The lush leaf growth will occur at the expense of the roots, creating thatch and weakening the overall plant. Also, those lawns will need much more frequent mowing.

The quick-fix nitrogen fertilizers most commonly used are ammonium nitrate and ammonium sulfate. They are less expensive than the slower-acting fertilizers, making them attractive to budget-conscious gardeners. However, they can be more costly in the long run. Quick-release nitrogen is designed to dissolve easily, but that means a heavy downpour may wash much of it out of the soil and off your lawn. Slow-release forms of nitrogen include sulfur-coated urea, resin-coated urea, urea formaldehyde, and organic fertilizers such as Milorganite. While these are more expensive up front, they do not have to be applied as often. As a rule, lawns fed with a slow-release form of nitrogen have better color and thickness and more reduced leaf growth than lawns treated with quick-release nitrogen.

Organic Fertilizers. More and more gardeners are opting for organic fertilizers that boost the lawn without damaging the environment. You'll need to use the organics in larger quantities than chemical fertilizers. However, with organic fertilizers, you are incorporating organic material into the soil in addition to feeding. This builds the quality of the soil and provides longer-term benefits than are provided by quick-acting, concentrated fertilizers.

Nitrogen Fertilizers

SLOW-RELEASE	Advantages	Disadvantages
Sulfur-coated urea Bone meal Dried poultry waste Soybean meal Composted manure Alfalfa meal	Nitrogen released gradually; low incidence of burning; fewer applications used; lasts longer	Higher initial costs; dependent on warm weather for release; takes longer for turf grass response

FAST-RELEASE	Advantages	Disadvantages
Ammonium nitrate Calcium nitrate Ammonium phosphate Ammonium sulfate Urea	Immediate nitrogen availability; generally costs less; better known release rate; releases even in cold weather	More apt to leach; more apt to burn foliage; more frequent applications required; may acidify soil; may make plants vulnerable to disease; requires more frequent watering

Fertilizing Tips

The best time to fertilize a lawn is when it is actively growing.

◙ *Cool-season grasses grow best in spring and fall, so fertilize cool-season grasses at the beginning of the growing season in spring or as cooler temperatures return in fall.*

◙ *If you plan to fertilize at regular intervals over a period of months in spring, stop as soon as the weather gets hotter. If you like, you can feed once more in autumn after the first frost to set up the lawn for next spring's growth.*

◙ *Feed warm-season grasses in late spring and again in August.*

◙ *If you are using a slow-release form of nitrogen, feed smaller doses every six to ten weeks until about eight weeks before the first frost date.*

◙ *If the lawn has good color and is growing well, delay additional feedings by a week or two.*

◙ *Overfeeding a lawn is wasteful and damaging to the environment. Excess fertilizer may be leached out by watering and carried into underground water systems.*

popular wisdom, these clippings do not build up a layer of thatch. If you mow before the grass gets too long so the clippings aren't left in large clumps that block light to the grass, the clippings will quickly decompose, adding organic matter to the soil as well as nutrients. A mulching mower is a great asset because it chops up the grass into little pieces that can decompose quickly. Decomposing grass clippings also encourage earthworms, which aerate the soil and add to the nutrient content with their castings. Instead of throwing your clippings away, leave them on the lawn. The clippings can reduce the need for fertilization by as much as 25 percent, helping your lawn and the environment.

Coping with Weeds. A healthy lawn will grow dense enough to crowd out weedy plants. Control any annual weeds that intrude simply by mowing. You'll remove the seed head before it matures, and the plant will die at the end of its growth cycle. Perennial weeds are more of a problem. If you have them in small quantities, hand-weed the lawn before they set seed, and work to remove each weed's

Biostimulants and Other Lawn Boosters. In addition to fertilizers, substances called biostimulants have recently become available. These compounds increase the grasses' ability to absorb important nutrients from the soil, thus improving growth and increasing resistance to pests and diseases. One product called Mycor contains mycorrhizal fungi. It works to create a favorable environment for nitrogen-fixing bacteria in the soil and improves the grasses' ability to take in nutrients through their roots. Another product, BioPro, contains peat derivatives and micronutrients. It provides three benefits to lawns: improvment of the structure, increase in the plant's ability to use available nitrogen, and introduction of organic material to the soil. Compost and seaweed products are also sources of biostimulants. Talk to an experienced nurseryman to find out what organic options are available in your community.

An easy way to add extra nutrients to your lawn is to leave the clippings in place when you mow. Contrary to

◄ *Poison ivy grows in recently disturbed soil, such as in new lawns. The three red leaves are distinctive, but be aware that the leaves turn green as they mature.*

▶ *Crabgrass is the bane of homeowners. Mowing high, removing seed heads, and maintaining dense turf are essential to control this common lawn weed.*

▶ **Ground ivy**, also called gill-over-the-ground, spreads by aboveground stolons, shown here, and by underground rhizomes.

◀ **Purslane** is a warm-season annual that thrives in hot, dry weather. Its fibrous roots are easy to pull, but new roots develop from stem fragments.

entire root system. It's easiest to weed by hand when the soil is moist and soft. An easy way to remove weeds is to pour boiling water on them. This is especially effective when trying to remove weeds from between the cracks of a patio or on the edge of the lawn. Another option is to use a fertilizer in early spring that is mixed with a preemergent weed killer. Be aware, however, that this is a nonselective herbicide. It will kill grass seed as well as weed seeds.

WATERING

Lawns grow best when they are watered deeply and infrequently. The deep water penetration encourages roots to grow down, rather than sideways, improving the root structure and drought tolerance of the grass. If your soil is dense clay, water slowly so that the water can soak in rather than run off. The average lawn needs about 1 inch of water on a weekly basis. If your soil is a heavy clay, it can take as long as 5 hours for 1 inch of water to penetrate properly. At the other extreme, sandy soil will absorb 1 inch of water in approximately 10 minutes. To determine how much water you are delivering, space shallow cans at regular intervals along your lawn and time how long it takes them to fill. One inch of water will penetrate about 12 inches in sandy soil, 7 inches in loam, and 4 to 5 inches in clay. If you have clay

soil and want to water the lawn to a depth of 6 inches, you would need to leave the sprinkler on until there is 1½ inches of water in each container. Ideally a lawn should be watered to a depth of 6 to 12 inches.

Water lawns early in the morning or late in the afternoon. It is generally less windy at those times of day, so the water won't blow into the air. The cooler temperatures and lack of wind also will minimize evaporation.

MOWING

Many lawn problems are a result of cutting grass too short. Grass that is shorn too close is more likely to succumb to stresses caused by drought, insect injury, foot traffic, or inadequate sun. Ideally you should never remove more than one-third of the leaf surface each time you mow. See the table on the following page for guidelines on ideal heights for different grasses. The lawn's rate of growth—and therefore how often you need to mow—will depend on how warm the weather is, how much water the lawn has received, and whether you fertilized. Those factors will vary throughout the season, although most people find that a schedule of weekly mowing works well.

At least once a year you should sharpen your lawn mower blades. Blunt mower blades can ruin a lawn by tearing the leaves. Each torn blade will die back ⅛ to ¼ inch, giving the lawn a brown tinge. The ragged edge on each blade of grass also makes the lawn more susceptible to disease.

Lawns mowed to the proper height are typically healthier and better able to resist disease than grass cropped short. Keep the mower blades sharp, and follow the recommended mowing heights given on the next page.

Recommended Mowing Heights

Grass Type	Finished Height
Bluegrass	2 inches
Perennial ryegrass	2 inches
Tall fescue	2 inches
Fine fescue	2 inches
St. Augustinegrass	2 inches
Buffalograss	2 inches
Bermudagrass	1½ inches
Zoysiagrass	1½ inches
Centipedegrass	1½ inches

Source: The Lawn Institute (Marietta, Georgia)

Adjust the cutting height of the mower. *By setting the mower to cut higher, you will reduce weed growth and slow the frequency of mowing. Short grass does not shade out weeds like taller grass, and its crown is exposed.*

Lawn Mowers

Today homeowners can choose from a variety of lawn mowers. Most of the newer models are mulching mowers, designed to pulverize the grass so that it breaks down quickly. When buying a mower, be sure the machine has a good warranty. Also check that it can be serviced at local shops and that parts are readily available. Once a year, have it tuned, cleaned, and serviced, and the blade sharpened; a good time is during the winter before the mowing season begins. Regular maintenance is a good long-range investment. The major mower types are described here.

Reel Mower. *The reel mower is the type with a cylinder of blades. Most have five blades, although for a finer cut (as on golf courses) there are seven- and nine-blade machines. There are gas-powered reel-style mowers, but most homeowners who select this option stick with the hand-push models. A reel-type hand mower is excellent for a small, level and even lawn. It is compact to store, quiet to use, doesn't pollute, and in a small space takes no more time to do the job than a motorized version.*

Electric Mower. *If you prefer a motorized mowing machine, the electric ones are ideal for small properties. They run quietly and are nearly maintenance-free. You can choose a cordless one that runs for an hour or more on a rechargeable battery, or opt for one with a long cord. In that case, take care that you don't run over the cord, cutting it along with the grass.*

Gas-Powered Mower. *Gas engines are often more powerful than electric motors, and they do not limit you by the length of the cord. There is a great range of gas mowers, including hand-propelled and self-propelled walk-behind designs as well as ride-on models for large properties. You can buy them with detachable bags for collecting the clippings and with mulchers that chop up the grass finely and spray it back onto the lawn. You will have a choice of horsepower, safety features, and starting features; you can choose a two-cycle engine, in which the oil is mixed with the gasoline, or a four-cycle engine, which runs on regular gasoline with a separate place for pouring in the oil. Gas-powered mowers need regular maintenance to run properly.*

Ground Covers

Ground covers are marvelous alternatives to lawns in garden areas that aren't subject to foot traffic. Ground covers add color and texture to the garden, and most don't require mowing or raking. Use them instead of grass around trees and shrubs to eliminate trimming, and in difficult areas where grass won't grow or mowing would be difficult.

Once established, most ground covers will block out weeds. Use ground covers to control erosion on steep slopes or to fill in space in beds until the slower growing plants mature.

GREAT VARIETY OF GROUND COVERS

Although many people think of ground covers as plants that hug the ground, almost any low-growing plant with a spreading habit is suitable for a ground cover. This includes small shrubs and conifers such as rockspray cotoneaster (*Cotoneaster horizontalis*) and creeping juniper (*Juniper horizontalis*). These shrubs grow as tall as 3 feet but cover the ground admirably. Rockspray cotoneaster provides three-season interest with small pink flowers in spring, glossy green foliage in summer, and red berries and foliage in autumn. Creeping juniper is a hardy plant that will grow in difficult situations where other plants won't survive, including steep slopes. It is an excellent choice for erosion control.

Vigorous clumping perennials such as daylilies also work well as ground covers; they are particularly useful on a steep slope because they require little care. Other perennials that cover the ground effectively if they are planted close together include lady's mantle (*Alchemilla mollis*), beach wormwood (*Artemisia stelleriana*), and showy sundrops (*Oenothera speciosa*). In addition to its silvery gray-green foliage, which catches water droplets and displays them like shiny jewels on velvet, lady's mantle produces pretty chartreuse blooms that combine well with blue flowers. Plant lady's mantle with catmint to create a mixed ground cover that resembles a tapestry. As its name suggests, beach wormwood does well by the seaside in sandy soil. It grows up to 2 feet tall with a 3-foot spread. Showy sundrops, which tolerate drought, will grow happily in full sun or partial shade. Harsh, difficult conditions are a good way to keep them under control; in moist, fertile soil they will invade. They are easy to grow and reward gardeners

▶ *A dense, carpet ground cover* is formed by Gaillardia, *also known as blanket flower, creating a prairie look to this drought-tolerant garden.*

Foliage creates cover. Phlox divaricata, hosta, foamflower, ajuga, and sweet woodruff foliage intermingle compatibly on this shady slope. In due course, their foliage will mask the dying daffodil leaves.

Bright ground cover adds light. Lamium maculatum 'White Nancy' sparkles under the shade of a large conifer. Even when out of bloom, the silver leaves margined with green brighten the otherwise dark spot.

with a pretty display of cup-shaped soft pink flowers in early summer.

Ferns that spread with underground runners are a lovely ground cover in shady areas, and fringed bleeding heart (*Dicentra eximia*) blooms in partial shade throughout most of the summer. Plant hostas close together as a ground cover in shady areas, both for their ornamental foliage and pretty flowers that grow on tall stalks in summer. Most hostas will tolerate both wet and dry conditions, adding to their usefulness.

GROUND COVERS AS PROBLEM SOLVERS

Within the plant kingdom there are ground covers that will grow in almost any difficult spot in the garden. In a hot, dry garden, consider planting pussytoes (*Antennaria dioica*) or hardy iceplant (*Delosperma cooperi*). Choose crown vetch (*Coronilla varia*) or creeping juniper (*Juniperus horizontalis*) on steep, sunny slopes where mowing is difficult. If sandy soil and salt spray are a problem, look into growing rugosa rose, mondo grass (*Ophiopogon japonicus*), bearberry (*Arctostaphylos uva-ursi*), or creeping lilyturf (*Liriope spicata*).

Ivy will grow in deep, dry shade and in areas where there is little root room. Snow-in-summer (*Cerastium tomentosum*) will tolerate clay soil and loves a hot, sunny bank; if the soil is too good, however, the plant can become invasive. Pachysandra is happy competing with tree roots and makes a pretty, tailored green collar when planted around trees.

Grow an evergreen ground cover such as periwinkle (*Vinca minor*) over spring-flowering bulbs. The dark green periwinkle leaves make a pretty backdrop when the bulbs are in bloom; later they help disguise the dying leaves. Also, you won't risk disturbing the bulbs by digging about in the bed later in the season. Choose bulbs such as *Narcissus* varieties, whose flowers are tall enough to be visible above the vinca (which can grow as high as 10 inches).

The obvious approach to ground covers is to mass-plant one species for uniform coverage. Another alternative is to intermingle different creeping plants with a variety of leaf and flower colors and textures to create a

This shady woodland slope has been planted with various hostas, ferns, and Siberian bugloss (Brunnera macrophylla), to create a varied, textured composition with little maintenance required.

dazzling tapestry effect. For best success, mix plants that require similar growing conditions. For example, mix different varieties of creeping thyme, such as caraway-scented thyme (*Thymus Herba-barona*), with its dark green leaves and matting growth, golden lemon thyme (*T. x citriodorus* 'Aurea'), with its green and yellow variegated leaves, and silver thyme (*T. vulgaris* 'Argenteus'), with silver and green variegated leaves.

When selecting ground covers, choose ones that are suited to the soil, light, and climate conditions in your garden. You'll be rewarded with a better appearance and minimal maintenance.

A weed barrier, Liriope muscari 'Big Blue' grows in a dense mass, so weeds cannot invade. In autumn, violet blue flower spikes brighten the display. The evergreen grass grows 10 to 18 inches tall.

Ground Covers for Difficult Situations

The tough, tenacious character that enables these plants to survive in difficult situations also makes some of them invasive. Keep a barrier, such as a wide strip of lawn, between these and flower beds.

DRY, SUNNY SPOTS

Achillea tomentosa (woolly yarrow), Zones 3–7

Aegopodium podagraria 'Variegatum' (variegated bishop's weed), Zones 3–9 (grows in sun or shade)

Antennaria dioica (pussytoes), Zones 4–7

Cerastium tomentosum (snow-in-summer), Zones 2–10

Ceratostigma plumbaginoides (leadwort), Zones 5–9

Helianthemum nummularium (sun rose), Zones 6–8

Oenothera speciosa (showy sundrops), Zones 3–8

Rosa rugosa (rugosa or saltspray rose), Zones 2–9

Saponaria ocymoides (soapwort), Zones 4–10

Sempervivum tectorum (hen and chickens), Zones 5–9

EROSION CONTROL

Coronilla varia (crown vetch), Zones 3–9

Euonymus fortunei (winter creeper), Zones 5–9

Hedera helix (English ivy), Zones 5–9

Hypericum calycinum (Aaron's beard/ St. John's Wort), Zones 6–8

Juniperus horizontalis (creeping juniper), Zones 4–10

POOR SOIL

Aegopodium podagraria 'Variegata' (variegated bishop's weed), Zones 3–9

Antennaria dioica (pussytoes), Zones 4–7, dry, sandy soil

Arctostaphylos uva-ursi (bearberry), Zones 2–7, dry, sandy soil

Artemisia stelleriana (beach wormwood), Zones 3–8, dry, sandy soil

Calluna vulgaris (Scotch heather), Zones 5–7, sandy, acidic soil

Cerastium tomentosum (snow-in-summer), Zones 2–10, needs good drainage

Ceratostigma plumbaginoides (leadwort), Zones 5–9

Chamaemelum nobile (Roman chamomile), Zones 3–8, poor, sandy soil

Hedera helix (English ivy), Zones 5–9

Juniperus horizontalis (creeping juniper), Zones 4–10

Opuntia compressa (prickly pear), Zones 5–9, dry, sandy soil

Santolina chamaecyparissus (lavender cotton), Zones 6–9, poor, but well drained

Sedum spurium (stonecrop), Zones 3–8, average to poor soil, needs good drainage

Juniperus horizontalis (creeping juniper)

Sempervivum (hen and chicks)

Saponaria ocymoides (soapwort)

Ground Covers for Shade

Asarum caudatum (British Columbia wild ginger), Zones 6–8, partial shade

Ceratostigma plumbaginoides (leadwort), Zones 5–9, full sun to partial shade

Chrysogonum virginianum (green and gold), Zones 5–8, partial shade in North, full shade in South

Convallaria majalis (lily-of-the-valley), Zones 3–8, partial to full shade

Cornus canadensis (bunchberry), Zones 2–7, partial shade

Epimedium spp., (bishop's hat), Zones 5–8, light to heavy shade

Euphorbia amygdaloides var. *robbiae* (spurge), Zones 7–9, partial shade

Galium odoratum (sweet woodruff), Zones 3–8, full shade

Gaultheria procumbens (wintergreen), Zones 4–8, light to full shade

Hosta species and cultivars (plantain lily), zones vary with variety, light to full shade

Lamium spp., Zones 4–9, partial to full shade

Lysimachia nummularia (creeping Jenny), Zones 3–8, full sun in North, full shade in South

Mazus reptans, Zones 5–8, full sun to partial shade

Paxistima canbyi (paxistima), Zones 3–8, partial shade

Phlox divaricata (wild sweet William), Zones 3–8, partial shade

Saxifraga x urbium (London pride), Zones 5–8, partial shade

Tiarella cordifolia (foamflower), Zones 4–9, partial shade

Vinca minor (periwinkle), Zones 4–8, light to moderately heavy shade

Ground Covers for Sun

Achillea tomentosa (woolly yarrow), Zones 3–7

Arabis caucasica (wall rock cress), Zones 4–8

Aurinia saxatilis (basket-of-gold), Zones 3–7

Cerastium tomentosum (snow-in-summer), Zones 2–7

Chamaemelum nobile (Roman chamomile), Zones 3–8

Cotoneaster horizontalis (rockspray cotoneaster), Zones 5–8

Euphorbia polychroma (cushion spurge), Zones 4–9

Geranium sanguineum (bloodred cranesbill), Zones 4–8

Iberis sempervirens (perennial candytuft), Zones 4–9

Juniperus communis 'Prostrata' (common juniper), Zones 3–9

Juniperus horizontalis (creeping juniper), Zones 4–10

Juniperus procumbens (Japanese garden juniper), Zones 5–9

Lithodora diffusa, Zones 7–9

Nepeta x faassenii mussinii (Persian catmint), Zones 4–8

Osteospermum fruticosum (freeway daisy), Zones 8–10

Phlox subulata (moss pink), Zones 3–9

Stachys byzantina (lamb's ears), Zones 4–9

Thymus spp. (low-growing varieties), zones vary with species

Veronica prostrata (prostrate speedwell), Zones 4–8

Potentially Invasive Ground Covers

The following ground covers can become invasive. They are easier to control if you grow them in less-than-ideal conditions. Don't plant them next to delicate perennials.

Aegopodium podagraria (bishop's weed), Zones 3–9

Cerastium tomentosum (snow-in-summer), Zones 2–10

Chamaemelum nobile (Roman chamomile), Zones 3–8, self sows

Coronilla varia (crown vetch), Zones 3–9

Hedera helix (English ivy), Zones 5–9

Hypericum calycinum (Aaron's beard/St. John's Wort), Zones 6–8

Houttuynia cordata 'Chameleon' (chameleon plant), Zones 5–9

Lamium galeobdolon (yellow archangel), Zones 4–9

Lamium maculatum (spotted lamium, deadnettle), Zones 3–8

Lysimachia nummularia (creeping Jennie), Zones 3–8

Mazus reptans, Zones 5–8

Oenothera speciosa (showy sundrops), Zones 3–8

Opuntia compressa (formerly *Opuntia humifusa*) (prickly pear), Zones 5–9, in South where birds sow

Lamium maculatum 'Beacons silver' (spotted nettle)

Cerastium tomentosum (snow-in-summer)

Ornamental Grasses

Ornamental grasses have grown remarkably in popularity in the past decade or so, as people appreciate their many positive qualities. The grass family is vast, with plants ranging in size from petite clumps suitable for edging a border or working as a ground cover, to monumental specimens that are excellent for using as screens or as a garden focal point. In addition to the diverse sizes, ornamental grasses come in many colors. As its nickname suggests, blood grass (*Imperata cylindrica* 'Red Baron') is a distinctive blood red, while blue oat grass

Ornamental grass creates a backdrop. *A screen of billowing fountain grass (*Pennisetum alopecuroides*) and eulalia grass (*Miscanthus sinensis*) backs the narrow lap pool. Many grasses are well suited to wet areas.*

(*Helictotrichon sempervirens*) has spiky, luminous blue leaves. Blue fescue (*Festuca ovina* 'Glauca') is particularly appealing, with its evergreen tufts of silvery blue foliage. There are variegated grass forms with silver or yellow stripes running the length of the leaves, as well as the amazing porcupine grass (*Miscanthus sinensis* 'Strictus'), with golden stripes running horizontally along each blade. Depending on the grass, the flower plumes (inflorescences) also come in a great range of colors, from burgundy red and soft pink to cream, ivory, and tawny shades of beige.

GRASSES IN THE LANDSCAPE

In a landscape, ornamental grasses add a special quality. Many of them are in almost constant motion, swaying gently in the slightest breeze to add a dynamic element to the garden. As the leaves brush against each other, they rustle pleasingly, soothing the ear. Silhouetted by backlighting, ornamental grasses glow and take on a magical quality.

There are ornamental grasses that work well in myriad garden applications. Some, such as the giant reed (*Arundo donax*), grow well along the edge of ponds or in bog gardens. Small, mounding grasses such as the fescues (*Festuca* species) keep tidy forms and make fascinating ground covers when massed. These small ornamental grasses adapt well to many garden situations. Generally, the large specimens such as eulalia grass (*Miscanthus* species) and the fall-blooming reed grass (*Calamagrostis brachytricha*) work better on a large property with a modern, informal garden. Grasses also can look at home in country-style and naturalistic gardens.

Ornamental grasses are touted for their year-round interest in the garden. Grasses such as maiden grass (*Miscanthus sinensis* 'Gracillimus') and fountain grass (*Pennisetum alopecuroides*) begin the growing season with fresh, green sprouts that develop into arching mounds. As the summer progresses, flower plumes wave from the tops of the plants; in winter the grass turns a

▶ **Foliage and flower panicles** *glow in the golden light when ornamental grasses are backlit. This creates a particularly dramatic look.*

An autumn flowering grass, *the diffuse flower panicles of Panicum virgatum 'Haense Herms' contrast pleasingly with the upright, narrow inflorescences of the feather reed grass (Calamagrostis x actiflora) at right. Striped ribbon grass (Phalaris arundinacea) fills the foreground.*

▶ **The horizontal stripes** *on zebra grass (Miscanthus sinensis 'Zebrinus') make this ornamental grass a striking landscape accent.*

tawny color that persists through the snowy season in many gardens (except in areas with winds or heavy snowfall). They are cut down in late winter to make room for the new growth in spring, and the cycle begins again.

A single, tall-growing ornamental grass makes a striking focal point or specimen plant in the garden. Pampas grass (*Cortaderia selloana*), with feathery plumes that stand tall among its saw-toothed grassy leaves in late summer, is a dramatic grass. Hardy from Zones 7–10, it will grow in wet or dry soil and acid or alkaline pH, and it tolerates dry desert winds, coastal fogs, and high humidity. (Avoid planting it in coastal areas of California, where it has become a nuisance weed.) In northern gardens silverfeather grass (*Miscanthus sinensis* 'Silberfeder'), giant Chinese silver grass (*Miscanthus floridulus*), or ravenna grass (*Erianthus ravennae*) are excellent large specimens.

Use one of the smaller fountain grasses, such as *Pennisetum setaceum,* as a centerpiece in a bed of low-growing annuals. Its green grassy leaves provide a pleasing contrast to red begonia flowers. Later in the summer, the red begonias are echoed in the fountain grass's pink or mauve flower panicles.

Grasses are Low Maintenance. Generally pestfree and easy to grow, ornamental grasses are great low-maintenance plants for hard-to-reach parts of the garden. Combine them with other plants to create an unexpected contrast of textures or colors. Plant them around the edge of a pond to make a soft transition between the hard edge and the water. Blur the edge of a path with mounds of blue fescue. Tall varieties make outstanding background plants in perennial borders. Plant a collection of grasses in a separate bed to enjoy

Interest through the Seasons

Ornamental grasses provide interest in the landscape every season. Below, *Pennisetum alopecuroides* (fountain grass) is shown in the same garden throughout the year.

Early Spring: *The daffodils are up and the grass has been cut.*

Early Summer: *Grasses hide the bare stalks of Allium aflatunense.*

Mid Summer: *Fountain grass underplanted with lilies (Lillium).*

Late Summer: *Grass mixes with black-eyed Susans (Rudbeckia).*

Fall: *Grass with seed heads takes on tawny fall colors.*

Winter: *Fountain grass pokes through deep snow.*

the great variety available. Some grasses, such as *Miscanthus*, are tolerant of the salt and humidity prevalent in coastal areas and make great screens or buffers. They are useful to create a protected microclimate for less-tolerant plants.

CHOOSE GRASSES WISELY

Consult the local Cooperative Extension Service or a reliable nearby nursery for recommendations on grasses suited to your area. A few grasses are invasive in some parts of the country. For example, feathertop grass (*Pennisetum villosum*) grows too aggressively in the Southwest, and the giant reed (*Phragmites australis*) is harming water birds by overtaking wetlands in the East. Pampas grass (*Cortaderia selloana*) is invasive in parts of the West, spreading rapidly by reseeding. Those same grasses are well behaved in other parts of the country. If possible, visit a nursery with a display garden that features ornamental grasses or a local botanical garden, park, or arboretum. You'll make better choices if you can see the grasses in their mature size in landscape situations. It's also helpful to observe how they perform throughout the year. Depending on where you live, some grasses that are touted for their year-round beauty actually get quite scruffy or look sickly in winter.

CARING FOR ORNAMENTAL GRASSES

Ornamental grasses are generally low maintenance and disease free. If you plant them in a spot that is well suited to their growing requirements, they'll reward you with almost carefree beauty. Like any newly planted specimen, ornamental grasses should be watered their first year in the ground. After that, their water requirements are minimal. They also need little or no supplemental fertilizer. In fact, adding high-nitrogen fertilizer can slow down flowering and cause the foliage to grow unattractively floppy. An annual dose of compost will supply a slow-release dose of all the necessary nutrients.

As with most plants, the care of ornamental grasses depends on where you live and the specific grass. A large number of the plants benefit from an annual cutting. You may find that a chain saw or hedge trimmer is the best tool to cut back large clumps of ornamental grass. Cut the grass to a few inches above the ground, being careful not to damage the crown. Wear gloves when handling ornamental grass; the term *blade* of grass is well-deserved.

If an ornamental grass clump grows too big, you will need to divide it. (See Chapter 12, pages 263–65 for information on dividing perennials.) Large clumps are too tough to pull apart by hand. You may need a sharp axe, hatchet, or machete to cut through the roots.

Seasonal Trimming

Although it isn't necessary for the plant's health, many ornamental grasses look better in spring if the old, dead growth is cut back in late winter before the new growth begins to show. Warm-season grasses, such as reed grass (*Calamagrostis arundinacea*) and pampas grass, should be cut to 3 or 4 inches above the ground; trim cool-season grasses, including large blue hairgrass (*Koeleria glauca*), at about two-thirds their height. Check the list on page 241 for trimming information for each specific plant.

A grass that was not cut back. The new leaves have grown up among the dead leaves, causing the grass clump to open up in the middle and flop.

◄ **Prepare for spring** by cutting grass down to about 8 inches in late winter. Within a few weeks this Miscanthus 'Giganteum' is already beginning to show signs of new growth.

TRANSPLANTING AND DIVIDING *MISCANTHUS* GRASS

Difficulty Level: Easy

Ornamental grasses occasionally need to be divided if they have outgrown their space or grown old and floppy in the middle. This task is similar to the process of dividing perennials shown in Chapter 12 on pages 264-65 except that a pruning saw is the best tool to cleanly cut through the tough clumps of grass. Divide ornamental grasses in the early spring after they have been cut back. Dig the new holes before you lift the divisions to minimize the time the plants spend exposed to the drying air.

Tools and Materials: Shovel, pruning saw, source of water, mulch, gloves.

Step 1: Dig Out the Grass. *Use a shovel to cut the soil around and under the grass clump. Pry the clump up, and lift the grass out of the ground. The grass shown here is Miscanthus.*

Step 2: Determine Where You Will Divide. *The shallow-rooted Miscanthus is out of the ground and ready for division. Choose a section that has a good balance of top growth and roots.*

Step 3: Make the Divisions. *After identifying where to divide, use a pruning saw to make a clean cut through the clump of roots. One clump of ornamental grass can easily yield several new divisions (shown in the inset).*

Step 4: Plant the Division. *The new divisions should be planted at the same depth at which they were originally growing. Fill the hole, and water. Add more soil if necessary. Tamp the soil down with your foot.*

Ornamental Grasses that Need an Annual Trim

The timing for trimming back ornamental grasses depends in part on your own style of gardening and the region where you live. In cold climates, you can remove the brown leaves in autumn or leave them on to enjoy through the winter and then cut them back very early in spring. In warm climates, a fall trim will stimulate new growth immediately, so that you can have new green foliage by winter. It is particularly important to remove dried foliage in places where risk of fire is severe.

Andropogon gerardii (big bluestem), Zones 4–9, cut back to 6 inches in early winter

Arrhenatherum elatius subspecies bulbosum (bulbous oat grass), Zones 4–9, cut back whenever it turns brown

Arundo donax (giant reed), Zones 7–10, cut dead stems to ground in winter

Bouteloua spp. (grama grass), zones vary with species,

Briza media (quaking grass), Zones 4–10, cut back old foliage in midsummer, cut back again in late fall

Calamagrostis spp. Zones 4–9, cut back in late winter

Chasmanthium latifolium (northern sea oats), Zones 5–9, cut back dead foliage in spring or fall

Cortaderia selloana (pampas grass), Zones 7–10, cut back every year or two in early spring

Erianthus ravennae (Ravenna grass), Zones 5–10, cut back dead leaves in late winter

Festuca glauca (blue fescue), Zones 4–9, cut back in early spring or fall for new growth

Helictotrichon sempervirens (blue oat grass), Zones 4–8, cut back to 3 inches in early spring

Miscanthus spp., zones vary with variety, cut back in late winter

Molinia caerulea (purple moor grass), Zones 5–8, cut back foliage in winter

Panicum virgatum and cultivars (switch grass), Zones 4–9, cut back in early spring

Pennisetum spp. (fountain grass), Zones 5–9, cut off seed heads to prevent selfsowing, cut back leaves in early spring

Phalaris arundinacea 'Picta' (ribbon grass), Zones 3–9, cut back in summer for new growth and in early spring

Schizachyrium scoparium (little bluestem), Zones 3–19, cut back in early spring

Sorghastrum nutans (Indian grass), Zones 4–9, cut back in early spring

Spodiopogon sibiricus (silver spikegrass), Zones 5–9, cut back in winter

Sporobolus spp. (dropseed), Zones 3–9, cut back in winter

Calamagrostis x acutiflora (feather reed grass)

Pennisetum alopecuroides 'Little Bunny' (dwarf fountain grass)

Cortaderia selloana (pampas grass)

CHAPTER 12

Flowers in the Landscape

Borders and Beds

Flowers touch our lives in a multitude of ways, soothing us with their scents and pleasing us with their delightful colors and forms. In the garden they bring sparkle, variety, and vibrancy.

Many gardens in North America are rich with floral interest in spring when so much is in bloom. Unfortunately, after the initial burst of color, some gardens quit, and for the rest of the growing season they are masses of unrelieved green. This lack of summer interest in the garden is unnecessary. Even in regions of the country where summers are the hottest and most humid, there are summer-blooming annuals, perennials, and bulbs that can grace the garden. All it takes is some thoughtful planning.

DESIGNING BORDERS AND BEDS

Borders. Traditionally perennial borders follow the line of paths, enhancing the journey from one part of the garden to another with a wonderful floral display along the way. But there are many other places you could site a border. For example, in lieu of a fence, you could create a perennial border across the front of your property to define your private space. Mix shrubs with perennials up against your home to transform a foundation planting into a mixed border. And you can line your driveway with perennial flowers.

Perennial borders generally look best against a background. Dark green hedges are a wonderful foil for flowers. Yew is often used as a formal background to a perennial border because it has finely textured foliage

Cottage-style borders flank the brick steps. Irises, yarrows, and coralbells are among the flowers shown.

and a deep color that sets off other plants to advantage. If you prefer an informal planted background, consider a screen of tall ornamental grass or a mixed collection of unpruned shrubs. Other options for backgrounds to perennial borders include trellises and fences. Look around your garden. You might find that an appropriate backdrop for a perennial border already exists.

Beds. Although beds and borders frequently are referred to in the same breath, there is a difference. A bed is an island of plantings. You can walk around a bed, viewing it from all sides. You can make a bed as large or small as you like, but make sure it complements the scale of other features in your garden. Also bear in mind maintenance issues. Unless you include maintenance paths to access the interior of a large bed, make the bed small enough so you can reach to the center to look after plants.

These pastel borders are displayed beautifully against a mellow-gray stone wall.

A bright border against a picket fence gives passersby a visual treat.

A lush island bed in a small town garden brims with cannas, daylilies, hostas, and potted plants.

This drought-tolerant border contradicts the notion that gardening in hot regions must be dull.

Designing with Plants

Choosing the plants and imagining them in all their glory is perhaps the most satisfying aspect of planning a perennial bed or border. Garden design experts recommend combining at least three to five of each plant in clumps or drifts to create an impact. Think about pleasing color combinations and bloom times.

Learn the mature heights of the plants. In a border you generally want the tallest plants in back so that all the plants can be seen, although you may move one or two forward to cast interesting shadows. Varied heights also increase the sense of depth in a border. In an island bed, plant the tallest plants in the center.

COLOR AND TEXTURE

Floral color is probably the most obvious feature of a bed or border. You can choose a color theme, such as a white garden, a red border, or a bed planted with pastel flowers. Remember that you don't have to be a slave to the concept. Think about introducing a pale lemon yellow flower to a blue garden to emphasize the blue flowers. Another idea, credited to the English gardener Gertrude Jekyll, is to gradually move through the color spectrum, making each section blend imperceptibly with the next. For example, a border that begins with yellow at one end could gradually move into the orange palette, followed by reds. A border that mixes colors throughout may be more to your taste.

Don't forget the value of gray foliage. Use it to create a restful spot in the midst of a lot of exciting color or as a buffer between two plants whose colors might clash. A large blob of white in a bed or border visually punches a hole in the design. Instead sprinkle white throughout to brighten the nearby colors and to add sparkle and life.

While designing your bed or border, also consider the shapes and textures of leaves and flowers. Aim to create an interesting rhythm throughout the bed or border.

When choosing plants for the bed or border, don't overlook shrubs, biennials, annuals, bulbs, and even small trees, particularly dwarf conifers. The trees and shrubs give year-round structure to the design. Many shrubs appropriate for perennial borders also produce

Well-placed pink roses punctuate the soothing colors of this mixed summer border.

flowers. Some give a lovely autumn display; others produce attractive berries or have pretty bark. All these features enhance the winter show. Annuals provide continual color spots throughout the summer, and bulbs bring interest from early spring through autumn. Think of your border as a mixed border.

Frame the Bed with Edging Plants. Like a picture on the wall, beds and borders generally look better if a frame sets them off. Consider edging the border with a mixture of low-growing plants such as ageratum, sweet alyssum, santolina, or dianthus.

There are basic principles and guidelines for designing a mixed perennial border, and it's important to know the rules. However, each garden is a reflection of the owner's own taste and personality. Be bold in experimenting with combinations of color, texture, and form. Nothing in a garden is permanent. No doubt your perennial bed will evolve as you gain more experience.

As Gertrude Jekyll wrote in her classic book *Colour Schemes for the Flower Garden*, "... Having got the plants, the great thing is to use them with careful selection and definite intention ... the duty we owe to our gardens and to our own bettering in our gardens is so to use the plants that they shall form beautiful pictures."

Yellow and orange tickseed and lilies happily mingle with violet balloon flowers and pink snapdragons.

▼ *Red poppies in a field of blue cornflowers* complement each other in a perfect patriotic combination.

▲ *Yellow yarrow, daylilies, and bright pink flowers* create a pleasing combination of color and texture.

Using Perennials in the Landscape

For many, the prospect of designing a perennial bed or border is fraught with uncertainty and anxiety. There is so much to coordinate from plant heights, bloom times, flower colors, care requirements, and hardiness. A few simple techniques can help you create a perennial border.

Larry Griffith, a horticultural research associate at Colonial Williamsburg, Virginia, has devised a technique that removes the fear and mystique from the process of designing with perennials.

GATHER PLANTS IN YOUR HEAD

First, draw to scale an outline of the border on a piece of paper. Choose a scale that fits comfortably on the paper. For example, if your border is going to be 21 feet long and 6 feet wide, you could tape two standard 8½-by-11-inch sheets of paper together to have a 22-inch width of paper, making your scale 1 inch to 1 foot. Then draw a diamond grid pattern on the paper, spacing the lines to scale so that they are 2 to 4 feet apart in the actual bed. (See illustrations at right.)

Meanwhile, start brainstorming about which flowers you might like to have in the border. A plant catalog full of photographs will give you an idea of what various plants look like. Cross check with local nurseries to know what is available and what does well in your area. Write down more plants than you'll actually need.

LAYING OUT THE BORDER

To design the border, you'll need to know the plant's projected height, the flower color, and the season of bloom. You easily can bring order to this information if you create a four-column chart. Run the plant names down the left column, and then create a column each for height, flower color, and bloom season. Now you can begin to put the jigsaw together. Start from the back of the border. Choose the tallest plants, and mark their proposed position in one of the diamond grids on the paper map. To help you visualize the color combinations you are creating, color the grid the approximate color of the flower. For a more natural look, plant clumps of flowers in drifts that blend into each other.

You may prefer a border that has moments of flower interest as you progress through the season or a border that knocks your socks off for a few weeks with a solid mass of bloom. In either case, put plants that will bloom about the same time with complementary flower colors near each other.

Also think about the shape of the flower. A perennial garden consisting only of blossoms with tall spires would be monotonous. Instead, mix spiky flower forms with round-headed flowers as well as others with cup formations and trumpet shapes.

When you've filled in the back space on the map, begin work on the middle section of the border. Select perennials of mid height, and mark their proposed position in the garden on the grid. The lowest-growing plants should be in front along the edges.

Repetition and rhythm are two features of a good garden design. You can introduce these elements to a long perennial border by repeating a basic design. If your border is long, divide it into thirds or quarters, and repeat the same placement and combination of plants three or four times down the length.

A perennial border takes two to three years to come into its own. Your border should look a little thin the first year with plenty of earth visible between the plants. You should space the plants far enough apart so that they have room to grow and spread to their mature sizes.

The perennial border at Barnsley House shows the beauty of using one dominant color sprinkled with dashes of another.

DESIGNING A PERENNIAL BORDER

The plan view and the perspective view are two different ways to look at the same garden. The numbers on the plants, in the diamonds, and at the left of the table correspond to one another. On the plan view, notice how the colors overlap the edges of the diamonds like drifts, blending seamlessly. This plan is intended to be repeated in a mirror image down the border.

Speaking at a garden symposium in Virginia, Penelope Hobhouse explained the technique of creating repetition and rhythm in a border with a story about her friend and colleague, Rosemary Verey. The story was that Verey and another colleague had worked all morning choosing plants for a border. By lunchtime they had done one-quarter of the length. "Oh dear," lamented Verey's colleague, "this is taking longer than I thought. We've still got three-quarters of the border to do." To this Verey retorted, "Don't be silly. We're done. We'll just repeat this plan four times!"

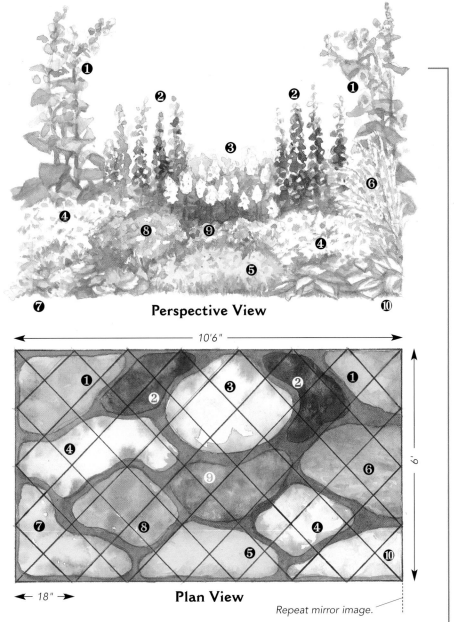

Perspective View

Plan View

Repeat mirror image.

Plant	Height and Spread	Season of Bloom	Hardiness Zone
❶ *Alcea rosea* (common hollyhock)	60"–96"H x 24"W	Early and Mid Summer	Zones 3–9
❷ *Delphinium* 'Bellamosum' (larkspur)	36"–48"H x 18"W	Early and Mid Summer	Zones 3–7
❸ *Phlox paniculata* 'David' (phlox)	40"H x 40"W	Mid to Late Summer	Zones 4–8
❹ *Leucanthemum x superbum* (shasta daisy)	30"H x 18"W	Early Summer and Fall	Zones 5–8
❺ *Coreopsis verticillata* (tickseed)	24"–32"H x 18"W	Summer to Autumn	Zones 3–8
❻ *Perovskia atriplicifolia* (Russian sage)	48"H x 36"W	Summer to Autumn	Zones 6–9
❼ *Alchemilla mollis* (lady's mantle)	24"H x 30"W	Summer to Autumn	Zones 4–7
❽ *Geranium* 'Johnson's Blue' (cranesbill)	18"H x 24"–30"W	Summer	Zones 4–8
❾ *Scabiosa columbaria* (scabiosa)	16"H x 16"W	Mid to Late Summer	Zones 3–8
❿ *Stachys byzantina* (lamb's ears)	18"H x 24"W	Summer to Autumn	Zones 4–8

Perennials

As the name suggests, a perennial is an herbaceous plant that continues to live for many years. In contrast, annuals grow, bloom, and die all in one season. Herbaceous perennials die down to the ground every winter and send forth new growth each spring. Woody plants, on the other hand, retain their branch structure year-round although they may drop their leaves in the autumn.

However, just because a plant is classified as a perennial doesn't mean it will survive in your climate. Some perennials are adapted to harsh winter weather; others are more tender and cannot tolerate cold temperatures. In fact, there is a large selection of tender perennials, including *Heliotrope* and *Pelargonium* (geranium) that are grown as annuals in most places, except the frost-free parts of the country.

Cold and Heat Tolerance Varies. Some perennials prefer cool summers; others require heat. When you are choosing perennials for your garden, find out how cold- and heat-hardy they are. (See Introduction, pages 14–15, for a description of the USDA Hardiness Zone System and the American Horticultural Society's newly introduced Heat-Zone Map). Also be aware of how much sun or shade they require and whether they prefer dry or moist conditions. Even when given the conditions that suit them perfectly, no perennial lives forever. Every perennial has a definite life span, although some live longer than others.

Perennials that Tolerate Hot, Humid Summers

While many perennials and biennials languish in hot, humid conditions, there is a large selection of beautiful plants that thrive in hot weather. The following are just a few of the many possibilities.

Achillea spp. (yarrow), zones vary with species

Agastache spp. (giant hyssop), zones vary with species

Allium spp. (flowering onion), zones vary with species

Asclepias tuberosa (butterfly weed), Zones 4–9

Bergenia spp. (elephant's ears), zones vary with species

Boltonia asteroides, Zones 4–9

Buddleia davidii (butterfly bush), Zones 6–9

Caryopteris x clandonensis (bluebeard), Zones 6–9

Centranthus ruber (red valerian), Zones 5–8

Chelone spp. (turtlehead), zones vary with species

Coreopsis spp. (tickseed), zones vary with species

Dendranthema x grandiflorum (hardy garden chrysanthemum), Zones 4–7

Echinacea purpurea (purple coneflower), Zones 3–9

Eryngium maritimum (sea holly), Zones 6–8

Hemerocallis spp. and cultivars (daylily), zones vary with species and cultivars

Hibiscus moscheutos (rose mallow), Zones 5–10

Hosta spp. and cultivars (plantain lily), zones vary with species and cultivars

Lamium maculatum (spotted deadnettle), Zones 4–8

Liatris spp. (gayfeather), zones vary with species

Lunaria annua (honesty, money plant), Zones 5–9

Nepeta x faassenii (catmint), Zones 4–8

Perovskia atriplicifolia (Russian sage), Zones 6–9

Physostegia virginiana (false dragonhead), Zones 4–8

Rudbeckia spp. (coneflower, black-eyed Susan), zones vary with species

Solidago spp. (goldenrod), zones vary with species

Stokesia laevis (Stokes' aster), Zones 5–9

Veronica spp. (speedwell), zones vary with species

To achieve a perennial border of varied texture plant poppies, irises, peonies, and alliums.

The planting of tall yellow butterfly weed (Alepias tuberosa) softens the picket fence.

The perennial ground cover, Ajuga, makes a lovely base for foliage annuals such as dusty miller and Perilla.

This perennial planting includes yellow Alchemilla (front), purple iris (center), and a pink poppy (center right).

To enhance the perimeter of a small lawn, ruffle the edge with hostas and Euonymus.

Annuals

True annuals are plants that complete their whole life cycle in one year. They grow, bloom, go to seed, and die. In nature's urge to propagate itself, annual plants will keep producing flowers if they are not allowed to set seed. This is why gardeners can enjoy such a long season of bloom from annuals.

Most of the plants we grow as annuals are frost-tender perennials that hale from warm climates such as Central and South America, South Africa, and the Mediterranean area. In fact, many of them are grown as perennials in the subtropical parts of southern California and south Florida. There homeowners enjoy the perpetual blooms of impatiens and wax begonias 12 months of the year. They manage the plants by trimming them back when they get leggy to encourage bushy growth and intense flowering.

The great advantage of many annuals is that they flower generously throughout the growing season, providing dependable color and interest in the garden. In cold-season climates, you can plant annuals in spring and enjoy a continous display of flowers until they succumb to the first killing frost in autumn.

Because of their energetic propensity to stay in flower all season long, annuals are an excellent choice for creating dramatic container displays. Because they need to be replanted each spring, you also have the opportunity to renew the container soil annually.

ANNUALS IN THE LANDSCAPE

Annuals are also an asset in the perennial border. Most perennials bloom for just a few weeks a year. Even gifted perennial border designers struggle with planting combinations that will flower from spring through autumn. That's where annuals come in handy. They grow quickly, so you can plug them into holes in the border and use them to extend the beauty of the display if there's a gap in the bloom cycle of the perennials.

Annuals were all the rage in the Victorian era when many of today's popular plants were first brought back to Europe and England by plant explorers. Home gardeners delighted in creating mass displays of them and planted them in colorful strips or elaborate patterns with bold color combinations. The technique, called bedding out or carpet bedding, fell out of favor when influential English gardeners wrote scathing, disparaging descriptions of these annual arrays, referring to the "ingenious monstrosity" of carpet bedding. As a result, the fashion for carpet bedding died, gradually giving way to the labor-intensive perennial beds and borders. However, many municipalities and homeowners with less time and staff to garden create stunning visual displays, perhaps because they can produce an eye-catching, season-long display relatively easily and inexpensively.

Because so many annuals flower throughout the growing season, they are ideal for cutting gardens. In fact, they benefit from being cut. With annuals, the more flowers you pick, the more the plants produce. Many annuals, such as zinnias, marigolds, and even impatiens, will last at least a week in a vase if they are picked fresh. Remove faded flowers promptly to encourage new blooms, as annuals stop blooming once they form seed. (See "Deadheading and Pinching," page 266.)

Annuals provide long color in the landscape. Shown here: ageratum and marigolds are still going strong in September.

The Victorian-style bedding of red begonias against the crisp, white staircase brilliantly displays the beauty of this annual.

This Persian-carpet design uses red, white, and pink annuals. The carpet effect is completed by its position in the lawn.

Annuals grow well in containers. Shown above: violas and impatiens

A rail fence acts as a convenient support for bouquets of blooming cosmos.

This cutting garden of annuals includes marigolds and ageratum. Annuals produce more flowers if they are cut.

Bulbs

In Holland, bulbs are a spring garden staple. In North America, we love spring-blooming bulbs, but we rarely think of them as an important element in the garden design. We also often ignore bulbs that bloom at other times of the year. In addition to the traditional spring displays of tulips and daffodils, there are bulbs that bloom in summer or autumn—and a few, such as *Galanthus nivalis* (snowdrops), *Iris reticulata*, and *Eranthis hyemalis* (winter aconite), that bloom in late winter.

Many of the minor bulbs (so-called because they are smaller than tulips and daffodils) are low-growing, ideal in rock gardens. These include *Muscari* spp. (grape hyacinth), *Anemone blanda* (windflower), winter aconite, and hardy cyclamen. Midsize plants such as many daffodils and tulips mix well in perennial borders. Very tall bulb plants such as *Fritillaria imperialis* (crown imperial), lilies, and *Eremurus* spp. (foxtail lily) are a wonderful backdrop to other plantings and are useful as vertical accents in a border. Of course, massed in a bed on their own, a single variety of bulb or a pleasing combination that blooms simultaneously makes a spectacular floral display. The disadvantage to such a massed display is the unsightly bulb foliage when the flowers are gone. One way of ameliorating the problem is to overplant the bulbs with annuals or a late-starting perennial such as hostas or daylilies in the bed with the bulbs. As the perennial grows, it will hide the dying bulb foliage.

BULBS IN CONTAINERS

Many bulbs also are ideal for containers because you can whisk the plants out of sight when they go through their unattractive dying-back stage. Pack as many as possible into each pot to obtain a full bouquet, and stick to one variety unless you are sure both will bloom at the same time. Plant bulbs in containers at same time as your bulbs in the garden. Because most spring-flowering bulbs need a period of chilling to bloom well, pots of these bulbs should stay outdoors or in a cold place over winter. Keep the containers out of direct sunlight so that the soil remains cool. Otherwise, the warmed soil will trigger the bulbs to sprout before they have developed adequate root systems. If that happens, the plants will flower poorly. Once the shoots appear, put the pots in a lightly shaded spot.

Plant Bulbs in Groups. Whether growing in pots or in garden beds, bulbs normally look better planted in tightly packed clumps of ten or more bulbs or in drifts that flow like rivers. For design purposes you should avoid buying fewer than 10 of any one bulb. Purchasing them in packages of 50 to 100 is even better. Brent Heath, owner of Brent and Becky's Bulbs (a mail-order bulb company based in Virginia), recommends planting five large daffodil bulbs per square foot. That means a small garden plot just 5 feet square should be planted

Summer-Blooming Bulbs

Agapanthus africanus and cultivars (African lily)

Allium caeruleum

Allium christophii (star of Persia)

Allium giganteum

Amaranthus x Amarcrinum memoria-corsii

Begonia Tuberhybrida Hybrids (tuberous begonia)

Canna x generalis and cultivars (canna lily)

Crocosmia cultivars (montbretia)

Dahlia cultivars

Gladiolus cultivars

Lilium species and cultivars (lily)

Lycoris squamigera (magic lily)

Tulbaghia violacea (society garlic)

Zantedeschia aethiopica (calla lily)

Zephyranthes grandiflora (zephyr lily)

Autumn-Blooming Bulbs

Colchicum species and cultivars, especially 'Waterlily'

Crocus goulimyi

Crocus niveus

Cyclamen hederifolium (hardy cyclamen)

Dahlia cultivars

Leucojum autumnale

Nerine bowdenii

Purple babiana complements yellow freesia to create a lovely bulb garden.

The essence of spring: *tulips bloom among flowering shrubs. Many bulbs of one color planted together add impact.*

Pale-pink forget-me-nots *among hot-pink tulips create a stunning scene.*

The purple iris *sits among a golden ring of the perennial yellow ice plant.*

This container garden includes: *yellow Narcissus (center) and Viola (front).*

Yellow and pale-pink lily bulbs *make an interesting display with goat's beard.*

with 125 daffodils! It takes even more small bulbs, such as crocuses and grape hyacinths, to fill a square foot. Arrange the bulbs so that they are grouped by color and type; if you want the display to peak all at once, mix varieties that bloom at the same time.

OVERPLANT BULBS

Another good tip is to overplant bulbs with a ground cover. Tulips especially benefit from this approach because they tend to stand tall and stately with not much foliage to cover the bare ground around them. Wild sweet William (*Phlox divaricata*) is ideal to combine with tulips. This type of phlox is an attractive ground cover while the bulbs are coming up, and it helps hide the dying leaves at the end of the season. If the phlox and tulips bloom simultaneously, the result is breathtaking.

Daffodils and crocuses are strong enough to force their way through sod; they are beautiful planted in the lawn. Choose early flowering varieties so that the foliage has a chance to die back before you mow the lawn.

Other low-growing, spring-blooming plants to combine with tulips and daffodils are forget-me-nots, primroses, pansies, and violas. Blue muscari, the 6-inch-tall bulb commonly called grape hyacinth, is another superb choice. Its lavender-blue flowers blend admirably with almost any floral colors; because they are planted only 2 or 3 inches deep, they can go right on top of the more deeply planted tulips and daffodils. Whatever flower you choose to put on top of the major

Break out of the winter doldrums with this bold planting of red-and-white 'Lucky Strike' tulips.

spring-blooming bulbs, generally the combination looks best if you mass-plant with just one type rather than create a busy mixture.

Annuals also mix well with spring-flowering bulbs, helping to make a smooth, colorful transition between spring and summer. As soon as annuals are available in the nurseries, plant them between the bulbs. By the time the bulb flowers and foliage are fading and dying back, the annuals will be big enough to mask the unsightly, withering leaves with cheerful summer flowers.

Daylilies are a great combination with daffodils. Plant one daylily for every five daffodil bulbs. The daylily foliage begins to emerge just as the daffodil leaves are fading, hiding the browning leaves. Other good perennial options for companion planting with daffodils include *Tanacetum coccineum* (painted daisies), *Achillea* spp. (yarrow), or any other perennial that is slow to emerge in spring.

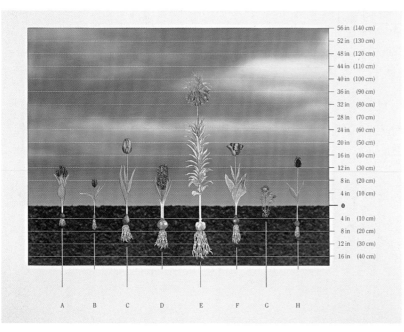

Planting depth and flower height chart. Initial A = Tulipa, B = Anemone blanda 'Pink Star', C = Tulipa 'Flaming Parrot', D = Fritillaria imperialis 'Rubra maxima', E = Hyacinthus orientalis 'Jan Bos', F = Tulipa, G = Tulipa humilis, H = Tulipa praestans 'Fusilier'. The scale on the right side of the table indicates the planting depth and height of each flower. Flower E is the tallest (40 inches) and the deepest planted (8 inches). G is the most shallow planted (2 inches).

BULBS FOR INDOORS

Some bulbs are well-suited to forcing into early bloom for out-of-season pleasure indoors. An excellent possibility is paperwhite narcissus, which will grow and bloom indoors in a bowl of water with no soil. Depending on the temperatures in your house, paperwhites will flower four to six weeks after you plant them. Plant the bulbs at two-week intervals from October through March for continual bloom throughout the winter months. You also can force hyacinths and amaryllis in the house. The scent of just one hyacinth will fill a room.

Chill Certain Bulbs. Some bulbs need chilling to flower properly indoors. In the deep South and Southwest, several bulbs need chilling before planting to bloom outdoors. Fortunately, prechilled bulbs are readily available at garden centers. Chilling times vary from 8 to 12 weeks, depending on the bulb.

Plant the bulbs in pots, placing the bulbs near the surface to allow a lot of root room. Jam the bulbs close together to get a good display. It's all right if they almost touch. Then put the planted pots in a spot that will stay cold but won't freeze. An unheated garage that doesn't

*A **festive display** of indoor flowering bulbs features red and white amaryllis. The huge, bright red flowers are Hippeastrum 'Hercules'. The smaller white flowers are H. 'Jewel', an unusually fragrant amaryllis. Amaryllis are easy to force into bloom and brighten the indoors for weeks in the dead of winter.*

freeze or a cellar hatchway are two good spots. The bulbs will grow roots during this cold period. Once the chilling time is over, bring the bulbs inside and let the warm air nurture them into flower. Don't forget to purchase the bulbs in autumn when they're available. If you decide in early December that you'd like to force bulbs, you will not likely find any bulbs still in stock.

Waves of Color

Plant spring bulbs in fall.   Daffodils and Muscari   Tulips and Muscari

While chrysanthemums are flowering and leaves are falling (left), plant bulbs "lasagna style" in layers with the largest bulbs on the bottom, the minor bulbs near the surface, and medium size bulbs in between. Dig down to maximum depth for the largest bulbs, and plant them under a few inches of soil. Then repeat the process for the medium and small bulbs. Daffodils and grape hyacinth (center) will come up after crocus (not shown), and will be followed by tulips (right).

Fragrant Flowers

Scent is an evocative thing. Memories of childhood or a well-known place can come flooding back on us with the whiff of a particular odor. The earthy smell of the newly awakened garden in spring is perfume to a gardener after a long, cold winter, as is the distinct odor of fresh rain.

People register and respond to scent differently. An iris or rose that has a strong fragrance to one person may have little or no scent to another. The potent fragrance of gardenia spells romance to some, while others find the odor a little too strong—almost nauseating.

Fragrance Attracts Pollinators. While people are drawn to scented flowers, the real motivation for the fragrance is to attract pollinators. A flower's scent is a siren call to bees and other pollinating insects, and each flower has evolved a scent that is most attractive to the pollinators it needs. For example, *Protea* have a yeasty smell designed to attract mice, which are their prime pollinator. Many night-blooming flowers are highly scented; in the dark these flowers need a way to advertise their presence to the night-flying moths and bats that are essential for their pollination.

In many cases, modern hybridizing has bred the scent out of flowers. For years people were so attracted to the dramatic, oversized, and unusually colored flower heads that they forgot about fragrance. The tide is turning, however, and now breeding work, particularly in the specialty of roses and other flowers once known for their fragrance, is giving new priority to perfume as well as flower color, form, and size.

You may want just one or two fragrant flowers as an accent in your garden or under an open window so that the scent wafts inside. Or you may choose to plant a space devoted entirely to sweet-smelling flowers and foliage. To get the most out of the potential fragrances, enclose the garden with a hedge or wall so that the scent is concentrated in a confined space. Don't overlook the potential for scented foliage. It is the oils in the leaves that give most herbs their pleasant odor.

Flowers and Leaves for Fragrance

There are hundreds of plants that have fragrant flowers or foliage. Some have a subtle scent; you need to bury your nose in the blossom to catch the delicious sweetness or alluring spicy smell. Others, such as gardenia, fill the nearby air with their fragrance.

Cestrum nocturnum (night jessamine), Zone 10
Convallaria majalis (lily-of-the-valley), Zones 2–7
Dianthus caryophyllus (border carnation), Zones 6–7
Gardenia jasminoides (gardenia), Zones 8–10
Heliotropium arborescens (heliotrope), Zone 11, elsewhere annual
Hosta plantaginea, Zones 3–8
Hyacinthus (hyacinth), Zones 4–10
Jasminum officinale (jasmine), Zones 9–10
Lathyrus odoratus (sweet pea), annual
Lavandula (lavender), Zones 6–10
Lilium regale (regal lily), Zones 4–9
Lobularia maritima (sweet alyssum), annual

Matthiola bicornis (night-scented stock), annual
Matthiola incana (stock), Zones 7–10, short-lived
Nicotiana sylvestris (tobacco plant), annual, short-lived perennial
Pelargonium spp. (scented geranium), Zones 9–10, elsewhere annual
Phlox paniculata 'David' (perennial phlox), Zones 4–8
Reseda odorata (mignonette), annual
Rosa spp. and cultivars (rose), zones vary
Rosmarinus officinalis (rosemary) Zones 6–10, depending on cultivar
Santolina chamaecyparissus (lavender cottton), Zones 6–9
Thymus (thyme), Zones 4–10

The scented garden features roses, fragrant petunias, bay, Antirrhinum, sweet pea, veronica, and nasturtium.

The **Lillium** *(lily) 'Star Gazer' is intoxicatingly fragrant.*

Convallaria majalis *(lily-of-the-valley) is always a favorite of perfume makers.*

▶ *It's all in the name:* Viola odorata (sweet violet), blooms in late winter.

The scent of Hyacinthus *(hyacinth) 'Sky Jack' is as perfect as its color.*

The traditional fragrant corsage flower has long been Gardenia augusta.

Antique roses *are full of fragrance.* Shown here, Rosa 'Charles de Mills'

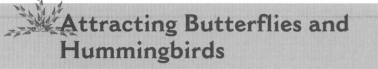

Attracting Butterflies and Hummingbirds

Butterflies and hummingbirds are a joy to watch in the garden; they add an extra dimension of movement, color, and life. Both creatures feed on nectar, which they need in large amounts to fuel their constant motion. You can increase their presence in your garden simply by choosing flowers that meet their needs. The lists that follow include just a small selection of the many possible plants that will lure these remarkable fliers to your personal domain.

ATTRACTING BUTTERFLIES

There are two ways to attract butterflies to the garden. The first is to plant a selection of nectar-rich flowers that will attract more butterflies than you otherwise would have. The second approach, which will attract a wider variety of butterfly species, is more comprehensive. In addition to providing for the adults, you need to provide caterpillar food plants as well as flowers for nectar.

Different species of butterfly larva prefer different plants, and needs vary from region to region. A few of the many possibilities to feed the larva include hop vine, *Ceanothus*, cherry, blueberry, aster, parsley, nasturtium,

and milkweed (*Asclepias*). Fortunately, butterfly caterpillars are not as voracious as the dangerous pests, such as the gypsy moth, which can defoliate an entire forest. In most cases, the foliage they eat won't spoil the overall look of the garden.

ATTRACTING HUMMINGBIRDS

There is a hummingbird to be found in just about every part of the country. The ruby-throated hummingbird summers in the eastern half of the country; Anna's hummingbird sticks to the West Coast area, particularly California; the broad-tailed hummingbird populates the Rockies and areas west in summer; and the Rufous hummingbird breeds in the northwestern part of the country.

Hummingbirds are beautiful to watch, with their ever-active hovering, darting motions and bright colors, and you can attract them to your garden with sugar-water filled feeders. But it's far better to lure them with suitable flowers. Because they feed through their long, needlelike beak, they prefer tubular or trumpet-shaped blossoms such as fuchsia, lilies, hollyhock, and gladiolus. Other nectar-rich flowers they enjoy include garden phlox, nasturtium, petunia, flowering tobacco, and daylilies.

Hummingbirds migrate north early in the season. To get them established in your garden when they first arrive, also include early-flowering choices such as columbine.

Plants for Butterflies

Try to combine a variety of plants that bloom at different times to keep continual interest in the garden and to provide a long season of nectar for the butterflies.

Alcea rosea (hollyhock), Zones 3–10

Allium schoenoprasum (chives), Zones 3–10

Asclepias tuberosa (butterfly weed), Zones 3–9

Aster novae-angliae (New England aster, or New York [*A. novae-belgii*]), Zones 5–9

Baptisia australis (false indigo), Zones 3–10

Borago officinalis, (borage), annual

Cimicifuga racemosa (snakeroot), Zones 3–9

Coreopsis (tickseed), Zones 4–10

Dictamnus albus (gas plant), Zones 3–8

Echinacea purpurea (purple coneflower), Zones 3–10

Heliotropium arborescens (heliotrope), Zone 11, elsewhere annual

Lantana camara & *L. montevidensis* (lantana), Zones 8–10, elsewhere annual

Matthiola incana (stock), Zones 7–10, short-lived

Monarda fistulosa (wild bee balm), Zones 3–9

Petroselinum hortense (parsley), biennial

Sedum spectabile (sedum), Zones 3–9

Tropaeolum majus (nasturtium), annual

Sedum spectabile *'Brilliant' (sedum) in flower lures butterflies.*

A broad-billed male hummingbird *drinks the nectar of a thistle flower.*

A planting *of coneflowers and black-eyed Susans draws butterflies.*

A mixed border *includes black-eyed Susans, pink petunias (front), sedum, daylilies, and cosmos against the house.*

The lively Zinnia *'Pinwheel' is a low-maintenance, long-blooming delight.*

Pink tulips, Alstroemeria, *and* yellow Coreopsis verticillata *'Moonbeam' (tickseed) surround a stone birdbath.*

To attract creatures in flight, *plant the spiky Cleome hassleriana (right) and Cosmos bipinnatus (left).*

Caring for Flowers

The most important aspect of caring for flowers is to put them in good-quality soil. If you have healthy soil, you will almost be guaranteed healthy plants. (See Chapter 3, pages 67–73 for detailed information on how to create good, productive soil.) Spend the time and money on that job before you invest in plants.

The second basic rule of successful gardening is to choose plants that are well adapted to the environment where you expect them to grow. If you put sun-loving plants in a too-shady setting, you are doomed to frustration. In most cases they will languish, possibly growing leggy and ungainly in search of the sun and probably not flowering at all. Plants that need a lot of moisture will wither and die in a dry garden, as will plants that hate to have wet feet if they are put in a boggy area.

Plant flowers suited to local conditions. Aloes, verbena, cactus, and agave thrive at a botanical garden.

Shade-tolerant plants growing under dappled light include perennial geranium and hostas.

Flowers grow best in weed-free, dark rich soil. Shown here: daffodils and a low-growing perennial.

BUYING PERENNIALS AND ANNUALS

When you purchase perennials and annuals in containers, whether they be the market packs of four, six, or eight tiny cells or in larger containers, the temptation is to select the plants that are in full bloom. That is a mistake. Those plants have been forced along at a rapid rate and have quickly outgrown their container space. You risk having long-term problems with roots damaged by being potbound, as well as plants that are exhausted before they've even begun to grow. In the case of perennials that bloom just once a year, that early bloom will quickly fade—and that's all you will get until next year.

You're much better off choosing a smaller plant with lots of buds not quite ready to bloom. Inspect the plant for any evidence of insect or disease problems. You want to see even, healthy growth without disfigured leaves or stems. Slide the plant out of its container. If the roots are curling around and around the bottom of the container, choose another plant; that one has been potbound for too long. Look for good green color and stocky, sturdy growth rather than a plant that is lanky and floppy. The tallest plant is probably not the best choice.

Some perennials ordered through catalogs arrive in bare-root form, meaning that the roots have been harvested after the plant died back in autumn, and the dormant roots are shipped without soil. These roots should be plump with no sign of mildew or rot. If you suspect a problem, call the company. Reputable houses stand by their product.

BUYING BULBS

Make sure that the bulbs you buy are healthy. Look for ones that are firm and blemish-free. As a rule, the larger bulbs of any genus will produce more and larger flowers.

Buying Healthy Plants

Choosing Perennials and Annuals

Be a savvy shopper when you are buying perennials and annuals. Be alert to clues about how healthy the plants are. You can tell a lot by a quick inspection of the plant. Here are points to check.

Signs of a Healthy Plant

Good Foliage Color

Symmetrical, Uniform Shape

Well Branched and Bushy

Plant Size in Proportion to Pot

Securely Attached ID Tag

Only a Few Small Roots Emerging or Visible through Pot Holes

Pot Filled with Soil to within 1" of Rim

Signs of an Unhealthy Plant

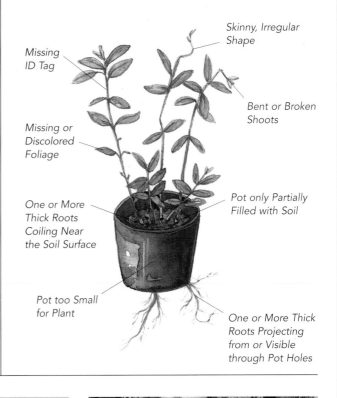

Missing ID Tag

Skinny, Irregular Shape

Missing or Discolored Foliage

Bent or Broken Shoots

One or More Thick Roots Coiling Near the Soil Surface

Pot only Partially Filled with Soil

Pot too Small for Plant

One or More Thick Roots Projecting from or Visible through Pot Holes

Choosing Bulbs

Healthy bulbs should be plump and firm. Soft or mushy bulbs are probably rotted. Bulbs that are too light have probably dried out and died. The top mail-order houses will go to great lengths to provide a good-quality product. If you receive a shipment containing bulbs that may not be healthy, call the supplier and let them know. In most cases they will send you replacements free of charge with no questions asked.

Two for the price of one. *This double-nosed narcissus bulb will eventually split into two bulbs.*

Healthy bulbs *should be firm and show some root growth. Avoid those with top growth.*

PLANTING PERENNIALS AND ANNUALS

Difficulty Level: ***Easy***

The best time to plant or transplant perennials and annuals is on a cool, overcast day. Cloudy weather spares the vulnerable transplants from having to cope with the stress of a hot sun beating on them.

If the plant is growing in a container, dig a hole large enough to accommodate the root ball. Fill the hole with water, and allow the water to soak in completely. Meanwhile, remove the plant from its container. Once the plant is out of the pot, break up the root ball slightly to free the roots. If the roots are in a tight root-bound ball, trim off the outer layer with a sharp knife. Another technique is to make two or three vertical cuts up into the root ball from the bottom and spread the sections apart, gently. (Don't do this for plants with only one or a couple fat tap-roots, such as Oriental poppies.) While these may seem like drastic measures, they are for the good of the plant. Either procedure will stimulate new feeder roots to grow, which can then spread out into the surrounding soil.

When you plant, study the roots to determine whether they naturally grow straight down or in a spreading fashion. If they want to grow downward, dig the hole deep enough to accommodate them. If the roots want to spread, dig the hole wide enough, and spread the roots over mounded soil in the planting hole. (See Chapter 10, pages 211–13 for information on planting bare-root and container-grown plants.)

Tools and Materials: Shovel, knife, water source, organic fertilizer, mulch, plant.

Step 1: Space the Transplant. *Before you dig any holes, position the plants. Remember to consider the plant's mature size, and allow room for growth.*

Step 2: Dig the Hole. *Make the hole deep enough to accommodate the root ball. Tease the roots apart with your fingers, so they don't retain the shape of the pot.*

Step 3: Fertilize the Plant. *Fill the hole with soil and compost. Sprinkle more organic fertilizer around the base of the new plant. Water the plant well.*

Step 4: Mulch the Transplant. *Apply several inches of mulch around the plant. Mulch out to the dripline, but do not cover the plant's crown.*

PLANTING BULBS

Plant spring-blooming bulbs in the fall around mid or late October once the ground has cooled, in soil that drains well. If you plant too early while the soil is still warm, the bulbs may send up foliage before winter. Depending on the size of the bulbs, they should be buried in 4 to 8 inches of soil. Daffodil bulbs are poisonous to burrowing rodents such as mice, voles, and moles. (The Latin *Narcissus* comes from the root word narcotic.) However, other bulbs, such as tulips and crocus, are very tasty to them. To protect the bulbs, line large planting holes with fine chicken wire, or if you are planting each bulb in a separate hole, toss a handful of sharp gravel in each hole to discourage hungry rodents.

To keep perennial bulbs coming back each year with vigor, fertilize them in the fall when the bulbs are developing their root systems. However, do not put the fertilizer directly into the hole when you plant the bulbs, or you could burn them. Instead, sprinkle a slow-release plant food over the ground as a topdressing where the bulbs are buried. A spring feeding will also give bulbs an added boost, although the autumn application is more important. Look for a fertilizer that is especially blended for bulbs, with a nutrient ratio such as 5-10-20 and with trace elements listed in the ingredients.

The dying leaves of perennial bulbs should be left undisturbed for at least six weeks to allow the nutrients to flow back into the bulbs. If you tie up or cut back the foliage before six weeks, you'll choke off the needed sunlight and fresh air they need to store sugars for next year's blooms. If you interrupt that process by disturbing the leaves, you'll weaken the bulbs and diminish the blooms you'll get in subsequent years.

DIVIDING PERENNIALS

Overgrown clumps of perennials won't bloom as prolifically as those with more root room; very old clumps will die in the center, leaving a ring of ailing plant material around the rim. If a perennial bed is densely overgrown, or if the plants in it haven't been divided for some time, it's worth your while to renovate the whole bed and recondition the soil. Remove all the plants to a tarp placed in the shade of a tree. (If there is no nearby shade, cover plants with another tarp to shade them and keep them from drying out.) Spread several inches of compost or well-aged manure and other nutrient-rich organic material over the bed, and dig it in thoroughly. As soon

In the fall, *plant bulbs among perennials. In the late spring, the perennials will hide the dying bulb foliage.*

as the bed is ready, divide and replant the perennials, breaking up large clumps of plants and spacing them so that they have room to grow and spread again. As you break up the plant clumps, discard old and woody inner parts. Each new division should have at least two roots and stems. Work as quickly as you can. The longer you leave the plants out of the ground exposed to the drying air, the weaker and more vulnerable they become. (Although some plants, such as irises and daylilies, are farily durable.) If you do need to delay replanting, wrap the plant roots in wet newspapers, and put them out of the sun. Keep the roots moist until you replant.

There are two approaches you can take to the job. The first is to unearth the entire plant and then pull or cut it apart into smaller portions and replant the new bits. The second is to insert your spade firmly into the middle of the clump, cutting it in half while it is in the ground. Then dig out one half, leaving the rest in place. Put fresh soil or a mix of half soil, half compost into the hole left by the plant half that's being removed; replant the divided piece in another location.

If the plants have been left undivided for too many years, the job isn't always as easy as described above. If the root clump is large, it may take two people tugging with all their might to get it out of the ground. These large root clumps can get so tough and woody that you have to chop them apart with a hatchet.

Divide Old Plants, Harvest Fresh New Plants. Throw away any tough or woody center parts of the divided plant; replant just the more vigorous outer bits. Dividing tough old plants may be a struggle, but you'll be rewarded with a collection of lovely rejuvenated plants.

In most cases you don't have to worry about being too rough with the plant. If the weather is cool and overcast, most perennials can take a lot of yanking about. The most important thing is to get a piece with a few good roots and some foliage with each division.

Spring and early to mid-autumn are the best times of year to divide plants. The easiest way to remember when to divide which plants is to know when the plant flowers, and not divide it while it is flowering or just before it flowers. Thus, perennials that flower in the spring can be divided in the fall. Perennials that bloom from summer through the fall, such as *Coreopsis* or daylilies, can be divided in the fall when they finish flowering or in the early spring. Perennials need at least a month before the ground freezes to set down new roots.

Divide Foliage Plants When Not in Leaf. Foliage plants can be divided either in the fall after the leaves have died back or in the early spring when they first emerge from the ground. However, if you have a friend who is desperate for a division of a plant in midsummer, go ahead and do it. Wrap the divided plant in wet newspaper, and put it in a plastic bag for travel. Plant it as soon as possible, and keep it well watered until you see new growth begin.

Depending on the plant and the weather conditions, newly divided plants may wilt severely the first few days after being replanted. In bright sunny weather you can minimize shock by covering new transplants with a cardboard box (or a few sheets of newspaper weighted down at the edges) for a few days. Make sure they have plenty of moisture. They will probably perk up in less than a week.

DIVIDING HOSTAS

Difficulty Level: Easy

A good way to get more plants for your money is to purchase perennials that have more than one growing crown. You often can divide one large plant into two or three smaller plants.

Tools and Materials: Knife and trowel or shovel for planting.

Step 1: Divide the Crown in Two. *Remove the plant from the pot. Spread the foliage to expose the space between two growing crowns, and then firmly cut, separating the crowns and sawing through the soil and roots.*

Step 2: Split the Plant into More Pieces. *This Hosta sieboldii 'Kabitan' has several growing crowns, so it can be split into four or five small plants. Make sure each division has at least a little foliage with roots attached.*

DIVIDING LAMB'S EARS

Difficulty Level: Easy

You can propagate a large variety of perennials by dividing them, and you can rejuvenate older plants by splitting them apart and removing old, woody growth. Candidates for division include perennials, such as daylilies, with fleshy roots; plants that expand the size of their clumps by growing new plants around them; and spreading plants, such as some sedum, that take root where stems touch the ground. For the example shown here, *Stachys byzantina* (lamb's ears) is being divided. *Stachys* plants are grown for their foliage, so you needn't be concerned about dividing at the wrong time and losing the season's flowers. Lamb's ears multiply by forming new plants at the base of the mother plant and take well to dividing.

Tools and Materials: Shovel and newspaper or drop cloth.

Step 1: Dig around the Clump of Plants to be Divided. *Don't worry about cutting through roots, or even crushing a few leaves. The plants can take a little rough handling.*

Step 2: Lift out the Clump. *While it is likely that soil will cling to the root ball, it is not essential to keep it one piece. You're going to pull it apart anyway when you make the divisions.*

Step 3: Pull Apart the Separate Plants. *Set them aside on newspaper or a drop cloth to keep debris off the lawn. It may help to use the shovel to cut through tough sections.*

Step 4: Plant the Divided Sections. *Plant the divisions with their crowns at about the same height they were originally. If you have more divisions than you need, give some away; meanwhile, keep the roots moist.*

DIVIDING BULBS

Most bulbs, including tubers, rhizomes, and corms, can be divided. In fact, after several years of multiplying underground and becoming more crowded in the process, they benefit from being spaced further apart. Dig up the bulb, pull apart the sections that have developed, and replant. The best time of year for dividing bulbs varies with the type of plant.

MULCHING

Flower beds that are cleanly edged and covered with an attractive mulch, such as shredded hardwood bark or cocoa bean hulls, have a pleasingly tidy and finished look. A thick layer of mulch will slow evaporation of moisture from the soil and reduce weeds.

DEADHEADING AND PINCHING

Deadheading and pinching may sound like terribly brutal things to do to your flowers, but they are in fact important jobs that help keep the flower garden healthy, beautiful, and productive. Deadheading is simply removing the dead flower heads. Except for the flower heads of a few plants such as *Sedum spectabile*, which look decorative as dried flowers, most are unsightly when they die. Also, rotting plant debris attracts insect pests. Remove spent flowers to keep the garden looking tidy and to maintain the vigor of the plants. In some cases, a perennial will rebloom later in the season if the spent flowers are removed in a timely way.

The generous annuals that flower throughout the season will slow down and eventually stop blooming if the fading flowers aren't removed. Annuals are "programmed" to bloom, set seed, and die. By removing spent flowers before they go to seed, you stimulate the plant to flower again in another effort to produce seed to perpetuate its kind. By deadheading you also stimulate new growth and provide room for the new flowers to grow.

Pinching well-shaped plants is another technique for stimulating new growth. When the plants are 2 to 4 inches high, pinch off the top part of the plant just above the top set of leaves. If the plant has multiple stems or branches, pinch off all the tips. For every branch tip you pinch off two or three more will grow, and each new branch has the potential to bear flowers. The result of your effort will be a fuller, more floriferous plant. Do not pinch back plants that grow in a low rosette; you'll remove the growing tip.

A mulch of shredded cedar bark retains moisture and keeps weeds out. Cedar bark is naturally resistant to insects.

▶ *Deadheading* prevents the plant from producing seeds and encourages more flowering. Shown here: deadheading an ageratum.

◀ *Pinching back plants* promotes bushy growth and full plants. Whether you use your fingers as shown here or pruners, the process is still called pinching.

FERTILIZING

Even in healthy soil perennials, annuals, and bulbs need to be fed periodically. After all, plants are continually drawing nutrients out, and at some point those nutrients need to be replenished.

There are two main kinds of fertilizers available: organic and synthetic. Ideally, you want to use organic fertilizer because the synthetic fertilizers, which are produced by industrial processes, contain high concentrations of mineral salts that can acidify the soil and repel earthworms. Do keep in mind, however, that organic fertilizers take longer than synthetics to break down in the soil and become available to plants. Apply them early in the season so that the nutrients are available to the plants when they need it. Because organic fertilizers are less concentrated and release their nutrients slowly, you won't need to apply them as often and you won't need to worry about burning plant roots. Organic fertilizers, are less likely to pollute groundwater than with synthetics .

Your best feeding program is to topdress the beds with a couple of inches of compost or aged manure. (See Chapter 3, pages 70–73 for more information on compost and fertilizers.) For people who prefer the convenience of bagged fertilizers, balanced all-purpose organic blends are now readily available. They supply more organic matter than synthetic fertilizers, though less than compost or aged manure. Annuals that bloom all season long, plus a few perennials, may appreciate the extra dose of nutrients that these blends supply. The formulas will be slightly different from those for standard fertilizers because the organic blends are generally less concentrated; expect to find formulas such as 4-5-4 or 3-2-2. Follow application rates on the package label.

WEEDING

Weeds are unsightly, but that is not their worst offense. To survive they have to be aggressive growers, so weeds have adapted to rob nearby plants of all available nutrients and water. If they grow large enough, they'll also hog growing space and light. If they are rampant enough, they may harbor harmful pests and diseases. A weedy garden is an eyesore as well as an unhealthy environment.

Weeds are controlled with a combination of gravel mulch, dense ground covers, and closely spaced plants.

It is impossible to completely eradicate weeds from the garden. Seeds will blow from the neighbor's garden or even from several blocks away. What the wind doesn't bring, birds may. However, careful maintenance goes a long way toward minimizing the weed problem.

The least labor-intensive approach to weed control is to mulch the garden. If the mulch is laid 4 to 6 inches deep, all but the most aggressive weeds will be stopped. The remainder will be relatively easy to pull. The other secret is to pull weeds before they go to seed. For the trouble of pulling one plant that is going into flower, you halt the potential of literally thousands of new weed plants that could sprout from the resulting seeds. In short, your best approach to weed control is vigilance and a willingness to spend frequent, hopefully short, sessions in the garden removing weeds.

If the weed plants are tiny and you know they aren't seedlings of wanted plants, slice off their roots just below soil level with a sharp hoe. Once they get larger, you're better off digging them out from the roots. Unless they've gone to seed, in which case you should dispose of them in a sealed container, use the pulled weeds as additional mulch, or throw them on the compost heap.

STAKING PLANTS

Some perennials and annuals grow taller than their stalks can support. If you have a very dense growing environment, the nearby plants may be enough to hold the heavy plants upright. In most cases, however, you'll need to stake or tie them up. There are several options available to gardeners, each well adapted to specific plants and situations. For best results, install stakes early in the season so that flower stems get support before they're tall enough to fall over. Tying up peonies after the rains have flattened them is less successful. Insert stakes with care to minimize damage to plant roots.

A simple stake can be made by driving a wooden stake, bamboo pole, or even a straight, sturdy tree branch into the ground and tying a single plant to it. This approach is excellent for particularly tall plants, such as delphiniums or taller cultivars of bearded irises, which send up a tall flower stalk.

Looped Stake. *A more expensive option for individual flower stems is the looped stake. This is a metal stake with an open loop bent at one end. Drive the stake into the ground near the plant, and then slide the tall stem into the encircling arms of the loop.*

Interweave twine to support tall stems.

Grow-Through Supports. *Shrubby perennials, such as peonies, do well when they are contained by grow-through supports. These are made of a coarse metal mesh set in a ring, which is supported on metal legs or stakes. The support is inserted in the ground over the young plant. As the plant gets taller, it grows through the mesh of the support, eventually hiding it altogether.*

Multiple Stakes and String. *You can support broad, floppy plants with multiple tall stems by surrounding them with stakes and then catching up all the falling pieces with green string or twine.*

WINTERIZING

Perennials need to be put to bed for winter. After the first frost, cut the plants down to the ground, and remove any debris and weeds that could harbor pests and diseases. Also remove annuals at the end of the season. After the first frost kills back their foliage, dig up tender bulbs, and store them in a cool, dry place over the winter. Leave ornamental grasses and plants with seed heads, which make an attractive winter display. Those plants should be cut down in early spring to allow room for new growth to develop.

Mulch with Evergreen Boughs to Prevent Heaving. In climates where winter heaving can uproot perennials, exposing roots to cold and drought, wait until the ground freezes for the first time. Then apply a layer of loose (nonmatting) mulch or evergreen boughs to help keep the ground frozen so it remains stable.

Although most plants will continue to grow throughout winter in warm climates, autumn is a good time to give the beds a good tidying. Remove the tired leaves from plants such as irises, and rake out any fallen leaves or debris. While you're at it, take the time to remove weeds. Once winter or spring rains start, they'll begin growing vigorously. Pull weeds out when they're young, and certainly before they go to seed.

Put perennials to bed for the winter. *After the first frost, lay evergreen boughs over plants to prevent heaving. The boughs keep the ground frozen.*

Look for the Beauty in Winter. Although many gardeners spend the winter dreaming of spring, there is something to be said for appreciating the quiet stillness of the winter landscape. If your landscape has good bones, it should have enough structure that it won't look bare during the winter.

Take a mental picture of your garden before you cut everything back. Remember how it looked in its spring glory. Use this slow season to catch up on your records, making note of which plants worked and which you'd like to move in the spring. If there is nothing interesting to look at from inside, plan to plant a tree or shrub (preferably one with winter interest) to fill the gap. (See Chapter 10, page 203 for a list of plants with winter interest.)

Shop the Catalogs with Purpose. After you've created your wish list, start browsing through garden catalogs. Refer back to your notes, and think about the conditions in your garden. Then you can shop the catalogs with purpose, and you won't be tempted with impulse purchases.

Keep your gardening gloves handy. And when that warm day comes in February, as it always does, get outside and poke around, looking and listening for signs of spring.

After a killing frost, *cut perennial plants down to the ground. After such a frost, the stems of herbaceous plants will turn black and mushy. Take time to appreciate the tranquility of this moment before cutting things back.*

CHAPTER 13

Vegetables and Herbs

Nothing beats the flavor of an ear of corn steamed just moments after harvest, or of crunching on crispy peas eaten straight from the pod while still in the garden. Freshly picked, juicy tomatoes sprinkled with homegrown basil are a treat not to be missed. All this and more is possible if you grow your own vegetables and herbs. And you don't have to devote a huge amount of space to grow food. In this chapter you'll get ideas for tucking an attractive vegetable or two into a flower garden and growing flowers and herbs in with the vegetables to make the most of your growing space. You'll also learn how to care for your crops to maximize your harvest and minimize pests and diseases.

Herbs are an intensely satisfying group of plants to grow. Many are both edible and ornamental; others have delightful scents. Read on to learn about traditional designs for herb gardens as well as new ideas for incorporating herbs into a home landscape.

Designing Your Vegetable Garden

Traditionally vegetable gardens have been considered unattractive production plots that are hidden away, out of sight of the ornamental portions of the garden. That doesn't need to be the case. Many fruits and vegetables, such as ruby chard, rhubarb, parsley, kale, and artichokes, are attractive plants in their own right; they can even be tucked into flower borders without jarring results. By the same token, flowers complement a vegetable plot, some with beneficial results as companion plants. French marigolds (*Tagetes patula*) add bright color to a food garden, at the same time discouraging nematodes and some insect pests. Some flowering favorites planted in the kitchen garden can help attract a variety of beneficial insects that devour pests; these flowers include yarrow (*Achillea* species), candytuft (*Iberis* species), evening primrose (*Oenothera* species), and goldenrod (*Solidago* species).

The French elevated vegetable gardening to a high art with their *potagers*, or kitchen gardens. More and more North American gardeners, too, are designing gardens of edibles that are ornamental as well as practical. This approach makes a lot of sense if you have limited space in which to garden.

In a *potager*, vegetables and fruits—with occasional flowers for decorative effect—are planted in a formal

◀ **Edible as well as ornamental,** *the orange marigolds are a stunning contrast to the purple cabbage heads. Marigold petals have a spicy citrus flavor and add a splash of color to food.*

▼ **This successfully designed vegetable garden,** *created by gardening author Rosalind Creasy, combines ornamental vegetables, herbs, flowers, and dwarf trees to create a pretty garden scene. Note her use of potted plants.*

▲ **A geometric vegetable garden** *can be high art, as shown in this famous potager at Villandry in France. Here the ornamental cabbage 'Lyssaka' is mass-planted within neatly clipped boxwood-lined parterres. Standard roses add vertical interest.*

design using the distinctive plant forms to create intricate patterns of color and texture. When you design an ornamental vegetable garden, think about the visual qualities of each vegetable in the same way you would think about the color, form, and texture of plants when you design a flower garden.

Villandry, a Renaissance chateau in France's Loire Valley, is home to the world's most famous *potager*. There, nine enormous square beds divided by wide, straight formal paths are mass-planted with vegetables of different shapes, colors, and textures to create eye-catching patterns. For example, one year the feathery, jade-green tops of carrots might be mixed with globular blue-green cabbages and bluish, spiky-leaved leeks to set off the red-veined leaves of beets. Within the large beds, called parterres, low boxwood hedges divide up the space and serve as frames for the decorative plantings of vegetables.

Most vegetables are either cool season or heat-loving annuals, so the beds at Villandry are planted twice a year. A spring crop of cool-season vegetables such as peas, broad beans, radishes, lentils, spring cabbage, and different kinds of lettuces is planted in mid-March and harvested in mid-June. In their place are planted summer and autumn crops, including brightly colored cabbages, pumpkins, zucchinis, carrots, leeks, eggplants, tomatoes, celeriac, chives, parsley, basil, and chicory.

PLANT IN PATTERNS

You can even incorporate the design qualities of a *potager* in a small suburban vegetable garden. Instead of planting vegetables in long rows, mass them to create patterns. Outline beds with attractive edging plants such as curly parsley. Plants with edible flowers—such as violas, nasturtiums, or pot marigolds (*Calendula officinalis*)—are ideal. Draw the pattern on paper before you go out to plant. Within your vegetable plot, draw a number of smaller beds that together form a pattern. Then, within each small bed, design a pattern of mixed plants or a mass planting of one vegetable to make a dramatic design. For example, you might plant quarter circles in each corner with stripes formed of ruby-red Swiss chard and bright green spring onions, or red and green lettuces. Think about incorporating a central focal point into your design, such as a dramatic single plant—perhaps an artichoke or a dwarf apple or pear tree—or a decorative frame or trellis covered with scarlet runner beans.

If formal, framed patterns are not to your taste, another option for an ornamental vegetable garden design is bold blocks. Divide your beds into a series of rectangles to create a geometric patchwork plan, and then plant each bed with a different crop. Think about the color and texture of each plant so you can put attractive combinations in beds next to each other.

Paths as Part of the Design. Early American colonists designed their dooryard gardens with a geometric structure of intersecting paths dividing the beds, but each bed was planted as an informal medley of vegetables, herbs, and flowers all jumbled together to

A bold yellow-and-red design is created by stripes of edible and ornamental plants. Don't overlook foliage color, such as the purple basil planted in front of the lettuce (center).

provide for the medicinal and culinary needs of the family. Beds were accessible from both sides (hence the pattern of paths) and narrow enough to reach across, so the gardener could easily weed and harvest without trampling on the soil and compacting it. These cottage-style gardens have a charm and practicality that make them appealing to this day. Colonial gardens were usually surrounded by a picket fence to keep out wandering livestock. Today most suburban gardeners don't need to worry about stray cows and goats; however, a picket fence is still an attractive garden enclosure.

◄ *This bed alongside a path is planted with parsley, marigolds, lavender, basil, chives, and thyme. The path is edged with a low woven fence, made when the twigs were young and supple.*

► *Shapes, colors, and textures can be used when combining herbs to create a picture that is a joy to behold whether there are flowers in bloom or not. A sundial is a traditional ornament to place in the center of a sunny herb garden; the path gives structure and adds a pattern to the design.*

PLACING THE GARDEN

Most vegetables and herbs require at least 6 hours of sun. Study the light patterns on your property before deciding where to place the vegetable garden. You may be able to eek out an early crop of cool-weather vegetables under deciduous trees before they leaf out. However, for summer vegetables, open sun is preferred.

Avoid planting on low ground. The soil may not drain properly, and a cold microclimate could exist. If the sunniest part of your property is on low ground, consider building a raised bed.

DECIDING ON YOUR CROPS

Home gardeners can choose from a wealth of vegetable varieties. When planning your garden, resist the temptation to have one of everything. Grow crops that your family likes to eat. Give priority to fruits and vegetables that are expensive to buy because they don't travel well, such as raspberries, and to ones that are less flavorful when purchased at the grocery store because they're picked for shipping before they are ripe. Although recent corn hybrids hold their flavor much better than the old varieties, it's still a treat to feast on corn on the cob cooked within minutes of being picked in the garden. Exotic varieties such as golden tomatoes, yellow-fleshed watermelons, blue potatoes, and heirloom vegetables that have been grown in gardens for hundreds of years are all fun possibilities.

Heirloom Vegetables. While many wonderful new vegetable varieties have been bred, there is still something about the old tried-and-true vegetables. Heirloom vegetables have not been genetically altered. Many have developed strong traits over the years that enable them to survive. But heirloom vegetables will continue to exist only if people continue to grow them and collect their seed. Look for catalogs that specialize in heirloom vegetables, or join the Seed Savers Exchange, a network of committed gardeners who grow and swap the seeds of heirloom vegetables.

Consider Climate. When choosing vegetables, keep in mind your local climate and growing conditions. The growing season varies from region to region. It is the number of days between the last frost of winter and the first frost of fall. And because the ground takes a while to warm up, the actual growing season is probably shorter

Vegetables and ornamentals can be grown together in a tiny garden. Here lettuce, zucchini, salsify, and spinach are planted in spokes that radiate out from the central millstone fountain.

▶ *'Storr's Green' heirloom zucchini* is a compact grower. The glossy green squash stands out sharply against the bright yellow flowers, which are edible.

◀ *This mound of heirloom vegetables* ('Brownwell' potatoes) is the crop from just one root.

than the frost-free season by a couple of weeks. Crops such as okra and watermelon, which we associate with the South, require a lot of warm weather to develop properly. While there are hybrids such as 'Sugar Baby' watermelon that mature quickly for regions with a shorter growing season, you are pushing the limits to grow them in cool climates. If you live in a climate where the growing season is as short as 90 days, find vegetable varieties that are bred to mature within that time.

You can also stretch your growing season by starting seeds indoors and transplanting the seedlings out into the garden.

Approximate Vegetable Yields

A common mistake many new vegetable gardeners make is to plant too much of one crop. Zucchini plants, for instance, are so prolific that an average family doesn't need more than one or two of them. Use the following table to help determine how much you want to plant of any one vegetable. This is just a guideline, but it should help you plant as much as you can eat without a lot of waste.

Vegetables	Length of Harvest	Season of Harvest	Average Yield for 10' Row	Average Harvest per Week
Asparagus	4–6 weeks	spring	3 lbs.	0.6 lb.
Bean, bush snap	2 weeks	summer	3 lbs.	1.5 lbs.
Bean, pole snap	6 weeks	summer	4 lbs.	0.7 lb.
Bean, bush lima	3 weeks	summer	2 lbs. with pod	0.7 lb.
Bean, pole lima	4 weeks	summer	4 lbs. with pod	1 lb.
Beet	4 weeks	summer through fall	2.4 dozen	7 beets
Broccoli	4 weeks	summer through fall	4 lbs.	1 lb.
Cabbage	3–4 weeks	spring, fall	4 heads	1 head
Cantaloupe	3 weeks	summer	4 melons	1 melon
Carrot	4 weeks	spring through winter	4 dozen	1 dozen
Chard	8 weeks	spring through fall	5 lbs.	0.6 lb.
Corn, sweet	10 days	summer	10 ears	1 ear/day
Cucumber	4 weeks	summer	5 lbs. (7 cucumbers)	2 cucumbers
Kale	4–20 weeks	spring, fall, winter	5 lbs.	0.5 lb.
Lettuce, leaf	6 weeks	spring, fall	15 stalks	2.5 stalks
Lettuce, head	4 weeks	spring, fall	8 heads	2 heads
Okra	6 weeks	summer	3 lbs.	0.5 lb.
Onion	4–24 weeks	summer and fall, depending on type	5 lbs.	0.4 lb.
Parsnip	4 months	late fall through winter	5 lbs.	0.4 lb.
Pea, green	2 weeks	spring	7 lbs. with pod	3.5 lbs.
Pepper, sweet	8 weeks	summer	40 peppers	5 peppers
Potato	4 months	spring through fall, depending on variety	6 lbs.	0.4 lb.
Potato, sweet	5 months	fall	8 lbs.	0.4 lb.
Pumpkin	2 months	fall	10 lbs.	1.25 lbs.
Radish	2 weeks	spring and fall	7 dozen	3.5 dozen
Rhubarb	4–6 weeks	spring	6 lbs.	1.2 lbs.
Spinach	4 weeks	spring and fall	10 lbs.	2.5 lbs.
Squash, summer	4 weeks	summer	7 lbs.	1.75 lbs.
Tomato	8 weeks	summer	8 lbs.	1 lb.
Turnip, root	5 months	late spring, fall	15 roots	3 roots
Watermelon	3 weeks	summer	2 melons	1 melon

CHOOSE PEST AND DISEASE RESISTANT PLANTS

Be aware of pests and diseases that are prevalent in your area. Call your Cooperative Extension Service, and talk to the experts to find out common problems. It's also helpful to talk to friends and neighbors who have experience growing vegetables. Nothing beats personal experience for excellent information. In the South and mid-Atlantic states, hot, humid summers breed fungal diseases. Avoid vegetables that are susceptible to fungal diseases, or choose resistant varieties. For example, melons are prone to diseases such as various mildews and fusarium wilt, but breeders have developed several, such as 'Athena', 'Ambrosia', and 'Classic', that are resistant. Opt for those or similar varieties, especially if you live in a humid climate.

Read seed catalog descriptions carefully to find out which varieties have been bred for resistance. (See Chapter 14, pages 290–305 for more information on managing pests and diseases.)

Specialty Tomatoes

Determinate and Indeterminate Tomatoes. There are two classes of tomato: determinate and indeterminate. Determinate tomatoes are bushier and don't get as tall; they slow or stop growing taller once they start producing. They are good canning tomatoes because all the fruit ripens at about the same time. (Technically, tomatoes are fruit, although they are widely referred to as vegetables.) The indeterminate varieties continue growing all season long, so they get much taller than determine types. Indeterminates are best as salad tomatoes because they will continue to bloom all summer long, producing fruit until frost.

Determinate 'Roma' VFN

Indeterminate 'Yellow Pear'

Indeterminate 'Tigerella'

Disease Tolerant Varieties. Tomatoes often have a series of initials after their name. These indicate the variety's resistance to some of the pests and diseases that plague tomatoes. It is especially important to select disease-tolerant varieties if you plant tomatoes in the same spot year after year. (See "Crop Rotation," page 282.)

Initial	Name of Disease	Description of Disease
V	Verticillium	Plant looks wilted with yellow patches on leaves that turn brown; thrives in cool temperatures
F	Fusarium	Plant looks wilted with yellow patches on leaves that turn brown; thrives in warm temperatures
N	Nematodes	Yellow, wilted, and stunted plant with reduced crop yield
T	Tobacco mosaic	Mottled yellowing leaves and fruit; twisted new growth

Determinate 'Celebrity' VFNT

Plant Combinations that Repel Pests

Plant	To Repel
Basil with tomatoes	Tomato hornworms
Thyme or tomatoes with cabbages	Flea beetles, cabbage maggots, white cabbage butterflies, and imported cabbageworms
Tomato with asparagus	Asparagus beetle
Catnip near eggplant	Flea beetles
Cucumber with corn	Raccoons (deterred by cucumbers)
Radishes with cucumber	Cucumber beetles
Rosemary with beans	Mexican bean beetle
Horseradish near potatoes	Colorado potato beetles
Onions with carrots	Rust flies and some nematodes
Onion with cabbages	Cabbage butterflies

This insect-repelling combination is ornamental and functional. The frilly edging of parsley sets off the tomato plants beautifully. In addition to parsley, tomatoes are compatible with chives, onion, marigold, nasturtium, and carrot.

COMPANION PLANTING

Companion planting makes use of the effects plants can have on other plants growing nearby. Strongly scented French marigolds (*Tagetes patula*) repel some insects as well as help reduce damaging nematodes in the soil. Basil grown near tomatoes is said to improve the tomato's flavor as well as to repel aphids, mosquitoes, and mites. To get the most from companion planting, make notes about which combinations work best in your garden. See Chapter 14, pages 293–97 for detailed information on companion planting, attracting beneficial insects, and plants that repel pests.

Growing Vegetables and Herbs

SOIL PREPARATION

Good-quality soil is the foundation for any successful garden. This is especially true of a vegetable garden because for the most part you're growing annual plants that need a lot of nutrients to grow quickly and produce bountifully. Have your soil tested to see whether you have any pH problems or nutrient imbalances that would interfere with growing vegetables. (See Chapter 3, page 68 for informa-

A close planting of purple and chartreuse kale, Italian parsley, and marigolds creates a pleasing picture of color and texture. Marigolds reduce nematodes in the soil.

tion on soil testing.) If the soil test suggests lime, try to add it the fall before you intend to plant, as it takes some time for lime to counteract soil acidity. If the soil test recommends sulfur (to correct alkaline soil) or fertilizer, these can be added a week or two before you plant. Also consider planting cover crops to fertilize the soil. (See page 282 for information on cover crops.)

SOIL TESTING BEFORE DIGGING

It's important to check the moisture level of the soil before you start digging. Although it's tempting to plant your vegetables in the early spring as soon as the snow melts, it's wiser to resist this urge. If you dig while the soil is too wet, you can damage the soil structure. Use these simple tests to determine whether the soil is ready to dig.

This soil is too dry. *If you squeeze a handful of soil, and it breaks apart when you open your hand, it is too dry to dig or plant.*

Too wet. *If the soil forms a tight clump when you squeeze it and your finger leaves a depression when you press the clump, it is too wet.*

Just right. *If the soil stays in a clump when it is squeezed but breaks apart when you tap it, the moisture content is just right.*

ADD ORGANIC MATTER

The best way to build the soil for vegetables is with organic matter such as compost and manure. (Use aged manure if you apply it in the spring. If the garden will be empty over the winter, you can spread fresh manure—it will have aged sufficiently by the following spring.)

Follow the instructions in Chapter 3, pages 70–73 for adding and digging-in amendments. Once the amendments have been tilled into the soil (either by hand digging or rototilling, depending on the size of your garden), rake the bed to smooth it out and to remove any stones that might have surfaced. At this point, the garden is ready for sowing seed or setting-in transplants.

Amend Soil with Leaves. If you have deciduous trees in your garden, you have a great source for improving the soil readily available. An easy way to amend the soil is to shred the leaves in the autumn and spread them over the bed, allowing them to decompose over the winter. In the spring, simply turn the leaves under. The decomposed leaves will provide plenty of nutrients. A more common procedure to maintain good-quality soil is to spread and turn under a 1-inch layer of compost, rotted manure, or other organic materials each fall or spring.

TIMING YOUR PLANTING

The temptation is strong to sow seed as early as possible. However, sometimes starting too soon can have detrimental results. Once seedlings sprouted indoors start to grow in earnest, they will become weak and spindly if they don't have enough light and room to grow. They need to be transplanted outside as soon as possible. However, if the air and soil temperatures are still too low for them to flourish outdoors, you are stuck caring for plants that are growing weaker by the day. Vegetables produce best if they can grow quickly without any setbacks. Younger plants set outside at the optimal time will quickly catch up to and even outpace larger plants that were started too soon indoors.

The same is true for planting seeds directly into the ground outdoors. Plants require a certain soil temperature before they will germinate. As a general rule, cool-season crops need the soil to be at least 45°F to sprout. Heat-loving vegetables need the soil to be at 60°F or warmer. Ask your extension educator about the ideal time to start vegetable seed indoors. The extension office has charts with schedules for different vegetables based on your region. Wait for the right time to plant. (A soil thermometer is a helpful tool.) Your patience will be rewarded with a successful crop.

STARTING SEEDS

Starting vegetables and herbs from seeds gives you a head start on your garden, and you can plant unusual varieties that you may not find locally. Pay attention to the information on the seed packet to time your planting. Seeds shouldn't be growing under the adverse conditions found indoors for too long.

Tools and Materials: Plastic tray with cover, soilless planting medium (mix of perlite, vermiculite, sand, sphagnum moss) or a commercial seed-starting blend mix, flat-edged piece of wood, sheet of paper folded in half, trowel, watering can with rosette or mister bottle, small pots.

Step 1: Fill the Tray. *Moisten the medium, and fill the tray. Smooth the surface by dragging the stick across, pressing firmly to eliminate air pockets as you go. Make row indents across the surface with the stick.*

Step 2: Spread the Seed. *Put the seeds in the folded paper, and sprinkle them along the rows. Mix very tiny seeds with sand first; then spread them with the paper. Press the seeds into the planting medium.*

Step 3: Bury the Seeds. *Use a small trowel to spread a thin layer of planting medium over the seeds. Some seeds require light to germinate and should not be covered. Follow the directions on the seed package.*

Step 4: Water the Seeds. *Use a watering can fitted with a rosette to trickle water over the medium until it is evenly moist. Use a mister bottle for fine seeds. The goal is to moisten the medium without dislodging the seeds.*

Step 5: Cover the Tray. *Place a cover or a sheet of clear plastic wrap over the tray to retain humidity. Place the covered tray in a bright spot. Remove the cover for a few hours once a day to allow air to circulate.*

Step 6: Transplant the Seedlings. *After the first leaves appear, keep the cover off for most of the day. When the seedlings have two to four sets of leaves, transplant each seedling to a pot of its own.*

SEED SOURCES

The quality of all seed is not alike. Old or poorly stored seeds are less likely to germinate. Buying cut-priced seeds or packets that have been marked down in price is a false economy. All your labor in preparing the soil, planning the garden, weeding, feeding, and tending will be for naught if your seed produces weak plants or doesn't germinate at all. Always buy seed that is dated to sell in the year you are planting, and buy from known, reliable sources.

The easiest way to find seed is to visit your local garden center, hardware store, or home supply store. For a wider array of choices, look at mail-order catalogs. You also can find small regional seed companies that sell varieties suited to your climate, stock heirloom varieties, or specialize in great selections of tomatoes, chili peppers, or edible flowers. By growing these special varieties, gardeners are helping to preserve genetic diversity.

Look for Locally Harvested Seed. Plants grown from seeds harvested from your local region are more likely to grow well than those shipped from across the country. From what the experts understand, part of the seed's genetic makeup includes qualities that make the plant especially well adapted to where the mother plant grew. Therefore, your optimal sources for seed are local or regional catalog companies. In addition to stocking more locally grown seeds, their selection of varieties is more likely to feature ones particularly suited to your area.

After you've planted the seeds, save the packet and the receipt. If you have problems, you can go back to the vendor; if you especially like particular seeds, you'll know which one it is if you want to reorder for another year. Keep notes about each plant, recording what went well and what failed or could be improved. Those notes will be invaluable to help you plan future gardens.

Make the most of limited space in a small vegetable garden. In the garden shown here, the sprawling vines are kept in the back of the bed, and beans are trained up vertical supports. There is just enough to harvest and no waste.

This heirloom pepper is called 'Jimmy Nardello's'. It is indeed a sweet pepper, although its shape suggests that it is hot.

MAXIMIZE SPACE

Grow quick-maturing plants such as lettuces and other greens together. After they're harvested, you can use the released space for another crop. This technique is called succession planting. (See page 281.) Place plants such as pumpkins, which sprawl, on the edge of the garden so that they don't take up as much valuable bed space. Locate perennial vegetables, such as asparagus and rhubarb, out of the way of the beds where you put the annual crops. That way you won't disturb the perennials when you till the soil for the annual beds each year. Another good tip is to grow vegetables from the same family (cole crops such as cabbages and broccoli; legumes, including all the pea and bean varieties; tomato and its relatives, eggplants and peppers) together to make crop rotation easier. (Crop rotation is explained on page 282.)

Once you've chosen the vegetables you want to grow, you've got to decide how to arrange them in your garden. In addition to the visual considerations discussed earlier, keep in mind the growing requirements of your plants. As a rule, locate tall plants such as corn or pole beans at the north end of the bed so that they don't shade their shorter companions. An exception is plants that appreciate relief from the sun, such as summer lettuce; in that case, place the plants that need shade on the north side of taller vegetables.

Vertical Vegetables

You can get a larger harvest out of a small plot of land and add vertical visual interest to your landscape by growing vegetables on trellises or other plant supports. Peas, pole beans, cucumbers, some melons, and indeterminate varieties of tomatoes are vining crops that grow better if they are kept off the ground. There are lots of different systems for growing vegetables vertically. The best choice depends on the plant you want to support and your own preferences.

Plant Teepees. A time-honored system for supporting peas, pole beans, vining squash, and pumpkins is a tripod or teepee. Use poles 6 to 8 feet long. Pound them firmly into the ground in a circle, and then tie the tops together in a clump to make a teepee shape. Plant one or two vining vegetables at the base of each pole, and train them to grow upward. To make even more intense use of the space, you can plant cool-loving vegetables such as lettuce and spinach inside the teepee, where they will appreciate the shade during the hot days of summer. Children also enjoy the secret hiding place plant teepees provide. They will have treasured memories of sitting inside one, picking fresh peas or beans, or watching the squash and pumpkins ripen. Ten-foot poles give children a little more room underneath and provide extra height for tall bean varieties such as 'Scarlet Runner'.

Crisscrossed Poles. This support system allows you to plant a large number of vining vegetables in rows. Pound 5- to 8-foot-long poles into the ground in a row about 12 inches apart. Create a second parallel row of poles about 30 inches from the first row. Tie opposite pairs of poles together about 6 inches from the top to form a small V shape, just wide enough to hold a pole. To give stability to the entire row, set a long pole across the tops of the Vs. For added stablilty, tie it to each crisscrossed pole.

Trellis Support. A simple alternative to crisscrossed poles is a trellis support, which serves as a partition in the landscape, dividing space to create individual rooms or to serve as a backdrop to other plantings.

For the frame, select sturdy poles 6 to 8 feet long. The support is relatively easy to set up, so you can take it down over the winter if you like or change its position from year to year as you rotate crops or alter your vegetable garden design. (See Chapter 6, page 144, for more information on trellis design.)

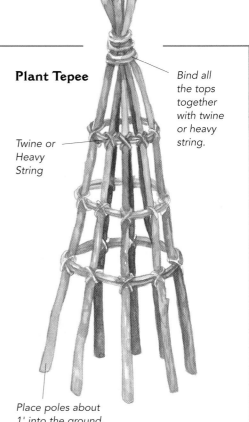

Plant Tepee

Bind all the tops together with twine or heavy string.

Twine or Heavy String

Place poles about 1' into the ground.

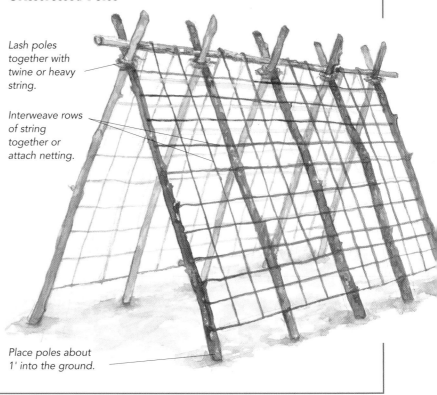

Crisscrossed Poles

Lash poles together with twine or heavy string.

Interweave rows of string together or attach netting.

Place poles about 1' into the ground.

When to Plant Your Produce

Crops that mature in less than 60 days, such as the following, are excellent for short-season gardens and for succession planting.

There are a few perennial vegetables and fruits. These long-lived plants benefit from the same good soil and feeding as other perennial plants.

FAST-MATURING VEGETABLES

Beta spp. (beets)
Brassica juncea (mustard greens)
Brassica oleracea (kohlrabi)
Brassica rapa (Chinese cabbage), many varieties
Cichorium endiva (endive)
Daucus carota (carrots), miniature varieties
Eruca vesicaria (arugula)
Lactuca sativa (lettuce)
Mesclun (a mix of salad greens)
Phaseolus spp. (bush beans)
Raphanus sativus (radishes)
Spinacia oleracea (spinach)

PERENNIAL VEGETABLES AND FRUITS

Actinidia spp. (kiwi)
Asparagus officinalis (asparagus)
Cynara cardunculus (cardoons)
Cynara scolymus (artichokes)
Fragaria x ananassa (strawberries)
Helianthus tuberosus (Jerusalem artichokes)
Rheum x cultorum (rhubarb)
Rubus fruticosus (blackberry)
Rubus idaeus (raspberry)
Vaccinium spp. (blueberry)
Vitis labrusca, V. rotundifolia & V. vinifera (grapes)

Beta (golden and spinel beets)

Phaseolus vulgaris 'Bench Mark' (bush snap bean)

Asparagus officinalis (asparagus)

Helianthus tuberosus roots (Jerusalem artichoke)

SUCCESSION PLANTING AND INTERPLANTING

Succession planting and interplanting are two excellent ways to get a bigger harvest.

Succession planting is simply seeding the same crop over a period of weeks during the growing season. It is an excellent way to extend the harvest for vegetables that do not produce continuously throughout the summer. Radishes, lettuce, carrots, beets, bush snap beans, spinach, onions, and corn all are excellent candidates for succession planting. Plant some of the seed, wait two or three weeks, and then plant some more. You can continue sowing until you run out of growing time. Check on the number of days each plant requires to reach maturity. (Also observe how long they take in your particular garden.) Then count back from the date of your region's first projected frost date in autumn. For example, if the first killing frost in your neighborhood on

Crop succession will allow you to get the most out of the space you allot to vegetables. Do so by replacing fast-maturing crops, such as lettuce and spinach, with a new planting when the first crop is finished.

average happens by November 15 and the vegetable needs 63 days to mature, then you can continue to plant up until about September 13. (Give yourself a margin of a couple of weeks, and plant until September 1.)

A second type of succession planting is crop succession. In warm regions with a long growing season, this technique is an excellent way to get the most out of your vegetable garden space. After you've harvested all of one crop, such as a cool-season lettuce planted in early spring, use the same space to plant a heat-loving summer vegetable, such as tomato or eggplant. You can use the same space to get a third harvest if you replace the summer produce with autumn vegetables, such as kale and broccoli.

Interplanting Crops. Interplanting, or intercropping, is growing two different crops in the same space. Native Americans grew corn, pole beans, and squash together for a highly efficient, mutually beneficial use of space. The beans grew up the corn stalks, while the squash spread about on the ground around the poles.

Another good use of interplanting is to combine a quick-growing vegetable with a slower-growing crop.

Grow a cover crop, such as the barley as shown here, and then plow it into the soil before seeds are set. You'll improve the soil and smother out weeds.

For example, space broccoli plants at the usual distance, tucking a couple of radish seeds between each, or sow rows of radishes at the edges of your squash bed. Radishes also make good markers for seeds that are slow to germinate. Or plant radish and turnip seeds together. The radishes will germinate within days, reminding you of where the turnips are. When the radishes are ready for harvest, the turnips will have sprouted and will benefit by the "cultivating" that results when the radishes are pulled. Then they will grow to fill the empty space. Quick-growing spinach and slower-growing brussel sprouts are other good companions.

CROP ROTATION

One of the best ways to foil diseases and insect pests in a vegetable garden is to move the annual crops around in the garden from year to year. That way, if a disease or pest that strikes down tomatoes remains in the soil, a planting of cabbages in the same spot the next year will be unaffected. Meanwhile, the disease will wither away because it has no host, and the pests will have to work hard and travel greater distances to find their preferred feeding source. The most simple approach to crop rotation is to wait several years before you replant a bed with any vegetable from the same family.

Cover Crops. If you have enough space, devote one bed each year to a *green manure*. Green manures are plants such as annual rye, buckwheat, or clover that you grow to improve and renew the soil, plowing or turning them under at the end of its season. Planting green manures can also help control weeds. (See "Weeding," on page 284, for more information.)

Care and Feeding of Vegetables

Growing vegetables is a labor-intensive but deeply satisfying occupation. Once your garden is laid out and growing well, your primary job will be to keep a regular eye on things to make sure no problems develop. It's much easier to deal with a pest or disease if you catch it in its early stages rather than after it has grown into an infestation. If you slip up on the regular maintenance, you'll make much more work for yourself or reduce your harvest. During the summer months, make it a habit to take a daily tour of the garden, checking on the growth, pulling a few weeds, perhaps harvesting a bit, and looking for signs of problems. Take along a trowel and clippers, so you have the tools handy if you spot a quick job that needs to be done.

WATERING

To keep growing at a consistently rapid rate, vegetables need a steady supply of water. Any time vegetable plants are stressed because of lack of water, they will turn their energies into surviving instead of producing. Monitor the moistness of the soil regularly, and irrigate when it begins to get too dry. To test the soil's dryness, take up a handful of soil and squeeze it. If the soil will not stay together in a lump, it is too dry and needs water.

The best time to water is early in the morning or late in the afternoon; you'll lose less water from evaporation. If you're watering by hand, try to keep the water away from the plants' foliage; direct the stream of water to the roots and soil, where it's most needed. Wet leaves are more vulnerable to sunburn and fungus infection. Run the water slow enough that it can soak in, rather than running off the top of the soil away from plant roots.

The most practical method for irrigating large vegetable beds is a drip-irrigation or soaker-hose system. These systems deliver water directly to the plants' root zones, so weeds are minimized, and it soaks in deeply rather than running off because it is delivered so slowly. Drip and soaker systems are adaptable, so you can modify the design as the vegetable-garden needs change from season to season and year to year. If you have mulched the garden with black plastic, run the lines under the plastic. Mark the plastic sheeting to indicate the location of each emitter, and then cut through the plastic and

Monitor your plants for early signs of pest or disease problems while taking a daily stroll through your vegetable garden to enjoy the fruits of your labor.

Drip irrigation delivers water directly to the roots of these young broccoli plants. It is easy to move the lines around to accommodate a different crop at a later date.

plant next to the emitter. (See Chapter 3, pages 80–83 for more information on drip-irrigation systems.)

When seeds are sprouting and plants are small, the soil needs to be kept continually moist. A daily light sprinkling (or twice daily if the weather is particularly hot and dry) is ideal until the seedlings are established. (Don't worry about wetting the foliage of young seedlings.) Then begin watering only the root zone.

Weeding

Weeds compete for water, nutrients, and light and can harbor insect pests. It's impossible to completely eradicate weeds, but you can go a long way toward controlling them.

Weeds are easiest to remove when they're young and the roots aren't well established. Uproot them with a hoe, being careful not to disturb the roots of nearby plants. You have to hand-dig well-established weeds. Don't wait until after the plants have set seed, or you'll be faced with a larger weed problem next year.

Cover crops such as clover, annual rye, vetch, barley, and buckwheat are great for weed control and adding organic matter to the soil. The most common procedure is to plant a cover crop after the vegetables have been harvested. Plow the cover crop into the ground the following spring, three to four weeks before planting the garden, and certainly before the cover crop goes to seed. The weeds will be gone, and the soil will be improved. Buckwheat is probably the best cover crop for shading out annual weeds. It requires a slightly different treatment because it needs warm weather to grow. Plant it in late spring (the same time as squash), and turn it under a few weeks later just as it starts to bloom; then plant a second crop, and turn it over a few weeks later. You'll have to wait until the following season to plant vegetables, but you will have added lots of organic matter to the soil and have eliminated many of the weeds.

The plantain weed self-sows prolifically. Pull it before it sets seeds.

Mulching

Mulch is a layer of material used to cover the soil surface in the garden to shade out weeds, slow the evaporation of moisture from the soil, and moderate soil temperatures. For the vegetable garden, you need organic mulches that will break down by the end of the season or can be turned into the soil; these include straw, chopped leaves, and grass clippings. Organic materials improve the quality of the soil as they decompose.

Mulch acts as an insulator. In cold climates, wait until the ground has warmed up for the season before you spread mulch. As a guideline, wait until seedlings are well established. They won't start growing until the soil is warm, and you won't risk burying them too deeply because you can't see where they are. If you are using a coarse-textured material such as shredded leaves, it takes a 4- to 6-inch layer of mulch to keep down weeds. Fine-textured mulches such as cocoa bean hulls need to be only 2 to 3 inches deep. In either case, you can get away with less in shady areas where weeds are less likely to thrive. To avoid the risk of introducing rot, take care to keep the mulch away from the stems of plants.

At the end of the growing season, turn organic mulch into the soil to add more organic material. It will break down over the winter months, adding nutrients, feeding earthworms, and improving the soil's structure.

Mulch insulates plants and feeds the soil when it breaks down.

Fertilizing

Gardeners can choose between organic and synthetic fertilizers. Organic products are derived from animals, plants, or minerals. These products, including well-rotted manure, fish meal and emulsion, compost, bone and blood meal, limestone, cottonseed meal, and wood ashes, improve soil structure, add nutrients, and help nourish the microbial life whose activity makes for a healthy soil that's a good growing medium for plants.

The synthetic fertilizers are manufactured by industrial processes. Their appeal is that they are easy to apply and get quick results. Unfortunately, while these synthetics supply concentrated nutrients to the plants, they don't supply any organic matter to feed earthworms and other beneficial soil organisms. If you like the convenience of synthetic fertilizers, be good to your soil, and use them in conjunction with compost or leaf mold to maintain good soil health and structure. Or try one of the balanced, blended granular organic fertilizers now available at most garden centers. If you prefer liquid fertilizers, try a combination liquid seaweed-fish emulsion product.

Too much fertilizer is worse than too little; it invites diseases and can reduce harvests. Follow label directions when applying fertilizers. If your soil is especially rich thanks to the addition of compost or manure, cut back slightly from the recommended rates.

Crops that take a long time to mature (such as tomatoes) benefit from a midseason boost of nutrients. Cut-and-come-again salad mixes should be fertilized after each harvest to encourage regrowth. One way to fertilize is to apply a top or side dressing of compost, well-rotted livestock manure, or a commercially available fertilizer. Another option is to soak the soil at the base of the plants with diluted liquid fertilizers such as fish emulsion or manure tea made by steeping manure in a bucket of water and straining the liquid, which you use as fertilizer. If you're planting a second crop in space vacated by a fast-maturing crop, spread a bit of fertilizer before replanting.

If your soil is undernourished to start, vegetables may have yellowing leaves and stunted growth, a sign of nitrogen deficiency. Many nutrient deficiencies are hard to diagnose, but fortunately there's a good general remedy. As soon as you notice these symptoms, fertilize the plants with a solution of 1 tablespoon each of liquid fish fertilizer (or emulsion) and liquid seaweed in a gallon of water. Pour the solution right onto the plants' leaves. Plants can absorb these nutrients through their leaves, and they need fast help to recover from the stress in time to produce a harvest. These fertilizers contain balanced amounts of phosphorus, nitrogen, and potassium, the three primary nutrients plants require, plus a good balance of all micronutrients. With luck and a timely application, you may be able to salvage your crop. If not, focus your energy on improving the soil for next season.

◄ *Healthy soil* will be dark, crumbly, and alive with earthworms.

Fertilize cut-and-come-again crops, such as leaf lettuce, after each harvest.

Organic Fertilizers

Organic fertilizers and soil amendments feed the plants and improve the texture and quality of the soil. All fertilizers have three numbers on the package, which indicate the amount of nitrogen, phosphorous, and potassium or N-P-K. The designation 0-0-22 for sulfate of mgnesium denotes there are 0 parts of nitrogen, 0 parts of phosphorous, and 22 parts of potassium.

Sulfate of potash magnesia (0-0-22) promotes vigor and disease resistance.

Green sand (0-0-0.1) promotes plant vigor. Long-term source of potash

Kelp meal (1-0-2) is an organic plant food.

Dried blood (4-2-2) is a natural source of nitrogen.

Granulated manure enriches soil and feeds plants. Soil amendment

Gypsum loosens clay soil and improves aeration. No nutritive value

Potash (0-0-60) promotes plant vigor and disease resistance.

Cotton seed meal (6-2-1) is an organic plant food.

Bone meal (4-12-0) is a source of natural phosphorus.

Compost enriches the soil and feeds plants. Nutrient content varies.

Landscaping with Herbs

The attractions of herbs are many. Most are easy to grow and tolerate poor soil, drought, and both full or partial sun. In addition, there is great satisfaction in stepping out into the garden to snip fresh herbs for summer salads or pasta dishes, or to make basting brushes for barbecues. Many herbs are fragrant, and their aroma adds an extra dimension to the pleasure of walking in the garden. It's not surprising that most gardeners grow at least one or two herbs.

A traditional herb garden has symmetrical paths that establish the structure of the garden and a central, decorative feature such as the stone planter shown here.

Herb gardens were planted by monks and nuns in medieval cloisters. In addition to ministering to the spiritual needs of the local people, the people in religious orders took care of the physical. The herb gardens were known as *physic* gardens, and the plants grown were ones known (or believed) to have properties for healing. The tradition of the herb garden devoted solely to the diverse range of plants we classify as herbs continues to this day, and the results are delightful.

Herbs Work Well in Geometric Patterns. If you want a traditional herb garden, create symmetrical beds divided by paths made of brick, gravel, flagstone, or even grass. Use the combination of beds and paths to create an interesting geometric pattern, such as triangles with a diamond bed in the center or arches in the corners and square beds in the center. Another motif for a traditional herb garden design is a round bed divided into sections like a sliced pie. Plant each section with a different herb or with a combination of herbs that fit well together. Choose an ornament such as a birdbath, fountain, or a statue to place in the center of the garden as a focal point.

Many people with small gardens want to grow herbs but don't want to limit themselves to just that family of plants. Herbs lend themselves to many garden situations. Incorporate them into the vegetable garden. Edible herbs are particularly appropriate in the food garden because you can harvest for the kitchen all in one place.

Sectioned herb beds of rosemary, chives, and creeping thyme are partitioned by a narrow brick walk with sweet alyssum rimming the design. The herbs are tucked into a small corner of the landscape.

Plant Edible Herbs Near the Kitchen. Grow edible herbs in a kitchen dooryard garden so they are easy to harvest for cooking. Popular culinary herbs include chives, basil, sage, mint, parsley, rosemary, and thyme. All these herbs grow well in containers. If the space near your kitchen door is paved, grow the herbs in pots combined in attractive clusters. (See Chapter 8, pages 172–75 for information on container planting.)

◀ *This ornamental herb garden* is full of texture and color. Some of the herbs shown include parsley (bottom left), purple and yellow pansies, chamomile, mint, and scented geranium.

▶ *This round herb garden* is framed by an old wagon wheel mounted on blocks. Raised beds are ideal for herbs that need good drainage.

Herbs for Flower Beds and Borders

Many of these herbs will survive in hotter zones in the dry Southeast. However, they aren't all edible. Some, like monkshood, are quite toxic. But they are all attractive whether you cook with them, use them for medicinal purposes, make potpourris, or simply enjoy them in the landscape or as cut flowers. Consult an herb book for specific information on each plant.

Achillea millefolium (yarrow), Zones 3–9

Aconitum napellus (monkshood), Zones 3–8

Agastache foeniculum (anise hyssop), Zones 4–8

Alchemilla mollis (lady's mantle), Zones 4–8

Allium schoenoprasum (chives), Zones 3–11

Angelica archangelica (angelica), Zones 4–10

Calendula officinalis (pot marigold), hardy annual

Carum carvi (caraway), Zones 4–11

Chamaemelum nobile (Roman chamomile), Zones 3–8

Digitalis purpurea (foxglove), Zones 4–8

Foeniculum vulgare 'Purpurascens' (bronze fennel), Zones 6–11

Hyssopus officinalis (hyssop), Zones 3–11

Inula helenium (elecampane), Zones 3–9

Lavandula angustifolia (English lavender), Zones 5–8

Lavandula dentata (French Lavender), Zones 9–11

Lavandula stoechas (Spanish Lavender), Zones 7–11

Monarda didyma (bee balm), Zones 4–8

Nepeta x faassenii (catmint) Zones 4–8

Pelargonium graveolens (rose geranium), Zones 9–11, elsewhere annual

Pelargonium odoratissimum (apple geranium), Zones 9–11, elsewhere annual

Pimpinella anisum (anise), halfhardy annual

Rosmarinus officinalis (rosemary), Zones 8–10

Salvia officinalis (sage), Zones 5–8

Satureja montana (winter savory), Zones 5–11

Stachys byzantina (lamb's ears), Zones 4–9

Tanacetum parthenium (feverfew), Zones 4–9

Tanacetum vulgare (tansy), Zones 4–11

Thymus species and cultivars (thyme), zones vary with species and cultivar

Tropaeolum majus (nasturtium), tender annual

Valeriana officinalis (valerian), Zones 4–8

Carum carvi (caraway)

Foeniculum vulgare (fennel)

Lavandula dentata (French lavender)

ORNAMENTAL HERBS

In addition to compelling flowers, many herbs have foliage that breaks out of the stereotype of green leaves, growing instead with distinct silver, blue-gray, reddish purple, yellow, or even variegated foliage.

Traditional Herb Knot Gardens. In Elizabethan times, gardeners used different herbs and shrubs to plant intricate intertwining designs, called knot gardens. Herbs that lend themselves to this treatment include lavender cotton (*Santolina chamaecyparissus*), lavender, germander (*Teucrium chamaedrys*), rosemary, and marjoram (*Origanum majorana*). Mix them with shrubs such as dwarf boxwood, myrtle, and 'Crimson Pygmy' barberry.

As an alternative to a knot garden, plant a zigzag design down the center of a long, narrow bed with a shrublike herb such as santolina or germander, and then plant the triangle shapes created by the miniature hedge with different herbs. Put tall plants in the back triangles and shorter ones in front.

Many low-growing or creeping herbs are excellent as ground covers and are delightful planted between stepping stones. Good possibilities include the many creeping thymes, pennyroyal (*Mentha pulegium*), and Roman chamomile (*Chamaemelum nobilis*). An herb walkway is both a visual and sensual delight. (See Chapter 11, pages 232–36 for more information on ground covers.)

Anise Hyssop. Many herbs sport beautiful flowers, making them prime candidates for perennial borders. A lovely addition to a sunny flower bed or herbaceous border is anise hyssop (*Agastache foeniculum*), also known as licorice mint or anise mint. A tall, upright plant that reaches to 5 feet tall, it produces showy spires of violet flowers in late summer. Bees and butterflies adore these flowers.

Lavender Brightens the Landscape. Brighten your garden and perfume the air with English lavender (*Lavandula angustifolia*). Lavender grows in dense clumps, making it ideal to create floral pools of violet-blue in a border. The silver-gray foliage makes a handsome display all season. In warm areas, lavender is evergreen. It thrives in slightly dry, sunny spots with good drainage.

Herbs are useful plants to soften hardscape elements. Here the center stones have been removed from the small courtyard patio, and planted with a collection of brightly colored and scented herbs.

Rosemary. Another blue-flowering ornamental herb is rosemary (*Rosmarinus* species). Upright varieties make excellent hedges or specimen plants in warm-climate gardens. They also can be trained as standards so that they resemble miniature trees. Choose cascading varieties for hanging baskets and to spill over the edge of retaining walls. Rosemary is drought-tolerant and prefers a warm, sunny spot.

Hundreds of Thyme Species. There are more than 400 species of thyme (*Thymus*), with as many as 60 named varieties favored in the garden or kitchen. Many of these varieties bear profuse and attractive flowers, while others have interesting, ornamental foliage. Of the many varieties, some grow tall and upright while others are low to the ground.

Sage. Another herb that has a long history of medicinal and culinary importance is sage. It is also an excellent hardy garden perennial. The most common sage, *Salvia officinalis*, produces violet flowers on tall spikes in early summer. There are scores of sage varieties, many with dramatic flowers. Some kinds, such as tricolor sage, have attractive foliage: tricolor sage has dark green leaves edged with creamy white and pink.

CHAPTER 14

Managing Pests and Diseases

Even in the most well-tended garden, pests and diseases will intrude on the personal paradise you've created. However, there are steps you can take to keep any pest or disease that does develop under control without dousing your garden with harmful chemicals.

If you launch a systematic program of organic pest management in your garden, you'll find that in most cases you can keep problems under control without resorting to measures that damage the environment and the natural balance.

Integrated Pest Management

Integrated pest management (IPM) is the phrase coined to describe an approach to pest control that utilizes regular monitoring of pests and diseases to determine whether and when control measures are needed. The goal is to avoid using chemicals by combining an integrated, multi-pronged strategy to fight garden problems.

IDENTIFYING THE PROBLEM

An important aspect of IPM is identifying the pests and diseases that target specific plants. The more you know, the better equipped you are to take action that will have the least negative effect on the environment. For example, early in the spring the cabbage root maggot can decimate crops of cabbages, broccoli, cauliflower, turnips, or radishes. The parent fly lays its eggs about two weeks before the frost-free date. Plants that are set out in the garden at about the time the eggs are laid will be vulnerable to the hungry maggots. If you delay planting by two weeks, you're unlikely to have a problem.

Integrated pest management starts with careful and regular monitoring of your plants. The paths and the narrow beds in this well-tended, healthy looking landscape make it easy to inspect the plants and catch any problems as they emerge.

MONITOR YOUR PLANTS

A second aspect of IPM is monitoring. It's a relatively easy task to handpick a few caterpillars off a plant or to control aphids in the early stages of their occupation. However, if you wait too long to deal with them, minor pest problems can escalate into major infestations. Keep an eye on your plants. During the growing season, try to find time to walk through your garden on a daily basis. Carry a pair of clippers with you. In addition to enjoying the garden experience, you can deadhead the odd flowers as you go, pull up a random weed, and notice whether there are any problems developing that need your intervention.

◀ *A benign, if somewhat whimsical, pest-control* method is demonstrated by this clay-pot scarecrow. If you look closely, you can see crows perched on the scarecrow's shoulder, making this scarecrow more ornamental than functional.

MAKE AN EDUCATED GUESS

Once you're aware of a problem, you can make an educated decision about which, if any, steps to take. In many cases, you may not have to do anything. For example, you may notice a small number of aphids on your roses. Before you reach for a spray, look for black-and-yellow or black-and-white striped flies that resemble small bees or wasps. These are syrphid flies. They lay their eggs in aphid colonies, and their larvae, which look like small, translucent slugs, feed on the aphids. This is an example of nature taking care of pests without human or chemical intervention.

▲ *Learn to recognize* syrphid flies and their larvae (inset). The translucent larvae have voracious appetites for aphids, and should keep the aphid population under control.

In some cases, the damage a pest may do is insignificant. For example, if the leaves of your dogwood are skeletonized, dogwood sawflies are probably the cause. Different species feed at different times, so damage may occur through the growing season. Early in the season, you need to control the pest with insecticidal soap or, in the case of severe infestations, with Rotenone. Late in the season, don't worry; the tree will send out new leaves in the spring.

In large-scale agricultural situations, IPM includes the use of chemicals, although usually as a last resort. In a home garden, you should be able to maintain a healthy environment without spraying harmful chemicals. Here are further suggestions to help you implement a program of organic pest management.

Grow Vigorous Plants

The healthier your plants are, the better equipped they will be to ward off damaging insects, fungi, and diseases. In fact, many insects and diseases target weakened plants and will avoid the healthy ones. If a healthy plant is attacked, it has the strength to withstand the setback.

BUY ONLY HEALTHY PLANTS

When you purchase plants, look for those that are growing well and are pest- and disease-free. You're better off paying more for a vigorous plant at a reputable nursery than taking on a weak specimen sold at a budget price. Before you choose a plant, check that it is not potbound and that the roots are healthy. Also inspect the leaves for insects and any discoloration or misshapen form that may be a sign of disease or fungus. If you suspect that a plant may be ailing, do not buy it. You don't want to introduce the problem into your garden, and you don't want to play nurse to a sickly plant.

Provide the Conditions to Keep Plants Thriving.

Once you're sure you have selected insect- and disease-free plants, help them stay that way. Good soil is the key to growing healthy plants. In a rich loam environment where the roots can spread easily and take up appropriate amounts of nutrients and moisture, a plant will thrive and be strong enough to resist almost anything nature throws at it.

Lastly, water your plants to encourage a deep and extensive root system. See Chapter 3, page 88 for details on correct watering techniques. During periods of drought, monitor the plants, and water them before they wilt. The less stress a plant has to undergo from other factors, the better it will hold up against disease.

SELECT FOR DISEASE AND PEST RESISTANCE

Hybridizers are constantly developing new varieties of plants that are disease-resistant. Whenever possible, opt for plants bred to withstand diseases that are prevalent in your area. For example, tomatoes often have initials after their name, including V, F, T, N, and L. The V indicates a resistance to verticilliulm wilt, F is resistance to fusarium wilt, T refers to tobacco mosaic virus, N to nematodes, and L to gray leaf spot.

Grow healthy plants. If you buy healthy plants and consistently provide optimal growing conditions, your plants will be stronger and therefore less likely to succumb to insects, fungi, and diseases.

Good soil keeps plants healthy. *The raised beds shown here are full of dark, crumbly (obviously improved) soil. Some of the plants growing in this photograph include: cabbage (bottom-left), roses (against the fence), chives (center), and lettuce.*

Bred for disease resistance, *the 'Roma' tomato is less prone to verticillium wilt and fusarium wilt than other cultivars.*

Hybrids Bred for Disease and Pest Resistance.
Cucumbers are particularly susceptible to leaf spot, anthracnose, cucumber mosaic, and downy mildew. The pickling cucumber, 'Little Leaf', has been bred to resist these diseases. 'Salad Bush' and 'Space Master', both bred to grow in small spaces, are resistant to cucumber mosaic and scab. You'll find many hybrids of cabbage, carrot, corn, green and pole beans, lettuce, onion, pepper, squash, tomato, and yellow bean that are bred to resist disease.

Some hybrids are even bred for pest resistance. 'Cocozelle' squash is less tasty to aphids than other varieties. In the world of cabbages, 'Danish Ballhead', 'Red Acre', and 'Early Jersey Wakefield' all tolerate cabbage looper and imported cabbageworm without sustaining major damage.

Good Sanitation

Many pests hide in neglected, weedy, overgrown sections of the garden. For example, stink bugs which damage cabbage- and squash-family crops, overwinter and lay eggs in weedy areas. It takes only five weeks from the time an egg is laid for a mature adult to begin gobbling up your crops and breeding the next generation. If you mow or weed their habitat, you'll go a long way toward stopping their onslaught.

Fungus spores are widely dispersed from leaf to leaf, especially when rain hits the leaves and sends the spores flying. Rake up fallen leaves, particularly if they show signs of disease.

Another good sanitation practice is to prune diseased branches. Sterilize the pruners between cuts with a solution of diluted bleach (1 or 2 tablespoons per gallon of water) or straight rubbing alcohol so you don't inadvertently spread the disease with your tools or your hands. Throw away diseased leaves and branches rather than composting them. You don't want to risk the infection's surviving in your compost heap.

Attract Beneficial Creatures

Not all insects and animals destroy plants. There are a host of creatures whose survival depends on having a steady diet of the damaging pests. Enlist these beneficials as your allies in the ongoing battle between you and the plant-sucking, plant-chewing enemy.

While you can purchase ladybugs or praying mantises from organic mail-order catalogs, you have no guarantee that these useful critters will stay in your garden once you release them. Ideally, you want to attract beneficial insects to your property by providing an attractive environment for them.

◀ *Praying Mantid egg cases, plus other beneficial insects, such as ladybugs, are shipped through the mail. Mantids are controversial, however, because they eat pests, beneficials, and each other with equal zest.*

◀ *A well-tended garden is a place where vegetables and herbs thrive. This mixed flower and vegetable bed, featuring marigolds and cabbage, is mulched and weeded.*

BATS, TOADS, BIRDS, AND LIZARDS

You may not want bats in your belfry or attic, but they are marvelous for insect control in the garden. They feast on nocturnal flying insects, devouring thousands in the course of a night. If you see a bat flying around your garden, be glad you've got this ally in your battle against pests. You can encourage a bat or two to settle by putting up a bat house, although bats tend to prefer their own roosts to man-made houses. They also appreciate a little water.

Toads, lizards, turtles, and nonpoisonous snakes are other strong resources in your battle against garden pests. Turn a broken pot upside down to create a shady retreat for one of these creatures, provide a source of water, and then sit back and let them do the work of insect control. Toads actually have adapted their hunting techniques to modern inventions. It's not unusual to see a toad sit by a pathway light at night waiting to catch unwary insects that are drawn by the illumination.

Birds Eat Insects. Lastly, many birds eat insects. Make birds feel welcome and comfortable in your garden by providing for their needs. At the basic level they need food, water, and some shrubbery for cover. To give the birds a treat, plant a few berry-producing shrubs. However, you may enjoy adding a few pretty garden ornaments, such as a birdhouse or two, bird feeders, and a birdbath, to please both yourself and the birds.

▲ *A Lesser Long-Nosed Bat* pollinating a saguaro cactus flower. Bats eat thousands of insects every night as well as pollinating flowers.

◄ *An American toad* (Bufo americanus) sits, fat and happy, after a meal of insects. Encourage toads with a source of water and a shady place to hide.

A five-lined skink lizard (Eumeces fasciatus) resting on a plant leaf. Lizards, especially young ones such as this, hungrily devour garden pests.

Baby birds, such as this bluebird fledgling, enjoy a steady diet of insects caught by their parents. A male Eastern bluebird (inset) perches among daylilies with an insect in its beak.

Companion Planting

Companion planting is an ancient practice, probably as old as agriculture itself. It is simply growing plants together for mutual benefit; or in the case of decoy plants, for the benefit of a preferred crop. A classic example of good plant companions is corn, squash, and climbing beans. This traditional combination, called "The Three Sisters," dates back at least to the Native Americans who passed on their wisdom to the Pilgrims. The beans release nitrogen into the soil that benefits the heavy-feeding corn and squash. The corn supports the climbing beans and the squash has plenty of room to sprawl across the ground beneath the vertical crops.

Mixed Plantings Are Less Appealing to Pests. In the wild, plants tend to grow together in a mixed up jumble. This is good survival practice because a mass planting of anything delicious to specific pests will draw pests like a beacon. But just one or two of the plants

Good companions repel pests. *Cabbage, coriander, and marigolds look beautiful together. The umbel-shaped coriander flowers, when blooming, attract beneficial insects; the strongly scented marigolds are intended to repel pests.*

*A **mixed planting** of angelica, marigolds, fennel, several kinds of lettuce, and tomatoes is not as likely to be wiped out by a pest or disease as a monoculture. The many umbel-shaped flowers attract beneficials, which will manage any pests.*

Attract beneficial insects, *such as hoverflies, lacewings, and ladybugs, by adding plants with small, shallow flowers to your garden. Shown above, the umbel-shaped clusters of Achillea 'Coronation Gold' are a beacon to mature beneficials.*

tucked among many others will hardly be noticed. As a result, any mixed group of plants will tend to be healthier than a cluster of one plant, called a monoculture. If, for example, you plant a cabbage patch, it will become a feast for all the pests that enjoy cole crops. On the other hand, if you combine cabbages with vegetables and flowers from other families, then the attraction to cole crop feeders is minimized.

In addition to generally mixing up plants to create a visually pleasing and diverse culture, specific plants are grown near each other to achieve particular results. The three primary reasons for specific companion planting are to attract beneficial insects, to repel unwanted pests, and to promote the general health and well being of nearby plants.

COMPANION PLANTING TO ATTRACT BENEFICIAL INSECTS

Herbs such as fennel, parsley, dill, anise, and coriander all produce clusters of tiny flowers grouped into an umbrella shape, called an *umbel*. This flower form is ideal for beneficial insects that sup on nectar and pollen and then produce larvae that eat unwanted pests. Some of the beneficials drawn to umbel-shaped flowers include the larvae of parasitic wasps, hoverflies, tachinid flies, lacewings, and ladybugs (also known as lady beetles). The mature adults in this group have short mouthparts, so they prefer small, shallow flowers. Later in the season, these same insects enjoy yarrow, sunflowers, zinnias, and asters. Include these herbs and flowers near any plants that are plagued by a wide array of pests, including aphids, mealybugs, soft scales, whitefly, moth and beetle larvae, codling moth, cabbageworm, hornworm, corn borer, and spider mites.

Planting to Attract Beneficial Insects

PLANT	BENEFICIALS IT ATTRACTS		PESTS CONTROLLED
 *Achillea* (yarrow)	Parasitic wasp	Syrphid (hover) fly	Aphids, moth and beetle larvae, flies, codling moth, cabbageworm, hornworm, corn borer, armyworm, other caterpillars
 *Archangelica* (angelica)	Ladybeetles (ladybugs)	Lacewing	Aphids, mealybugs, soft scales, spider mites, whiteflies, moth eggs, small caterpillars, soft-bodied insects, thrips
 *Ipomoea purpurea* (morning glory)	Ladybugs		Aphids, mealybugs, soft scales, spider mites, white-flies
 *Tanacetum vulgare* (tansy)	Lacewing (larvae stage)		Aphids, mealybugs, mites, moth eggs, scales, small caterpillars, soft-bodied insects, thrips
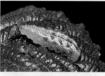 *Iberis* (candytuft)	Syrphid fly (larvae stage)		Aphids
 *Oenothera biennis* (evening primrose)	Ground beetle		Cabbage root maggots, cutworms, snail and slug eggs, armyworms, tent caterpillars
 *Solidago* (goldenrod)	Soldier beetle	Pirate bug	Aphids, insect eggs, leafhoppers, rust mites, spider mites, small caterpillars, thrips, moth larvae, beetle larvae, grasshopper eggs

The images in the beneficials column:

(*Solidago* also attracts ladybeetles and parasitic wasps)

COMPANION PLANTING TO REPEL UNWANTED PESTS

Horticulturalists are wary of claiming definitive evidence that certain plants repel pests. However, some gardeners have noticed improved results when they combine certain plants. Many believe rue will deter Japanese beetles. It also is useful in keeping rats out of the garden.

Decoy Plants Serve as Bait. As a variation on repelling pests, some gardeners plant a decoy crop to protect the plants they want to harvest. For example, if you plant dill and lovage near tomatoes, hornworms will gravitate to the decoy crop, leaving your tomatoes to flourish. Chervil is great slug bait. Plant it among vegetables and ornamentals. Flowering mustard will lure cabbageworms and harlequin bugs away from your cabbage crops.

The trick, however, is to remove and destroy the trap crop as soon as it is infested with the pest. (You will be able to see the pests and their damage.) Otherwise, you'll simply encourage the pests to reproduce and cause more of a problem. If the pests you are trying to catch could fly away while you're pulling up the decoy crop, cover it first with a cloth or bag.

COMPANION PLANTING FOR GENERAL HEALTH

Some plants grow well together because they have different nutrient and space needs. They can grow near each other without horning in on each other's territory, and you get more intense use out of the space. Good examples are corn and squash as described earlier. Spinach is useful between pea rows. The spinach matures and is harvested long before the peas need the extra space. Spinach also is a good companion with brussels sprouts.

Plant Slow and Fast Growers Together. Plant a row of slow-to-mature vegetables, such as turnips, with radishes. The quick-germinating radishes will be ready for harvest about the time the slower-growing vegetables begin to spread. When you pull the radishes, you'll give the soil around the plants a useful tilling.

▶ *Planting slow- and fast-growing crops together makes good use of space. Here the 'Green Arrow' peas are almost ready to harvest when the younger broccoli has just sprouted. The broccoli also benefits from the shade provided by the pea plants.*

Rue may repel Japanese beetles. *Many gardeners notice good results when rue is planted among crops. It also keeps rats out of the garden.*

Other Symbiotic Plant Combinations. Tomatoes, basil, and marigolds are another symbiotic combination. Basil is said to improve the flavor of tomatoes (both in the garden and on the dinner plate), and the strong scent of marigolds is believed to deter insects. The three plants growing together make a pretty display.

Plant lettuces and spinach in the shade of staked tomatoes, beans, cucumbers, or tall growing corn. The cooler microclimate produced by the shade will extend the growing season for these cool-season leafy vegetables.

◀ *Another winning combination: tomatoes and marigolds (Tagetes patula). The strong scent of marigolds is said to keep insect pests away.*

Physical Controls

In many cases you can control a pest by keeping it away from its intended feast. Put a paper collar around young plants to foil the cutworm. Possible materials for the collar include cardboard rolls from paper towels, bathroom tissue, or foil; quart-sized milk cartons cut into multiple rings; or layers of newspaper cut into strips and stapled or taped into rings. Each collar should be 2 to 3 inches tall. Tuck the collars into the soil about an inch so that the cutworms don't burrow underneath.

A floating row cover protects young lettuce plants from crawling and flying pests, as well as rabbits. The row cover allows light and water to pass through and provides a measure of insulation, thereby extending the growing season.

FLOATING COVERS

Floating row covers keep unwanted creatures away from young plants. These specially-made fabrics are water- and light-permeable, so the plants thrive despite the covering. The best floating row covers are those made of spun-bonded polyester, polypropylene, and polyethylene. The fabric is so light that you can lay it directly on top of the plants without flattening them. Although a floating row cover cannot stop pests that emerge from the soil after the cover is in position, it will effectively exclude insect pests that can crawl or fly to the plants, as well as birds, rabbits and other animal pests. As an added bonus, you'll prevent the transmission of plant diseases spread by insects.

An example of a physical control is this wire cage around a blueberry bush. The cage prevents rabbits and other creatures from eating the blueberries. Add netting over the top of the cage if birds become a nuisance.

Netting or wire cages are a great help to keep birds from eating fruit as well as to keep rabbits and other unwanted feeders away from your crops. If you are serious about growing soft fruit such as berries, consider building a fruit cage and growing them inside.

Mulch, Abrasive Material, Sticky Traps. A 6-inch layer of straw mulch discourages weeds, retains moisture, and ultimately breaks down to improve the soil. Straw is also an effective barrier against Colorado potato beetles that overwinter in the soil. It takes the beetles so long to crawl through the thick mulch that the potato seedlings have a chance to mature before the beetles emerge.

Straw mulch protects plants from insect pests. It is especially effective against the Colorado potato beetle. A heavy layer of straw also retains moisture, inhibits weeds from growing, and ultimately breaks down to feed the soil.

Keep snails and slugs off plants by laying down a 2-inch wide strip of abrasive material around each plant. The scratchy surface will tear the tender skin, and the mollusks die of dehydration. Effective abrasive materials include diatomaceous earth (a mineral created from the remains of fossilized diatoms), wood ash, talc, lime, and

A sticky trap captures apple tree moths before they can do serious damage. This physical control works because the moths are attracted to its color and cannot escape from its sticky surface.

crushed eggshells. Wood ash and lime increase the soil's alkalinity. Do not use them if your soil pH is already high, say 8 or more.

Special sticky traps work on aphids, thrips, whiteflies, cabbage root flies, carrot rust flies, cucumber beetles, and imported cabbageworms, which are attracted to the color yellow. You can purchase commercially-made sticky traps at garden centers, or make your own. Paint sturdy cardboard or a piece of wood with paint containing the pigment called Federal Safety Yellow No. 659. When the paint is thoroughly dry, staple the yellow trap to a stake, and then spread the painted surface with glue formulated to remain tacky for about 2 weeks. Place the traps near infested plants about level with the top of the plant. You'll need one trap for every five to six plants.

ORGANIC PESTICIDES

While it's not a good idea to spray chemical poisons for every pest problem that arises, there are some biological substances that are toxic to insect pests but harmless to other life forms.

Bacillus Thuringiensis. Perhaps the best-known organic pesticide is *Bacillus thuringiensis*. BT is a microbe that paralyzes the stomach of caterpillars, ultimately causing them to starve to death. This substance is harmless to birds, mammals, bees, and other insects. BT specifically targets chewing pests, including cabbage loopers, tomato hornworms, European corn borers, gypsy moth caterpillars, and beetle larvae.

Pyrethrum. Another organic pesticide is pyrethrum. Derived from the pyrethrum or painted daisy (*Tanacetum cineraniifolium*, also called *Chrysanthemum cinerariifolium*), this contact insecticide kills aphids, beetles, caterpillars, leafhoppers, mites, stink bugs, thrips, and whiteflies. However, the pest must be directly hit with the material. Pyrethrum is highly toxic to fish, aquatic insects, and some beneficials. Having said that, once sprayed on the plants, pyrethrum breaks down within an hour. It is available commercially in dust form, liquid concentrate, and ready-to-use spray. Don't confuse natural pyrethrums with a synthetic compound called pyrethroids. Be sure to read the label closely, as the names are so similar, but the products are not.

Recipe for Pyrethrum Spray

- ❧ 1 cup pyrethrum flowers
- ❧ ⅛ cup rubbing alcohol
- ❧ Water
- ❧ 8 oz. jar with lid
- ❧ Cheesecloth

If you grow the pyrethrum daisy, you can make your own pyrethrum concentrate. Put 1 cup of tightly-packed pyrethrum flowers into an 8-ounce jar. Pour ⅛ cup rubbing alcohol over the flowers. Cover the jar, and steep the mixture overnight. Strain the mixture through cheesecloth, and discard the flowers. To make a spray, dilute the concentrate at a ratio of 1 part pyrethrum/alcohol to 48 parts water (1 ounce of pyrethrum concentrate to 6 cups of water). Test the mixture on a leaf before you spray the entire plant, and don't use it on hairy-leafed plants.

Insecticidal Soap. Insecticidal soap is a contact insecticide useful against soft-bodied and sucking insects, including aphids, mites, leafhoppers, mealybugs, scale, spider mites, thrips, and whiteflies. You can make your own insecticidal soap if you use pure bar soap. Do a test spray on a few leaves, and wait a couple of days to check for signs of injury. Never use soap on ferns or nasturtiums. When you spray the plant, do both the top and undersides of the leaves to catch the pests where they are hiding.

Recipe for Insecticidal Soap

- ❧ Pure bar soap
- ❧ Soft water

Make insecticidal soap spray by dissolving 1 teaspoonful of pure bar soap shavings in ⅛ cup of boiling softened water. Hard water is not effective. Soften hard water by straining it through peat moss. Once the soap is dissolved, add ⅞ cup of soft water to make a full cup of the spray. If you want to make a larger batch, the ratio is 1 part shaved soap to approximately 50 parts water.

Animal Pests

There's nothing more discouraging than to watch an Oriental lily bud for days, waiting for it to open, only to wake up one morning and find the bud gone with only the stalk left and the telltale angled cut that indicates the teeth marks of a deer. Rabbits and deer can decimate a vegetable or flower garden in one night, and squirrels will industriously dig up and eat a field of crocus bulbs, as well as graze on tomatoes, sweet corn, and sunflower seeds. As much as we enjoy these creatures in the wild, replacing damaged plants is time-consuming and costly as well. Here are some tips for keeping them out of the garden.

FENCE OUT RABBITS, MICE, AND VOLES

Rabbits. Fence with a wire mesh no larger than 1½ inches. The fence should be at least 2 feet above the ground and buried at least 6 inches below the soil level. As an added precaution, sprinkle dried blood meal, cow manure, or wood ashes near plants, replenishing them after rain.

Mice and Voles. Fence with a mesh no larger than ¼ inch. Extend the barrier 1 foot above and below the soil level. To keep mice from eating bulbs, plant clusters of bulbs in fine wire mesh, or toss a handful of sharp gravel into each planting hole with the bulb. The mice won't want to burrow through the gravel to get to the bulb. Household ammonia sprinkled on the ground around plants will help repel voles.

Raccoons and Woodchucks. Raccoons are partial to ripe corn and melons. Woodchucks will eat anything in the vegetable garden, pulling up entire plants. Install a two-strand electric fence around your plot, the top strand 1 foot from the ground, the lower one 6 inches. A wire-mesh fence three feet tall aboveground and buried 2 feet below also will keep out woodchucks.

Deer. Deer can jump more than 7 feet high. To be effective, a deer fence needs to be at least 8 feet tall. You can purchase inexpensive plastic-mesh fencing that is easy to staple to trees and other supports. Or you can install electric fencing with three levels of wires. The wires should be evenly spaced, with the top wire about 8 feet off the ground.

▶ **Wire cages** protect plants from foraging deer and rabbits. The cages are effective and less intrusive than a long stretch of fence. Such cages can be easily made by stapling heavy wire netting to a stake.

◀ **Wire that surrounds** the plant and is placed in the planting hole keeps moles and voles away from the 'Birchwood Parky's Gold' hosta.

An electric fence is a no-nonsense way to keep deer out of the garden. The inset shows a sapling surrounded by a wire cage, which keeps bucks from rubbing their antlers against the tree. Immature trees often do not recover from antler rub.

Other measures that people sometimes find helpful to deter deer include hanging net bags filled with mothballs or human hair around the garden; hanging bars of soap from trees and shrubs, sprinkling blood meal around the perimeter of the garden, and spraying commercially-available deer repellents on prized plants.

Hot Pepper and Garlic Sprays. Garlic and hot pepper are organic repellents to aphids, cabbage loopers, leafhoppers, squash bugs, whiteflies, birds, cats, deer, dogs, and rabbits. You can purchase premixed sprays at nurseries, or make your own using the recipe below. Begin using the spray before pests begin feeding, and reapply pepper spray after a rain or overhead watering. Garlic should be applied twice each season. These substances will deter but not kill pests. For sensitive people, the oils of pepper or garlic can be extremely painful if they get in the eyes or even on bare skin. Most people are not sensitive to external contact with garlic.

Recipe for Hot Pepper and Garlic Sprays

- ½ cup hot peppers or 15 cloves of garlic
- Water
- Insecticidal soap
- Protective gloves
- Blender
- Plant sprayer
- Cheesecloth

Hot pepper deters dogs, cats, rabbits, and insects. Make your own spray by combining ½ cup of hot peppers with 2 cups of water. Puree the peppers and water in a blender, strain the liquid through cheesecloth, and spray on the plants daily for 5 to 7 days until the pests go elsewhere. Peppers can burn your skin, so wear protective gloves while making the mixture and spraying it.

A variation on the pepper spray is one made of garlic. Puree 15 garlic cloves with 2 cups of water. Strain the liquid through cheesecloth, and add a few drops of insecticidal soap.

Battling Diseases

As with mammals, in the plant world there are infectious diseases and noninfectious ones. Infectious diseases generally are caused by invasive pathogens such as fungi, bacteria, and viruses. Noninfectious diseases are caused by external factors such as mineral and nutrient deficiencies in the soil, weather conditions including drought or excess rains, lack of air circulation, and improper watering practices.

There are three factors that must all be present for a plant disease to successfully take hold: the presence of a pathogen, a hospitable environment for the pathogen, and a susceptible host plant. If any one of these conditions is missing, the disease will not occur. If you choose disease-resistant varieties of plants, practice good garden hygiene, and grow your plants in excellent quality soil with good air circulation, the incidence of disease in your garden will drop significantly.

Manure Tea to Boost Immunity. Healthy plants have their own built-in immune system. You can boost their natural immunity by brewing your own manure tea and spraying it on the plants and saturating their roots systems with it. The manure is rich in nutrients and good bacteria that protect the plants. Compost tea, made the same way, but with compost instead of manure (see box) is also effective against fungal diseases.

Recipe for Manure Tea

- Manure or compost
- Water
- Bucket
- Shovel
- Plant sprayer
- Cheesecloth

Steep a shovelful of manure (or compost) in a bucket of water for a few days. Strain the mixture through cheesecloth, and then pour it into a spray bottle. Spray the tea on plant leaves, and pour a small amount at the base of plants.

FUNGI

There are good types of fungi and damaging varieties. The beneficial fungi contribute to the decomposition of dead leaves and are an important part of the ecology of your garden. The disease-causing ones feed on growing plants, releasing toxins in the process. A fungus such as powdery mildew is an eyesore but doesn't damage the plant itself. Other fungi, such as needle cast, turn pine needles brown, causing them to drop early in the summer. A severely infected tree that isn't treated will die.

Water, wind, insects, birds, animals, and even humans spread fungi seeds, called spores. Good cultural practices go a long way to controlling the spread of fungi disease.

❧ *Rake leaves away from plants that are particularly susceptible to anthracnose or other fungal diseases.* Otherwise, water splashing on the fallen leaves will splash back up on the plant, possibly spreading infection. Camellias and mountain laurels (*Kalmia*) benefit from keeping fallen leaves away from the plants. Don't put these leaves in the compost heap; instead, throw them away. Otherwise, you'll risk spreading the disease.

❧ *Site plants where they will get good air circulation.* Roses and pine trees benefit from plenty of space around them. Avoid putting them in corners where breezes never stir the air. Another way to increase air movement around a plant is to prune it to open up the structure.

❧ *Avoid wetting leaves when you water them.* Damp environments foster fungi; the spores need a moist environment to germinate. That's why you'll encounter less fungi disease in dry climates or during dry periods. Water directly to the plants' roots, or install drip irrigation or soaker hoses that allow the water to soak in gradually, thus giving the plants a healthy, deep watering.

❧ *Remove all fungus-infected leaves from the shrub.* If you leave them in place, insects, wind, water, and even your hands when you touch the plant will spread the disease. Throw away the infected leaves rather than composting them.

▶ **There is plenty of room for air** to circulate, which will help keep fungal diseases from flourishing. Avoid putting roses, which are prone to fungus, in corners or up against buildings where there is little air movement.

◀ **Fungal diseases** such as powdery mildew, shown here on a rose, are unsightly but don't cause the plant any permanent damage. Other fungal diseases are more serious.

▲ **Clear debris away from plants** such as the mountain laurel (Kalmia) shown here and camellias, which are particularly susceptible to anthracnose and other fungal diseases.

❧ *Use baking soda or fungicide sprays.* Environmentally safe fungicide sprays are commonly available. Lime-sulfur spray is excellent to control plant diseases such as mildew, anthracnose, leaf spot, and brown spot. Spray deciduous trees in late winter or early spring before the plants leaf out. The mixture will burn leaves and growing shoots. Baking soda spray is effective against powdery mildew, leaf blight, and leaf spots. As a preventive measure, begin spraying vulnerable plants in spring, and continue throughout the summer.

Mosaic virus is evident on a pea plant. Mosaic virus is usually spread by aphids and leafhoppers. Floating row covers will keep these insects off the plants and therefore slow the spread of viral diseases.

Recipe for Baking Soda Spray

- ❧ 1 tablespoon baking soda
- ❧ ⅛ teaspoon insecticidal soap
- ❧ 1 gallon water

Dissolve the baking soda in the water then add the soap, which helps the solution adhere to the leaves. Spray leaves on both sides, repeating every 5 to 7 days until the problem is solved.

BACTERIA

Most bacteria in the garden are beneficial. They break down dead plant tissue and release nitrogen back to the plant. However, all bacteria are not beneficial. The bad bacteria get inside plants through the mouths of infected feeding insects, by way of open wounds, or through natural pores and openings in the plant. Once inside, bacteria either damage a plant's ability to distribute water through its cells or rob the plant of nutrients. The telltale sign of the presence of bacteria is rotting tissue that is slimy or smells disgusting, or both.

❧ *Crop rotation.* By planting vegetables in different beds each year, bacteria specific to one host plant are deprived of a food source and will die.

❧ *Garden sanitation.* Many disease-carrying pests overwinter in dense clumps of weeds or under debris. Clean away these nesting areas.

❧ *Resistant plant varieties.* Select plant varieties that are bred to resist specific diseases.

VIRUSES

Viruses are spread both by insect saliva and by nematodes. Another culprit is the gardener. If you are pruning away diseased branches on a tree or shrub, cut the branch well below the infected part, and disinfect the pruners between cuts with a solution of household bleach and water (1 or 2 tablespoons of bleach to a gallon of water) or straight rubbing alcohol.

Indications of viral infections include stunted foliage, foliage that is abnormally curled, abnormal patterns in the leaf, and atypical leaf color, such as yellow.

❧ *Amend the soil.* The symptoms of viral infections closely resemble nutrient deficiencies. If you notice symptoms, first amend the soil, adding appropriate minerals or nutrients. If the problem persists, you are wise to destroy the plant because there are no known remedies for viruses and the only way to get a definitive diagnosis is through a laboratory.

❧ *Keep insects away.* In the case of vegetables that may be infected with the mosaic virus, which is spread primarily by aphids and leafhoppers, you can avoid the problem by keeping the insects off the plants. Cover the crops with a floating row cover. Light and water can penetrate, but the insects cannot. (See page 298.) Leafhoppers also spread curly top, a viral infection that causes leaves to curl, become stiff, turn yellow, and die. Vegetables such as beets, tomatoes, beans, melon, and spinach are susceptible, as are many perennials. Plant resistant varieties; use floating row covers where appropriate; use insecticidal soap, pyrethrin spray, and other natural leafhopper controls; and encourage the presence of predatory flies, bugs, and parasitic wasps, which are the leafhopper's natural enemy.

Disease Symptoms and Solutions

FUNGAL DISEASES	Symptoms	Plants Affected	Solutions
Anthracnose	Yellow or brown spots	Many woody and herbaceous plants, including dogwood, maple, sycamore, and mountain laurel; vegetables, inlcuding beans, cucumbers, melons, peppers, and tomatoes.	Rake up and destroy infected leaves; choose resistant vegetable varieties; plant in well-drained soil; apply copper-based fungicide for deciduous trees and shrubs.
Black spot	Circular black spots on leaves	Roses	Avoid wetting leaves; prune shrubs to increase air circulation; plant resistant cultivars; remove and destroy infected leaves and canes.
Botrytis blight	White, gray, or tan fluffy growth on flower stems; brown spots on leaves; mold on fruit	Herbaceous perennials; vegetables such as cabbage and onions; fruit, including strawberries and grapes	Remove infected fruit; provide good air circulation; destroy infected perennial tops when they die back.
Downey mildew	Yellow spots on leaf tops; white, tan, or gray cottony spots on leaf undersides	Grapes; woody and herbaceous plants	Provide good air circulation; grow resistant cultivars; remove and destroy infected leaves; apply copper-based fungicides.
Powdery mildew	White, powdery dusting on plant surfaces	Woody and herbaceous plants, including lilacs, phlox, bee balm, squashes, roses, zinnias	Provide good air circulation; plant resistant cultivars; apply baking soda spray or lime-sulfur spray.
Rust	Yellow or white spots on leaf tops; yellow or orange streaks on underside	Woody and herbaceous plants	Avoid getting leaves wet; provide good air circulation; remove infected leaves.
Sooty mold	Grows on sticky excretions produced by aphids, scales, and mealybugs; black film on leaves; sticky leaves	Woody and herbaceous plants	Not directly harmful, although can reduce photosynthesis and is very ugly; control insects; wipe small plants clean.

FUNGAL DISEASES (continued)	Symptoms	Plants Affected	Solutions
 Verticillium wilt	Leaves turn yellow, and then plant wilts	Tomatoes, peppers, melons, asters, chrysanthemums, peaches, cherries, strawberries, maples, plus others	There is no cure; plant wilt-resistant cultivars; soil solarization may help.

BACTERIAL DISEASES

	Symptoms	Plants Affected	Solutions
 Leaf spot	Discoloration on leaves, usually brown, sometimes surrounded by yellow ring; holes in leaves	Woody and herbaceous plants	Rotate crops; practice good garden sanitation; plant resistant cultivars; apply copper sprays.
 Bacteria wilt	Limp, wilted leaves; collapsed stems; long sticky strands of white ooze inside stems	Cucumbers, melons, squash, herbaceous plants	Plant resistant cultivars; control cucumber beetles and grasshoppers (using floating row covers); remove and destroy infected plants.
 Slime flux	Smelly, slimy liquid exuding from bark wounds	Elms, maples, poplars, other trees	Ugly but not life-threatening; no known controls

VIRAL DISEASES

	Symptoms	Plants Affected	Solutions
 Curly top	Twisted, curled leaves that turn stiff and leathery; stunted plants; reduced fruit production	Beets, tomatoes, beans, melons, spinach	Plant resistant cultivars; remove weeds where virus can overwinter; use floating row covers to keep off infected pests.
 Mosaic	Leaves mottled with yellow, white, and green spots or streaks	Woody and herbaceous plants	Plant resistant cultivars; use floating row covers to keep infected insects off vegetables; remove and destroy infected plants.

GLOSSARY

Acidic A pH measure less than 7 (neutral), indicating a low level of hydrogen. Woodland plants, including rhododendrons, azaleas, and ferns, do best in slightly acidic soil with a pH between 5 and 7. The pH of acidic soils can be raised by adding lime products.

Aggregate Crushed stone, gravel, or other material added to cement to make concrete or mortar. Gravel and crushed stone are considered coarse aggregate; sand is considered fine aggregate.

Alkaline A pH measure above 7 (neutral), indicating a high level of hydrogen. The pH of alkaline soils can be reduced by adding acidic materials, such as leaf mold or pine needles, or by adding products derived from sulfur or iron.

Anvil pruner A hand tool designed to cut through branches ½ to ¾ inch in diameter. Its single cutting blade closes on a plate or "anvil" made of soft metal. Anvil pruners are easier to use than the "bypass" pruners, but more likely to crush bark.

Apex (plural: apices) The tip (tips) of branches or the end buds of a growing plant.

Apical dominance Concentration of growth hormone in the tips of branches.

Arbor An arched, open structure that spans a doorway or provides shelter for a seat. Often covered with vines and used as a garden focal point.

Arborist A professional who has been trained and equipped to prune and care for trees.

Arborize Pruning overgrown shrubs to a primary stem, so that they resemble small trees. The technique works best with single-stemmed shrubs, such as camellias, or multi-stemmed shrubs with prominent major stems, such as hollies.

Arch An upright support structure for vines or climbing plants, often used to mark an entry or transition area in the garden.

Ashlar Stone cut at a quarry to produce smooth, flat bedding surfaces that stack easily. Walls made from such stones have a formal appearance.

BT (Bacillus thuringiensis) A microbe that is toxic to caterpillars—including cabbage loopers, European corn borers, and other pests—but that is harmless to birds, mammals, bees, and other insects. Sold commercially as an organic pest control product.

Backfill To fill in an area, such as a planting hole, trench, or around a foundation, using soil or gravel.

Base map A drawing or survey that details the location of all property boundaries, structures, slopes, significant plantings, and location of sunrise and sunset. An important first step in landscaping.

Bat A brick cut in half lengthwise.

Batten A cross-piece used to reinforce a gate or door.

Bed joint Horizontal masonry joint, as opposed to a vertical masonry joint (called a head joint). Also called beds.

Beneficials Animals, microbes, and insects; such as ladybugs, parasitic wasps, and hoverflies, that prey upon garden pests.

Berm A mound of earth that directs or retains water. A 6-inch berm built around the drip line of a tree or shrub will create a basin, ensuring that water reaches the plant's roots.

Bond The arrangement of bricks that creates a pattern in a wall or other masonry structure.

Bond stones Support stones that extend through the full thickness of a wall. They are staggered and placed every few feet along the length of the wall for extra strength.

Bow saw A pruning tool with a narrow blade and arched back. The blade allows it to cut more quickly than other saws; however, its wide back makes it unsuitable for cutting between tight tree notches and dense shrub branches.

Bud An unopened cluster of leaves or of a flower, where growth occurs.

Butyl synthetic rubber flexible liner A very durable material used to line ponds. Safe for all aquatic life, it is unaffected by sunlight or frost and will last for decades. Butyl rubber liners are 30 mil thick, black, and have a slightly textured surface.

Bypass pruner A hand tool used to cut through branches up to ½ to ¾ inch in diameter. Like a scissor, it has two sharpened blades that overlap as they cut. When the blades are sharp, they give a cleaner cut than do anvil style pruners.

Cap The top, flat layer of a masonry structure. Often ornamental, it also keeps out water, thus preventing the expansion and contraction caused by freezing and thawing of water caught in the seams. (*see* Coping)

Catch basin An underground reservoir to collect excess water. Usually located in the lowest part of the garden.

Circuit A system for watering small, designated areas rather than an entire area at once.

Clay Soil that consists of extremely fine particles that pack together tightly, so that water drains through slowly. Contains very little oxygen; plant roots have difficulty pushing through it.

Collar The slight swelling that occurs where a branch of a tree or shrub meets the trunk. (*see* Saddle)

Collar joint The vertical joint between two stacks of bricks or stones.

Commons The cheapest grade of bricks; made for all-purpose building.

Compost Decomposed organic materials, such as grass clippings, fallen leaves, plant trimmings, and kitchen scraps. The crumbly, black product holds and slowly releases nutrients and water. Rich in earthworms and healthy soil bacteria, it is ideal for amending soil, topdressing lawns, and mulching beds.

Computer-assisted design programs (CAD) Computer programs that allow homeowners to design their own landscapes without the effort of drawing on paper. The programs include mapping symbols for plants as well as for hardscape elements, such as decks, walls, and fences. Some include information on the plants' growing requirements; others allow the user to envision the landscape in the future.

Concrete bonder A material applied to concrete block to help stucco adhere to the surface.

Coping The top, flat layer of a masonry structure. Often ornamental, it also keeps out water, thus preventing the expansion and contraction caused by freezing and thawing of water caught in the seams. (*see* Cap)

Course A horizontal row of bricks or stones.

Cover crop Crops, such as clover, annual rye, vetch, barley, and buckwheat, used to blanket the ground and choke out weeds. When turned under, the decaying crops also improve the soil.

Crown Where the upper part of the plant joins the roots, usually at soil level.

Cultivar Short for cultivated variety. A plant variety developed in cultivation, rather than occurring naturally in the wild. Cultivars may be bred for desirable traits, such as double flowers, compact growth, cold hardiness, or disease resistance. The cultivar name usually is shown within single quotation marks, as in *Euonymus alatus* 'Compactus', here indicating a compact form.

Determinate tomatoes Tomato varieties that are bushy in form and that slow or stop growing when they begin producing their crop. Preferred for canning or making sauces, as the fruit tends to ripen all at once.

Diatomaceous earth A mineral created from the fossilized remains of ancient marine creatures. Its abrasive quality makes it an excellent control for soft-bodied pests, such as slugs and snails. Use only horticultural grade diatomaceous earth, not the type sold for swimming pools.

Double dig A method for improving soil at a deeper level than usual. By digging a trench, loosening and amending the soil at the bottom of the trench, and then backfilling with amended topsoil, a gardener can create a raised bed filled with an extra-thick layer of rich and fluffy soil.

Drip irrigation A system that delivers water at a slow rate directly to plant roots, thus ensuring that plants are thoroughly watered, even in clay soils which absorb water at a slow rate. Little or no water is wasted from run-off or evaporation.

Drip line An imaginary line in the soil around a tree or shrub that mirrors the circumference of the canopy above. The plant's roots are found in this area, although some extend further.

Dry-laid walk A masonry path installed without mortar.

Dry wall A stone wall that does not contain mortar.

Emitter Water delivery device on a drip irrigation system. The number of emitters and their rate of flow can be adjusted every season to meet the changing needs of the plants and the garden.

Engineering brick Top-grade brick. The hardest and most impervious to weathering.

English bond A brick pattern that contains periodic headers in each course, adding strength to the wall.

EPDM Ethylene Propylene Diene Monomer; an extremely durable and flexible rubber material used for lining ponds. It is safe for all aquatic life, impervious to sunlight and frost, and resistant to air pollution. EPDM liners are 45 mil thick and charcoal gray in color.

Extension saw A curved pruning saw attached to a long pole that allows work on branches that would otherwise be out of reach.

Facing brick A type of brick used when consistency in appearance is required. A batch of facing brick will be quite uniform in color, size, texture, and face structure.

Flemish bond A brick pattern that alternates courses of headers with stretchers, adding strength to the wall.

Float A steel, aluminum, or wood object used to smooth the surface of poured concrete by driving large aggregate below the surface.

Floater A plant that grows on the surface of water and draws its nutrients from water, rather than from soil.

Footing The concrete base that supports a masonry wall or other structure. It is built below the local frost line to prevent heaving.

Footprint The perimeter of a house or other significant structures, shown on a property survey.

Friable Refers to a soil texture that is crumbly and easy to work, such as with loam.

Gallery A tunnel-like structure with an arched roof, usually covered with vines. Often serves as a shaded garden passageway or wall. (*see* Pergola)

Garden room Outdoor space bordered by hedges, trellises, or constructed walls, creating a sense of privacy or seclusion.

Genus (plural: genera) A closely related group of species sharing similar characteristics and probably evolved from the same ancestors. In scientific, or botanical, language the genus name begins with a capital letter and is followed by the species name, which begins with a lower-case letter. Both words are italicized, as in *Acer palmatum*.

Girdling When the roots of a potbound plant encircle a trunk or stem, restricting the flow of nutrients and water and eventually resulting in the plant's death.

Green manure A cover crop grown and turned or plowed under the soil to improve its texture and nutrient content.

Growth bud Usually the tip or end bud of a branch, where growth chemicals are concentrated.

Hardiness A plant's ability to survive winter cold or summer heat without protection.

Hardscape Parts of a landscape constructed from materials other than plants, such as walks, walls, and trellises, made of wood, stone, or other materials.

Hardware cloth A flexible, wire mesh. Sometimes used to roughen a base coat of stucco.

Hardwood cutting The removal of pencil-thick tips of branches (5 to 8 inches long) at the end of the growing season when the wood has completely hardened. The cuttings are rooted, then planted outdoors. Good candidates include boxwood, forsythia, and gardenia.

Headers Bricks turned horizontal to the stretcher courses.

Hedge clippers A hand tool with long, scissor-like blades designed for trimming and shaping hedges and bushes.

Heeling in Planting bare-root stock in a temporary but protected location, with the trunk tilted on a sharp diagonal to discourage rooting.

Heirloom vegetables Plants grown from seed that has been collected and saved over many generations; the varieties have not been genetically altered, but have often developed traits that allow them to survive specific conditions.

Humus   Decayed organic material rich with nutrients. Its spongy texture holds moisture.

Indeterminate tomatoes   Tomato varieties with vines that continue to grow and bear fruit until killed by frost.

Inflorescense   The "flower" of an ornamental grass. A cluster of seeds which is borne on top of the grass blade.

Interplanting   To combine plants with different bloom times or growth habits, making it possible to fit more plants in a bed, thus prolonging the bed's appeal. Also, to combine vegetables of different heights or forms (such as corn, beans, and squash) or those that mature at different rates (such as radishes and squash) within the same growing area.

IPM (Integrated Pest Management)   An approach to pest control that utilizes regular monitoring of pests to determine if and when control is needed. By using a multi-pronged strategy that includes minimizing stress on plants, monitoring for pests, and proper pest identification, chemicals can be avoided. When control measures are needed, the least toxic methods are used.

Jointing   The finish given to the mortar that extrudes from each course of bricks.

Landscape fabric   A synthetic fabric, sometimes water-permeable, spread under paths or mulch to serve as a weed barrier.

Lateral branch   A side branch that connects to the trunk or primary branch of a tree or shrub.

Limbing up   Pruning a tree's lower branches as high as 30 to 40 feet to allow more light to reach lawn and plants below.

Loam   An ideal soil for gardening, containing plenty of organic matter and a balanced range of small to large mineral particles.

Loppers   A long-handled pruning tool for cutting wood that is 1¼ to 1¾ inches in diameter. Available with bypass and anvil-style blades.

Marginal plants   Plants that grow around the edges of water bodies, so that their roots are submerged while their leaves and flowers are above the surface of the water. Yellow flag (*Iris pseudacorus*) is one example.

Microclimate   Small area with unique growing conditions, usually as a result of a land formation (such as a valley or pond) or nearby structure (such as a building or stone wall). Individual plants, such as tomatoes or beans, can produce enough shade to create a cooler microclimate for smaller plants, such as lettuce, to grow.

Monoculture   The practice of growing only one type of plant in a given area; plants grown this way are more susceptible to insect and disease problems.

Node   The area of a stem where leaf growth occurs.

Organic matter   Plant and animal debris such as leaves, garden trimmings, and manure, in various stages of decomposition.

Overwinter   To keep a marginally hardy plant alive during the winter so that it can resume growth the following spring. Also can refer to the ability of insects to survive the winter.

Oxygenator   Underwater plants that absorb nutrients and carbon dioxide from fish wastes and decaying materials, thus helping to starve out algae.

Parterre   Diminutive hedges, such as boxwood, used to divide space and serve as decorative frames for other plantings in formal gardens.

Pathogen   A disease-causing agent.

Pergola   A tunnel-like walkway or seating area with columns or posts to support an open "roof" of beams or trellis-work; usually covered with vines. (*see* Gallery)

Perlite   Volcanic glass that has been heated until it expands, resulting in very lightweight particles that are used to improve drainage and aeration in potting mixes.

Perspective   Because objects in the distance appear smaller, it is possible to use plants to alter the way a garden is perceived. For instance, placing a small statue at the end of a small garden makes the garden seem larger. Staggering planting heights and narrowing a walkway also can create optical illusions based on perspective.

pH   The measure of hydrogen content on a scale of 0 to 14, with 7 considered neutral. A pH above 7 is considered alkaline, while a pH below 7 is considered acidic. Soil pH affects the availability of nutrients to plants.

Pinching   Removing the growing tips of branches or shoots to encourage lush, bushy growth. Removing the end buds sends chemical signals that stimulate the growth of side buds. (*see* Apical dominance)

Plat   Prepared by professional surveyors, it shows precise property lines and any easements. It is used for making a base map for landscaping and is available from a tax assessor's office or given to homeowners when purchasing their property.

Pointing   The process of repairing or adjusting the joints of a stone wall.

Poly   Short for polyethylene.

Polyethylene   A material used as a lining for temporary pools. Extended exposure in sunlight causes it to crack or tear within two to three years.

Potager   A French kitchen garden in which vegetables and fruits, and occasionally flowers are planted in a formal design using the plant forms to create patterns of color and texture.

Potbound   Excessive roots encircle the inside of the pot and sometimes emerge from its drainage holes.

Preprune   To cut the roots of a tree or shrub by digging around the drip line with a spade, several months to a year before digging up the plant. This encourages the growth of new feeder roots and increases the plant's chances of survival after it is moved.

Pruning knife   A hand tool used to smooth rough edges on a cut when pruning.

PVC (Polyvinyl Chloride)   Material used for irrigation pipes; also used to make flexible pond liners. PVC pond liners are moderately priced and have a life span of 10 to 15 years, but are not as durable as pond liners made of synthetic rubber sheeting.

PVC-E   A stronger and more flexible version of standard PVC used for flexible pond liners.

Reinforcing rod   Steel bar inside the concrete foundation of a wall, used for extra support.

Rooting hormone powder   A substance applied to the end of a cutting to promote the growth of roots.

Run wild   To allow decking boards to overhang the edges of the deck during construction. When all boards are installed, the ends are then cut off in a straight line.

Saddle   The slight swelling where the branch of a tree or shrub meets the trunk. (*see* Collar)

Sailor   An upright brick with the broad face positioned out.

Scratch coat   A rough, base coat used when applying stucco.

Secateurs   Hand pruners designed to cut through branches up to ½ to ¾ inch in diameter. Two kinds are available: the bypass type has two sharpened blades that overlap as they cut; the anvil type has a single cutting blade.

Semi-ripe   Neither new growth nor mature growth; cuttings taken from branches in early summer for the purpose of starting new plants.

Shearing   Using hedge shears or electric hedge trimmers to shape the surface of a shrub, hedge, or tree, with the goal of producing a smooth, solid mass of greenery.

Shears   A tool (manual, gas-powered, or electric) used for trimming the surface of a shrub, hedge, or tree.

Silt (silty)   Soil that is sedimentary and fine in texture, but coarser than clay. It feels slippery and compacts easily.

Single dig   To excavate or turn soil to the depth of the head of the shovel or spade, about 8 to 12 inches.

Snap a chalk line   Mark a temporary line using string coated in chalk to ensure that construction lines will be straight. The tool for doing this is called a "chalk line box."

Soap   A brick cut to half of its width.

Softscape   The palette of plants used in a landscape, as opposed to the hardscape, which refers to nonliving landscape objects, such as paths, stones, patios, and walls.

Softwood cutting   Growing tips (at least 3 to 4 inches long) of branches removed in late spring before growth has fully hardened, used for starting new plants.

Soldier   An upright brick with the narrow edge facing outward.

Species   Among plants, a group that shares many characteristics, including essential flower types, and that can interbreed freely. In scientific, or botanical, language the species name always follows the genus name and begins with a lowercase letter. Both words are italicized, as in *Acer palmatum*.

Sphagnum moss   A moisture-absorbent, partially decomposed plant material harvested from bogs and sold commercially as a soil amendment. Sometimes used as a liner for wire hanging baskets because of its ability to hold water.

Split A brick cut to half of its height.

Stack bond The arrangement of bricks in which mortar joints are not bridged by courses above and below. Considered the weakest bond.

Stretchers Bricks laid horizontally in the direction of the wall.

Swale A naturally occurring wetland area where water tends to flow or accumulate during heavy rains.

Synthetic rubber The most durable and most expensive material used for pond liners. Holds up to sunlight and freezing temperatures for decades. Two types: EPDM and butyl.

Tilth Soil with an easy-to-work texture which is the result of a balanced mix of small and large particles and plenty of organic matter.

Topdress To cover the surface of soil with a thin layer of compost or fertilizer.

Umbel The umbrella-shaped cluster of tiny flowers found on certain plants, such as fennel, parsley, and dill.

Underplant To plant low-growing plants, such as ground covers, under taller plants such as shrubs.

Vista An avenue or line of sight that allows a distant view. In small gardens, even a short, straight path leading to a focal point will create a vista that makes the garden appear larger. (*see* Perspective)

Weep holes Holes that allow water to seep through a retaining wall, so that it does not build up behind it.

Wythe A vertical section of a wall that is equal to the width of the masonry unit.

Xeriscape Landscape design that utilizes drought-tolerant plants and various techniques for minimizing water use.

Zones Climate divisions on a map indicating extreme cold or heat for that area, used to determine a plant's suitability. Also refers to divisions of a garden based on types of plants and their watering needs.

METRIC EQUIVALENTS

All measurements in this book are given in U.S. Customary units. To find metric equivalents, use the following tables and conversion factors.

Inches to cm (*1 in = 2.54cm*)

in.	cm
7/64	0.2778
1/8	0.3175
1/4	0.6350
3/8	0.9525
1/2	1.2700
5/8	1.5875
3/4	1.9050
1	2.5400
5	12.70
10	25.40

Feet to meters (*1 ft = 0.3048m*)

ft.	m
1	0.3048
5	1.5240
10	3.0480

Square feet to square meters
1 ft.^{2} = 0.09290304m^2

Ounces/pounds (Avoirdupois) to g
1 oz. = 28.349523g
1 lb. = 453.5924g

Pounds to kilograms
1 lb. = 0.45359237k

Ounces/quarts to liters
1 oz. = 0.02957353l
1 qt. = 0.9463l

Gallons to liters
1 gal. = 3.7852l

Fahrenheit to c (*°C = °F − 32 × 5/9*)

°F	°C
50	10.00
60	15.56
70	21.11
80	26.67

INDEX

PHOTO CREDITS

Photo credits by the author, Catriona Tudor Erler, are abbreviated CTE.
p. 1: Positive Images/Jerry Howard. **p. 2:** Janet Loughrey. **p. 6** (top to bottom): Ken Druse; Grant Heilman/Larry Lefever; H. Armstrong Roberts/Ralph Krubner. **pp. 8–9** (left to right): Jessie Walker; Charles Mann; Photos Horticultural. **p. 10** (clockwise, from top right): Photos Horticultural; Garden Picture Library/Nigel Francis; Positive Images/Jerry Howard. **p. 11** (clockwise, from top left): Jerry Pavia; Jerry Pavia; Andrew Lawson. **p. 12** (clockwise, from top right): Jerry Pavia; John Glover; Charles Mann. **p. 14:** courtesy USDA. **p. 15:** The American Horticultural Society. **pp. 16–17:** John Glover. **pp. 18–19** (clockwise, from top): Grant Heilman/Larry Lefever; Grant Heilman/Lefever/Grushow; Rosalind Creasy. **p. 20** (clockwise, from top left): CTE; Jon-Joseph Russo; Jon-Joseph Russo. **p. 21:** Richard Fish. **p. 22** (top to bottom): CTE; Jerry Pavia. **p. 23:** Michael Thompson. **p. 24:** Richard Fish. **p. 25** (left to right): CTE; Jerry Pavia. **p. 26** (top to bottom): CTE; CTE; Derek Fell. **p. 27** (clockwise, from top left): CTE; Derek Fell; James Walsh Erler. **p. 28** (clockwise, from top left): Garden Picture Library/Ron Sutherland; Derek Fell; Garden Picture Library/Ron Sutherland. **p. 29** (clockwise, from top): CTE; Garden Picture Library/Ron Evans; CTE. **p. 30** (clockwise, from top right): James Walsh Erler; Rosalind Creasy; Allan Mandell. **p. 31** (top to bottom): Grant Heilman/Lefever/Grushow; Grant Heilman/Lefever/Grushow; CTE. **p. 32** (clockwise, from top right): CTE; New England Stock/Michael Shedlock; CTE. **p. 33** (clockwise, from top right): CTE; CTE; Grant Heilman/Lefever/Grushow; New England Stock/Lou Palmieri. **p. 34** (all): CTE. **p. 35** (clockwise, from top left): CTE; CTE; Richard Fish. **p. 36:** CTE. **p. 37:** Neil Soderstrom. **p. 38:** Osterreichische Galerie. **p. 39** (clockwise, from top right): CTE; CTE; Derek Fell. **p. 40:** Garden Picture Library/Howard Rice p. 41 (all): CTE. **p. 42** (all): CTE. **p. 43** (top to bottom): James Walsh Erler; CTE. **p. 44:** CTE. **p. 46** (top to bottom): Positive Images/Jerry Howard; CTE. **p. 48:** CTE. **p. 49** (all): CTE. **p. 50** (all): CTE. **p. 51:** James Walsh Erler. **p. 52** (all): CTE. **p. 54** (all): CTE. **p. 55** (all): CTE. **p. 56** (top to bottom): Jerry Pavia; CTE. **p. 57** (all): CTE. **p. 59** (all): CTE. **p. 60** (top to bottom): CTE; Derek Fell; Jerry Pavia. **p. 61:** CTE. **p. 62:** J. Paul Moore. **p. 63** (all): CTE. **pp. 64–65:** Grant Heilman/Larry Lefever. **pp. 66–67** (top to bottom): John Glover; Photo Researchers/Alan Detrick. **p. 68** (clockwise, from top left): Neil Soderstrom; Carl Weese/Joe Provey; Carl Weese/Joe Provey; Carl Weese/Joe Provey. **p.**

69: Grant Heilman/Barry Runk. **p. 70:** CTE. **p. 71** (top to bottom): Neil Soderstrom; Neil Soderstrom; Derek Fell. **p. 72** (all): Neil Soderstrom. **p. 75** (all): CTE. **p. 76:** CTE. **p. 79** (all): D. Cavagnaro. **p. 80:** James Walsh Erler. **p. 82** (all): Crandall & Crandall. **pp. 86–87:** Crandall & Crandall. **p. 89** (top to bottom): Crandall & Crandall; Garden Picture Library/Gary Rogers. **p. 90** (all): CTE. **p. 91** (clockwise, from top): CTE; Malibu Lights; Malibu Lights; Malibu Lights; Malibu Lights. **p. 93** (top to bottom): Photo Images/Margaret Hensel; Garden Picture Library/D.S. Sira. **pp. 94–95** (clockwise, from top): CTE; CTE; Jerry Pavia; CTE. **p. 96** (all): CTE. **p. 97** (clockwise, from top left): CTE; Rosalind Creasy; Charles Mann. **p. 98** (top to bottom): H. Armstrong Roberts/H. Abernathy; CTE. **p. 99** (clockwise, from top left): Jerry Pavia; CTE; CTE; Jerry Pavia. **p. 100:** Positive Images/Jerry Howard. **p. 101** (all): Neil Soderstrom. **pp. 102–103** (all): CTE. **pp. 104–105** (all): CTE. **p. 106:** Jerry Pavia. **p. 108** (top to bottom): Ken Druse; Jerry Pavia. **p. 109** (all): CTE. **pp. 110–111** (clockwise, from top): FPG/Jose Luis Banus-March; Crandall & Crandall; FPG/Maria Pape. **p. 112** (clockwise, from top left): Jacqueline Murphy; CTE; Garden Picture Library/Gill Hanly. **p. 113** (left to right): Derek Fell; CTE; CTE. **p. 114:** Crandall & Crandall. **p. 115** (top to bottom): CTE; Garden Picture Library/Brian Carter; Balthazar Korab. **p. 116** (top to bottom): Derek Fell; Positive Images/Jerry Howard; Michael Thompson. **p. 117** (top to bottom): Michael Thompson; CTE. **p. 118** (top to bottom): CTE; Crandall & Crandall; Michael Thompson. **p. 120** (all): Crandall & Crandall. **p. 121:** Crandall & Crandall. **pp. 124–125** (all): John Parsekian. **p. 126** (top to bottom): CTE; Jacqueline Murphy. **p. 127:** Crandall & Crandall. **pp. 128–129** (clockwise, from top): Crandall & Crandall; Jerry Pavia; CTE. **p. 130** (all): Jerry Pavia. **pp. 132–133** (all): Crandall & Crandall. **p. 134:** Crandall & Crandall. **p. 136:** CTE. **p. 137** (all): CTE. **p. 138** (all): Neil Soderstrom. **p. 139** (top to bottom): Jerry Pavia; Crandall & Crandall. **p. 141** (all): courtesy California Redwood Association/Scott Zimmerman. **p. 142** (top to bottom): David Goldberg; Photo Researchers/G.M. Bryant. **p. 144:** Andrew Lawson. **p. 145** (top to bottom): CTE; David Goldberg. **p. 147** (all): CTE. **pp. 148–149** (clockwise, from top): Derek Fell; Michael Thompson; Charles Mann. **p. 150** (top to bottom): Grant Heilman/Jane Grushow; Positive Images/Jerry Howard. **p. 152** (all): Derek Fell. **p. 153** (top to bottom): Photos Horticultural; FPG/Peter Grindley; Garden Picture Library/Lynne Brotchie.

p. 154 (top to bottom): Derek Fell; Photos Horticultural. **p. 156** (top to bottom): Positive Images/Pam Spaulding; CTE; Photo Researchers/Christine Douglas. **p. 157** (top to bottom): Bruce Coleman/Wendell Metzen; Dembinsky Photo Assoc./Dan Dempster. **p. 158:** Derek Fell. **p. 159** (top to bottom): Derek Fell; Ken Druse; CTE. **p. 160** (clockwise, from top right): John Glover; Garden Picture Library/Jane Legate; Garden Picture Library/Howard Rice. **p. 162** (top to bottom): Derek Fell; Positive Images/Jerry Howard. **p. 163** (clockwise, from top): Garden Picture Library/Bob Challinor; CTE; CTE. **p. 164:** Michael Thompson. **p. 165** (clockwise, from top left): CTE; Photo Researchers/Alan & Linda Detrick; Charles Mann; Garden Picture Library/Lynne Brotchie. **p. 166:** CTE. **p. 167** (clockwise, from top left): CTE; Nancy Engel; CTE; CTE. **p. 168:** Garden Picture Library/Bob Challinor. **p. 169** (clockwise, from top left): Garden Picture Library/J.S. Sira; Derek Fell; John Glover; Michael Thompson. **p. 170:** Jerry Pavia. **p. 171** (clockwise, from top left): Garden Picture Library/Eric Crichton; CTE; Garden Picture Library/Howard Rice; Positive Images/Jerry Howard; John Glover. **p. 172:** Dembinsky Photo Assoc./Darryl Beers. **p. 173** (top to bottom): Positive Images/Pam Spaulding; Photo Researchers/C. Seghers; Garden Picture Library/Lynn Brotchie. **pp. 174–175** (all): CTE. **p. 176:** Photos Horticultural. **p. 177** (top to bottom, left): H. Armstrong Roberts/F. Sieb; David Goldberg; (top right): Positive Images/Pam Spaulding; (middle left): Photo Researchers/Charlie Ott; (middle right): Positive Images/John Parker; (bottom right): Derek Fell. **p. 178:** Garden Picture Library/Howard Rice. **p. 179** (clockwise, from top left): Garden Picture Library/Howard Rice; Jerry Pavia; Photo Researchers/Alan & Linda Detrick. **pp. 180–181:** Photos Horticultural. **pp. 182–183** (left to right): John Glover; Hugh Palmer; John Glover. **p. 185:** Dembinsky Photo Assoc./Richard Shiell. **p. 186** (top to bottom): Photo Researchers/E.R. Degginger; CTE. **p. 187** (all): Neil Soderstrom. **p. 190:** CTE. **p. 193** (all): CTE. **p. 194:** Rick Mastelli. **p. 195** (all): CTE. **p. 196** (top to bottom): Grant Heilman/Jim Strawser; Neil Soderstrom. **p. 197:** Photo Researchers/Jeff Lepore. **pp. 198–199** (all): CTE. **pp. 200–201** (counterclockwise, from top): Derek Fell; Garden Picture Library/John Glover; Garden Picture Library/Brigitte Thomas. **p. 202** (top to bottom): Bruce Coleman/Joy Sporr; Positive Images/Jerry Howard; Bruce Coleman/Erwin & Peggy Bauer. **p. 203** (left to right): Positive Images/Pam Spaulding; CTE; D. Cavagnaro. **p. 204** (left to right): D. Cavagnaro;

Photo Researchers/Robert Isaacs; Bruce Coleman/Robert Falls. **p. 205** (top to bottom): John Glover; Garden Picture Library/Lamontagne; Garden Picture Library/Howard Rice; Grant Heilman/Lefever/Grushow. **p. 206** (clockwise from top left): Garden Picture Library/Eric Crichton; Positive Images/Jerry Howard; John Glover. **p. 207** (top to bottom): John Glover; Michael Dirr. **p. 208** (top to bottom): Positive Images/Patricia Bruno; Garden Picture Library/Lamontagne. **p. 209** (all): CTE. **p. 212** (all): CTE. **p. 213** (all): Neil Soderstrom. **p. 215:** Stephen E. Munz. **p. 216:** Photo Images/Jerry Howard. **p. 217** (top to bottom): Photo Researchers/Renee Lynn; Charles Mann. **p. 218** (clockwise, from top right): Dr. Peter Landschoot; Dr. Peter Landschoot; Dr. Peter Landschoot; Dr. Shirley Anderson; Dr. Shirley Anderson; Dr. Shirley Anderson. **p. 219** (clockwise, from top left): Derek Fell; Joe Provey; Karen Williams; Steve Weist/Jack Fry. **p. 220** (left to right): Carl Weese/Joe Provey; Carl Weese/Joe Provey; Renald Provey/Joe Provey. **p. 221** (clockwise, from top): Neil Soderstrom; Grant Heilman/Runk/Schoenberger; Photo Researchers/R.J. Erwin; Photo Researchers/Charles Belinsky. **p. 222** (left to right): Carl Weese/Joe Provey; Carl Weese/Joe Provey; Dwight Kuhn. **p. 223** (all): Carl Weese/Joe Provey. **p. 224** (clockwise, from top left): Karen Williams; Carl Weese/Joe Provey; Carl Weese/Joe Provey; Carl Weese/Joe Provey; Karen Williams. **p. 225** (all): Carl Weese/Joe Provey. **p. 226** (left to right): Carl Weese/Joe Provey; Carl Weese/Joe Provey; Crandall & Crandall. **p 227** (clockwise, from top right): Carl Weese/Joe Provey; Carl Weese/Joe Provey; Carl Weese/Joe Provey; Crandall & Crandall. **p. 229** (top to bottom): Neil Soderstrom; Grant Heilman/Jim Strawser. **p. 230** (counterclockwise, from top): Carl Weese/Joe Provey; Carl Weese/Joe Provey; Grant Heilman/Barry L. Runk. **p. 231:** Carl Weese/Joe Provey. **p. 232** (top to bottom): Charles Mann; Positive Images/Pam Spaulding; Charles Mann. **p. 233** (top to bottom): Grant Heilman/Larry Lefever; CTE. **p. 234** (left to right): Charles Mann; Photo Researchers/John Kaprielian; Charles Mann. **p. 236** (top to bottom): CTE; Charles Mann; CTE. **p. 237** (top to bottom): Photo Researchers/Alan & Linda Detrick; Photo Research-

ers/Alan Detrick; David Goldberg. **pp. 238–240** (all): Carol Ottesen. **p. 241** (left to right): CTE; Photo Researchers/Alan & Linda Detrick; Derek Fell. **p. 242:** CTE. **p. 243** (clockwise, from top left): Jerry Harpur; John Glover; CTE; Charles Mann. **p. 244:** Garden Picture Library/Gill Hanly. **p. 245** (clockwise, from top): Lynn Karlin; Jessie Walker; Garden Picture Library/Juliette Wade. **p. 246:** CTE. **p. 249** (clockwise from top left): Grant Heilman/Lefever/Grushow; CTE; CTE; CTE; Positive Images/Jerry Howard. **p. 250:** Michael Thompson. **p. 251** (clockwise, from top left): CTE; CTE; CTE; Photo Researchers/Tom Hollymen; CTE. **p. 253** (clockwise, from top left): Positive Images/Jerry Howard; CTE; Garden Picture Library/J.S. Sira; Positive Images/Margaret Hensel; Garden Picture Library/John Glover; Charles Mann. **p. 254** (top to bottom): Derek Fell; courtesy Netherland Flower Bulb Info. **p. 255** (top to bottom): courtesy White Flower Farm; courtesy Netherland Flower Bulb Info. **p. 257** (clockwise, from top left): Garden Picture Library/Lynn Brotchie; Positive Images/Harry Haralambou; Jerry Pavia; D. Cavagnaro; John Glover; John Glover; John Glover. **p. 259** (clockwise, from top left): CTE; Photo Researchers/D.C. Kelly; Jerry Pavia; D. Cavagnaro; Jerry Pavia; Jerry Pavia. **p. 260** (counterclockwise, from top): Dembinsky Photo Assoc./Darrel Beers; Garden Picture Library/J.S. Sira; Michael Thompson. **p. 261** (all): courtesy Netherland Flower Bulb Info. **p. 262** (all): Derek Fell. **p. 263:** Garden Picture Library/Jane Legate. **pp. 264–265** (all): CTE. **p. 266** (top to bottom): CTE; D. Cavagnaro; D. Cavagnaro. **p. 267:** Allan Mandell. **p. 269** (top to bottom): Derek Fell; Garden Picture Library/Roger Hyam. **pp. 270–271** (clockwise, from top right): CTE; Rosalind Creasy; John Glover. **p 272** (clockwise, from top): D. Cavagnaro; Grant Heilman/Jane Grushow; Garden Picture Library/Lamontagne. **p. 273** (top to bottom): CTE; D. Cavagnaro; Photo Researchers/Joyce Photographics. **p. 275** (clockwise, from top left): Crandall & Crandall; Crandall & Crandall; Crandall & Crandall; Photo Researchers/Alan Detrick. **p. 276** (top to bottom): Derek Fell; D. Cavagnaro. **p. 277** (all): Neil Soderstrom. **p. 278** (all): David Van Zanten. **p. 279** (top to bottom): D. Cavagnaro; Lynn Karlin. **p. 281** (left to right): D Cavagnaro; D. Cavagnaro; Photo Research-

ers/Michael Gadomski; Derek Fell. **p. 282:** (top to bottom): John Glover; Derek Fell. **p. 283** (top to bottom): Lynn Karlin; Derek Fell. **p. 284** (left to right): Neil Soderstorm; Jerry Pavia. **p. 285** (left to right): Grant Heilman/Runk/Schoenberger; Derek Fell. **p. 286** (all): CTE. **p. 287** (clockwise, from top): CTE; John Glover; Photos Horticultural. **p. 288** (top to bottom): CTE; Jerry Pavia; CTE. **p. 289:** John Glover. **pp. 290–291** (counterclockwise, from top left): CTE; Hugh Palmer; Photo Researchers/Ken Brate; Photo Researchers/Harry Rogers. **p. 292** (top to bottom): David Goldberg; Jerry Pavia; Crandall & Crandall. **p. 293** (left to right): John Glover; Photo Researchers/Harry Rogers. **p. 294** (clockwise, from top right): Photo Researchers/ Merlin Tuttle; Bruce Coleman/Joe McDonald; Photo Researchers/Suzanne & Joseph Collins; Dembinsky Photo Assoc./George Stewart; Photo Researchers/Adam Jones. **p. 295** (clockwise, from top left): John Glover; Derek Fell; John Glover. **p. 296** (1st row, left to right): D. Cavagnaro; Photo Researchers/Dwight Kuhn/Bruce Coleman; Photo Researchers/Stephen Parker; (2nd row): Photo Researchers/Okapia/G. Buttner; Bruce Coleman/J.C. Carton; Photo Researchers/Joe McDonald/Bruce Coleman; (3rd row): D.Cavagnaro; Bruce Coleman/E.R. Degginger; (4th row): D.Cavagnaro; Photo Researchers/L. West; (5th row): Photo Researchers/Bonnie Sue; Photo Researchers/Stephen Dalton; (6th row): Photo Researchers/Rod Planck; Photo Researchers/Holt Studios; (7th row): Jerry Pavia; Photo Researchers/Harry Rogers; Photo Researchers/S.J. Krasemann. **p. 297** (top to bottom): Jerry Pavia; Derek Fell; Jerry Pavia. **p. 298** (top to bottom): D.Cavagnaro; CTE; Derek Fell; Photo Researchers/Noble Proctor. **p. 300** (all): CTE. **p. 302** (top to bottom): Photo Researchers/Holt Studios; Joseph Strauch; CTE. **p. 303:** Photo Researchers/Holt Studios/Nigel Cattlin. **p. 304** (top to bottom): Derek Fell; Photo Researchers/Dan Guravich; Photo Researchers/Holt Cattlin; Photo Researchers/Holt Studios/Nigel Cattlin; Photo Researchers/Alan Detrick; Photo Researchers/Holt Studios/Nigel Cattlin. **p. 305** (top to bottom): Photo Researchers/Holt Studios/Nigel Cattlin; Derek Fell; Derek Fell; Purdue Univ./Dr. Peggy Sellers; USDA/Dr. R. T. Lewellen; Photo Researchers/Holt Studios/Nigel Cattlin.

I L L U S T R A T I O N   C R E D I T S

pp. 40, 45, 47, 49, 53, 58, 61, 62, 73, 76, 77, 78, 81, 83, 84, 85, 88, 92, 100, 103, 106, 107, 119: Nancy Hull. (sepia tones **pp.61,62,83,84,85,88:** Clarke Barre **pp. 121, 122, 123:** Rick Daskam. **pp. 131, 134, 135, 136, 140, 143, 144, 146, 151:** Nancy Hull. **p. 155:** Mavis Augustine Torke. **p. 158:** Michele Angle Farrar. **p. 161:** Mavis Augustine Torke. **pp. 184–185, 187:** Michele Angle Farrar. **pp. 188–89:** Todd Ferris. **pp. 191–192:** Mavis Augustine Torke. **pp. 195, 196, 210, 211, 214:** Michele Angle Farrar. **p. 231:** Todd Ferris. **p. 247:** Nancy Hull. **p. 261:** Michele Angle Farrar. **pp. 268, 280:** Nancy Hull.

Have a home gardening, decorating, or improvement project? Look for these and other fine Creative Homeowner books wherever books are sold.

An impressive guide to more than 100 flowering plants. More than 500 color photos. 208 pp.; 9"×10"
BOOK #: 274032

How to prepare, cultivate, and harvest a successful garden. Over 400 color photos. 176 pp.; 9"×10"
BOOK #: 274244

A four-season step-by-step guide to growing flowers. Over 500 photos & illustrations. 224 pp.; 9"×10"
BOOK #: 274791

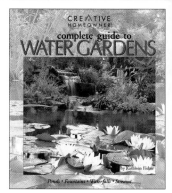

A comprehensive tool for the aspiring water gardener. Over 400 color photos. 208 pp.; 9"×10"
BOOK #: 274452

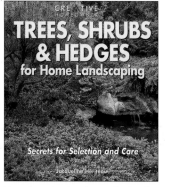

How to select and care for landscaping plants. Over 500 illustrations. 208 pp.; 9"×10"
BOOK #: 274238

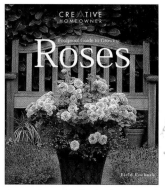

A growing guide for beginners and experienced gardeners. Over 400 color photos. 160 pp.; 9"×10"
BOOK #: 274055

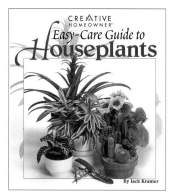

Complete houseplant guide 200 readily available plants; more than 400 photos. 192pp.; 9"×10"
BOOK #: 275243

Home landscaping guides that cover six regions: Mid-Atlantic (274537); Midwest (274385); Northeast (274618); Southeast (274762); Northwest (274344); California (274267). 400 illustrations each.

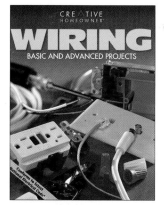

New, updated edition of best-selling house wiring manual. Over 700 color photos. 256 pp.; 8¹/₂"×11"
BOOK #: 277048

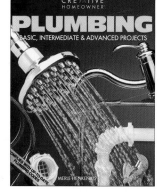

Take the guesswork out of plumbing repair. More than 750 illustrations. 272 pp.; 8¹/₂"×10⁷/₈"
BOOK #: 27820

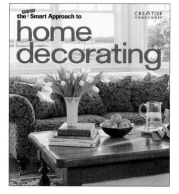

How to work with space, color, pattern, texture. Over 400 photos. 288 pp.; 9"×10"
BOOK #: 279672

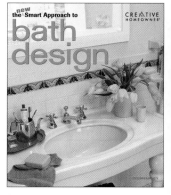

All you need to know about designing a bath. Over 260 color photos. 208 pp.; 9"×10"
BOOK #: 279234

For more information, and to order direct, call 800-631-7795; in New Jersey 201-934-7100.
www.creativehomeowner.com